1986

OPERATING SYSTEM DESIGN
THE XINU APPROACH

PRENTICE-HALL SOFTWARE SERIES
Brian W. Kernighan, advisor

OPERATING SYSTEM DESIGN
THE XINU APPROACH

DOUGLAS COMER

Bell Laboratories
600 Mountain Avenue
Murray Hill, NJ 07974

PRENTICE-HALL, INC.
Englewood Cliffs, New Jersey 07632

Library of Congress Cataloging in Publication Data

Comer, Douglas.
    Operating system design, the Xinu approach.

    (Prentice-Hall software series)
    Bibliography: p.
    Includes index.
    1. Xinu (Computer operating system)   2. System
design.   I. Title.   II. Series.
QA76.6.C6275   1984   001.64′2   83-19270
ISBN 0-13-637539-1

Editorial/production supervision: Nancy Milnamow
Cover design: Photo Plus Art (Celine A. Brandes)
Manufacturing buyer: Gordon Osbourne

This book was set by the author using TROFF and other UNIX text-processing
software, and the typesetting facilities at Bell Laboratories, New Jersey.

LSI 11, PDP 11, and VAX are registered trademarks of Digital Equipment Corporation.
UNIX is a trademark of Bell Laboratories.

Printed in the United States of America

10   9   8   7   6   5

ISBN 0-13-637539-1

Prentice-Hall International, Inc., *London*
Prentice-Hall of Australia Pty. Limited, *Sydney*
Editora Prentice-Hall do Brasil, Ltda., *Rio de Janeiro*
Prentice-Hall Canada Inc., *Toronto*
Prentice-Hall of India Private Limited, *New Delhi*
Prentice-Hall of Japan, Inc., *Tokyo*
Prentice-Hall of Southeast Asia Pte. Ltd., *Singapore*
Whitehall Books Limited, *Wellington, New Zealand*

To my wife, Chris, and our children, Sharon and Scott.

Contents

Chapter 8   Memory Management   **101**

Chapter 9   Interrupt Processing   **113**

Chapter 10   Real-Time Clock Management   **123**

Chapter 11   Device Independent Input and Output   **141**

Chapter 18   File Systems   309

Chapter 19   Exception Handling and Support Routines   347

Chapter 20   System Configuration   367

Foreword

The quasars are so remote and the quarks so minute, it seems impossible to comprehend all dimensions of our physical universe.

For example, the most distant quasar is on the order of 10^{27} meters distant and the quarks are on the order of 10^{-18} in diameter. This is a span of 45 orders of magnitude from the largest known distance to the smallest. The ratio of the largest to the smallest known distance, 10^{45}, is miniscule when compared to the number of subatomic particles in the universe, approximately 10^{80}.

When physical constraints are removed, human thought will routinely attempt to grapple with numbers incomprehensibly larger than these. For example, the largest known Fibonacci number exceeds 10^{208} and the largest known prime exceeds 10^{3374}. One of the largest numbers to appear in a mathematical proof (Skewes' number) is on the order

$$10^{10^{10^{10^{34}}}}$$

The combinatorial spaces through which our computer programs must search for solutions can easily reach such staggering sizes.

How can the human mind overcome barriers of such incomprehensible size? How can we assemble comprehensible computers and programs capable of dealing with vast spaces of abstract objects, the largest of which are many orders of magnitude bigger than the smallest?

Nature long ago solved this problem. It is the hierarchical ordering principle of building up structures by levels and clusters. Issac Asimov has, over the years, explored this principle by studying "ladders" measuring the universe by length, area, volume, mass, density, pressure, time, speed, and temperature.[†] There is a film, *Powers of Ten*, that explores the ladder of length with fascinating visual simulations; it can be seen in a display at the Smithsonian Air and Space Museum in Washington, DC.

The *Powers of Ten* film simulates a viewscreen spanning a distance of 10^n meters for a range of integers n, "steps" on a ladder of length. Initially, the viewscreen is 1 meter wide (Step 0) and shows a picnicker on a Chicago football field. The viewer ascends the ladder of length as the viewscreen expands its scope by a factor of 10 every 10 seconds. For example, at Step 2, the screen contains the entire football field; at Step 5, the Chicago metropolitan area; at Step 8, the planet earth; at Step 13, the solar system; at Step 19, the local star group; at Step 21, the

---

[†] See *The Measure of the Universe*, Harper and Row, New York, 1983; and *Asimov on Numbers*, Pocket Books, New York, 1977.

Milky Way Galaxy; and at Step 22, the local cluster of galaxies. Finally, at Step 27, the screen shows a few faint blips, each a quasar or cluster of galaxies. The film then returns to the starting point and begins descending the ladder by shrinking the screen's scope by a factor of 10 every 10 seconds. For example, at Step -2, the screen shows a small patch on the picnicker's arm; at Step -5, individual cells in the picnicker's skin; at Step -9, molecules; at Step -10, atoms; at Step -13, protons and neutrons. Recent advances in physics have measured quarks, the smallest subatomic particles known, at Step -18.

These explorations of the universe, ascents and descents on ladders of measure, show the same striking patterns:

a. The universe is mostly empty space.

b. At each step there are well-defined objects with well-defined rules of interaction.

c. The objects of a given step are composed of objects of lower steps and are constituents of objects of higher steps.

The hierarchical ordering principle — *the Principle of Steps* — is nature's way of structuring the universe. It applies across all known steps of all ladders of measure, and probably applies at new steps yet to be discovered.

By the middle 1960s, computer scientists were becoming seriously concerned about the sizes of computer programs. On a ladder of storage, the largest user programs of the day were Step 5 — i.e., when compiled, occupied on the order of 10^5 words of file store. The largest programs of all, operating systems, were then at Step 6 and were threatening to reach Step 7. You will not be surprised, then, when I tell you that, of all computer scientists, operating systems designers were the most anxious to apply nature's Principle of Steps to impose order on large programs.

At the First ACM Symposium on Operating Systems Principles (SOSP) in 1967, Dijkstra reported organizing the software of the THE operating system into seven levels (steps). Each level consisted of a collection of abstract objects and a set of rules governing their behavior. (The rules were enforced by encoding them into operating system procedures called "primitive operations" or simply "primitives.") The internal structure of an object at a given level was invisible at that level but could be explained in terms of objects and operations of levels below. Dijkstra had applied nature's Principle of Steps to the design of a large program and, in so doing, had constructed a comprehensible Step 5 operating system.

The Principle of Steps was employed in other experimental operating systems such as Liskov's VENUS operating system (4 levels, 1972) and SRI's Provably Secure Operating System (17 levels, 1975). This principle has influenced programming language design as well, under the somewhat mystical name of "data abstraction"; examples include Simula (1967), Concurrent Pascal (1975), Ada (1980), and Smalltalk (1981). It has influenced software engineering, under the name "top-down refinement." It has influenced computer communications, under the name "layered network protocols."

Despite its presence in some rivulets of computer science for many years, the Principle of Steps has been slow to flow into the mainstream of computer systems design. Skeptics argue that systems constrained by this principle are inherently less efficient than systems constructed by expert programmers not so constrained. They offer two lines of argument. The first, which shows up most clearly in "layered network protocols," is that each level of software has access *exclusively* to the next lower level. This leads to a design in which messages must be passed down through intermediate levels to gain access to objects several steps down in the hierarchy. In fact, the Principle of Steps merely requires objects to be composed solely of lower objects; it does not rule out direct access to any visible lower object. The second argument is that constraints on structure increase system size by removing opportunities for optimizations. This remarkably persuasive argument has never been supported by data. In fact, all operating systems designed with explicit attention to hierarchical ordering have been significantly *smaller* than other systems of similar function.

Doug Comer's book, − this book − is about XINU, an operating system for a set of LSI 11 computers capable of cooperative computation via a store-and-forward ring network. (XINU stands for "XINU is not UNIX," and is pronounced "zee-new.") XINU incorporates the concepts of UNIX into a level-structured operating system that can run in as little as 4000 bytes (2000 words) of main store. The entire set of XINU source files include, with comments, just under 5850 lines of C code and 650 lines of assembler code. (Without comments, there are 4300 lines of C code and 550 lines of assembler.)

So there you have it: a real, Step 5 operating system with all the functionality of the Step 7 operating systems of the early 1970s. Pretty impressive, isn't it? Nature's Principle of Steps works.

Peter J. Denning

August 7, 1983

Preface

Building a computer operating system is like weaving a fine tapestry — it consists of producing a large, complex object in many small steps. Like stitches in a tapestry, details are important because mistakes are noticeable. But understanding details and the mechanics of assembling pieces is only a small part of the problem; a masterful creation requires a pattern that the artisan can follow.

Surprisingly, few operating system textbooks or courses explain that there is a pattern from which systems can be built. Some students still hear the rhetoric that often was taught a decade ago: "operating system design is mostly black art and little science." Textbooks reenforce these ideas by focusing on details that have especially elegant explanations, independent of how such topics pertain to modern systems. As a result, students are left with the feeling that operating systems consist of a few well-understood pieces that are somehow connected by what is otherwise a morass of mysterious code containing many machine-dependent tricks.

Now that inexpensive microprocessors have become abundant more programmers are being asked to design software systems starting with the bare machine. It is important that programmers working with such hardware know the fundamentals of operating system design for two reasons. First, operating system primitives provide incredible intellectual leverage — it is impossible to devise systems that exploit the power of these new computers without understanding operating systems. Second, the effort that has been expended in operating system research is staggering — it is unlikely that any programmer would ever stumble onto a good design without rigorous training.

This book attempts to remove the magic from operating system design, and to consolidate the body of material into a systematic discipline. It reviews the major system components and a structure that organizes them in an orderly, understandable manner. Unlike texts that survey the field by presenting as many alternatives as possible, it guides the reader through the construction of a conventional process-based system, using practical, straightforward primitives. It begins with a bare machine, and proceeds step-by-step through the design and implementation of a small, elegant system. The system, called Xinu, serves as an example and a pattern for system design.

Although Xinu is small enough to fit into the text, it includes all the components that constitute an ordinary operating system: memory management, process management, process coordination and synchronization, interprocess communication, real-time clock management, device drivers, intermachine communication

(networks), and a file system. These components are carefully organized into a
hierarchy of layers, making the interconnections among them clear, and the design
process easy to follow. Despite its size, Xinu retains much of the power of larger
systems. Readers accustomed to commercial microcomputer "operating systems"
will be pleasantly surprised by its sophistication. An important lesson to be learned
is that good system design can be as important on small machines as it is on large
ones.

With only a few exceptions, the book covers topics in the sequence that a
designer follows when building a system. Each chapter describes a component in
the design hierarchy and presents software that illustrates how to implement primitives in that layer. This approach has several advantages. First, each chapter explains a larger subset of Xinu than the previous ones, making it possible to think
about the design and implementation of a given layer independent of the implementation of preceding or succeeding layers. Second, the details of any chapter can be
skipped on first reading — a reader need only understand what services the routines
in that chapter (layer) provide, not how those routines are implemented. Third, the
reader sees the implementation of a procedure before that procedure is used to
build others, making clear how each layer is built out of previous ones. Fourth, in-
tellectually deep subjects like concurrency come up early, before many procedures
have been introduced, while the bulk of the code (intermachine communication and
file systems) comes at the end when the reader is better prepared to understand the
details.

Chapters 1-13 describe a "minimal" system that supports concurrent processing, terminal input and output, and real-time clock management. Although the
minimal system may not seem useful at first, it has served as the basis for several
applications, including a VLSI chip tester. Later chapters describe machine-to-
machine communication (computer network) software, and the file system that are
built on top of the minimum system.

Unlike many other books on operating systems, this one does not attempt to review every alternative for each system component, nor does it survey existing commercial systems. Instead, it shows the implementation details of one set of primitives, usually the most popular set. For example, the chapter on process coordination explains semaphores (the most widely accepted process coordination primitives), relegating a discussion of other primitives (e.g., monitors) to the exercises.
Our goal is to remove all the mystery about how primitives can be implemented on
conventional hardware. Once the essential magic of a particular set of primitives is
understood, the implementation of alternative versions should be easy to master.

The book is designed for advanced undergraduate or graduate-level courses.
Although there is nothing inherently difficult about any topic, covering most of the
material in one semester demands a rapid pace (usually unattained by undergradu-
ates).

In lower-division system courses, class time may be needed to help students
understand the motivation and details that are presented. Although such exposition
may seem unnecessary, experience has shown that students at this level find concurrency an extremely difficult notion. Many are not adept at reading sequential

programs, and fewer still really understand the details of a run-time environment or machine architecture; they need to be guided through the chapters on process management carefully. It helps immensely if students have hands-on experience with the system so they can observe it in action. The host software runs on a VAX computer under the UNIX operating system. Ideally, students will have the opportunity to *use* Xinu during the first few day or weeks before they try to understand its internal structure. Chapter 1 provides a few examples and encourages experimentation. (It is surprising how many students take system courses without ever writing concurrent programs.)

In advanced courses, students understand concurrent programming and machine architecture. They can pick up details from the text, leaving time in the classroom to discuss alternative sets of primitives, alternative implementations, and proof of correctness. Students should be encouraged to read some of the many journal articles and books on operating systems, and to see how the primitives in Xinu extend into more complex hardware systems.

Programming projects are strongly encouraged at all levels. Many exercises suggest modifying or measuring the code, or trying alternatives. (The software is available for a nominal charge). Many of the exercises suggest improvements, experiments, and alternative implementations. Larger projects are also possible. Examples that have been used include: a virtual circuit protocol layer to go on top of the present datagram layer; the design of an internet naming and addressing scheme; a remote file server; a remote login facility to allow machines to log into a host operating system across the ring network; and the design of a text editor that minimizes the cost of sending files across the network. Other students have transported Xinu to processors like the Intel 8086 and Motorola 68000.

Some background in basic programming is assumed. The reader should understand basic data structures like linked lists, stacks, and queues, and have written programs in a high-level language like Pascal, PL/I, or C.

I encourage designers to code in high level languages whenever possible, reverting to assembly language only when necessary. Following this approach, I have written most of Xinu in C. Appendix 1 contains a quick introduction to C for readers who are interested only in reading the programs. It explains C constructs by comparing them to similar constructs in Pascal. Readers have an opportunity to develop their ability to read C code in Chapter 3 which deals with a familiar subject (linked lists). The linked list procedures form an especially easy introduction to C because they do not contain any explicit references to concurrent process control constructs. Readers who want to write programs or make substantial changes to Xinu can find more detail about C in the book by Kernighan and Ritchie [1978].

A few machine dependent routines are written in LSI 11 assembler language (almost identical to that of the popular PDP 11). However, the explanations and comments accompanying these routines make it possible to understand them without learning assembler language in detail.

I gratefully acknowledge the help of many people who contributed ideas, hard work, and enthusiasm to the Xinu project. At Purdue, a group of graduate students helped with the initial design and implementation. They also gathered together most of the cross-development software.

Andre Bondi and Subhash Agrawal read through early versions of the process manager and context switch code before a viable compiler and downloader were available.

Steve Salisbury built a C library for Xinu that was compatible with the UNIX C library.

Matt Bishop, Ken Dickey, and Bhasker Parathasarathy adapted a PDP 11 C compiler to the LSI 11.

Dave Schrader devised a process structure for the store-and-forward ring network, and suggested the ports mechanism for passing frames between layers.

Sean Arthur and Professor Vincent Shen spent many hours wiring together a reconfigurable star-shaped ring network and connections to the host computer.

Derrick Burns, a student at Princeton University, transported Xinu to a Motorola 68000 system.

Bob Brown and Chris Kent wrote the downloader, uploader, and post-mortem debugger. Both made helpful suggestions about the choice of primitives and the implementation details. Bob put together an early version of *kprintf* that helped immensely with debugging, and contributed several pieces of code including the routine to size memory, an early version of the communication ports, and modifications to defer the clock.

Several colleagues provided valuable suggestions. Peter Denning first suggested the use of layering. He gave me a draft of Denning *et. al.* [1981], and provided pointers to the other literature, all of which influenced the design.

Tom Murtagh helped work through several layering details.

Janice Cuny, Brian Kernighan, Edmund Lien, and Jacobo Valdes, all commented on an early draft. Bob Brown and Ran Ginosar provided especially helpful suggestions on later versions.

I thank my wife, Chris, for patiently reading many drafts for technical accuracy and syntactic correctness.

I owe much to my experiences, good and bad, with commercially available operating systems. Although Xinu differs internally from existing systems, the fundamental ideas are not new. Several of them came from the UNIX Time-Sharing System developed at Bell Laboratories (see Ritchie and Thompson [1974]). Readers familiar with UNIX should be aware, however, that although many of the ideas, techniques, and names come from UNIX, the two systems are quite different internally — programs written for one system do not usually run on the other.

Finally, I am indebted to Purdue University and Bell Laboratories for support of the project, and to Bell Laboratories for the excellent typesetting facilities that made this book possible.

OPERATING SYSTEM DESIGN
THE XINU APPROACH

1

Introduction and Overview

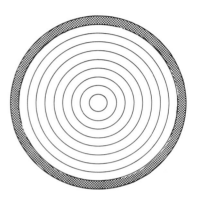

1.1 Operating Systems

Hidden in every computer system is the software that controls processing, manages resources, and communicates with external devices like disks and printers. Collectively, the programs that perform these chores are sometimes referred to as the *executive*, *monitor*, *task manager*, or *kernel*. We will use the broader term *operating system*.

Computer operating systems are among the most complex objects created by mankind: they allow multiple users to share the machine simultaneously, protect data from unauthorized access, and keep dozens of independent devices operating correctly. All this is done at blinding speed by issuing detailed commands to incredibly intricate hardware. But the operating system is not usually an independent machine that sits around all day controlling the computer — it is itself a program that is executed by the same processor that executes user's programs. When the computer is executing a user's program, the operating system is inactive.

Arranging details so the operating system will always regain control is complicated enough, but it is even more impressive that an operating system manages to provide reasonably high-level services with unreasonably low-level hardware. As this book proceeds we will see how crude hardware is, and how much system software it takes to manage even simple devices like terminals. The philosophy behind our design is that operating systems need not be confined by the hardware; they can hide the low-level details of the real machine and provide the high-level services of an abstract machine.

Operating system design is not an old craft; an understanding of it has evolved slowly along with our understanding of machine architectures. In the beginning, machines were scarce and expensive; only a few programmers had an opportunity to use them, and fewer still had an opportunity to build operating systems. Because the basic problems of concurrent computation and automated resource management had not been solved, commercial systems often contained major design flaws. They were unnecessarily complex and riddled with bugs. Their internal details varied from machine to machine because they were intimately concerned with hardware resources. Their external capabilities and human interfaces also varied widely as vendors sought new ways to attract customers.

As technology grew, machines became less costly and more abundant. Advances in micro-electronic technology reduced fabrication costs, and made possible inexpensive single-board and single-chip computers. Vendors now offer customized chips. Designing and implementing software systems for microcomputers is no longer a task reserved for a few specialists; it is a skill expected of competent systems programmers.

Fortunately, our understanding of operating system design has grown along with the technology used to produce new machines. As researchers examined fundamental issues and experimented with system design, they began to formulate principles and techniques of good design. They identified the abstract services common to all operating systems, and explored the many variations possible. They defined the basic operating system components that carry out these machine-independent abstractions, and discovered a technique called *layering* that organizes the components, simplifies system design, and eases implementation.

Compared to its early counterpart, a modern system is simple, clean, and portable. A modern system is easier to design because it follows a pattern, and easier to understand or modify because it is cleanly partitioned into layers. At the heart of the layered organization is the raw machine. Building out from this core, higher layers of software provide more powerful primitives, and shield the user from the machine beneath. Each layer of the system provides an abstract service, implemented in terms of the abstract services provided by lower level layers.

1.2 Our Approach

This book is a guide to the design and implementation of layered operating systems. It takes a practical approach, showing the details of a real system. We begin with a microcomputer, an easy machine to understand, and proceed step-by-step through the construction of a layered system capable of supporting multiple processes, network communication, and a file system. Each chapter explains the role of one layer in the system, illustrating the details with programs. The design ends with a complete, working system that fits together in a clean and elegant way. The resulting system is not a toy; it is a powerful operating system shoehorned into a microcomputer.

Our approach provides two advantages. First, every part of the system is present; the reader will see how an entire system fits together, not merely how one or two important parts interact. Because the code for every piece is included there can be no mystery about any part of the implementation. Second, the reader can obtain a copy of the system to modify, instrument, measure, extend, or transport to another architecture.

Learning from a real system means that the programs form an integral part of the text that cannot be ignored. They are the centerpiece of discussion, and must be read and studied to appreciate the underlying subtlety and engineering detail. Many of the exercises, for example, suggest improvements or modifications that require the reader to delve into details. A skillful programmer will find additional ways to improve the code.

The key to a successful design lies in ordering the layers so services needed to implement a given layer are defined in layers beneath it. In practice, design is a trial-and-error process where the layering is reorganized as design proceeds. To eliminate futile attempts and the consequent backtracking, we can use the results of research and the accumulated experience of other designers. Instead of considering alternative organizations, we simply begin with a layering scheme that is known to work well, and follow it consistently. The organization selected is a process-based layering scheme that is versatile and widespread. It has several other useful properties that will become apparent as well (e.g., successively larger subsets form successively more powerful systems). By the end of the book, the reader will see how each piece of the system fits into this scheme, and be prepared to tackle alternative organizations.

1.3 What An Operating System Is Not

Before proceeding into the design of an operating system, we should all agree on what it is we are about to study. Surprisingly, many programmers do not even have a correct intuitive definition of an operating system. Perhaps the problem arises because vendors and computer professionals often use one name to refer to the set of all software supplied with an operating system as well as the system itself. Perhaps it arises because the available support software usually makes it unnecessary for programmers to access system services directly, or perhaps because the user interface gives the system its characteristic personality. In any case, we can clear the air quickly by ruling out well-known items that are not part of the operating system core.

First, an operating system is not a language or a compiler, even though vendors usually supply compilers with their systems. All programs, even the operating system, must be written in some language. Although recent languages like Concurrent Pascal and Edison aid in writing operating systems, we will see that a system can be constructed using a conventional language and a conventional compiler.

Second, an operating system is not merely a *command interpreter*, although most vendors supply a command interpreter as the human interface to their systems. In older systems, designers chose to build command interpreters that users could not replace easily, causing users to assume that command interpretation was inherently linked to the operating system. In modern systems command interpreters are like other programs; individual users can choose one that suits them, or write their own.

Third, an operating system is not a library of commands. Utility programs that edit files, send mail, compile programs, or link them are just that — utility programs that any competent programmer can write and run without changing the operating system. Vendors usually supply a set of utilities with their operating systems, but local installations often change or replace them without modifying the system itself. Modern systems extend the freedom to replace commands to users so they can tailor the computing environment according to their individual tastes.

1.4 An Operating System Viewed From The Outside

The essence of an operating system lies in the services it provides to user programs. Programs access these services by making *system calls*. System calls look like procedure calls when they appear in a program, but transfer to operating system routines when invoked at run-time. Taken as a set, the system calls establish a well-defined boundary between the running program and the operating system. They define the services that the system provides and the interface to those services.

To appreciate the interior of an operating system, one must first understand the characteristics of the services it provides, and how to use those services. This book describes an operating system called *Xinu*. We will begin by reviewing a few of the services it provides. Later we will return and describe, in detail, the implementation of each.

Xinu runs on a microcomputer along with code from user's programs. It performs chores such as reading characters from a keyboard; displaying characters on a terminal; managing multiple, simultaneous computations; operating timers; saving files on disk storage devices; and relaying messages between programs. The description that follows will help you understand, in general terms, how to use Xinu, and the examples that follow will help explain some of its services.

1.4.1 The Xinu Small Machine Environment

Small computers, like the one described in this book, are often incapable of compiling operating systems as large as the ones that control them. Of course, if a microcomputer has enough speed, storage, and system software, it behaves like any other general-purpose computer system: the programmer can create programs, compile them, save them, and run them using only the micro. One version of the operating system can be used to create the next version just as it can be used to create any new program. But many machines do not have enough resources for these activities because compiling an operating system would take days or weeks. How do programmers create software systems for machines that are slow or small?

How do they create the original version of the system for any new computer? The answer is simple — they do not use an inadequate system; they use another comput-er instead.

Xinu is a good example. The minimum configuration runs on a small, slow microcomputer without using any external storage devices. The entire system, in-cluding user's programs, is prepared on a larger machine, called a *host*, and *down-loaded* onto the microcomputer. To run a program, the user compiles it on the host computer using a cross-compiler, and combines it with code from the Xinu library using a cross-loader. The cross-compiler produces code for the micro. The cross-loader produces an exact memory image for the micro by combining the compiler output with previously compiled code for Xinu. After a memory image has been produced, a downloader copies the memory image from the host machine into the memory of the micro over a standard serial connection like those used to connect terminals to computers. Once the downloader has filled the micro's memory, exe-cution proceeds on the micro independent of the host.

1.4.2 Xinu Services

Programs running under Xinu access services by calling operating system rou-tines. For example, the system routine *putc* writes a single character on an I/O device. It takes two arguments: the device identifier and the character to write. Here is a C† program that writes the message "hi" on the console when run under Xinu:

```
/* ex1.c - main */

#include <conf.h>

/*-----------------------------------------------------------------------
 * main  --  write "hi" on the console
 *-----------------------------------------------------------------------
 */
main()
{
        putc(CONSOLE, 'h'); putc(CONSOLE, 'i');
        putc(CONSOLE, '\r'); putc(CONSOLE, '\n');
}
```

The code introduces several conventions used in Xinu and in this book. The state-ment, *#include <conf.h>* inserts a file of configuration declarations in the source program. The configuration file contains, among other things, a definition for *CONSOLE*. Usually, *CONSOLE* refers to a terminal connected to the micro through which the user interacts. Later we will see the contents of *conf.h* and learn how names like *CONSOLE* become synonymous with devices; all a user needs to

---

†Appendix 1 contains an quick introduction to C that should be sufficient to understand programs in this book.

know is that the include statement must appear in any program that uses device names.

The program writes four characters to the terminal: "h", "i", a carriage return, and a line feed. The latter two are control characters that move the cursor to the beginning of the next line. Xinu does not perform any special operations when the program sends special characters — it merely passes them on to the terminal. They have been included to illustrate that *putc* is not line-oriented; it leaves the programmer responsible for cursor control.

The source file also introduces an important convention followed throughout this book. It begins with a one-line comment that gives the name of the file, *ex1.c*. If a source file contains several procedures, their names all appear on this line. Knowing the names of files will help you locate them if you have a machine-readable copy of Xinu. In addition, a comment of the form

```
/*----------------------------------------------
 * procedure name  --  description
 *----------------------------------------------
 */
```

precedes all procedure or program definitions to help highlight them.

1.4.3 Concurrent Processing

Conventional programs are called *sequential* because the programmer imagines a machine executing the code statement-by-statement. At any instant, the machine is executing exactly one statement. Operating systems support a much larger view of computation called *concurrent processing*. Concurrent processing means that many computations proceed "at the same time."

It is not difficult to imagine several independent programs each being executed statement-by-statement on several machines, but it is exceedingly difficult to imagine several independent computations being performed on a processor that can execute only one instruction at a time. Is concurrent computation real or imagined? If it is real, how does the hardware keep each program from interfering with the others? How do the programs cooperate so that only one takes control of an input or output device at a given time?

Computer systems usually do have some concurrent capabilities, but the most visible form of concurrency, multiple independent programs executing simultaneously, is a grand illusion. To create the illusion, an operating system switches a single processor among multiple programs, allowing it to execute one for only a few thousandths of a second before moving on to another. When viewed by a human, the programs appear to proceed concurrently. The technique, called *multiprogramming*, appears in almost all commercial systems. Interactive *multiprogramming* systems are called *timesharing systems* if the policy used to switch the processor around gives all users equal amounts of CPU time. The chief characteristic of a timesharing system is that the service received by a single user is inversely proportional to the load on the system.

Multiprogramming is a misleading term because concurrent processing encompasses more than "many instances of conventional programs". To be more accurate we should say that an operating system switches the CPU among many "computations" called *processes*, *jobs*, or *tasks*. Because terminology varies from system to system, it is difficult to choose a term that accurately reflects the notion of "computation" in Xinu. The terms *process* or *job* usually connote an isolated computation, while *task* often refers to one of a set of cooperating computations. In particular, concurrent programming languages often use the term *task* to refer to computations that share memory.

Xinu refers to "computations" as *processes*, the term used throughout the rest of this book. The next section helps distinguish the notion of "process" from the usual notion of "sequential program" by giving some examples. As we will see, this difference plays a central role in operating system design — everything must be built with it in mind.

1.4.4 The Distinction Between Programs And Processes

When programmers write a conventional (sequential) program, they imagine a single processor executing the program step-by-step without interruption or delay. However, a programmer writing code for concurrent processes must take an entirely different view. The operating system itself is a good example of a concurrent program. At any given instant, several processes (computations) may be executing. It may be that no two of them are executing the same program, but it may happen that they are all about to execute the same statement of one program. To further complicate matters, switching the processor among processes may cause one process to overtake another; no guarantees are made about their relative speeds. Designing the system procedures to operate correctly in a concurrent environment provides a tough intellectual challenge because they must all cooperate no matter which ones the user processes call or in which order. An example will help explain the problem.

In Xinu, a single process starts executing at the beginning of the user's main program when the system begins. The initial process may continue execution by itself, or it may create new, independent processes. When one process creates a new one, the original continues to execute, and the new process begins executing concurrently. For example, the code from file ex2.c consists of a main program and two procedures, *prA* and *prB*.

```
/* ex2.c - main, prA, prB */

#include <conf.h>

/*------------------------------------------------------------------
 * main  --   example of creating processes in Xinu
 *------------------------------------------------------------------
 */
main()
{
        int     prA(), prB();

        resume( create(prA, 200, 20, "proc 1", 0) );
        resume( create(prB, 200, 20, "proc 2", 0) );
}


/*------------------------------------------------------------------
 * prA  --   repeatedly print 'A' without ever terminating
 *------------------------------------------------------------------
 */
prA()
{
        while( 1 )
                putc(CONSOLE, 'A');
}


/*------------------------------------------------------------------
 * prB  --   repeatedly print 'B' without ever terminating
 *------------------------------------------------------------------
 */
prB()
{
        while( 1 )
                putc(CONSOLE, 'B');
}
```

The main program never calls either procedure directly. Instead, it calls two operating system procedures, *create* and *resume*, passing the addresses of *prA* or *prB* as the first argument (other arguments to *create* specify such things as the stack space needed, a scheduling priority, process name, the count of arguments for the process, and the process arguments). Each call to *create* forms a new process that will begin executing instructions at the address specified by its first argument. *Create* sets up the process, leaving it ready to run, but temporarily suspended. It returns the process id of the new process to its caller (in some languages *create* would be called a "function" instead of a procedure). The *process id* is an integer that identifies the created process so it can be referenced later. In the example, the main program passes the process id returned by *create* to *resume* as an argument. *Resume* starts (unsuspends) the process so it begins executing. The distinction between normal procedure calls and process creation is this:

> *A procedure call does not return until the called procedure completes. Create and resume return to the caller after starting the process, allowing execution of both the calling procedure and the named procedure to proceed concurrently.*

All Xinu processes execute independently and concurrently. In the example, the first new process executes code in procedure *prA*, printing the letter `A' continuously; the second executes code in procedure *prB*, printing the letter `B' continuously. Because processes execute concurrently, the output is a mixture of `A's and `B's. What happens to the main program? Remember that each independent computation is a process, so we should ask, "What happens to the process executing the main program?" The process executing the main program exits after the second call to resume because it has reached the end of the main program. Its exit does not affect the new processes at all. They go on spewing out `A's and `B's forever.

The example below shows that independent processes need not execute independent code. Just as in the previous example, a single process begins executing the main program. It calls *create* twice to start two new processes; both execute the code from procedure *prntr*.

```
/* ex3.c - main, prntr */

#include <conf.h>

/*------------------------------------------------------------------------
 * main  --  example of 2 processes executing the same code concurrently
 *------------------------------------------------------------------------
 */
main()
{
        int     prntr();

        resume( create(prntr, 200, 20, "print A", 1, 'A') );
        resume( create(prntr, 200, 20, "print B", 1, 'B') );
}


/*------------------------------------------------------------------------
 * prntr  --  print a character indefinitely
 *------------------------------------------------------------------------
 */
prntr( ch )
        char    ch;
{
        while ( 1 )
                putc(CONSOLE, ch);
}
```

The two processes proceed concurrently without any effect on one another, even
though they happen to be executing the same piece of code. The key point here is
that the notion of *process* is different from the usual notions of *program*:

> *A program consists of code executed by a single process. In
> sharp contrast, processes are not uniquely associated with a piece
> of code; multiple processes can execute the same code simultane-
> ously.*

This gives us some hint of the difficulty involved in designing operating systems.
Not only must each piece be designed to operate correctly by itself, the designer
must also guarantee that it does not interfere with other pieces, no matter how
many processes execute simultaneously.

    Although processes share code, it is important that each one have at least some
local variables. If every variable was shared by every process, chaos would result
whenever two processes tried to execute the same code. One can imagine what
would happen if two processes tried to use a single variable as the index of a *for*

loop. To avoid such interference the system creates an independent set of local variables for each process.

Create even allocates an independent set of arguments for each process, as the example demonstrates. The code in file ex3.c shows how two processes are passed different arguments even though they execute the same code. In the call to *create*, the last two arguments specify a count of arguments that follow, and a character that the system passes to the newly created process. The first new process created is passed character 'A', so it begins execution with formal parameter *ch* set to 'A'. The second new process begins with *ch* set to 'B'. Although these processes execute the same code, they each have their own copy of *ch*, just as recursive invocations of a procedure have their own copy of formal parameters. As in the earlier example, the output contains a mixture of both letters. This points out another significant difference between programs and processes:

> *Storage for local variables and procedure arguments is associated with the process executing the procedure, not with the code in which they appear.*

In terms of the implementation, each process has its own stack of local variables, formal parameters, and procedure calls.

1.4.5 Process Exit

The previous example consisted of a concurrent program with three processes: the initial process, and the two processes started with the system call *create*. We said that the initial process ceased when it reached the end of the code in the main program; this is referred to as *process exit*. Other processes can exit in the same way, namely, by reaching the end of the procedure in which they start (or by returning from it). Once the process exits, it disappears forever; there is simply one less computation in progress.

You should not confuse process exit with normal procedure call and return, or with recursive procedure calls. Just like a sequential program, each process has its own stack of procedure calls. Whenever it executes a call, the called procedure is pushed onto the stack. Whenever it returns from a procedure, the procedure is popped off the stack. Process exit occurs only when the process pops the last procedure (or main program) off its stack.

The system routine *kill* provides another mechanism to terminate a process. In a sense, *kill* is the inverse of *create*. It takes a process id as an argument, and stops that process immediately. A process can be killed at any time, and at any level of procedure nesting. When terminated, the process ceases execution, and its local variables disappear. The entire record of local variables and procedure calls on the stack disappears as well, of course. A process can exit by killing itself as easily as it can kill another process. To do so, it uses system call *getpid* to obtain its own process id, and *kill* to terminate:

```
kill( getpid() );
```

When used in this manner, the call to *kill* never returns because the calling process exits.

1.4.6 Shared Memory

In Xinu, each process has its own copy of local variables, formal parameters, and procedure calls, but all processes share the set of global (external) variables. Sharing data is sometimes convenient, but it can be dangerous, especially for programmers who are unaccustomed to writing concurrent programs. Sharing also introduces the need for more operating system services. Consider a simple example of two processes that want to communicate through a shared integer, *n*.

```
/* ex4.c - main, produce, consume */

int    n = 0;        /* external variables are shared by all processes */

/*------------------------------------------------------------------
 * main  --  example of unsynchronized producer and consumer processes
 *------------------------------------------------------------------
 */
main()
{
        int     produce(), consume();

        resume( create(consume, 200, 20, "cons", 0) );
        resume( create(produce, 200, 20, "prod", 0) );
}


/*------------------------------------------------------------------
 * produce  --  increment n 2000 times and exit
 *------------------------------------------------------------------
 */
produce()
{
        int i;

        for( i=1 ; i<=2000 ; i++ )
                n++;
}


/*------------------------------------------------------------------
 * consume  --  print n 2000 times and exit
```

```
 *-------------------------------------------------------------------------
 */
consume()
{
        int i;

        for( i=1 ; i<=2000 ; i++ )
                printf("n is %d \n", n);
}
```

In the code, global variable n is a shared integer, initialized to zero. The process executing *produce* loops 2000 times, incrementing n; we call this process the *producer*. The process executing *consume* also loops 2000 times; it prints the value of n in decimal. We call this process the *consumer*.

1.4.7 Synchronization

Try running *ex4.c* under Xinu — its output may surprise you. Most programmers suspect that the consumer will print at least a few, perhaps all, of the values between 0 and 2000, but it does not. In a typical run n has the value 0 for the first few lines; after that, its value is 2000. Even though the two processes run concurrently, they do not require the same amount of time. The consumer process must format and write a line of output, an operation that requires hundreds of machine instructions. Although formatting is expensive it does not dominate the timing; output does. The consumer quickly fills the available output buffers, and must wait for the output device to send characters to the console before it can proceed. While the consumer waits, the producer runs. Because it executes only a few machine instructions per iteration, the producer runs through its entire loop and exits in the short time it takes the output device to print a few characters. When the consumer resumes execution again, it finds that n has the value 2000.

Production and consumption of data by independent processes is common. The question arises "how can the programmer synchronize producer and consumer processes so that the consumer receives every datum produced?" Clearly, the producer must wait for the consumer to access the datum. Likewise, the consumer must wait for the producer to manufacture it. However, the mechanism for synchronization must be designed carefully, because the crucial constraint is this:

> *In a single processor system, no process should use the CPU while waiting for another.*

A process that executes instructions while waiting for another is said to be *busy waiting*. To understand our prohibition on busy waiting, think of the implementation. If a process uses the CPU while waiting, the CPU cannot be executing other processes. At best, the computation will be delayed unnecessarily, and at worst the waiting process will use all the CPU time and wind up waiting forever.

Xinu avoids busy waiting by supplying coordination primitives called *sema-phores*, and system calls that operate on them. Each semaphore consists of an integer value, initialized when the semaphore is created. The system call *wait* decrements a semaphore and causes the process to delay if the result is negative. *Signal* performs the opposite action, incrementing the semaphore and allowing a waiting process to continue. To synchronize with semaphores, the producer and consumer need two semaphores, one on which the consumer waits, and one on which the producer waits. Semaphores are created dynamically with the system call *screate*, which takes the desired initial count as an argument, and returns an integer by which the semaphore is known.

In the example below, the main process creates two semaphores, *consumed* and *produced*, and passes them as arguments to the processes it creates. Because the semaphore named *produced* begins with a count of 1, *wait* will not block the first time it is called in *cons2*. So, the consumer is free to print the initial value of *n*. However, semaphore *consumed* begins with a count of 0, so the first call to *wait* in *prod2* blocks. In effect, the producer waits for semaphore *consumed* before incrementing *n* to guarantee that the consumer has printed it. When the example runs, the consumer prints all values of *n* from 0 through 1999.

```
/* ex5.c - main, prod2, cons2 */

int     n = 0;                     /* n assigned an initial value of zero  */

/*------------------------------------------------------------------------
 *   main  --   producer and consumer processes synchronized with semaphores
 *------------------------------------------------------------------------
 */
main()
{
        int     prod2(), cons2();
        int     produced, consumed;

        consumed = screate(0);
        produced = screate(1);
        resume( create(cons2, 200, 20, "cons", 2, consumed, produced) );
        resume( create(prod2, 200, 20, "prod", 2, consumed, produced) );
}


/*------------------------------------------------------------------------
 * prod2  --   increment n 2000 times, waiting for it to be consumed
 *------------------------------------------------------------------------
 */
prod2(consumed, produced)
```

```
{
        int i;

        for( i=1 ; i<=2000 ; i++ ) {
                wait(consumed);
                n++;
                signal(produced);
        }
}


/*-------------------------------------------------------------------
 * cons2  --  print n 2000 times, waiting for it to be produced
 *-------------------------------------------------------------------
 */
cons2(consumed, produced)
{
        int i;

        for( i=1 ; i<=2000 ; i++ ) {
                wait(produced);
                printf("n is %d \n", n);
                signal(consumed);
        }
}
```

1.4.8 Mutual Exclusion

Semaphores provide another important purpose in Xinu, namely, mutual exclusion. Two or more processes engage in *mutual exclusion* when they cooperate so that only one of them obtains access to a resource at a given time. For example, suppose two executing processes each, from time to time, want to insert an item into a linked list. If they both happen to access the list concurrently, they could leave pointers set incorrectly. Synchronization is not the answer because the two processes do not want to alternate accesses; they merely want to exclude each other.

To mutually exclude for use of a resource like a linked list, the processes must create a semaphore (with an initial count of 1). Before accessing the resource, each process executes *wait* on the semaphore, and calls *signal* after it has completed. Often, the calls to *wait* and *signal* can be imbedded at the beginning and end of a procedure designed to perform the update. For example, file ex6.c shows an array, and a procedure to add items to it:

```
/* ex6.c - additem */

int     mutex;                    /* assume initialized with screate    */
int     a[100];
int     n = 0;

/*------------------------------------------------------------------------
 * additem  --  obtain exclusive access to array 'a' and add item to it
 *------------------------------------------------------------------------
 */
additem(item)
{
        wait(mutex);
        a[n++] = item;
        signal(mutex);
}
```

The assumption here is that a process created semaphore *mutex* using *screate* before any process called *additem*.

The code in file ex6.c provides a final illustration of the difference between the way one programs in sequential and concurrent environments. In the world of sequential programs, a procedure often acts to isolate changes to a data structure. By localizing code that changes a data structure in one procedure, the programmer gains a sense of security — only a small amount of code need be checked for correctness, because nothing else in the program will interfere with the data structure. In a multiprocess environment, however, isolating the code into a single procedure is insufficient. The programmer must also guarantee that its execution is exclusive, because interference can come from some other process executing the same procedure!

1.5 An Operating System Viewed From The Inside

If designed well, the interior of an operating system can be as elegant and clean as the best sequential program. The design described in this book achieves elegance by partitioning the system functions into roughly eight major components, and organizing those components into a layered hierarchy. Examining this particular system is especially helpful in understanding layered organization because it demonstrates how all the functions in a conventional operating system fit together.

Figure 1.1 shows an overview of the components we will discuss, as well as their ultimate organization. Although it is shown in final form, it was designed one layer at a time. At the heart of the system lies the scheduler and context switch. They are responsible for switching the CPU among the processes that are ready to run. Procedures in the next layer constitute the rest of the process manager, providing primitives to create, kill, suspend, and resume processes.

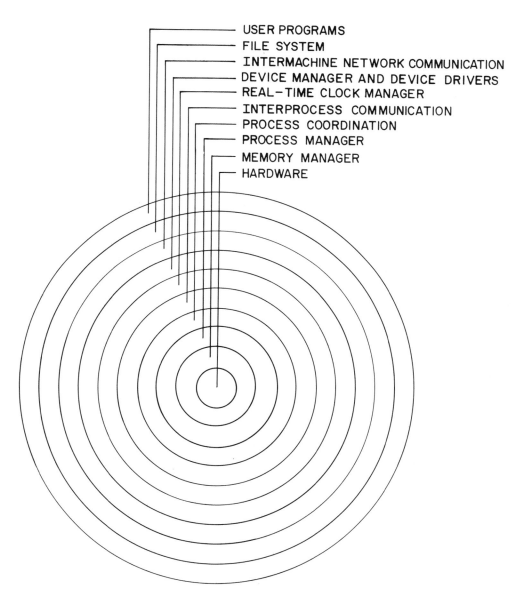

USER PROGRAMS
FILE SYSTEM
INTERMACHINE NETWORK COMMUNICATION
DEVICE MANAGER AND DEVICE DRIVERS
REAL-TIME CLOCK MANAGER
INTERPROCESS COMMUNICATION
PROCESS COORDINATION
PROCESS MANAGER
MEMORY MANAGER
HARDWARE

Figure 1.1 The layering of components in Xinu

Just beyond the process management layer comes the process coordination layer
that implements semaphores. Next come the procedures for real-time clock
management that allow, among other things, processes to delay for a specified time.
On top of the real-time clock layer lies a layer of device-independent input and out-

put routines. Above the device routines, a layer implements machine-to-machine communication, and the layer above that implements a file system.

The internal layering of a system should not be confused with the services it provides. The components are organized into layers to make the design and implementation cleaner; layering does not restrict procedure calls at run-time. Once the system has been built, procedures in higher layers can call routines like *wait* and *signal* that reside in the process coordination layer directly, just as they can call routines like *putc* that reside in outer layers. Thus, the layered structure describes only the implementation, not the flow of control.

The remainder of this book proceeds through the design of a system that follows the layered organization shown above. We consider the layers in roughly the same order as they are designed and built, from the innermost outward. Although this may seem awkward at first, the organization should start to seem meaningful by Chapter 6. By the end of Chapter 13, we will have designed a minimal kernel capable of supporting programs like those in the examples above. Network communication capability will be added to the system by the end of Chapter 16, and the design will include a complete core of operating system routines (including a file system) by the end of Chapter 18.

1.6 Summary

Operating system design has become a task expected of systems programmers. Unlike conventional, sequential programs, operating systems support a broad notion of computation in which multiple, independent processes execute concurrently, and high-level abstract services are provided. To design operating systems intelligently, programmers must appreciate concurrent processing, and the services like mutual exclusion and process synchronization needed to support it.

The examples given here show how programs use a few of the basic operating system services. They illustrate the differences between sequential programs and concurrently executing processes, and show how processes begin and end in Xinu. The examples illustrating the use of semaphores show how processes synchronize, and how they cooperate to guarantee mutual exclusion.

This introduction has focused on the exterior of an operating system, showing how programs use the services it provides. Later chapters concentrate on the interior of an operating system, showing how to design and build it, instead of how to use it. They proceed through the system one layer at a time, beginning with the raw hardware, and ending with a working system.

FOR FURTHER STUDY

Good surveys of operating system facilities can be found in Calingaert [1982], Habermann [1976], Peterson and Silberschatz [1983], and Tsichritzis and Bernstein [1974]. Warwick [1970] provides a somewhat older view. Books by Brinch Hansen [1973], Habermann [1976], and Shaw [1974] all consider design issues. Readers interested in more information will find that journal papers provide deeper treatments of the subject. Selected references can be found at the end of each chapter, and in the Bibliography.

Details about Xinu system calls and library routines are given throughout the text. They are summarized in the manual in Appendix 2, which also describes the cross-development commands.

EXERCISES

1.1   Explore the system calls available on your favorite operating system, and write a few programs that use them.

1.2   The program in file ex3.c has 3 processes running at one point. Modify it to use only 2 processes.

1.3   Under Xinu, the output from the programs in file ex2.c and ex3.c usually consists of alternate A's and B's. Speculate about the implementation of *putc*. What happens if one of the processes runs at a higher priority than another?

1.4   Test the program in file ex4.c repeatedly. Does it always print the same number of zeroes? Does it ever find a value of *n* other than 0 or 2000?

1.5   Modify the producer-consumer code in file ex5.c to use a buffer of 15 integers. Have the producer write integers 1, 2, ... in successive locations of the buffer, wrapping around to the beginning after filling the last slot, and have the consumer read and print them. Do you appreciate how to use counting semaphores with a buffer of size $k > 1$?

1.6   In file ex5.c, the semaphore *consumed* is created with a count of 1. Modify the code so *consumed* is created with a count of 0, and have the producer wait on it *after* signalling *produced*. Does it affect the output?

1.7   Write a program to find out what happens to a process that executes *wait* on a nonexistent semaphore, and an existing semaphore that no other process signals.

2

An Overview of the Machine and Run-Time Environment

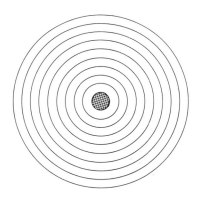

2.1 The Machine

Operating systems deal with the details of devices, processors, and memory — they cannot be designed without some notion of a machine. This book uses the Digital Equipment Corporation LSI 11/2 16-bit microcomputer. The LSI 11/2 was chosen because of its simplicity, popularity, and well-known instruction set. It is sufficiently simple to serve as a model of the general purpose microprocessor, and sufficiently complex to illustrate the details of operating system software. Finally, the 11/2 is a microcomputer version of the PDP 11 computer, a popular and well-known minicomputer.

The remainder of this chapter introduces the 11/2 hardware, describing pertinent features of the processor, memory, and communication devices. It explains the architecture, asynchronous communication, disk storage devices, and mechanisms like the stack, vectored interrupts, and device addressing. Although the details are not important, the basic ideas are.

2.1.1 Physical Organization Of The 11/2

An LSI 11/2 is constructed from a set of printed circuit boards that are roughly 5" X 9". Each of these *cards* is populated with integrated circuits, connected to form a functional unit. The card contains metal contacts or *fingers* at one end that plug into a slotted *backplane*. Sockets on the backplane perform two functions: they hold the boards in place, and provide electrical connections to them.

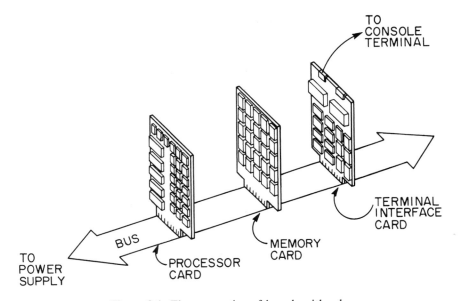

Figure 2.1 The connection of boards with a bus.

Conceptually, the sockets are wired together to form a *bus*. The vendor has named the bus used by an 11/2 the *Q-bus*. Some bus wires, like the power lines, attach to all boards in parallel. Other signals travel to the board on one contact and away on another so the board can decide whether to pass the signal through or to stop it. These are used, for example, to decide which board will use the bus at a given time.

One board contains the 11/2 processor itself; it must reside at the beginning of the bus. Other boards contain memory or I/O devices. Instead of one specific set of boards, the vendor offers a variety of boards so that each customer can plug together a customized configuration. For example, one type of board contains memory. Another contains less memory but also includes a device that communicates with a terminal. Yet another contains 4 terminal interface devices but no memory.

A board can communicate with other boards only by passing signals across the bus. When the processor board needs to write to memory, it places the address and data on the bus for the memory board to retrieve and store. When it needs to read data or fetch instructions, it places the address on the bus and asks the memory board to supply the data value. Naturally, the details of the bus design specify exactly how the boards manipulate and respond to signals to make these operations work correctly; for our purposes, such details are unimportant.

Independent of the physical arrangement and number of boards, memory must always be logically contiguous. To permit memory from several boards to be mapped into a contiguous address range, each board contains switches or hardwired jumpers that can be changed. Thus, it is possible to configure two identical memory boards so that one responds to low memory addresses while the other responds to higher addresses. Likewise, the I/O device interfaces contain jumpers so two boards can be configured to represent two distinct devices even though they happen to be the same physical type.

The physical order of boards along the Q-bus determines their priority, something that will come up in later chapters. We said that some signals enter a board on one connector and leave on another so the board can decide whether to intercept the signal or to pass it on down the bus. The signal that grants service to a board is one such signal. Suppose that two devices, say two terminals, are waiting for service. The CPU sends a grant signal down the bus. It passes along from board to board until it reaches a board that is waiting for service. The first board with a device waiting responds to the signal without passing it on. Boards further down the bus wait until the CPU finishes servicing the first board and reissues the grant.

2.1.2 Logical Organization Of The 11/2

The operating system is concerned with the logical organization of the machine, not its physical organization. The next sections describe the highlights of the 11/2 hardware that affect some of the code described later. It is not important to understand all the details now. Programmers familiar with the LSI 11 or PDP 11 architecture can skip most of the material; other readers should skim through the text to learn the basic ideas, and refer to it when specific details arise in later chapters.

2.1.3 Registers In The LSI 11/2

Figure 2.2 illustrates that the LSI 11 processor contains eight 16-bit registers, and one 16-bit processor status word (PS).

Notation	Register	Use
R0	0	general purpose
R1	1	general purpose
R2	2	general purpose
R3	3	general purpose
R4	4	previous display
R5	5	current display
SP	6	stack pointer
PC	7	program counter
PS	status	processor status

Figure 2.2 Registers in the 11/2

Registers 0-5, denoted R0 - R5, are general purpose registers that can contain an integer, an address, or two 8-bit characters. Register 6 is always a stack pointer (SP), and register 7 is the program counter (PC). The C compiler uses R5 to point to the frame (display) on the run-time stack for the currently active procedure, and R4 to point to the calling procedure's frame.

2.1.4 The Address Space

Memory on the 11/2 is divided into 8-bit quantities called *bytes*, with the byte being the smallest addressable unit. The term *character* is often used in place of *byte* because bytes are commonly used to hold characters. Most instructions can operate on either bytes or *words* (16 bits). Word operations may refer to even or odd byte addresses; the operation always affects the addressed byte and the next higher byte. Programmers unfamiliar with the 11/2 should note that unlike many machines one accesses the low-order byte of the word at the same address as the word itself.

The 11/2 can address up to 64K bytes of memory (K=1024) because addresses are 16 bits long. However, on the Q-bus the highest 8K addresses are reserved for devices. (Figure 2.3 shows where device addresses reside in this space.) Thus, a system can contain at most 56K bytes of real memory, addressed from 0 through 0157777 (octal†). All addresses refer to one physical address space; there is no memory management hardware. By convention memory addresses 0 through 0777 are reserved for interrupt and exception vectors (as described below), so programs and data start at location 01000. Because the stack manipulation hardware grows stacks from high memory to low, a program stack is usually allocated starting at the highest available memory address (which may be less than 0157777 if the machine has less than 56K bytes of real memory).

---

† Throughout the text we will use the C convention of starting octal constants with a leading 0.

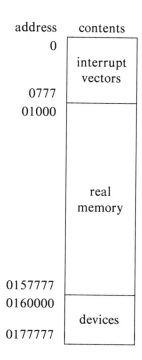

address   contents
0
interrupt
vectors
0777
01000

real
memory

0157777
0160000
devices
0177777

Figure 2.3 The address space of the 11/2 microcomputer Q-bus.

2.1.5 Processor Status Word

The processor status word contains the condition code bits and processor priority level. Figure 2.4 shows the layout of the PS.

15 through 8	7-6-5	4	3-2-1-0
...	Processor Priority	Trace mode	Condition codes

Figure 2.4 The bits of the 11/2 processor status word.

The condition codes (bits 3-0) are set whenever an instruction like *add* produces an arithmetic result or when a comparison is performed; they record whether the result is negative or zero, or whether an overflow or carry occurred. Conditional branch instructions examine the condition codes to determine whether to branch.

Bits 7-5 of the PS give the processor priority, a value from 0 to 7. These bits are sometimes called the *processor mask*, or *interrupt mask*. On the 11/2, processor levels 4 and higher mean that external interrupts are *disabled*, while values 0-3 mean that interrupts are *enabled*. When it becomes necessary to disable interrupts, the Xinu software will set the interrupt level to 7 by assigning the PS octal 0340.

2.1.6 Vectored Interrupts

The 11/2 processor employs the conventional *vectored interrupt* scheme for handling exceptions and interrupts from external devices. Whenever an external device needs to communicate with the processor, the device places a signal on the interrupt bus line. If the processor is running with interrupts enabled, it checks the interrupt line after executing each instruction to see whether an interrupt needs processing. To handle the interrupt, the processor sends an acknowledgement over the bus, and requests that the interrupting device return an *interrupt vector address*. The first device with a pending request receives the acknowledgement and responds by returning its interrupt vector address, *v*. When it receives the interrupt vector address from the bus, the processor pushes the current PC and PS on the stack, loads the PC and PS from two words in memory starting at location *v*, and continues executing instructions beginning at the new location. Each device is assigned a unique interrupt vector address with switches or jumpers before it is inserted in the bus, enabling the system software to distinguish among them. Thus, there is no need to poll devices to find out which one needs service when an interrupt occurs because the software can identify devices based on their interrupt vector address.

It is the programmer's responsibility to insure that an appropriate environment has been established before the interrupt occurs. The interrupt vector locations in memory must contain a valid PC and PS, and the stack pointer register, SP, must point to a valid stack address that can hold at least two 16-bit words. The stored PC points to an *interrupt service routine* or *interrupt handler* for the interrupting device. For all intents, the interrupt acts like a procedure call (except that the hardware forces it to occur "between" the execution of two instructions in the user's code). The processor executes code in the interrupt routine, eventually returning to the place at which the user's program was interrupted. To make the interrupt transparent to a running program, the interrupt handler must save and restore the state of the machine. On the 11/2, saving the state consists of saving registers R0 through R6 (the hardware saves R7 and the PS). In practice, the stack pointer (R6) need not be saved provided that the interrupt routine pops off whatever it pushes on the stack before returning (i.e., restores the stack to its original position).

To prevent the interrupt service routine from itself being interrupted by another device, the PS stored in the interrupt vector usually specifies a processor level of 7. Thus, as soon as interrupt processing begins the processor operates with interrupts disabled.

Interrupt processing ends when the processor executes a *return from interrupt* instruction (rti or rtt). In a single step, the return-from-interrupt restores the PC and PS from the stack, and returns the stack pointer to its original value, reversing the action taken by the processor when it detected an interrupt, and allowing processing to continue where it was interrupted.

2.1.7 Exceptional Conditions

Exceptional conditions are handled by the 11/2 exactly like interrupts. An exception, like a reference to nonexistent memory, execution of an invalid instruction code, or power failure, can be thought of as hardware detected errors. When an exception occurs, the processor pushes the current PC and PS onto the stack and loads a new PC and PS from a vector location in memory. As with interrupt vectors, the programmer assumes responsibility for storing a valid PC and PS in each exception vector. Unlike interrupt vector locations that can be changed, however, exception vectors are permanently assigned by the hardware to memory locations 0-27. Also unlike interrupts, exceptions cannot be disabled by changing the processor level.

2.1.8 Asynchronous Communication

An asynchronous communication device, often called a *serial line unit*, sends and receives characters (e.g., to a conventional terminal). At least one board in any 11/2 system contains an asynchronous communication device that connects that computer to a terminal. This section describes the basic hardware and gives the reader some intuition about programming it; later chapters describe device driver software in detail.

The cable connecting the device to a terminal consists of three wires: one carries data into the computer, one carries data away from the computer, and one provides an electrical "ground" against which voltages on the other wires are measured. Signals on the data wires consist of a series of positive or negative pulses corresponding to the 0 and 1 bits of the data being transmitted. Signals are *serial* because they travel down the wire one bit at a time, and *asynchronous* because the transmitter sends a character whenever one is available; there is no synchronization between the transmitter and receiver to control the start of a character.

When the CPU instructs a serial transmitter to send a character, the transmitter converts it to a sequence of zeros and ones, and sends them down the line contiguously. The transmitter then delays at least as long as it takes to send a bit to give the receiver time to process characters. Once finished sending a character the line remains idle (e.g., in the 0 state) until the CPU gives the transmitter the next character. In practice, the transmitter may also send an additional 1 bit, before and after each character to help the receiver recognize when to start reading bits, or a parity bit that helps the receiver detect errors. The number of such *start*, *stop*, and *parity* bits must be agreed upon by both the transmitter and receiver.

Much of the work involved in converting characters into a series of pulses or a series of pulses back into a character is carried out by a single integrated circuit that is controlled by a precise clock. The circuit is called a *Universal Asynchronous Receiver and Transmitter* (UART). Using its clock, the UART transmitter controls the duration of pulses, allowing no delay between them as it sends a character. The pulse rate, given in units of *baud*, can be thought of as the number of bits per second being sent. Common baud rates include 150, 300, 600, 1200, 2400,

4800, 9600, 19200, and 38400, with 9600 baud being a popular speed for CRT terminals and 300 baud being popular for electromechanical terminals. (Lower baud rates are used when signals must be sent greater distances.) Usually, the UART is configured with other components that can switch the baud rate. Sophisticated interfaces allow the CPU to change the baud rate at will; on less sophisticated ones switching may require changing physical switches or wiring jumpers on the interface board. Most devices on the 11/2 fall into the "unsophisticated" category.

An asynchronous receiver always monitors the incoming line, starting its timer when the first pulse arrives. It uses its clock to time the duration of pulses, sampling each pulse several times to insure that it has correctly timed the pulse boundaries. When the receiver collects 8 pulses, it records them in an 8-bit character and stops sampling.

Errors occur when the receiver cannot make sense out of the signals it receives. If the samples of a given pulse include a mixture of zeroes and ones, the receiver knows that either the transmitter sent at a different baud rate than it expected, or the signal was distorted by interference. It declares that a *framing error* occurred. *Character overrun errors* occur because the system cannot keep up with the transmitter. The receiver itself holds only one character at a time. The CPU must extract each character before subsequent characters arrive or the receiver indicates an overrun condition and replaces the earlier characters with the latest one.

A final form of "error" occurs when the line remains idle in the wrong state for an extended period (greater than the time it takes to transmit a character). Transmitters create this condition, calling it a *break*. Receivers report breaks as framing errors. Some systems use the break condition to trigger special handling. For example, the 11/2 can be wired so breaks on the console terminal line cause the processor to halt, a mechanism that the Xinu downloader uses to gain control of the system.

2.1.9 LSI 11 Asynchronous Serial Line Hardware

Conceptually, asynchronous transmitters and receivers are grouped into pairs consisting of one receiver and one transmitter. We will call each pair a *serial line unit* (SLU). The operating system treats each SLU as an independent device, assigned a unique device address and a unique interrupt vector address. Within an SLU, the transmitter and receiver function independently to allow simultaneous transfer in both directions. They are paired only because most serial connections involve two-way communication.

2.1.10 Addressing A Serial Line Unit

The CPU communicates with a serial line unit by reading and writing to addresses beyond the end of real memory. Boards containing devices watch the bus for addresses that correspond to their devices, and respond accordingly. From the programmer's point of view, each SLU contains 4 16-bit registers, denoted RCSR (receiver control and status), RBUF (received data buffer), XCSR (transmitter control and status), and XBUF (transmitter data buffer). Figure 2.5 shows their arrangement.

Name	High-Order Byte	Low-Order Byte
RCSR:	unused	receiver control
RBUF:	receiver errors	received data
XCSR:	unused	transmitter control
XBUF:	unused	transmitted data buffer

Figure 2.5 The arrangement of SLU registers.

Hardware on the interface board maps these registers into 4 contiguous words in the LSI 11/2's address space. For example, the console terminal usually uses addresses 0177560, 0177562, 0177564, and 0177566. To communicate with the device, a program reads or writes the address corresponding to the device register address, just as it reads or writes to a real memory address.

Device registers are not actually storage locations. When the CPU reads or writes to a device address, the interface board containing the device intercepts the transfer and interprets it as an instruction to transfer data between the device and CPU or to control the device. Thus, I/O can be viewed as a side effect of manipulating certain locations in the address space. For example, writing a character to the XBUF register address causes the SLU to capture that character and start transmitting it on the serial output line. Once the board accepts the character, it operates independent of the CPU; processing continues while the transmitter sends the character.

The CPU retrieves a character that has been received over the serial input line by reading from the RBUF address. Because the LSI 11 bus is 16 bits wide, the SLU transfers the character it has read in the low-order byte, and uses the high-order byte to report any errors that occurred during reception. Figure 2.6 shows the format of data read from the RBUF address.

Bit:	15	14	13	12	11	10	9	8	7	...	0
Contents:	E	V	F	P	0	0	0	0		character	

Figure 2.6 The format of data read from RBUF.

Bit E is 1 if any error occurred, V is 1 if an overflow error occurred, F is 1 if a framing error occurred, and P is 1 if a parity error occurred. The RBUF is *read-only* in that writes directed to that address are ignored by the hardware. Accessing the received data buffer has the side effect of clearing the receiver and enabling it to receive the next character.

2.1.11 Polled vs. Interrupt-Driven I/O

So far we have only described the basic mechanics of transfers between the CPU and the SLU; we have not discussed how they coordinate. Coordination is important because the CPU will interfere with the SLU if it accesses the receiver or transmitter data buffers while an I/O operation is in progress. How does the CPU know when a character has been received or when the transmitter is idle and ready to send a character? It uses one of two techniques: *polled I/O* or *interrupt-driven I/O*.

Polling requires the CPU to check the device repeatedly until it finds that a character is waiting. The CPU uses information from the CSR register to determine whether the device is idle. When read, the receiver's CSR returns the status information shown by Figure 2.7:

```
  Bit:     15      ...      8   7   6   5      ...        0
Contents: |      unused       | D | I |      unused       |
```

Figure 2.7 The format of data read from RCSR.

Bit 7 of the RCSR (marked D) returns 1 if the SLU has received a character from the serial input line, and is ready for the CPU to access it; otherwise it returns 0. To poll, the CPU reads from the RCSR address until bit 7 becomes 1, after which it reads from the RBUF address to obtain the character and restart the receiver for the next character.

Polled transmission follows the same approach. Bit 7 of the transmitter's CSR (marked T in Figure 2.8 below) returns 0 as long as the transmitter remains busy, after which it returns 1.

```
  Bit:     15      ...      8   7   6   5      ...    1   0
Contents: |      unused       | T | I |      unused     | B |
```

Figure 2.8 The format of information in XCSR.

To poll, the CPU repeatedly reads from the XCSR until bit 7 becomes 1, after which it writes a character to the XBUF address to start the transmitter again. Figure 2.9 shows a character in XBUF.

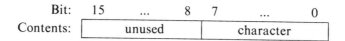

Figure 2.9 The format of data in XBUF.

We will see an example of polled output in Chapter 19 in the routine *kprintf* that is used for diagnostic output.

Polling is impractical except for debugging or other special applications because it requires the CPU to attend to devices constantly. To use interrupt-driven processing instead of polling, bit 6 of the transmitter and receiver CSRs must be set. If bit 6 (denoted I in Figure 2.7) is set to 1 in the receiver CSR, the SLU will post an input interrupt as soon as a character has been received. To obtain the character, the driver must read from the receiver's data buffer address, just as is done when polling is used. Once set, the receiver interrupt bit remains on, so each subsequent character will also cause an interrupt.

Bit 6 of the transmitter CSR enables it to interrupt the CPU when the transmitter becomes idle. If the bit is on, the SLU posts an output interrupt whenever the transmitter finishes sending a character. As expected, the interrupt handler must write a character to the transmitter data buffer address to start it sending again.

Bit 0 of the XCSR, marked B, controls transmission of breaks. When bit 0 is set to 1, the transmitter forces the line into a break condition independent of characters sent to the transmitter data buffer. The CPU must reset bit 0 to clear the break condition.

2.2 Disk Storage Organization

Computer systems often use magnetic storage devices for storage of bulk information. The name *disk* implies that the recording surfaces are shaped in round, flat platters that spin. The platter surfaces are coated with a material that records magnetic fields just as a magnetic recording tape does. The mechanism that changes or senses this magnetic coating is called a *read-write head*. A mechanical *arm*, actuated electrically, positions the head(s) to a specified location on the disk, and analog sensing hardware reads or writes data as the disk spins under the head. To increase the capacity, multiple platters are often built on one *spindle*, accessed by an arm with multiple heads attached. Normally, disk heads do not contact the magnetic surface; they "fly" incredibly close to it on a cushion of air. Accidents that occur when mechanical shock or dust particles on the surface cause the heads to bounce up and down and ruin the magnetic surface are called *head crashes*.

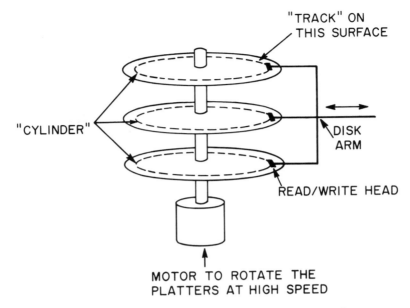

Figure 2.10 A disk arm with multiple read/write heads.

At a given arm position, the surface area under one head forms a ring called a *track*. In a multiple platter disk the set of all tracks for a given head position is called a *cylinder* because they outline a cylinder in 3-dimensional space. Each track is divided into fixed-length *sectors*; a sector is the smallest unit of storage that can be read or written in a single operation. Data transferred to or from a sector is often called a *block*; Xinu software assumes a sector length of 512 bytes when it allocates storage for blocks.

Compared to main memory, which operates at speeds measured in nanoseconds, disk devices are slow and awkward. Moving the arm usually requires tens of milliseconds. Even reading a track once the arm is in place is nontrivial because the disk must revolve at least once. That may take another 10 milliseconds. Thus, a disk access is on the order of 300,000 times slower than a memory access. To put this in perspective, imagine that you need to retrieve a pencil before you continue some task. Suppose it takes 10 seconds to walk to your desk (high speed memory) and retrieve one. A retrieval operation that took 300,000 times as long would last roughly 34.7 days. After a few such retrieval operations, you would quickly learn to save pencils in your desk drawer to avoid the trip. Operating systems use an analogous technique — they often contain complex algorithms that save copies of blocks to avoid unnecessary disk accesses.

If disks are so slow, why use them at all? Disk storage offers two important features that main memory does not. First, disk storage is less expensive. Second, it provides permanent, long-term storage. Unlike main memory which is called *volatile* because data "evaporates" when power is removed, data on disk is *nonvolatile*; it persists even if the system stops.

2.2.1 Disk Interface And Control Hardware

Disk hardware is much more complex than the asynchronous line hardware described above. In addition to the *disk drive*, which consists of the physical arm, platter(s), and read/write head(s), disk hardware includes a complicated electronic *controller* and *host interface*.

Disk controllers, which often contain a microprocessor themselves, position the disk arm, control transfer of data, and sense any errors that occur. Each controller can operate multiple disk drives (although they may not be able to transfer data to more than one disk simultaneously).

A host interface connects the controller to the standard computer system bus. It passes requests from the processor to the controller to start an I/O operation, and interrupts the CPU when the controller signals that the operation is complete. The host interface also passes data between the controller and memory during a data transfer operation.

The most significant difference between the disk and asynchronous line hardware is this:

> *Unlike asynchronous line hardware which interrupts the CPU for each character received or transmitted, the disk interface transfers large blocks of data directly to or from memory, interrupting only when the transfer is complete.*

The technique of transferring large blocks of data without interrupting the CPU is called *direct memory access* (DMA). It dramatically increases system throughput by allowing simultaneous data transfer to several peripherals while the CPU continues to execute instructions.

2.2.2 The Pieces Of Disk Hardware

The disk hardware has no notion of *file* or *directory* built in; they are all added by the system software, as we will see in Chapter 18. The hardware considers each disk device to be an array of 512-byte blocks (sectors), addressed 0, 1, 2, ..., *n*. On a small drive *n* is about 1000. Intermediate drives have between 10000 and 30000 blocks.

The hardware reads data by copying a sector on the disk to a block in memory, and writes data by copying a block from memory onto a sector of the disk.

Using the disk hardware consists of passing requests to the host interface, which carries them out and reports the results. Part of the information passed to the interface constitutes a request for the controller; the other part consists of a block to which data is to be transferred. The next section describes the request format used by one particular set of disk interface hardware.

2.2.3 Interface And Controller Request Formats

This section describes some of the details of the disk hardware used for Xinu. It is included only to give the reader some feel for the 6-byte controller request record and the interface device registers. Although sufficient to explain the code in the disk driver routines, this description is far from complete. The reader should consult the vendor's manuals before attempting to make significant changes to the software.

The disk driver described in Chapter 17 was built for an International Memories, Incorporated 5018H Winchester disk drive, a Data Technology Corporation DTC-11-1 host interface, and a Xebec Systems Incorporated S1410 Winchester Disk Controller. Despite being manufactured by three vendors, these pieces of equipment work well together.

Figure 2.11 shows the Xebec controller request record arrangement.

Byte:	Contents:
0	Command
1	disk unit (0)
2	high byte of block #
3	low byte of block #
4	block count (1)
5	Control (0)

Figure 2.11 Format of a request record for the disk controller.

The values shown in parentheses are the ones Xinu uses; the values in other fields depend on the request.

Like an SLU, the disk interface has a set of device registers that occupy locations in the address space above real memory. For example, the DTC-11-1 interface has six 16-bit registers starting at the device address. Figure 2.12 shows their arrangement. The CAR register gives the address in memory of the request record (see Figure 2.11). Registers XDAR and XCAR are used to hold the upper part of a memory address on machines that have memory addresses larger than 16 bits. They are always set to 0 on an 11/2.

Name:	Contents:
CCSR	Completion Status Register
CSR	Control and Status Register
DAR	DMA Address Register
CAR	Control Request Address Register
XDAR	Extension for DAR (always 0)
XCAR	Extension for CAR (always 0)

Figure 2.12 Host interface device register layout.

Like the control and status registers of other devices, the interface *CSR* register contains several bits that report errors and control interrupts. Figure 2.13 shows its format.

Bit:	15	14	13	12 ... 8	7	6	5 ... 2	1	0
Meaning:	E	-	P	-	D	I	-	F	G

Figure 2.13 Disk interface CSR layout.

Bit *E* is set if any error occurs, *P* is set if a parity error occurs, *D* is set if the operation is complete, *I* controls whether the interface will interrupt when the operation is complete, *F* forces the interface to reset the controller, and *G* is a "go" bit. The interface starts an I/O operation whenever the CPU sets the *G* bit to 1. The bit remains set until the controller responds and begins the operation.

2.3 The C Run-Time Environment

Operating systems should be written in high-level languages because it makes them easier to write, understand, debug, and move to other machines. We have chosen the C programming language for the example system in this book. C is a concise and powerful systems language that is well-suited to operating system implementation. It allows the programmer to manipulate addresses and specify storage layouts. It is also a high-level language that supports parameterized procedures, reasonable control statements, and separate compilation.

For the most part, it is possible to write an operating system without knowing the details of the compiler, the code it produces, or the conventions used by that code when it runs. From time to time, however, it will be necessary to peek beneath the covers and manipulate the run-time environment. This section reviews a few of the pertinent details.

The C compiler expects that each program will be run in an address space laid out in four *segments*. Figure 2.14 shows the arrangement of segments at run-time.

Figure 2.14 Storage layout for a C Program

The *text segment*, which includes code for the main program and all procedures, occupies the lowest part of the address space. The *data segment*, which contains all initialized data, occupies the next region of the address space. The uninitialized data segment, called the *bss segment*, follows the data segment. Finally, the *stack segment* occupies the highest part of the address space and grows downward. On the LSI 11, C programs allocate free space by growing the stack downward into it and by allocating heap storage from the bottom upward.

When Xinu runs multiple processes, it allocates a stack segment for each of them (but places the text, data, and bss segements for all processes together). These stacks are allocated from the free block with the highest memory address. Thus, if three processes start, their stacks are allocated contiguously from the highest memory address downward as shown in Figure 2.15:

```
0       _etext    _edata    _end
| text | data |  bss  |     FREE     ... | stack #3 | stack #2 | stack #1 |
```

Figure 2.15 Storage layout when Xinu runs.

Because the hardware does not protect one user from another, stack overflow in one process will, unfortunately, destroy the data in a stack that belongs to another process. A later chapter will discuss how the software can check for this error. Stack space is returned to the free list whenever a process exits.

Xinu also provides a system call that allocates space to user processes for general use. This space is allocated from the free block with the lowest address.

The symbols _etext, _edata, and _end refer to global variables inserted into the object program by the loader. They are initialized to the first address beyond the text, data, and bss segments, respectively. Thus, a running program can find out how much memory remains between the end of the loaded part and the current top of stack by taking the address of _end.

There is an important distinction between names in the object program and names in C source programs. It is this:

> *The compiler adds an underscore to all external symbols in C programs, and truncates them to eight characters.*

Thus, names like _end are declared in C without the underscore (i.e. "extern end"), and names like "reschedule" become "_resched" in the object code. The reader must remember this distinction when comparing C to assembler programs in which external symbols have explicit underscore prefixes.

The C procedure calling conventions are extraordinary. During a procedure call, the *calling* procedure is easiest to understand. It pushes actual arguments on the stack *in reverse order*, pushes a return address on the stack, and then branches to the called routine. The latter two actions are carried out with a single machine instruction called the *jump subroutine*:

jsr   pc,address-of-called-routine

Pushing parameters in reverse order allows procedures like *printf* to be called with a variable number of arguments. Even though the called routine cannot determine the number of arguments from the information on the stack, it can always find the first argument by looking on the stack just beyond the return address. Under the C conventions, the calling procedure is also responsible for popping arguments off the stack after the called procedure returns.

The *called* procedure is responsible for saving and restoring the machine state (e.g., registers that it will use), and popping the return address off the stack before it returns. One reason for allowing the called procedure to pop the return address is that the hardware provides a single instruction, *rts* (return from subroutine), that pops an address off the stack and jumps to that address.

The C calling sequence becomes more complex after the called procedure begins. The machine registers must be saved and then restored before returning to the caller. Instead of inserting code to save the registers in-line, the compiler inserts another procedure call, this time to *csv*. An assembler language routine, *csv* behaves unlike other procedures. First, it saves the registers and then it jumps back to the called procedure. The called procedure then executes, using registers if necessary. When finished executing, the called procedure uses another special assembler language routine, *cret*, to restore the registers. After *cret* restores the registers and the stack pointer, it returns control to the original caller. The reader is left to ponder over the rationale behind this mechanism.

The assembler language code for *csv* and *cret* follows. Operation codes *mov*, *jsr*, and *rts* stand for "move", "jump to subroutine", and "return from subroutine". Registers are referred to as *rx*, the stack pointer as *sp*, and the program counter as *pc*. The notation (*rx*) denotes indirect reference using the address in register *x*. In word instructions, prefixing a minus sign to an indirect reference first decrements the register (by two, the word length), and then uses it as a pointer. Suffixing a plus sign causes the register to be incremented (by two) after it has been used as a pointer.

```
/* csv.s - csv, cret */


/* C register save:  upon entry here, procedure A has called B, and B   */
/* has called csv to save registers.  r5 contains return address in B.  */
/* The stack has old r5, return address in A, and arguments on it.       */
/* C return: cret (below) is used to restore regs when the called proc. */
/* finally exits.  Comments are my best guess; code originally had none.*/


        .globl  csv, cret
/*------------------------------------------------------------------------
/*  csv  --  C register save routine (something to ponder on cold nights)
/*------------------------------------------------------------------------
csv:
        mov     r5,r0               / r0 not saved at call (C convention)
        mov     sp,r5               / r5 points to called routine's frame
        mov     r4,-(sp)            / push r4 -r2 on stack
        mov     r3,-(sp)
        mov     r2,-(sp)
        jsr     pc,(r0)             / jsr pushes PC onto stack goes to
                                    / address in r0 (originally in r5)


/*------------------------------------------------------------------------
/*  cret  --  C register restore routine
/*------------------------------------------------------------------------
cret:
        mov     r5,r2               / put copy of called frame ptr in r2
        mov     -(r2),r4            / reload r4 - r2 from start of frame
        mov     -(r2),r3
        mov     -(r2),r2
        mov     r5,sp               / restore SP
        mov     (sp)+,r5            / restore r5 saved on stack by call
                                    / to csv at procedure entry
        rts     pc                  / return to caller
```

2.4 Summary

We have reviewed the architecture of the LSI 11/2 computer. The LSI 11/2 is a conventional 16-bit microcomputer, organized around a bus through which the CPU accesses memory and devices. Output (input) is performed by writing to (reading from) addresses in the highest 8K bytes of the address space. When a device recognizes its address on the bus, it either transmits data to the CPU, reads data from the CPU, or controls the device. Simple devices like serial line units that connect the computer to asynchronous terminals require the CPU to explicitly control each character. More complicated devices like disks can perform I/O a block at a time. They only need the CPU to start a block transfer. Transmission is carried out by direct memory access (DMA) where the device uses the bus to interact directly with memory.

This chapter also reviewed the C programming language run-time environment and calling conventions. At run-time, C places program text, global data, and uninitialized global data at one end of memory, and grows a program stack downward from the other end. Its calling conventions are strange, but easy to follow if the called routine does not destroy the register contents.

FOR FURTHER STUDY

More information on the LSI 11/2, LSI 11/23, and Q-bus can be found in the vendor's handbooks *Microcomputers and Memories* and *Microcomputer Interfaces*. Myers [1978], Stone [1972], and Tanenbaum [1976] all provide general discussions of computer architecture; Stone [1975] looks at memory addressing in more detail. These books also review procedure calling conventions, as does Knuth [1968]. The C language calling conventions are described by Johnson and Ritchie [1981].

EXERCISES

2.1   Compare the 11/2 to Digital Equipment Corporation's PDP 11 computers. What are the most important differences? What is the stack "red-line"?

2.2   Find out about memory management on systems like the LSI 11/23 or a Motorola 68000-based system. Compare these to the 11/2.

2.3   Write a program that does polled output to the console terminal, and use it to output a string.

2.4   After an asynchronous communication interface finds one framing error, it often finds more framing errors. Explain.

2.5   Device interrupt vector addresses are called *programmable* if they can be changed after the hardware has been purchased from the vendor. Why are programmable vector addresses needed?

2.6   Because the disk interface accesses memory directly during DMA transfers, curious errors can result. Find out what happens if you read a 512-byte block of data into a memory location that is within 512 bytes of the highest memory address.

2.7   Find out why and how disks are *formatted* into sectors.

2.8   If a disk surface contains a physical flaw, it may make one or more sectors unusable. Some operating systems remap blocks on the disk, placing data for flawed blocks on unflawed sectors. Try to discover how your favorite operating system tolerates flawed disks (if it does).

2.9   Build a stand-alone program to format disks and check for flaws.

2.10 Find out what the keyword *register* means in C.

2.11 Look at the routine *csv* and figure out how it saves and restores registers. Explain how to save and restore registers with fewer instructions.

3

List and Queue Manipulation

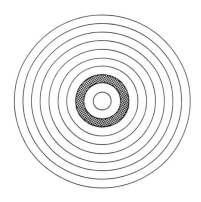

Linked list processing is fundamental in operating systems — it seems to pervade every component. This chapter introduces the set of procedures that form the backbone of linked list manipulation in the Xinu process manager. The routines described here are used to maintain queues ordered by time of insertion, and queues ordered by priority. They perform such actions as: inserting an item at the tail of a list, inserting an item in an ordered list, removing an item at the head of a list, and allocating a new list.

The linked list routines in this chapter provide a good introduction to the programming language C and to the programming conventions used throughout this book. Starting with these routines is especially helpful because they deal with a familiar subject, and because only one process executes them at a given time. Thus, the reader can think of the code as being part of a sequential program — there is no need to worry about interference from other processes executing concurrently.

3.1 Linked Lists Of Processes

The process manager deals with objects called *processes*, moving them to and from various lists frequently. The items actually stored in these lists are small,

nonnegative integers called *process identifiers* (or *process ids*); we will use the
terms "process", "process identifier", and "process id" interchangeably throughout
this chapter. Constant *NPROC* gives the range of process identifiers. If it helps,
assume *NPROC* is 10 and the items to be stored are integers between 0 and 9.

An early design called for many process lists, each with its own data structure.
Some of the lists were first-in-first-out (FIFO) queues, others were ordered by key.
Some were singly-linked, while others had to be doubly-linked. After the requirements were formulated, it became obvious that centralizing the linked-list processing into a single data structure would eliminate many special cases in the code.

To accommodate all these cases, we have chosen a representation in which: all
lists are doubly-linked (each node points to its predecessor as well as its successor),
each node contains a key (even though key values are not used in FIFO lists), and
each list has both a head and tail. In essence, they all have the form shown in Figure 3.1.

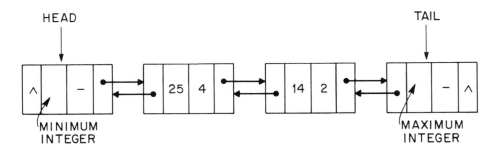

Figure 3.1 A doubly-linked list containing 4 (key=25) and 2 (key=14).

The key field in the head node contains the minimum possible integer; the key field
in the tail contains the maximum possible integer. As expected, the successor of
the tail and the predecessor of the head are null. When a list is empty, the successor of the head is the tail, and the predecessor of the tail is the head.

The diagram above is only a logical one. In practice, memory requirements
have been reduced by storing the data field implicitly. Such optimization is only
possible because of the following property:

A process appears on at most one list at any time.

To understand how data elements can be stored implicitly, look at Figure 3.2. It
shows an array called the *Q* structure, each entry of which has three fields: a key
field, a next field, and a previous field. Positions 0 through *NPROC*-1 correspond
to the integer process ids that are stored in the list; positions *NPROC* and higher
are used for heads and tails of lists. To place item *i* on a list, the node with index *i*
is linked into the list. It is only possible to reserve a node for each item because the

range of values is small (typically, *NPROC*=20), and no item ever appears on more than one list simultaneously. A closer look at the code should make the operations clear.

	key	next	prev
0			
1			
2	14	33	4
3			
4	25	2	32
5			
		.	
		.	
		.	
NPROC-1			
NPROC			
		.	
		.	
		.	
Head at 32	MININT	4	-1
Tail at 33	MAXINT	-1	2
		.	
		.	
		.	

Figure 3.2 The list from Figure 3.1 stored in the q array.

3.2 Implementation Of The Q Structure

In C, the *Q* structure pictured above is *q*, an array of *qent* structures. File *q.h* contains the declarations of both *q* and *qent*:

```
/* q.h - firstid, firstkey, isempty, lastkey, nonempty */

/* q structure declarations, constants, and inline procedures              */

#ifndef NQENT
#define NQENT                 NPROC + NSEM + NSEM + 4 /* for ready & sleep   */
#endif

struct  qent     {                      /* one for each process plus two for */
                                        /* each list                         */
        short    qkey;                  /* key on which the queue is ordered */
        short    qnext;                 /* pointer to next process or tail   */
        short    qprev;                 /* pointer to previous process or head */
        };

extern  struct   qent q[];
extern  int      nextqueue;

/* inline list manipulation procedures */

#define isempty(list)    (q[(list)].qnext >= NPROC)
#define nonempty(list)   (q[(list)].qnext < NPROC)
#define firstkey(list)   (q[q[(list)].qnext].qkey)
#define lastkey(tail)    (q[q[(tail)].qprev].qkey)
#define firstid(list)    (q[(list)].qnext)

#define EMPTY   -1                       /* equivalent of null pointer        */
```

Each *q* entry either corresponds to the head of a list, the tail of a list, or an item to be placed on a list. For now, remember that items stored on lists are process id integers in the range 0 to *NPROC*-1. The implicit assumption throughout the code is that *q*[0] through *q*[NPROC-1] correspond to these process ids, while *q*[NPROC] through *q*[NQENT] correspond to the heads or tails of lists.

File *q.h* introduces several new features of C and conventions used throughout the book. Because the name ends in *.h*, it implies that this file will be included in other programs (the "h" stands for "heading"). Such files often contain the declarations for global data structures, symbolic constants, and in-line procedures. File *q.h* is no exception. It defines *q* to be global (external) so every program in Xinu will be able to access it. It also defines symbolic constants like *EMPTY*. Constants are referenced by name throughout the code because it helps make their purpose clear.

Symbolic constant *NQENT* defines the number of entries in the *q* array; its definition in file *q.h* introduces conditional definition. The statement "#ifndef NQENT" means "compile the code down to the corresponding #endif, if and only if *NQENT* has not been defined previously." In file *q.h*, *NQENT* is assigned a value only if it has not been defined earlier. The value assigned, "NPROC+NSEM+NSEM+4" will allocate enough room in the *q* structure for *NPROC* processes as well as head and tail pointers for *NSEM* semaphore lists, a ready list, and a sleep list. Conditional compilation is used so the size of the *q* structure can be changed without modifying this file.

The contents of entries in the *q* array are defined by structure *qent*. (This file contains only a declaration of the shape of elements in the *q* array; we will see the definition of its contents in Chapter 13.) Field *qnext* points forward, *qprev* points backward, and *qkey* contains an integer key for the node. When the forward and backward pointers do not contain valid indexes, they are assigned *EMPTY*.

3.2.1 In-Line Q Functions

The functions *isempty* and *nonempty* are predicates (Boolean functions) that test whether a list is empty or not, given the index of its head as an argument. *Isempty* determines whether a list is empty by checking to see if the first node on the list is a process or the list tail; *nonempty* makes the opposite test. Remember that an item is a process if and only if its index is less than *NPROC*.

The other in-line functions should also be easy to understand. Functions *firstkey*, *lastkey*, and *firstid* return the key of the first process on a list, the key of the last process on a list, or the *q* index of the first process on a list. Usually, these functions are applied to nonempty lists, but they do not abort even if the list is empty because *qkey* is always initialized.

3.2.2 FIFO Queue Manipulation

To produce a FIFO queue, items are inserted at the tail of a list and removed at the head of a list. Procedures *enqueue* and *dequeue*, found in file *queue.c*, perform the FIFO operations in Xinu. The code is straight-forward, once you understand how pointers operate. Variables *tptr* and *mptr* are pointers to *qent* structures. The first two executable statements in *enqueue* assign these pointers the addresses of the *q* entries corresponding to the tail of the list and the process to be inserted. Once the address of an element has been recorded, individual fields of the structure are referenced using the "−>" operator. The point of recording addresses in pointers is efficiency − it avoids recomputing array subscripts again and again.

```
/* queue.c - dequeue, enqueue */

#include <conf.h>
#include <kernel.h>
#include <q.h>

/*------------------------------------------------------------------------
 * enqueue  --  insert an item at the tail of a list
 *------------------------------------------------------------------------
 */
int     enqueue(item, tail)
        int     item;                   /* item to enqueue on a list   */
        int     tail;                   /* index in q of list tail     */
{
        struct  qent    *tptr;          /* points to tail entry        */
        struct  qent    *mptr;          /* points to item entry        */

        tptr = &q[tail];
        mptr = &q[item];
        mptr->qnext = tail;
        mptr->qprev = tptr->qprev;
        q[tptr->qprev].qnext = item;
        tptr->qprev = item;
        return(item);
}


/*------------------------------------------------------------------------
 * dequeue  --  remove an item from a list and return it
 *------------------------------------------------------------------------
 */
int     dequeue(item)
        int     item;
{
        struct  qent    *mptr;          /* pointer to q entry for item */

        mptr = &q[item];
        q[mptr->qprev].qnext = mptr->qnext;
        q[mptr->qnext].qprev = mptr->qprev;
        return(item);
}
```

File *queue.c* includes three other files: *conf.h*, *kernel.h*, and *q.h*. File *q.h* is needed because procedures *enqueue* and *dequeue* both reference the *q* structure. But why are the other two included? It turns out that neither are needed by the code contained explicitly in *queue.c*. However, *queue.c* includes file *q.h* which references constants like *NPROC* and *NSEM* that are defined in *kernel.h* and *conf.h*. As a general rule, so many important constants have been collected into these two files that most system routines must include them. We will simply include them for now, and postpone looking at them until later.

3.3 Priority Queue Manipulation

The process manager often needs to select from a set of processes one with the highest priority, so the linked list routines must be able to maintain sets of processes that have an associated *priority*. (Priorities in Xinu are easy to understand: for now, think of them as integer values assigned to the processes.) In general, the task of selecting a process with highest priority is performed frequently compared with the tasks of inserting processes in the set and deleting them, so the idea is to design a data structure that makes selection efficient compared to insertion.

A variety of data structures have been devised to store sets when selection by priority is important. Such data structures are called *priority queues*. Although not all "priority queues" use a queue, the term accurately describes the Xinu implementation — Xinu priority queues are merely linked lists in which processes are ordered by their priority. The highest priority process can always be found at the tail of the list. Of course, insertion in a priority queue is more expensive than insertion in a FIFO queue because the list must be searched to determine where the new item should be located.

When many items appear in a priority queue, or if the number of insertions is high compared to the number of times items are extracted by priority, using linear lists for priority queues would not be efficient (the exercises discuss this point further). However, in a small system like Xinu, where we expect 2 or 3 elements to be on a given priority queue at any time, simple lists suffice.

The procedures that maintain ordered lists are straightforward. *Insert*, shown below, takes as an argument a process id, an integer giving the head of a list in the *q* structure, and a priority, and inserts the process into its correct position in the list. It uses the *qkey* field of a process' node to store that process' priority. To find the correct location in the list, *insert* searches for an existing element with a key greater than or equal to the key of the element being inserted. During the search, integer *next* moves along the list. The loop must eventually terminate because the key of the tail element contains the largest possible integer. Once the correct location has been found, *insert* changes the necessary pointers to link the new node into the list.

```
/* insert.c  -  insert */

#include <conf.h>
#include <kernel.h>
#include <q.h>

/*------------------------------------------------------------------
 * insert.c  --  insert an process into a q list in key order
 *------------------------------------------------------------------
 */
int     insert(proc, head, key)
        int     proc;                   /* process to insert           */
        int     head;                   /* q index of head of list     */
        int     key;                    /* key to use for this process */
{
        int     next;                   /* runs through list           */
        int     prev;

        next = q[head].qnext;
        while (q[next].qkey < key)      /* tail has MAXINT as key      */
                next = q[next].qnext;
        q[proc].qnext = next;
        q[proc].qprev = prev = q[next].qprev;
        q[proc].qkey  = key;
        q[prev].qnext = proc;
        q[next].qprev = proc;
        return(OK);
}
```

Elements can be extracted from a FIFO queue by removing them from the head; they can be extracted from a priority queue at either the head or tail. Procedures *getfirst* and *getlast* provide the operations of removing items from queues. *Getfirst* takes the list head index as an argument, and *getlast* takes the list tail index as an argument. If the list is a priority queue, *getfirst* removes an item with the smallest key and *getlast* removes an item with the largest key; for FIFO queues, *getfirst* removes the oldest item in the list. Both routines return the index of the item removed. These returned values are either process ids or *EMPTY*.

```
/* getitem.c - getfirst, getlast */

#include <conf.h>
#include <kernel.h>
#include <q.h>
```

```
/*-----------------------------------------------------------------------
 * getfirst  --  remove and return the first process on a list
 *-----------------------------------------------------------------------
 */
int     getfirst(head)
        int     head;                   /* q index of head of list    */
{
        int     proc;                   /* first process on the list  */

        if ((proc=q[head].qnext) < NPROC)
                return( dequeue(proc) );
        else
                return(EMPTY);
}




/*-----------------------------------------------------------------------
 * getlast  --  remove and return the last process from a list
 *-----------------------------------------------------------------------
 */
int     getlast(tail)
        int     tail;                   /* q index of tail of list    */
{
        int     proc;                   /* last process on the list   */

        if ((proc=q[tail].qprev) < NPROC)
                return( dequeue(proc) );
        else
                return(EMPTY);
}
```

3.4 List Initialization

The procedures described so far all assume that even though the lists may be empty, their head and tail nodes have been initialized. We now consider how to create empty lists in the first place. It is appropriate that this material occurs at the end of this chapter because it brings up an important point about the design process:

Initialization is the final step in design.

This may sound strange because it is not possible to postpone thinking about initialization altogether, but the point is simple: design the data structures needed to keep the system running first, and then figure out how to initialize them. Partitioning the "steady state" part of the system from the "transient state" part helps avoid the temptation of sacrificing good design for easy initialization.

Initialization of entries in the *q* structure is performed on demand as entries are needed. Running programs call *newqueue* to create a new list. *Newqueue* allocates a pair of adjacent positions in the *q* array to use as head and tail nodes, and initializes the list to empty by pointing the successor of the head to the tail and the predecessor of the tail to the head. Other pointers are assigned the value *EMPTY*. When it initializes the head and tail, *newqueue* also sets the key fields to the smallest and largest possible integers, respectively, so the head and tail can be used with an ordered list. Finally, *newqueue* returns the index of the list head to its caller.

```
/* newqueue.c  -  newqueue */

#include <conf.h>
#include <kernel.h>
#include <q.h>


/*------------------------------------------------------------------------
 * newqueue  --  initialize a new list in the q structure
 *------------------------------------------------------------------------
 */
int     newqueue()
{
        struct  qent    *hptr;          /* address of new list head     */
        struct  qent    *tptr;          /* address of new list tail     */
        int     hindex, tindex;         /* head and tail indexes        */

        hptr = &q[ hindex=nextqueue++ ];/* nextqueue is global variable */
        tptr = &q[ tindex=nextqueue++ ];/*  giving next used q pos.      */
        hptr->qnext = tindex;
        hptr->qprev = EMPTY;
        hptr->qkey  = MININT;
        tptr->qnext = EMPTY;
        tptr->qprev = hindex;
        tptr->qkey  = MAXINT;
        return(hindex);
}
```

3.5 Summary

The code in this chapter described linked-list manipulation in the process manager. Linked lists of processes are kept in a single data structure, the q array. Primitive operations for manipulating the lists of processes can produce FIFO queues or priority queues. All lists have the same format: they are doubly-linked, each has both a head and tail, and each node has an integer key field. Keys are used when the list is a priority queue; they are ignored if the list is a FIFO queue.

FOR FURTHER STUDY

Knuth [1968] describes linked-list manipulation in detail. Good algorithms for priority queues and related data structures can be found in Aho et. al. [1974]. Wirth [1976] contains examples in Pascal. Habermann [1976] explains the use of a priority queue in operating systems.

EXERCISES

3.1 Duplicate the procedures in this chapter to work with singly-linked lists. How much storage does the second set of routines require? How much CPU time do they save?

3.2 Implement procedures to manipulate lists using pointers instead of subscripts into an array of structures. How much storage/time do they save? Comment on the complexity of routines like *isempty* when implemented with pointers.

3.3 Does *insert* work correctly for all possible keys? If not, for which does it fail?

3.4 Larger systems sometimes use a data structure known as a *heap* to contain a priority queue. What is a heap? Will its use be more or less expensive than an ordered, doubly-linked list when the list size is between 1 and 3?

3.5 Finding the address of an item in an array may require multiplication. If the compiler you are using converts multiplication by a power of 2 into a shift, try padding the size of a *qent* to 8 bytes. How much faster does it make the routines? Investigate the relative speed of multiplication and shifting on the 11/2.

3.6 Modify *insert* to use pointers instead of subscripting. Is it faster? Larger?

3.7 Rewrite all the list manipulation routines so they reference a list by a single integer, k, and assume that $q[k]$ is the list head and $q[k+1]$ is the list tail. Are they faster or slower?

3.8 Modify *newqueue* to check for an error caused by allocating more than *NQENT* entries.

4

Scheduling and Context Switching

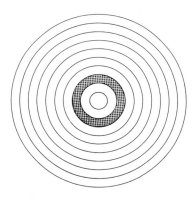

An operating system achieves the illusion of concurrent processing by rapidly switching one processor among several computations. Because the speed of the computation is extremely fast compared to that of a human, the effect is impressive — many activities appear to proceed simultaneously.

Context switching lies at the heart of the process juggling act. It consists of stopping the current computation, saving enough information so it may be restarted later, and restarting another process. What makes such a change difficult is that the CPU cannot be stopped at all — it must continue to execute the code that switches to a new process.

This chapter describes the basic context switching mechanism, showing exactly how a process saves its state information, chooses another process to run from among those that are ready, and relinquishes control to that process. It describes the data structure that holds information about processes while they are not executing, and shows how the context switch uses that data structure. For the present, we ignore the questions of when or why processes choose to switch context. Later chapters address these issues, showing how higher layers of the system use the context switch built here.

4.1 The Process Table

The system keeps all information about processes in a data structure called the *process table*. There is one entry in the process table for each process. Because exactly one process is running at any time, one of those entries corresponds to an active process — its saved state information is out of date. All other process table entries contain information about processes that have been stopped temporarily. To switch context the operating system saves information about the currently running process in its process table entry, and restores information from the process table entry corresponding to the process it is about to execute.

Exactly what information must be saved in the process table? The system must save any values that will be destroyed when the new process runs. For example, in Xinu each process has its own separate stack memory, so a copy of the stack need not be saved. However, the new process will change the machine registers when it executes, so their contents must be saved. In addition to data that must be reloaded when it resumes a process, the system also keeps information in the process table that it uses to control processes and account for their resources. These details will become clear as we see how the process table is used.

The Xinu process table, *proctab*, is an array with entries for up to *NPROC* processes. It is declared in file *proc.h*, below. Each entry in *proctab* is a structure named *pentry* that defines the information kept for each process.

```
/* proc.h - isbadpid */

/* process table declarations and defined constants            */

#ifndef NPROC                      /* set the number of processes */
#define NPROC         10           /*   allowed if not already done */
#endif

/* process state constants */

#define PRCURR        '\01'        /* process is currently running */
#define PRFREE        '\02'        /* process slot is free         */
#define PRREADY       '\03'        /* process is on ready queue    */
#define PRRECV        '\04'        /* process waiting for message  */
#define PRSLEEP       '\05'        /* process is sleeping          */
#define PRSUSP        '\06'        /* process is suspended         */
#define PRWAIT        '\07'        /* process is on semaphore queue*/

/* miscellaneous process definitions */

#define PNREGS        9            /* size of saved register area  */
```

```
#define PNMLEN          8           /* length of process "name"   */
#define NULLPROC        0           /* id of the null process; it */
                                    /*  is always eligible to run  */


#define isbadpid(x)     (x<=0 || x>=NPROC)


/* process table entry */


struct  pentry  {
        char    pstate;             /* process state: PRCURR, etc. */
        short   pprio;              /* process priority           */
        short   pregs[PNREGS];      /* saved regs. R0-R5,SP,PC,PS  */
        short   psem;               /* semaphore if process waiting */
        short   pmsg;               /* message sent to this process */
        short   phasmsg;            /* nonzero iff pmsg is valid    */
        short   pbase;              /* base of run time stack       */
        short   pstklen;            /* stack length                 */
        short   plimit;             /* lowest extent of stack       */
        char    pname[PNMLEN];      /* process name                 */
        short   pargs;              /* initial number of arguments  */
        short   paddr;              /* initial code address         */
};


extern  struct  pentry proctab[];
extern  int     numproc;            /* currently active processes   */
extern  int     nextproc;           /* search point for free slot   */
extern  int     currpid;            /* currently executing process  */
```

Throughout Xinu, each process is identified by an integer. The following rule gives the relationship between those integers and the process table:

> Processes are referenced by their process id, which is the index of the saved state information in proctab.

Only the *pregs* field of the Xinu process table entry contains copies of registers needed to restart the process; other fields contain information for bookkeeping and error checking. For example, the fields *pbase*, *pargs*, and *pname* contain the address of the process stack, the number of arguments passed to the process when it was created, and a character string identifying the process. Some of these values are used to free memory when a process completes; others are merely for debugging.

4.2 Process States

The system uses the *pstate* field of the process table to help it keep track of what the process is doing and, consequently, the validity and semantics of operations performed on it. The system designer must evolve this set of process states as the initial design proceeds. The set should be well-defined before implementation begins because many of the routines that manipulate processes base their actions on the process' state, requiring the programmer to carefully consider each case.

In Xinu, the initial design produced the following six states: *current*, *ready*, *receiving*, *sleeping*, *suspended*, and *waiting*. File *proc.h* contains symbolic constants for each of these that are used throughout the code: *PRCURR*, *PRREADY*, *PRRECV*, *PRSLEEP*, *PRSUSP*, and *PRWAIT*. In addition to the above values, the *pstate* field contains *PRFREE* when no process is using that process table entry. Later, we will explore each state in detail, seeing why they arose and how a process moves between them. Only the current and ready states concern us at this time.

4.3 Selecting A Ready Process

Almost every system needs *ready* and *current* process states. Processes are classified *ready* when they are eligible for CPU service but are not currently executing; the single process receiving CPU service is classified as *current*. Switching context consists of two things: selecting a process from among those that are ready (or current), and giving control of the CPU to the selected process. Software that implements the policy used to select a process from among those that are ready to run is called a *scheduler*. In Xinu, procedure *resched* makes that selection according to the following well-known scheduling policy:

> *At any time, the highest priority process eligible for CPU service is executing. Among processes with equal priority scheduling is round-robin.*

By *round-robin* we mean that processes are selected one after another so that all members of the set have an opportunity to execute before any member has a second opportunity. Priorities, kept in the *pprio* field of the process table entry, are nothing more than positive integers that give the user some control over how processes are selected for CPU service. (More complex systems adjust priorities from time-to-time, based on observed behavior of the process.)

To make the selection of a new process faster, all ready processes appear in a list ordered by priority, such that the highest priority process is immediately accessible. *Resched* uses the queue mechanisms from Chapter 3 to examine and update that list. It uses process priorities as keys, and keeps the list ordered by key, so highest priority processes are found at the tail. Global variables *rdyhead* and *rdy-*

tail point to the head and tail of the ready list in the *q* structure. Whether the current process should also be kept on the ready list is determined largely by the details of each implementation, but the entire system must be designed to obey the same rule. In Xinu,

> *The current process does not appear on the ready list, but its process id is always given by the global integer variable currpid.*

Consider what happens to the currently executing process during a context switch. Often, the currently executing process remains eligible to use the CPU even though it must temporarily pass control to another process. In such situations, the context switch must change the current process' state to *PRREADY*, and move it onto the ready list so it will be considered for CPU service again later.

How does the rescheduler, *resched*, decide whether to move the current process onto the ready list? It does not receive an explicit parameter telling the disposition of the current process. Instead, the system routines cooperate to save the current process in the following way: if the currently executing process will not remain eligible to use the CPU, system routines assign the current process' *pstate* field the desired next state before calling *resched*. Whenever *resched* prepares to switch context, it checks *pstate* for the current process, and makes it ready only if the state still indicates *PRCURR*.

In addition to moving the current process to the ready list, *resched* completes every detail of scheduling and context switching except saving and restoring machine registers (which cannot be done directly in a high-level language like C). It selects a new process to run, changes the process table entry for the new process, removes the new process from the ready list, marks it current, and updates *currpid*. It also resets the preemption counter, something we will consider later. Finally, it calls *ctxsw* to do the dirty work of saving the current registers and restoring those for the new process. The code is shown below.

```
/* resched.c  -  resched */

#include <conf.h>
#include <kernel.h>
#include <proc.h>
#include <q.h>

/*------------------------------------------------------------------------
 * resched  --   reschedule processor to highest priority ready process
 *
 * Notes:        Upon entry, currpid gives current process id.
 *               Proctab[currpid].pstate gives correct NEXT state for
 *                      current process if other than PRCURR.
 *------------------------------------------------------------------------
 */
int     resched()
{
        register struct pentry  *optr;  /* pointer to old process entry */
        register struct pentry  *nptr;  /* pointer to new process entry */

        /* no switch needed if current process priority higher than next*/

        if ( ( (optr= &proctab[currpid])->pstate == PRCURR) &&
           (lastkey(rdytail)<optr->pprio))
                return(OK);

        /* force context switch */

        if (optr->pstate == PRCURR) {
                optr->pstate = PRREADY;
                insert(currpid,rdyhead,optr->pprio);
        }

        /* remove highest priority process at end of ready list */

        nptr = &proctab[ (currpid = getlast(rdytail)) ];
        nptr->pstate = PRCURR;                  /* mark it currently running   */
#ifdef  RTCLOCK
        preempt = QUANTUM;                      /* reset preemption counter    */
#endif
        ctxsw(optr->pregs,nptr->pregs);

        /* The OLD process returns here when resumed. */
        return(OK);
}
```

Resched uses procedure *ctxsw* to change registers because they cannot be manipulated in a high-level language. The code for *ctxsw* is, of course, machine dependent. Obviously, the program counter must be reset last, because as soon as it has been reset, the CPU will resume executing code in the new process, wherever that happens to be (the text segment for the new process will be present in memory because Xinu keeps all parts of the program resident). The trick is to reload the process status and stack pointers before reloading the program counter. On the 11/2, the *rtt* instruction pops both the PS and PC from the stack, and reloads them in one step. After saving the registers associated with the "old" process in its register save area, *ctxsw* switches stacks to the "new" process stack. By pushing copies of the stored values for the PS and PC onto the new stack, *ctxsw* is able to restore the process status register, program counter, and stack pointer to their correct values in one *rtt* operation. After the *rtt* sets the program counter, the machine will resume executing instructions associated with the new process.

```
/* ctxsw.s - ctxsw */


/*---------------------------------------------------------------------
/* ctxsw  --  actually perform context switch, saving/loading registers
/*---------------------------------------------------------------------
   / The stack contains three items upon entry to this routine:
   /
   /     SP+4 => address of 9 word save area with new registers + PS
   /     SP+2 => address of 9 word save area for old registers + PS
   /     SP   => return address
   /
   / The saved state consists of: the values of R0-R5 upon entry, SP+2,
   / PC equal to the return address, and the PS (i.e., the PC and SP are
   / saved as if the calling process had returned to its caller).

           .globl   _ctxsw            / declare the routine name global
_ctxsw:                               / entry point to context switch
           mov      r0,*2(sp)         / Save old R0 in old register area
           mov      2(sp),r0          / Get address of old register area
           add      $2,r0             /  in R0; increment to saved pos. of R1
           mov      r1,(r0)+          / Save registers R1-R5 in successive
           mov      r2,(r0)+          /   locations of the old process
           mov      r3,(r0)+          /   register save area.  (r0)+ denotes
           mov      r4,(r0)+          /   indirect reference and, as a side
           mov      r5,(r0)+          /   effect, incrementing r0 to next word.
           add      $2,sp             / move sp beyond the return address,
                                      /   as if a return had occurred.
           mov      sp,(r0)+          / save stack pointer
           mov      -(sp),(r0)+       / Save caller's return address as PC
           mfps     (r0)              / Save processor status beyond registers
           mov      4(sp),r0          / Pick up address of new registers in R0
                                      / Ready to load registers for the new
                                      /   process and abandon the old stack.
           mov      2(r0),r1          / Load R1-R5 and SP from the saved area
           mov      4(r0),r2          /   for the new process.
           mov      6.(r0),r3         / NOTE: dot following a number makes it
           mov      8.(r0),r4         /   decimal; all others are octal
           mov      10.(r0),r5
           mov      12.(r0),sp        / Have now actually switched stacks
           mov      16.(r0),-(sp)     / Push new process PS on new process stack
           mov      14.(r0),-(sp)     / Push new process PC on new process stack
           mov      (r0),r0           / Finally, load R0 from new area
           rtt                        / Load PC, PS, and reset SP all at once
```

The code in *ctxsw* reveals how to resolve the dilemma caused by trying to save registers while a process is still using them. Think of an executing process that has called *resched* (which called *ctxsw*). Instead of trying to save the program counter and stack pointer as the process executes, *ctxsw* saves the program counter and stack pointer as if the process had just returned from the call to ctxsw. The saved value of the program counter is taken from the return address because this is the address to which *ctxsw* would return if it were a normal procedure. The saved value for the stack pointer is the address of the first argument because this is the value the stack pointer would have if *ctxsw* returned to its caller.

It is interesting to note that all processes call *resched* to perform context switching, and *resched* calls *ctxsw*, so all suspended processes will resume at the same place — just after the call to *ctxsw* in *resched*. Each process has its own stack of procedure calls, however, so the return from *resched* will take them in various directions.

Building all procedures to return to their caller is a key ingredient in keeping the system design clean. It would be impossible unless the scheduler returned to its caller. So, both *resched* and *ctxsw* have been designed to behave just like any other procedures — they eventually return. Of course, there may be considerable delay before a call to *resched* returns because the CPU may execute other processes arbitrarily long before restarting the calling process (depending on the process priorities).

4.4 The Null Process

Resched only switches the processor among the current and ready processes; it does not create new processes. It assumes that at least one process is available, and does not bother to verify whether the ready list is empty. There is a strong consequence:

> *Resched, can only switch context from one process to another, so at least one process must always remain ready to run.*

To insure that a ready process always exists, Xinu creates an extra process, called the *null process*, when it initializes the system. The null process has process id zero, and priority zero; its code, which will be shown in Chapter 13, consists of an infinite loop. Because user processes must have a priority greater than zero, the scheduler switches to the null process only when no user process remains ready to run.

4.5 Making A Process Ready

When *resched* needed to move the current process onto the ready list, it manipulated the list directly. Making a process eligible for CPU service occurs so frequently that we have invented a procedure to do just that. It is named *ready*:

```
/* ready.c - ready */

#include <conf.h>
#include <kernel.h>
#include <proc.h>
#include <q.h>

/*------------------------------------------------------------------------
 * ready  --  make a process eligible for CPU service
 *------------------------------------------------------------------------
 */
int     ready (pid, resch)
        int     pid;                    /* id of process to make ready  */
        int     resch;                  /* reschedule afterward?        */
{
        register struct pentry  *pptr;

        if (isbadpid(pid))
                return(SYSERR);
        pptr = &proctab[pid];
        pptr->pstate = PRREADY;
        insert(pid,rdyhead,pptr->pprio);
        if (resch)
                resched();
        return(OK);
}
```

Besides the process id, *ready* requires a Boolean argument that controls whether or not it calls *resched*. Symbolic constants RESCHYES and RESCHNO are used for this argument throughout the system code. Usually, *ready* needs to call *resched* after placing a process on the ready list to ensure that the CPU is executing the highest priority ready process. When the caller needs to move several processes from some other list onto the ready list, rescheduling in the midst of the move makes things messy. The answer is to temporarily suspend the scheduling policy and call *ready* several times specifying RESCHNO. Then, after all processes have been moved and the list manipulation is complete, a call to *resched* reinstates the policy by assuring that the highest priority ready process is currently executing. We will see an example of delayed rescheduling in Chapter 6.

4.6 Summary

Scheduling and context switching are closely related activities that make concurrent execution possible. Scheduling consists of choosing a process from among those that are eligible for execution. Context switching consists of stopping one process and starting a new one. To keep track of the processes, the system uses a global data structure called the process table. Whenever the scheduler temporarily suspends a process, it saves all pertinent information about that process in its process table entry, along with a value that indicates the process state. This chapter considered procedures *ready*, *resched*, and *ctxsw* that performed transitions between the *current* and *ready* states.

FOR FURTHER STUDY

Many scheduling algorithms have been devised and analyzed. Coffman and Denning [1973] contains a formal treatment of the subject. Less formal are Bull and Packham [1971], and Bunt [1976]. Lampson [1968] discusses scheduling based on priorities.

Other books, by Habermann [1976], Calingaert [1982], and Shaw [1974] emphasize the consequences of various scheduling schemes.

EXERCISES

4.1 Identify fields in the process table used only for error checking.

4.2 Investigate another processor (e.g., the Motorola 68000 series), and determine what information needs to be saved during a context switch.

4.3 Write *ctxsw* for another processor, trying to minimize the number of instructions.

4.4 Because each process has its own stack, information like register values could be saved on the stack during a context switch. Does this reduce or increase the amount of assembly code required? What are the advantages of each approach?

4.5 It would be possible for *ctxsw* to reach into the run-time stack to obtain enough information to have the process resume in the routine that called *resched* instead of in *resched*. What are the advantages and disadvantages of doing so?

4.6 The C compiler used to build Xinu does not require registers R0-R3 to be saved and restored across procedure calls. Suggest a way to speed up context switching in such an environment. Give three reasons for not adopting such an approach.

4.7 Rewrite *resched* to have an explicit parameter giving the disposition of the currently executing process. Does it require more time?

4.8 Describe the relationship between coroutines and the context switch in this chapter.

5

More Process Management

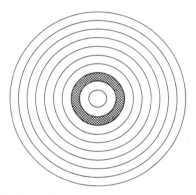

Chapter 4 discussed context switching, and showed how processes move between the ready and current states. This chapter shows how new processes come into existence in the first place, and how they eventually exit. It also introduces a new process state, namely, *suspended*, and explores routines that move processes among the current, ready, and suspended states.

5.1 Process Suspension And Resumption

Having a way to temporarily stop a process from executing and then to restart it proves to be quite useful. We will say that a stopped process has been placed in a state of "suspended animation". Suspended animation can be used, for example, when a process wants to wait for one of several restart conditions without knowing which will occur first.

The first step in implementing suspended animation consists of defining operations that will be used to suspend processes. In this case, the choice is obvious because only two are needed: *suspend*, to stop a process, and *resume* to restart it.

Because suspended processes are not eligible to use the CPU, a new process state is needed to distinguish them from *ready* and *current* processes. We will call the new state *suspended*. Figure 5.1 summarizes the actions that *suspend* and *resume* perform, showing how processes move among the *ready*, *current*, and *suspended* states.

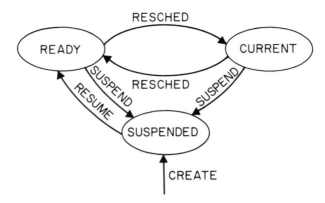

Figure 5.1 Transitions among the current, ready, and suspended states

The details of *suspend* and *resume* are obvious. *Suspend* needs an argument that specifies the process to be suspended. It must verify that the process to be suspended is either *ready* or *current*. *Resume* also needs an argument that specifies the process to be restarted; it must verify that the specified process is in the *suspended* state.

Process resumption is straightforward. *Resume* only needs to move the process back to the ready list and change its state. Suspension is not much more complex. Suspending a ready process involves changing the state recorded in its process table entry, and removing the process from the ready list so *resched* will not switch to it. The currently executing procedure can suspend itself by passing *suspend* its own process id:

$$suspend(\ getpid(\ )\ );$$

Suspending the current process involves moving it to the suspended state and then rescheduling to allow another process to execute.

5.1.1 Implementation Of Resume

Procedure *resume* moves a suspended process back to the ready state where it becomes eligible for processor service. The code, is contained in file *resume.c*.

```
/* resume.c - resume */

#include <conf.h>
#include <kernel.h>
#include <proc.h>
```

```
/*-------------------------------------------------------------------
 * resume  --  unsuspend a process, making it ready; return the priority
 *-------------------------------------------------------------------
 */
SYSCALL resume(pid)
        int     pid;
{

        char    ps;                     /* saved processor status    */
        struct  pentry  *pptr;          /* pointer to proc. tab. entry */
        int     prio;                   /* priority to return        */

        disable(ps);
        if (isbadpid(pid) || (pptr = &proctab[pid])->pstate != PRSUSP) {
                restore(ps);
                return(SYSERR);
        }
        prio = pptr->pprio;
        ready(pid, RESCHYES);
        restore(ps);
        return(prio);
}
```

Although *resume* calls *ready* to link the process into the ready list, it performs important chores that *ready* does not. It checks to be sure that its argument specifies a valid process, and that the referenced process is suspended. It also disables interrupts before calling *ready*. These actions make *resume* callable from a user's program.

Sometimes it is useful for the process calling resume to know the priority of the process it restarts, so *resume* returns that priority as its value. Care must be taken to capture the priority before the call to *ready* because the resumed process may start running when *ready* calls *resched* (before the process executing *resume* completes). The delay that occurs between the call to *ready* and the next instruction can be arbitrarily long because an arbitrary number of processes can execute before the calling process is rescheduled. To be sure that the returned priority reflects the resumed process' priority at the time of resumption *resume* makes a copy in local variable *prio* before calling *ready*, and returns the value in *prio*.

5.1.2 The Return Values SYSERR And OK

File *resume.c* includes file *kernel.h* along with *conf.h* and *proc.h*. *Kernel.h*, shown later in this chapter, defines several constants used throughout Xinu, including the integers *SYSERR* and *OK*. By convention, Xinu procedures always return SYSERR to indicate that their arguments were unacceptable or that something else prevented successful completion of the operation they tried to perform. Similarly, routines like *ready* that do not use the returned value to carry information back to the caller return the integer OK to indicate successful completion.

5.2 System Calls

The precautions that *resume* takes to verify an operation is legal make it a general purpose routine that can be invoked by any process at any time. It is our first example of what are generally referred to as *system calls*. System calls stand between a naive user's program and the rest of the operating system, so they must protect the internal system from illegal use. As the examples in Chapter 1 illustrate, systems calls do more than merely protect the system. To the programmer, system calls define the exterior of the operating system by providing an interface through which the user accesses all system services.

When a process executes a system call like *resume* and the procedures that *resume* calls, it changes the process table and other system data structures like the *q* structure. There is only one process table in the system, shared by all processes in the system. How can a process be sure that no other process will interfere by trying to change the process table at the same time? For one thing, it must not call *resched*, because rescheduling could mean a context switch to another process that needs to change the system tables. We will see that rescheduling can also result when a device interrupts, because interrupt routines sometimes call *resched* as well. To prevent interrupts, *resume* invokes the inline procedure *disable* to set the processor priority high enough to prevent all interrupts. *Disable* records the current processor priority in its argument, *ps*, and then sets the processor interrupt mask high enough to prevent interrupts. The definition of *disable*, shown in *kernel.h* later in this chapter, resorts to using assembler language instructions to record and modify the processor status register, something the programmer cannot do in a high-level language. Just before leaving *resume*, the process calls procedure *restore* to reset the processor priority to its original value. *Resume* cannot merely enable interrupts before returning to its caller because the caller may have been executing with interrupts disabled. Therefore, *resume* restores them to their original value before returning.

5.2.1 Implementation of Suspend

Suspending a process is not much more complex than resuming a suspended one. File *suspend.c* contains the code. *Suspend* first checks to see that argument *pid* specifies a valid process that is currently executing or ready. If the process to be suspended is in the ready state, it must be removed from the ready list and moved to the suspended state.

```
/* suspend.c - suspend */

#include <conf.h>
#include <kernel.h>
#include <proc.h>

/*------------------------------------------------------------------
 *  suspend  --  suspend a process, placing it in hibernation
 *------------------------------------------------------------------
 */
SYSCALL suspend(pid)
        int     pid;                    /* id of process to suspend   */
{
        struct  pentry *pptr;           /* pointer to proc. tab. entry */
        char    ps;                     /* saved processor status     */
        int     prio;                   /* priority returned          */

        disable(ps);
        if (isbadpid(pid) || pid==NULLPROC ||
          ((pptr= &proctab[pid])->pstate!=PRCURR && pptr->pstate!=PRREADY)) {
                restore(ps);
                return(SYSERR);
        }
        if (pptr->pstate == PRREADY) {
                dequeue(pid);
                pptr->pstate = PRSUSP;
        } else {
                pptr->pstate = PRSUSP;
                resched();
        }
        prio = pptr->pprio;
        restore(ps);
        return(prio);
}
```

5.2.2 Suspending The Current Process

Although suspending the currently executing process may seem odd, it turns out to be quite useful, and the code brings up two interesting points. First, the currently executing process will stop executing, at least temporarily, so it must arrange to switch to another process. To do so, it merely marks its process state suspended (*PRSUSP*), and calls *resched*. If you remember, *resched* looks at the process state to determine the disposition of the current process. In this case, it will switch context without moving the current process back onto the ready list.

Second, *suspend*, like *resume*, returns the priority of the suspended process to its caller. However, *suspend* records the process priority *after* it has suspended the process. When a process suspends another one the code makes perfect sense because nothing can change the priority while *suspend* executes with interrupts disabled. But when a process suspends itself, it calls *resched*, allowing other processes to execute. They may change the process' priority. When *suspend* eventually resumes executing, it reports the priority at the time of resumption. The exercises consider the motivation for this arrangement.

You may have noticed that *suspend* and *resume* do not maintain a separate linked list of suspended processes as *ready* did. The reason is simple. Ready processes are kept on an ordered list only to speed the search for the highest priority process during rescheduling. Because the system never searches through suspended processes looking for one to resume, the set of suspended processes need not be kept on a list.

5.3 Process Termination

Suspend freezes processes, but leaves them in the system so they can be resumed later. Another system call, *kill* stops a process immediately and removes it from the system completely. Once a process has been removed, it cannot be restarted because *kill* eradicates its entire record, freeing the process table entry.

The actions taken by *kill* depend on the process' state. Before writing the code, the designer needs to have some notion of the possible states and what it would mean to terminate a process in that state. For example, processes that are ready, sleeping, or waiting are all kept on linked lists in the *q* structure, so *kill* must dequeue them. If the process is waiting for a semaphore, *kill* must adjust the semaphore count as well. Not all these cases will make complete sense until you know more about the process states.

The code for *kill* appears in file *kill.c*, below. Consider how it operates for a process in the *ready* state. *Kill* checks its argument, *pid*, to ensure that it corresponds to a valid, active process by verifying that it is in the correct range and that the process table entry is not free. It then decrements *numproc*, the global variable that records the number of active user processes. Next, *kill* calls procedure *freestk* to free memory that the process used for a stack. It unlinks the process from the ready list with procedure *dequeue*, and frees the process table entry by assigning its state field *PRFREE*. Because the process no longer appears on the ready list, it will never regain control of the CPU.

Now consider what happens when *kill* needs to terminate the currently executing process. As before, it validates its argument and decrements the count of active processes. If the current process happens to be the last user process, decrementing *numproc* makes it zero, so *kill* calls procedure *xdone*, shown below. After *kill* marks the current process' state free, it calls *resched* to pass control to another ready process.

```
/* kill.c - kill */

#include <conf.h>
#include <kernel.h>
#include <proc.h>
#include <sem.h>
#include <mem.h>

/*------------------------------------------------------------------------
 * kill  --  kill a process and remove it from the system
 *------------------------------------------------------------------------
 */
SYSCALL kill(pid)
        int     pid;                    /* process to kill          */
{
        struct  pentry *pptr;           /* points to proc. table for pid*/
        char    ps;                     /* saved processor status   */

        disable(ps);
        if (isbadpid(pid) || (pptr= &proctab[pid])->pstate==PRFREE) {
                restore(ps);
                return(SYSERR);
        }
        if (--numproc == 0)
                xdone();
        freestk(pptr->pbase, pptr->pstklen);
        switch (pptr->pstate) {

        case PRCURR:    pptr->pstate = PRFREE;  /* suicide */
                        resched();

        case PRWAIT:    semaph[pptr->psem].semcnt++;
                                                /* fall through */
        case PRSLEEP:
        case PRREADY:   dequeue(pid);
                                                /* fall through */
        default:        pptr->pstate = PRFREE;
        }
        restore(ps);
        return(OK);
}
```

```
/* xdone.c - xdone */

/*-------------------------------------------------------------------
 * xdone  --  print system completion message as last process exits
 *-------------------------------------------------------------------
 */
xdone()
{
        printf("\n\nAll user processes have completed.\n\n");


}
```

5.4 Kernel Declarations

The file *kernel.h* defines inline procedures *disable* and *restore* mentioned above, as well as a few other variables and symbolic constants used throughout Xinu. Although not all the names that appear in it make sense yet, they will by the end of the chapter.

```
/* kernel.h - disable, enable, halt, restore, isodd */

/* Symbolic constants used throughout Xinu */

typedef char            Bool;           /* Boolean type             */
#define FALSE           0               /* Boolean constants        */
#define TRUE            1
#define NULL            (char *)0        /* Null pointer for linked lists*/
#define SYSCALL         int             /* System call declaration  */
#define LOCAL           static          /* Local procedure declaration */
#define INTPROC         int             /* Interrupt procedure  "   */
#define PROCESS         int             /* Process declaration      */
#define RESCHYES        1               /* tell ready to reschedule */
#define RESCHNO         0               /* tell ready not to resch. */
#define MININT          0100000         /* minimum integer (-32768) */
#define MAXINT          0077777         /* maximum integer          */
#define SP              6               /* reg. 6 is stack pointer  */
#define PC              7               /* reg. 7 is program counter */
#define PS              8               /* proc. status in 8th reg. loc */
#define MINSTK          40              /* minimum process stack size */
#define NULLSTK         300             /* process 0 stack size     */
#define DISABLE         0340            /* PS to disable interrupts */
#define OK              1               /* returned when system call ok */
#define SYSERR          -1              /* returned when sys. call fails*/
```

```
/* initialization constants */

#define INITARGC      1                 /* initial process argc       */
#define INITSTK       200               /* initial process stack      */
#define INITPRIO      20                /* initial process priority    */
#define INITNAME      "main"            /* initial process name       */
#define INITRET       userret           /* processes return address    */
#define INITPS        0                 /* initial process PS          */
#define INITREG       0                 /* initial register contents   */
#define QUANTUM       10                /* clock ticks until preemption */

/* misc. utility inline functions */

#define isodd(x)      (01&(int)(x))
#define disable(ps)   asm("mfps ~ps");asm("mtps $0340")
#define restore(ps)   asm("mtps ~ps") /* restore interrupt status   */
#define enable()      asm("mtps $000")/* enable interrupts          */
#define pause()       asm("wait")     /* machine "wait for interr."  */
#define halt()        asm("halt")     /* machine halt instruction    */

extern  int     rdyhead, rdytail;
extern  int     preempt;
```

5.5 Process Creation

The system call *create* creates a new, independent process. The idea is to lay down an exact image of the process as if it had been stopped while running, so *ctxsw* can switch to it. *Create* finds a free (unused) slot in the process table, allocates space for the new process' stack, and fills in the process table entry.

A look at the code in file *create.c* explains most of the details. Procedure *newpid* searches the process table for a free process id, returning *SYSERR* if none exists. *Create* uses procedure *roundew* to round the specified stack size to the next largest even word, and calls *getstk* to allocate space for the stack (Chapter 8 discusses both of these memory management routines).

We refer to the initial process stack as a *pseudo-call* because *create* carefully pushes values on it to simulate a procedure call. In C, the pseudo-call consists of arguments and a return address. When started, the new process begins executing the code for the designated procedure, obeying the normal calling conventions for accessing arguments and allocating local variables. In short, it behaves exactly as if it had been called from another procedure.

How does the designer choose a return address value to use in the pseudo call? Fortunately, there is a guideline for what happens when a process returns from its initial procedure: it should exit. *Create* makes the return address in the pseudo call

the address of procedure *userret*. If the process does attempt to return from the initial procedure, control passes to *userret*. Procedure *userret* terminates the calling
process with *kill*.

    Create also fills in the process table entry. Knowing that *ctxsw* switches to
processes by picking up register contents from the *pregs* field, *create* fills in appropriate values for stack pointer, program counter, and processor status word.
Create makes the state of the newly created process *PRSUSP*, leaving it suspended,
but otherwise ready to run. Finally, *create* returns the process id of the newly
created process. The id must be passed to *resume* to start the new process executing.

    Many of the process initialization details depend on the C run-time environ-
ment — there is simply no way to start a process without facing them. For example, *create* pushes arguments onto the process stack so the first argument is near
the top of the stack. Although not all C compilers adhere to this convention, most
do. The code that pushes arguments is difficult to understand because *create* copies
those arguments directly from its own run-time stack onto the stack that it has allocated for the new process. To do so, it finds the address of the arguments on its
own stack and moves through the list using pointer arithmetic. This is clearly a
machine (and compiler) dependent trick. One alternative is to have the caller construct an array of argument pointers, and have *create* copy pointers from the list
onto the new process' stack.

```
/* create.c - create, newpid */

#include <conf.h>
#include <kernel.h>
#include <proc.h>
#include <mem.h>


/*------------------------------------------------------------------------
 *  create  -  create a process to start running a procedure
 *------------------------------------------------------------------------
 */
SYSCALL create(procaddr,ssize,priority,name,nargs,args)
        int     *procaddr;              /* procedure address            */
        int     ssize;                  /* stack size in words          */
        int     priority;               /* process priority > 0         */
        char    *name;                  /* name (for debugging)         */
        int     nargs;                  /* number of args that follow   */
        int     args;                   /* arguments (treated like an   */
                                        /* array in the code)           */
{
        int     pid;                    /* stores new process id        */
        struct  pentry  *pptr;          /* pointer to proc. table entry */
```

```
        int     i;
        int     *a;                     /* points to list of args     */
        int     *saddr;                 /* stack address              */
        char    ps;                     /* saved processor status     */
        int     INITRET();
        disable(ps);
        ssize = roundew(ssize);
        if ( ssize < MINSTK || ((saddr=getstk(ssize)) == SYSERR ) ||
                (pid=newpid()) == SYSERR || isodd(procaddr) ||
                priority < 1 ) {
                restore(ps);
                return(SYSERR);
        }
        numproc++;
        pptr = &proctab[pid];
        pptr->pstate = PRSUSP;
        for (i=0 ; i<PNMLEN && (pptr->pname[i]=name[i])!=0 ; i++)
                ;
        pptr->pprio = priority;
        pptr->pbase = (short)saddr;
        pptr->pstklen = ssize;
        pptr->plimit = (short) ( saddr - ssize + 1);
        pptr->pargs = nargs;
        for (i=0 ; i<PNREGS ; i++)
                pptr->pregs[i]=INITREG;
        pptr->pregs[PC] = pptr->paddr = (short)procaddr;
        pptr->pregs[PS] = INITPS;
        a = (&args) + (nargs-1);        /* point to last argument       */
        for ( ; nargs > 0 ; nargs--)    /* machine dependent; copy args */
                *saddr-- = *a--;        /* onto created process' stack  */
        *saddr = (int)INITRET;          /* push on return address        */
        pptr->pregs[SP] = (int)saddr;
        restore(ps);
        return(pid);
}


/*-----------------------------------------------------------------------
 * newpid  --  obtain a new (free) process id
 *-----------------------------------------------------------------------
 */
LOCAL   newpid()
{
        int     pid;                    /* process id to return          */
        int     i;
```

```
        for (i=0 ; i<NPROC ; i++) {        /* check all NPROC slots        */
                if ( (pid=nextproc--) <= 0)
                        nextproc = NPROC-1;
                if (proctab[pid].pstate == PRFREE)
                        return(pid);
        }
        return(SYSERR);
}


/* userret.c - userret */

#include <conf.h>
#include <kernel.h>


/*------------------------------------------------------------------------
 * userret  --  entered when a process exits by return
 *------------------------------------------------------------------------
 */
userret()
{
        kill( getpid() );
}
```

5.6 Utility Procedures

Three additional system calls help manage processes: *getpid*, *getprio* and *chprio*. *Getpid* allows a process to obtain its process id. *Userret* shows one reason a procedure may need to know the id of the process executing it. *Getprio* allows a process to obtain a process' scheduling priority. Another useful system call, *chprio*, allows a process to change a process' priority. The implementation of all three routines is exceedingly simple:

```
/* getprio.c - getprio */

#include <conf.h>
#include <kernel.h>
#include <proc.h>


/*------------------------------------------------------------------------
 * getprio -- return the scheduling priority of a given process
 *------------------------------------------------------------------------
 */
```

```
SYSCALL getprio(pid)
        int     pid;
{

        struct  pentry  *pptr;
        char    ps;

        disable(ps);
        if (isbadpid(pid) || (pptr = &proctab[pid])->pstate == PRFREE) {
                restore(ps);
                return(SYSERR);
        }
        restore(ps);
        return(pptr->pprio);
}
```

After checking its argument, *getprio* extracts the scheduling priority for the specified process from the process table entry, and returns the priority to the caller.

```
/* getpid.c - getpid */

#include <conf.h>
#include <kernel.h>
#include <proc.h>


/*------------------------------------------------------------------------
 * getpid  --  get the process id of currently executing process
 *------------------------------------------------------------------------
 */
SYSCALL getpid()
{
        return(currpid);
}
```

It may seem that procedure *getpid* is useless because it returns the value of variable *currpid*, a value that the process could obtain directly with less overhead. Why not have processes access *currpid*? If Xinu is transported to a machine in which user processes cannot access the address space occupied by the system, it may not be possible for a user process to obtain the value of *currpid* directly.

```
/* chprio.c - chprio */

#include <conf.h>
#include <kernel.h>
#include <proc.h>


/*------------------------------------------------------------------------
 * chprio  --  change the scheduling priority of a process
 *------------------------------------------------------------------------
 */
SYSCALL chprio(pid,newprio)
        int      pid;
        int      newprio;                          /* newprio > 0                    */
{
        int      oldprio;
        struct   pentry *pptr;
        char     ps;

        disable(ps);
        if (isbadpid(pid) || newprio<=0 ||
            (pptr = &proctab[pid])->pstate == PRFREE) {
                restore(ps);
                return(SYSERR);
        }
        oldprio = pptr->pprio;
        pptr->pprio = newprio;
        restore(ps);
        return(oldprio);
}
```

This implementation of *chprio* seems to do exactly what is needed. It checks to be sure the specified process exists before changing the priority field in its process table entry. As the exercises point out, however, it contains a serious flaw.

5.7 Summary

This chapter has expanded the ideas of process management by discussing how to add another layer of software on top of the scheduler and context switch. The new layer includes routines to *suspend* and *resume* execution as well as routines that *create* processes and *kill* them. Finally, we looked at three utility procedures that obtain a process' identifier (*getpid*), obtain a process' scheduling priority (*getprio*), or change a process' priority (*chprio*). Despite its brevity, the code built thus far forms the basis of a process manager. With proper initialization and a few support routines, it will multiplex the CPU among multiple computations.

The following chapters discuss the design of synchronization and interprocess communication, components that are built on top of the existing layers. Chapter 8 will discuss the only low-level layer that we have ignored so far, the memory manager. Following that, we will continue the pattern of building layers one on top of the other.

FOR FURTHER STUDY

Primitives for process creation and management vary widely among systems. Calingaert [1982] includes a good survey of process creation techniques. Knuth [1968] gives the details of coroutine activation; Ritchie and Thompson [1974] describe the *fork* primitive used to create processes in the UNIX system.

EXERCISES

5.1 Processes can tell which of several events triggered their resumption if their priority is set to a unique value before each call to *resume*. Use this method to create a process that suspends itself and determines which of two other processes resumes it first.

5.2 Why does *create* build a pseudo-call that returns to *userret* at process exit instead of one that calls *kill* directly?

5.3 Modify *create* to call kill directly, pushing the process id onto the stack as an argument to *kill*.

5.4 Global variable *numproc* tells the number of active user processes. Considering the code in *kill* can you tell whether the count in *numproc* should include the null process or not?

5.5 Find out how the *trap* instruction can be used to pass control to a system call on the 11/2. What are the disadvantages of this mechanism? Hints: think of the memory needed, and the number of possible system calls.

5.6 *Create* leaves the new process suspended instead of running. Why?

5.7 Procedure *resume* saves the resumed process' priority in a local variable before calling *ready*. Show that if it referenced *pptr->prio* after the call to *ready*, *resume* could return a priority value that the resumed process never had (not even after resumption).

5.8 In procedure *newpid*, the variable *nextproc* is a global integer that tells the next process table slot to check for a free one. Starting the search from where it left off eliminates looking past the used slots again and again. Speculate on whether the technique is worthwhile.

5.9 *Getpid* simply returns the value of *currpid* to the caller. Discuss reasons for hiding the operating system internals with system calls. Find out about address space mapping on a machine more complex than an 11/2, and consider why it might be necessary to have a system call instead of allowing user processes to access *currpid* directly.

5.10 Procedure *chprio* contains a serious design flaw. Find it, describe its consequences, and repair it.

6

Process Coordination

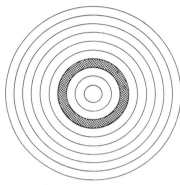

Independent processes use coordination primitives to synchronize their actions, and to cooperate in sharing resources. Chapter 1 introduced *counting semaphores*, the basic process coordination mechanism in Xinu, and gave examples of their use. In one example, two processes coordinated to guarantee that the "consumer" received every value emitted by the "producer." In another example, a set of processes used a semaphore to obtain exclusive access to a data structure they shared.

Semaphores are perhaps the easiest process coordination primitives to understand and implement. Conceptually, each semaphore, *s*, consists of an integer count. Processes call *wait*(*s*) to decrement its count, and *signal*(*s*) to increment it. If the semaphore count becomes negative when a process executes *wait*(*s*), that process is delayed. From the point of view of the process, the call to *wait* just does not return for a while. A delayed processes becomes ready to run again each time *signal* is called. If no process ever calls *signal*, the delayed process continues to wait forever.

Exactly how does procedure *wait* delay its caller? It is important to remember that even though processes run concurrently, we are discussing a system that usually executes on a single processor. A process cannot execute instructions while waiting without depriving other processes of CPU service. For example, waiting that involves testing a memory location in a tight loop is dangerous — if the CPU spends all its time executing the "waiting" process, no other process can ever call *signal* to terminate the wait. Even in systems with many processors, so-called *busy waiting* techniques may interfere with processing because each processor contends with others while using the memory or bus systems to fetch instructions or data. To minimize system overhead, the coordination primitives in Xinu follow this principle:

> *Waiting processes do not execute instructions; when all user processes are waiting, the system does not execute code.*

Whether a system executes code when all user processes are waiting depends somewhat on the machine architecture. Like most machines, the 11/2 includes a *wait* instruction to halt the CPU while all processes wait. For the time being we will defer the problem of halting the CPU when all processes wait, and consider the simpler case of how to avoid busy waiting when at least one process remains ready to run. Remember that Xinu always has a ready process — the null process.

6.1 Low-Level Coordination Techniques

The previous chapter contained examples of process coordination techniques in the code for routines like *ready* and *resume*. When a process executing one of these routines needs to modify a shared data structure like the process table, it must be sure that no other process attempts concurrent access. Coordination between these low-level system routines involves disabling interrupts and being careful not to call *resched*. Why not use this solution again? Disabling interrupts has an undesirable global effect on the system: it stops all but one process, and limits what that process can do. We need general purpose coordination primitives so that arbitrary subsets of the processes can coordinate without stopping other processes, without disabling device interrupts for long periods of time, and without limiting what running processes can do. For example, it should be possible for one process to prohibit changes to a large data structure long enough to print it, without stopping those processes that do not need to access it.

6.2 Implementation Of High-Level Coordination Primitives

The Xinu implementation of counting semaphores avoids busy waiting by denying CPU service to waiting processes. When a process needs to wait for some semaphore, the system places it on a list of processes associated with that semaphore. Naturally, each semaphore must have its own, independent list of waiting processes. To delay the current process, *wait(s)* enqueues it on the list for *s*, and calls *resched* allowing other processes to run. *Signal(s)* checks the list associated with *s* whenever it is called. Provided the list of waiting processes is nonempty, *signal* restarts a process by moving it back to the ready list.

In what state should a process be placed while it is waiting for a semaphore? It is clearly not *current* or *ready* because it is neither using the CPU nor eligible to use it. The *suspended* state, introduced in Chapter 5, will not suffice either, because it is used by procedures like *suspend* and *resume* that have no connection

with semaphores. More importantly, processes waiting for semaphores appear on a
list, but suspended processes do not — *kill* needs to distinguish the two cases.
Whenever the existing process states cannot adequately indicate how operations
should be carried out, the designer can invent a new state. In this case we will call
the new state "waiting", and refer to it in the code with the symbolic constant
PRWAIT. Figure 6.1 shows the expanded state transitions.

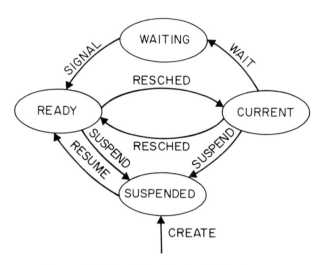

Figure 6.1 Transitions for the 'waiting' state

6.2.1 Semaphore Data Structures

In Xinu, semaphore information is kept in the global semaphore table, *semaph*.
Each entry in *semaph* contains the integer count and list of processes corresponding
to one semaphore; its definition is given in C by structure *sentry*. File *sem.h* contains the details:

```
/* sem.h - isbadsem */

#ifndef NSEM
#define NSEM              45        /* number of semaphores, if not defined */
#endif

#define SFREE     '\01'             /* this semaphore is free               */
#define SUSED     '\02'             /* this semaphore is used               */

struct  sentry  {                   /* semaphore table entry                */
        char    sstate;             /* the state SFREE or SUSED             */
        short   semcnt;             /* count for this semaphore             */
        short   sqhead;             /* q index of head of list              */
        short   sqtail;             /* q index of tail of list              */
};
extern  struct  sentry  semaph[];
extern  int     nextsem;

#define isbadsem(s)     (s<0 || s>=NSEM)
```

In structure *sentry*, field *semcnt* contains the current integer value of the semaphore. The list of processes waiting for a semaphore resides in the *q* structure; *sentry* fields *sqhead* and *sqtail* only give the index of the head and tail. The state
field, *sstate* tells whether each semaphore entry is currently free (unallocated) or in
use.

Throughout the system, semaphores are identified by an integer. As with
processes, the semaphore identifiers are meaningful values, chosen to connect the
semaphore and its table entry:

> *Semaphores are identified by their index in the global semaphore
> table, semaph.*

System calls *wait* and *signal* implement the basic semaphore operations.
Wait(*s*) decrements the count of semaphore *s*. If the count remains nonnegative,
wait returns to the caller immediately. Otherwise, it enqueues the calling process
on the list for *s*, changes the process state to *PRWAIT*, and calls *resched* to switch
to a ready process. The list is maintained as a FIFO queue with insertions at the
tail and deletions at the head. In essence, a process executing *wait* on a semaphore
with a nonpositive count voluntarily gives up control of the CPU after *wait* records
its id on the list of waiting processes.

Once enqueued on a semaphore list, a process remains there (and hence, not
executing) until it reaches the head of the queue and some other process signals the
semaphore. When the call to *signal* moves the waiting process back to the ready
list, it becomes eligible to use the CPU, and eventually resumes execution. From

the point of view of the waiting process, its last act consisted of calling *ctxsw*. The call to *ctxsw* returns to *resched*, the call to *resched* returns to *wait*, and the call to *wait* returns to wherever it was called.

```
/* wait.c - wait */

#include <conf.h>
#include <kernel.h>
#include <proc.h>
#include <q.h>
#include <sem.h>

/*------------------------------------------------------------------
 * wait  --  make current process wait on a semaphore
 *------------------------------------------------------------------
 */
SYSCALL wait(sem)
        int     sem;
{

        char    ps;
        register struct sentry *sptr;
        register struct pentry *pptr;

        disable(ps);
        if (isbadsem(sem) || (sptr= &semaph[sem])->sstate==SFREE) {
                restore(ps);
                return(SYSERR);
        }
        if (--(sptr->semcnt) < 0) {
                (pptr = &proctab[currpid])->pstate = PRWAIT;
                pptr->psem = sem;
                enqueue(currpid,sptr->sqtail);
                resched();
        }
        restore(ps);
        return(OK);
}
```

The code for *signal* is straightforward. It increments the semaphore count, and makes the first waiting process ready to run.

```
/* signal.c - signal */

#include <conf.h>
#include <kernel.h>
#include <proc.h>
#include <q.h>
#include <sem.h>


/*------------------------------------------------------------------
 * signal  --  signal a semaphore, releasing one waiting process
 *------------------------------------------------------------------
 */
SYSCALL signal(sem)
register int    sem;
{
        register struct sentry  *sptr;
        char    ps;

        disable(ps);
        if (isbadsem(sem) !! (sptr= &semaph[sem])->sstate==SFREE) {
                restore(ps);
                return(SYSERR);
        }
        if ((sptr->semcnt++) < 0)
                ready(getfirst(sptr->sqhead), RESCHYES);
        restore(ps);
        return(OK);
}
```

Although it may seem difficult to understand why *signal* makes a process ready even though the semaphore count remains negative, or why *wait* does not enqueue the process every time, the reason is both easy to understand and easy to implement. *Wait* and *signal* keep the following condition invariant:

> *A nonnegative semaphore count means that the queue is empty; a semaphore count of negative n means that the queue contains n waiting processes.*

Both *wait* and *signal* change the semaphore count, so they adjust the queue length, if necessary, to reestablish the invariant. Because *wait* decrements the count, it adds the current process to the queue if the new count is negative. Because *signal* increments the count, it removes a process from the queue if the queue is nonempty.

6.3 Semaphore Creation and Deletion

The need for semaphores may come and go as execution progresses, so it would be foolish to allocate each semaphore a specific purpose. Rather than fix the use of semaphores at compile time, Xinu allows processes to request a semaphore, use it, and then release it. Processes can create an arbitrary number of semaphores in arbitrary order, as long as the number allocated simultaneously does not exceed the maximum table size. To help minimize the cost of creating semaphores, the system preallocates head and tail nodes in the *q* structure for each semaphore list at system initialization time. Thus, only a small amount of work need be done at semaphore creation time.

System calls *screate* and *sdelete* allocate and release semaphores. *Screate*, shown below, takes the initial semaphore count as an argument, and returns the semaphore id of a semaphore with that count. The method is simple: search for an unused entry in the semaphore table *semaph*, and initialize it. *Screate* uses procedure *newsem* to search for a free entry. It then initializes the count, and returns the index of the semaphore just allocated.

```
/* screate.c - screate, newsem */

#include <conf.h>
#include <kernel.h>
#include <proc.h>
#include <q.h>
#include <sem.h>

/*------------------------------------------------------------------------
 * screate  --  create and initialize a semaphore, returning its id
 *------------------------------------------------------------------------
 */
SYSCALL screate(count)
        int     count;                          /* initial count (>=0)        */
{
        char    ps;
        int     sem;

        disable(ps);
        if ( count<0 || (sem=newsem())==SYSERR ) {
                restore(ps);
                return(SYSERR);
        }
        semaph[sem].semcnt = count;
        /* sqhead and sqtail were initialized at system startup */
        restore(ps);
        return(sem);
}


/*------------------------------------------------------------------------
 * newsem  --  allocate an unused semaphore and return its index
 *------------------------------------------------------------------------
 */
LOCAL   newsem()
{
        int     sem;
        int     i;

        for (i=0 ; i<NSEM ; i++) {
                sem=nextsem--;
                if (nextsem < 0)
                        nextsem = NSEM-1;
                if (semaph[sem].sstate==SFREE) {
                        semaph[sem].sstate = SUSED;
                        return(sem);
```

```
                }
        }
        return(SYSERR);
}
```

Sdelete reverses the actions of *screate*. It takes the index of a semaphore as an argument, and releases the semaphore table entry for use again.

```
/* sdelete.c - sdelete */

#include <conf.h>
#include <kernel.h>
#include <proc.h>
#include <q.h>
#include <sem.h>

/*------------------------------------------------------------------------
 * sdelete  --  delete a semaphore by releasing its table entry
 *------------------------------------------------------------------------
 */
SYSCALL sdelete(sem)
        int     sem;
{
        char    ps;
        int     pid;
        struct  sentry  *sptr;          /* address of sem to free      */

        disable(ps);
        if (isbadsem(sem) || semaph[sem].sstate==SFREE) {
                restore(ps);
                return(SYSERR);
        }
        sptr = &semaph[sem];
        sptr->sstate = SFREE;
        if (nonempty(sptr->sqhead)) {   /* free waiting processes      */
                while( (pid=getfirst(sptr->sqhead)) != EMPTY)
                        ready(pid,RESCHNO);
                resched();
        }
        restore(ps);
        return(OK);
}
```

If processes remain enqueued when *sdelete* tries to delete a semaphore, it must dispose of them. When faced with an active semaphore, *sdelete* places waiting processes back on the ready list, allowing each to resume execution as if the semaphore had been signalled. This is only one possible disposition of the waiting processes; the exercises suggest some other alternatives.

6.4 Summary

This chapter discussed process synchronization primitives known as counting semaphores. In addition to showing how to build procedures that create and delete semaphores, it showed how the primitive semaphore operations *wait* and *signal* cooperate to suspend processes and resume them such that waiting processes do not use any CPU time. In essence, a process that needs to wait for a semaphore voluntarily enqueues itself on the list of processes waiting for the semaphore, and calls the scheduler to allow other processes to execute. Eventually, when another process signals the semaphore, it moves the waiting process back to the ready list, so it can regain control of the CPU once again.

FOR FURTHER STUDY

Dijkstra [1965] introduced semaphores, and showed how to use them for synchronization. Initially, semaphores had only binary values, and the operations were known as *P* (wait) and *V* (signal). These are summarized in the appendix of Dijkstra [1968]. Although binary semaphores are sufficient to provide basic synchronization and mutual exclusion, the addition of counts makes them much more convenient to use. Patil [1971] and Kosaraju [1973] consider whether binary semaphores can solve all synchronization problems.

Brinch Hansen [1970, 1972] showed how to synchronize by exchanging messages. Another process synchronization tool, the monitor, is described by Hoare [1974]. Its beginnings can be seen in the "secretary" of Dijkstra [1971] and in Brinch Hansen [1973]. Although high-level primitives like monitors make it easier to express the intended process interaction, they can be implemented with semaphores.

EXERCISES

6.1 It is sometimes convenient to reset the count of a semaphore without going to the trouble of deleting the semaphore and acquiring a new one. Write a system call *sreset* that resets a semaphore to a new count.

6.2 Deleting a semaphore while processes remain enqueued waiting for it might be considered an error. Rewrite *sdelete* to refuse to delete a busy semaphore.

6.3 Another way to handle the deletion of an active resource is to defer the deletion. Rewrite *sdelete*, *wait*, and *signal* to place deleted semaphores in a state such that *signal* releases the semaphore table entry when it removes the last waiting process from the queue. What unexpected effects might deferring deletion have?

6.4 Instead of placing responsibility for deletion of active semaphores on the process calling *sdelete*, consider allowing waiting processes to handle the problem. Modify *wait* so it returns an integer *DELETED* in case the semaphore was deleted while the calling process was waiting. (Choose a value for *DELETED* that will not interfere with *SYSERR* or *OK*.) How can the process calling *wait* know when to return *DELETED*? Checking the state of the semaphore is insufficient because a higher priority process may reuse the table entry before all the deleted processes resume execution and examine *sstate*. Hint: add a sequence field to *sentry*.

6.5 Instead of allocating a central semaphore table, arrange to have each process allocate space for semaphore entries as needed, and use the address of an entry as the semaphore id. Compare this method to that of a centralized table. What are the advantages? Disadvantages?

6.6 *Wait*, *signal*, *screate*, and *sdelete* coordinate among themselves for use of the semaphore table. How much easier would it be to code them if semaphores were used?

6.7 Why does *sdelete* call *ready* without rescheduling? Why does it call *resched* directly? Modify the code so it allows *ready* to reschedule on the last call.

6.8 Assuming procedure calls are expensive, *sdelete* could check the priority of processes as it added them to the ready list and not bother calling *resched* if none had higher priority than the current process. Speculate about the wisdom of adding this optimization.

6.9 Construct a new system call, *signaln(sem, n)* that signals semaphore *sem n* times. Try to make it more efficient than *n* calls to *signal*.

6.10 Languages meant specifically for writing concurrent programs often have coordination and synchronization imbedded in the language constructs directly. For example, it might be possible to declare procedures in groups such that the compiler automatically inserts code to prohibit more than one process from executing in any group. Find an example of a language designed for concurrent programming, and compare process coordination with the semaphores in Xinu. What types of mistakes can a programmer make when required to manipulate semaphores directly?

6.11 Because it is much more likely that an incorrect expression will evaluate to 0 or 1, *newsem* begins allocating semaphores from the high end of the table to reduce the chance of inadvertently waiting on the wrong semaphore. If all entries are allocated, the problem persists. Suggest better ways of identifying semaphores.

6.12 Draw a call graph of all procedures in Chapters 1 through 6, showing which procedures each procedure calls. Can the layered structure be deduced from the graph?

7

Message Passing

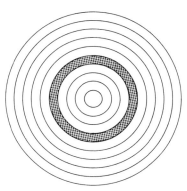

Message passing refers to a form of inter-process communication in which one process requests that the operating system send data directly to another. In some systems, processes deposit and retrieve messages from named "pickup points"; in others, each message must be addressed directly to a process. Message passing is both convenient and powerful, and many systems use it as the basis for all communication. For example, operations like sending data to a terminal or across a network to another machine can all be designed on top of message passing primitives.

Messages also provide a form of process coordination, because the receiver can delay until the arrival of the next message. The chief difference between coordinating with messages and semaphores is that semaphores require precise synchronization between the processes that *wait* and those that *signal* because there must be a call of *wait*(*s*) for every call to *signal*(*s*). By contrast, message passing can be unsynchronized. Unsynchronized messages are easier to use if a process does not know how many messages it will receive, when they will be sent, or which processes will send them. For example, one process in the Xinu network routines uses messages to help it "time out" acknowledgements — it transmits data over the network and waits for an acknowledgement message (indicating that the data arrived) or a timer message (indicating that it should retry the operation).

7.1 Message Passing In Xinu

Xinu supports two forms of message passing that serve to demonstrate two design approaches. This chapter deals with the first form, messages passed from one process directly to another. Chapter 14 discusses the second form, messages left at rendevous points. Separating messages into two classes has the advantage of making process-to-process messages more efficient, but the disadvantage of requiring the user to know the destination of messages when writing programs. (Readers with special interest in message passing facilities should think about the potential benefits and liabilities of unifying all message passing as they read this material.)

Process-to-process message passing has been carefully designed to ensure that processes do not block (i.e. delay) while sending messages, and waiting messages do not consume all of memory. To make these guarantees, the message passing facility limits each message to one word (the size of an integer or pointer), and permits only one unreceived message per process at any time. The implementation of these restrictions is well-defined: if several messages are sent to a process before it attempts to receive any of them, only the *first* message will be received. Thus, a process can use message passing to determine which of several events completed first by having them each send a unique message upon completion.

Three Xinu system calls manipulate messages: *receive*, *recvclr*, and *send*. *Send* takes a message and a process id as arguments, and delivers the message to the specified process. *Receive* waits for a message to arrive, and then returns that message to its caller; it requires no arguments. *Recvclr* is the asynchronous analog of *receive*; it never waits for a message to arrive. If the process has a message when it calls *recvclr*, the call returns the message exactly like *receive*. But if no message is waiting, *recvclr* returns the value *OK* to its caller without delaying to wait for a message to arrive. As the name implies, *recvclr* is often used to clear away any old messages that might be waiting.

Again, the question arises: "in what state should a process be while waiting for a message?" Because waiting for a message differs from waiting for a semaphore, waiting for the CPU, suspended animation, or currently executing, none of the existing states exactly solves the problem. So, it is time to add another state to our design. The new state, "waiting to receive a message", is referenced in the software with the symbolic constant *PRRECV*. Adding it to the other states produces the transition diagram shown in Figure 7.1.

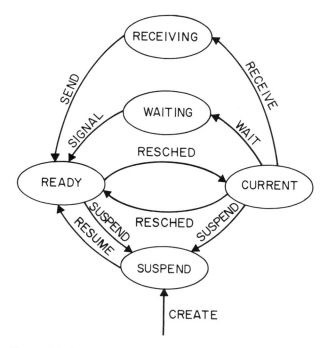

Figure 7.1 Process state transitions for the 'receiving' state

7.2 Implementation Of Send

Send must store messages where the recipient can *receive* them. They cannot be kept in the sender's memory because the sending process might exit before the message was received. They cannot be kept in the recipient's memory because allowing the sender to write into it poses a security threat. We have solved the problem by allocating space for messages in the process table entry.

To deposit a message, *send* first checks that the specified recipient process exists. It verifies that the recipient does not have a message outstanding by examining the *phasmsg* field of its process table entry. If the process has no outstanding messages, *send* deposits the new message in the *pmsg* field, and makes the *phasmsg* field nonzero to indicate that a message is waiting. Finally, if the process is waiting the arrival of a message, *send* moves it to the ready list, enabling it to access the message and continue execution.

```
/* send.c - send */

#include <conf.h>
#include <kernel.h>
#include <proc.h>


/*------------------------------------------------------------------------
 *  send  --   send a message to another process
 *------------------------------------------------------------------------
 */
SYSCALL send(pid, msg)
int     pid;
int     msg;
{
        struct  pentry  *pptr;          /* receiver's proc. table addr. */
        char    ps;

        disable(ps);
        if (isbadpid(pid) || ( (pptr= &proctab[pid])->pstate == PRFREE)
            || pptr->phasmsg != 0) {
                restore(ps);
                return(SYSERR);
        }
        pptr->pmsg = msg;               /* deposit message             */
        pptr->phasmsg++;
        if (pptr->pstate == PRRECV)     /* if receiver waits, start it */
                ready(pid, RESCHYES);
        restore(ps);
        return(OK);
}
```

7.3 Implementation Of Receive

A process, *P*, calls *receive* (or *recvclr*) to obtain a message that has been sent to it. *Receive* examines the *phasmsg* field of its process table entry to determine if there is a message waiting. If not, it changes *P* to the receiving state and calls *resched*, allowing other processes to run. Eventually, when another process, *Q*, sends *P* a message, *send* places *P* back on the ready list. When *P* executes, the call to *resched* returns, allowing *receive* to pick up the message and return it to the caller.

```
/* receive.c - receive */

#include <conf.h>
#include <kernel.h>
#include <proc.h>


/*------------------------------------------------------------------------
 *  receive  -  wait for a message and return it
 *------------------------------------------------------------------------
 */
SYSCALL receive()
{
        struct  pentry  *pptr;
        int     msg;
        char    ps;

        disable(ps);
        pptr = &proctab[currpid];
        if (pptr->phasmsg == 0) {        /* if no message, wait for one */
                pptr->pstate = PRRECV;
                resched();
        }
        msg = pptr->pmsg;                /* retrieve message            */
        pptr->phasmsg = 0;
        restore(ps);
        return(msg);
}
```

Recvclr operates much like *receive* except that it always returns immediately. The implementation is straight-forward:

```
/* recvclr.c - recvclr */

#include <conf.h>
#include <kernel.h>
#include <proc.h>


/*------------------------------------------------------------------------
 * recvclr  --  clear messages, returning waiting message (if any)
 *------------------------------------------------------------------------
 */
SYSCALL recvclr()
{
        char    ps;
        int     msg;

        disable(ps);
        if (proctab[currpid].phasmsg) {          /* existing message?    */
                proctab[currpid].phasmsg = 0;
                msg = proctab[currpid].pmsg;
        } else
                msg = OK;
        restore(ps);
        return(msg);
}
```

7.4 Summary

Message passing allows one process to send information to another. This
chapter explored a simple form of interprocess message passing that used the central process table as an exchange point. The chief advantages of such an implementation are small size and efficient code; the chief disadvantage is the limitation
to one outstanding message per process. Later chapters will explore a generaliza-
tion of message passing in which processes rendevous at common message exchange
points called ports.

FOR FURTHER STUDY

Brinch Hansen [1970, 1972] introduced the notion of message passing, and
showed how it can be used in the RC 4000 system. The text by Peterson and Silberschatz [1983] surveys the area, discussing the advantages and disadvantages of
allowing multiple messages to be enqueued for a receiver.

EXERCISES

7.1 Write a program that prints a prompt, and then loops printing the prompt again every 8 seconds until someone types a character. (Hint: sleep(8) delays the calling process for 8 seconds).

7.2 It is often best to try a new facility before installing it. Assume *send* and *receive* did not exist, and write experimental versions without using the *PRRECV* process state. (Hint: suspend and resume almost suffice; make sure that the resumption came from *send*).

7.3 Xinu records the first message sent to a process and rejects others. When is message order important?

7.4 Implement versions of *send* and *receive* that record all messages.

7.5 Discuss the use of a message passing scheme in which each process can have at most *k* outstanding messages.

7.6 Discuss a message passing mechanism in which each process is allowed at most *k* outstanding messages, with the added restriction that successive calls to *send* block (e.g. by waiting on a semaphore) until the receiving process makes room for additional messages by receiving some of those that are waiting.

7.7 Investigate systems in which the innermost layer implements message passing instead of context switching. What is their chief liability?

7.8 What facility in Xinu handles the case where a process wants to receive the most recent message sent instead of the first message sent?

7.9 Implement *sendf*, a modified form of *send* that forces delivery of a message by destroying any existing message. (Chapter 14 describes one use of *sendf*.)

8

Memory Management

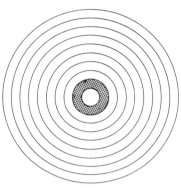

Main memory ranks high among the important resources that an operating system manages because it is essential for program execution. The operating system keeps track of the location and size of available free space, allocating it on demand, and recovering it when processes complete. In large computer systems, where the demand for memory at a given time often exceeds the total available, the system must multiplex real memory among processes waiting to use it. Memory multiplexing can take the form of *swapping*, where entire processes are written to secondary store when they are not using the CPU, or *paging*. A paged system divides each program into small fixed-size pieces called *pages*, keeping all but the most recently referenced pages on secondary storage. Programmers do not worry about swapping or paging because the system performs these activities in a way that is transparent to the running programs.

Often, paged systems do more than multiplex the real memory among processes — they supply each process with its own, independent address space. These so-called *virtual* address spaces can be larger than the real memory on the machine because the paging system keeps the virtual image on disk, moving only the small subset of pages being referenced to main memory. When a process references memory location i in its address space, the hardware consults memory mapping tables to determine if the page on which the reference lies currently resides in main memory. If not, the system suspends the process, and loads the page, writing some other page back to secondary storage if necessary to make room for the new one. Finally, when the page has been loaded, process execution resumes.

To be efficient, memory management (especially paging) requires hardware support. If a memory management mechanism is designed well, the operating system can use it to partition memory in such a way that the hardware prevents one process from reading or writing memory allocated to another process. Such protection is essential in environments where processes are not friendly, or where security is important; it is convenient in almost any environment, because it helps detect programming errors.

8.1 Memory Management On The 11/2

Unfortunately, the 11/2 hardware cannot manage multiple address spaces nor can it protect processes from one another. As a consequence, the Xinu system and all processes occupy portions of the same address space which is arranged as shown in Figure 8.1:

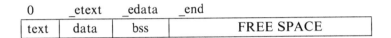

Figure 8.1 Storage layout when Xinu begins

The program text occupies the lowest part of memory, followed by the global variables in the segments called *data* and *bss*. Variables in the *bss* segment are uninitialized. Following the conventions in C, the current version of Xinu writes zeroes into *bss* memory before execution begins. (However, programs should not be written to depend on uninitialized data.) As described in Chapter 2, the loader defines external symbols *etext*, *edata*, and *end* so a running program can determine its size. At system startup, Xinu initializes global variable *maxaddr* to the address of the highest valid memory location, so the initial size of the free space can be determined in a C program.

Maintaining processes in a single address space is certainly not ideal, but it does have some advantages. For one thing, processes can pass pointers among themselves and the operating system easily because the interpretation of an address does not depend on the process context. The ability to share data is another advantage: because the processes share global variables, they can exchange large amounts of data without copying it. Finally, having just one address space makes the memory management routines much simpler to implement than those found in other systems.

8.2 Dynamic Memory Requirements In Xinu

Xinu requires program text and all global data to remain resident in main memory at all times. However, program text and global data account for only part of the space required by an executing process. Each process also needs space for a stack to hold procedure frames and local variables, as well as so-called *heap* space for other dynamically allocated variables. Xinu allocates stack memory from the highest addresses in free space, producing a run-time allocation like that shown in Figure 8.2.

0	_etext	_edata	_end					
text	data	bss	heap	FREE	...	stack3	stack2	stack1

Figure 8.2 Storage layout during execution

This Chapter explores the procedures and data structures that manage the free memory, allocate space for stack and heap storage, and keep track of storage that has been released. At this level, free space is treated as an exhaustable resource — the system simply hands it out as long as requests can be satisfied. A process that cannot obtain memory must decide for itself whether to try again. Exhaustive allocation works only when processes cooperate to keep from consuming all free memory. (Chapter 15 explores a set of high level memory management routines that prevent exhaustion by partitioning memory and blocking requesting processes until memory becomes available.)

8.3 Low-Level Memory Management Procedures

Two procedures, *getstk* and *freestk* obtain and release process stack space. Recall that *create* used procedure *getstk* to allocate stack space when forming a new process. *Getstk* obtains a block of memory and returns its highest address, the address at which the stack pointer initially starts. *Create* records the size and location of the allocated space in the process table entry. Later, when the process terminates, *kill* calls procedure *freestk* to return the process' stack space to the free list again. *Freestk* expects as arguments the highest address of the block being returned and the size.

Two additional procedures, *getmem* and *freemem*, also obtain and release blocks of free space. By convention, these procedures allocate and release memory for all purposes other than process stacks. Unlike the stack allocation procedures, *getmem* and *freemem* reference blocks of memory by their lowest address.

Because only *create* and *kill* allocate and free process stacks, Xinu guarantees that the stack space allocated to a process will be released at process exit. Unfortunately, the system cannot guarantee that space allocated by *getmem* will be released, because it does not record such allocations on a process-by-process basis.

Thus, the burden of returning heap space is left to the user program:

> *A process must release storage that it allocates from the heap before it exits.*

Of course, returning allocated space does not guarantee that the heap will never be exhausted. The demand could still exceed the available space, or the free space could be fragmented into small, discontiguous pieces. But releasing space avoids needless exhaustion.

8.4 The Location Of Allocated Storage

Xinu allocates stack space and heap storage from opposite ends of the available space. Because the hardware grows stacks downward, *getstk* allocates space for a stack at the highest available address. *Getmem* allocates space for other dynamic variables at the lowest possible address in the free space. Separating stack and heap storage works best when a single user process executes because all remaining free space separates the heap and stack. If the stack overflows accidentally, it runs into free space located between the stack and heap, instead of data. When more than one process executes concurrently, the situation is not as pleasant. Stack overflow in one process corrupts data in the stack of another because the system allocates stacks contiguously. In fact, stack overflow is one of the most common problems in Xinu. The exercises in Chapter 4 suggested one solution — place an uncommon value at the base of each process stack and have *resched* check both the current process stack size and the value at the base of the stack for the process it is about to run. If either indicate stack overflow, print an error message and halt.

8.5 The Implementation Of Xinu Memory Management

Xinu keeps blocks of free memory linked together on a list with global variable *memlist* pointing to the first free block. An important invariant maintained by all these procedures is:

> *Blocks on the free list are ordered by increasing address.*

While on the free list, each block contains, in the first two words, a pointer to the next block and the size of the current block. The record *memlist* is also declared to have the same form as all blocks on the free list. File *mem.h* contains the pertinent definitions in C:

```
/* mem.h - freestk, roundew, truncew */


/*-------------------------------------------------------------------
 * roundew, truncew - round or truncate address to next even word
 *-------------------------------------------------------------------
 */
#define roundew(x)      (int *)( (3 + (int)(x)) & (~3) )
#define truncew(x)      (int *)( ((int)(x)) & (~3) )


/*-------------------------------------------------------------------
 * freestk  --  free stack memory allocated by getstk
 *-------------------------------------------------------------------
 */
#define freestk(p,len)  freemem((unsigned)(p)                   \
                            - (unsigned)(roundew(len))          \
                            + (unsigned)sizeof(int),            \
                            roundew(len) )


struct  mblock  {
        struct  mblock  *mnext;
        unsigned int    mlen;
        };
extern  struct  mblock  memlist;        /* head of free memory list    */
extern  int     *maxaddr;               /* max memory address          */
extern  int     end;                    /* address beyond loaded memory */
```

Structure *mblock* gives the shape of each node on the free list. Field *mnext* always points to the next block (or contains *NULL*), and field *mlen* gives the length of the current block in bytes, including the two-word header.

File *mem.h* introduces two in-line functions, *roundew* and *truncew*. Because only blocks of two words (4 bytes) or more can be linked onto the free list, Xinu refuses to allocate or free smaller quantities of memory. To be sure that requests specify correct amounts of memory, the memory management routines use *roundew* or *truncew* as needed to round or truncate to an even number of words, by making the number of bytes a multiple of four.

8.5.1 Allocating Heap Storage

Procedure *getmem* allocates heap storage. The code for *getmem* appears in file *getmem.c*, below. It uses *roundew* to round up the memory request, and then searches the memory list to find the first block of memory large enough to satisfy the request. Because the list of free blocks is singly-linked, *getmem* uses two pointers, *p* and *q*, to search it. When *p* points to a block of suitable size, *q* points

to its predecessor on the list (possibly the head, *memlist*). If the size of a free
block exactly matches the size of the request, *getmem* merely deletes the block
from the free list and returns its address. If the size of the free block is greater
than the size requested, *getmem* partitions off a piece of size *nbytes*, and links the
remainder back on the free list. It returns the address of the allocated piece to the
caller.

When a block on the free list must be divided, variable *leftover* points to the
piece that must be left on the free list. Computing such an address is conceptually
simple: the leftover piece lies *nbytes* beyond the beginning of the block. However,
adding *nbytes* to pointer *p* does not produce the desired result because C performs
pointer arithmetic. To force C to use integer arithmetic instead of pointer arithmetic, *p* is changed to type *unsigned* with a cast (i.e., "(unsigned)p"), and then
the result is changed back into a pointer with another cast.

```c
/* getmem.c - getmem */

#include <conf.h>
#include <kernel.h>
#include <mem.h>

/*------------------------------------------------------------------------
 * getmem  --  allocate heap storage, returning lowest integer address
 *------------------------------------------------------------------------
 */
int     *getmem(nbytes)
        unsigned nbytes;
{
        char    ps;
        struct  mblock  *p, *q, *leftover;

        disable(ps);
        if (nbytes==0 || memlist.mnext==NULL) {
                restore(ps);
                return( (int *)SYSERR);
        }
        nbytes = (unsigned) roundew(nbytes);
        for (q= &memlist,p=memlist.mnext ; p!=NULL ; q=p,p=p->mnext)
                if ( p->mlen == nbytes) {
                        q->mnext = p->mnext;
                        restore(ps);
                        return( (int *)p );
                } else if ( p->mlen > nbytes ) {
                        leftover = (struct mblock *)( (unsigned)p + nbytes );
                        q->mnext = leftover;
```

```
                           leftover->mnext = p->mnext;
                           leftover->mlen = p->mlen - nbytes;
                           restore(ps);
                           return( (int *)p );
                }
        restore(ps);
        return( (int *)SYSERR );
}
```

8.5.2 Allocating Stack Storage

Getstk must search the entire list of free blocks when allocating space because the list is kept in ascending order by block address, and the desired block is the one with the highest address that satisfies the request. During the search, variables *fits* and *fitsq* record the values of *p* and *q* each time a block satisfies the request. When the search completes, *fits* points to the free block that last satisfied its request (or remains *NULL* if none do); *fitsq* points to its predecessor.

```
/* getstk.c - getstk */

#include <conf.h>
#include <kernel.h>
#include <mem.h>

/*------------------------------------------------------------------------
 * getstk  --  allocate stack memory, returning address of topmost int
 *------------------------------------------------------------------------
 */
int     *getstk(nbytes)
        unsigned  int nbytes;
{
        char    ps;
        struct  mblock *p, *q; /* q follows p along memlist          */
        struct  mblock *fits, *fitsq;
        int     len;

        disable(ps);
        if (nbytes == 0) {
                restore(ps);
                return( (int *)SYSERR );
        }
        nbytes = (unsigned int)roundew(nbytes);
        fits = NULL;
        q = &memlist;
        for (p = q->mnext ; p != NULL ; q = p,p = p->mnext)
                if ( p->mlen >= nbytes) {
                        fitsq = q;
                        fits = p;
                }
        if (fits == NULL) {
                restore(ps);
                return( (int *)SYSERR );
        }
        if (nbytes == fits->mlen) {
                fitsq->mnext = fits->mnext;
                len = nbytes;
        } else {
                len = fits->mlen;
                fits->mlen -= nbytes;
        }
        fits = ((int)fits) + len - sizeof(int);
        *( (int *) fits ) = nbytes;
        restore(ps);
```

```
      return( (int *)fits );
}
```

Once a block has been found, two cases arise. If the size of the free block is exactly the size requested, *getstk* merely unlinks it from the free list and returns its address. Otherwise, *getstk* divides the block in two, allocating *nbytes* bytes from the top to return, and revising the length field in the piece that remains on the free list. *Getstk* always returns the address of the highest integer location in the block it allocates under the assumption that it will be used for a stack that grows downward.

8.5.3 Releasing Storage

Processes return previously allocated memory to the list of free blocks when they finish using it so it can be given out again. System call *freemem* returns a block of storage by inserting it in the proper location of the free list, and coalescing it with any adjacent free blocks. As in *getmem*, pointers *p* and *q* run down the list of free blocks. Because the list is kept in order by block address, *freemem* stops searching as soon as the address of the block to be returned lies between *p* and *q*.

Special cases complicate the code that links the returned block into the free list. The new block may lie adjacent to free blocks above or below, or both. When these cases arise, *freemem* groups adjacent free blocks together to form larger blocks. (Failure to do so would eventually *fragment* the free list into small pieces.)

A pitfall can be avoided by remembering that the new block may be adjacent to free blocks on both sides. As shown in file *freemem.c*, the code always checks to see whether the new block is adjacent to the block following, even if it coalesces the new block with the previous one:

```c
/* freemem.c - freemem */

#include <conf.h>
#include <kernel.h>
#include <mem.h>


/*------------------------------------------------------------------------
 *  freemem  --  free a memory block, returning it to memlist
 *------------------------------------------------------------------------
 */
SYSCALL freemem(block, size)
        struct  mblock  *block;
        unsigned size;
{
        char    ps;
        struct  mblock  *p, *q;
        unsigned top;

        if (size==0 || (unsigned)block>(unsigned)maxaddr
                        || ((unsigned)block)<((unsigned)&end))
                return(SYSERR);
        size = (unsigned)roundew(size);
        disable(ps);
        for( p=memlist.mnext,q= &memlist ; p!=NULL && p<block ;
                        q=p,p=p->mnext )
                        ;
        if ((top=q->mlen+(unsigned)q)>(unsigned)block && q!= &memlist ||
                        p!=NULL && (size+(unsigned)block) > (unsigned)p ) {
                restore(ps);
                return(SYSERR);
        }
        if ( q!= &memlist && top == (unsigned)block )
                q->mlen += size;
        else {
                block->mlen = size;
                block->mnext = p;
                q->mnext = block;
                q = block;
        }
        if ( (unsigned)( q->mlen + (unsigned)q ) == (unsigned)p) {
                q->mlen += p->mlen;
                q->mnext = p->mnext;
        }
        restore(ps);
        return(OK);
}
```

Because releasing stack memory is the same as releasing heap memory, procedure *freestk* can be written in terms of *freemem*. In this implementation, *freestk* is coded as an in-line procedure, defined in file *mem.h*, in Section 8.5. It merely computes the lowest address in the block of memory to be released, and calls *freemem*, passing the address and length as arguments.

8.6 Summary

The lowest level of the Xinu memory manager maintains a linked list of all free storage, allocating storage on demand and adding it back to the free list when requested to do so. The free list is ordered by address. Heap memory is allocated from the lowest free memory addresses, while process stack space is allocated from the highest free memory addresses. Because the list is singly-linked, allocating stack space requires searching the entire free list.

At this level, memory is considered an exhaustable resource, given out without constraint until none remains free. The low-level memory manager simply rejects requests that cannot be satisfied; there are no mechanisms to prevent processes from using all the free memory or to block processes until their requests can be satisfied. Higher layers of the memory manager that provide these mechanisms are discussed in Chapter 15.

FOR FURTHER STUDY

Memory management has received wide attention in the literature. The basic algorithm used here is called "first-fit" in Knuth [1968], where alternatives like "best-fit" and "buddy" are also considered. Comparisons of first-fit and best-fit can be found in the articles by Shore [1975] and Bays [1977].

Much of the research in memory management has centered on discovering and analyzing policies for paging and swapping on systems that support virtual address spaces. Peterson and Silbershatz [1983] devote an entire chapter to virtual memory. A key problem involves selecting which program or part of a program to write back onto secondary store when a new page must be brought into memory. Denning [1970, 1980] surveys virtual storage systems, describing the research. Madnick and Donovan [1974] describe commercial hardware that supports paging, and describe its use. Other good descriptions of memory management can be found in Calingaert [1982], Habermann [1976], and Tsichritzis and Bernstein [1974].

EXERCISES

8.1 An early version of *getstk* and *getmem* had no provision for returning memory to the free list. Speculate about microcomputer applications: is *freemem* necessary?

8.2 Implement the smallest routines possible for memory allocation, assuming there is no need to return storage to a free list. How do the sizes of the new allocation routines compare to the sizes of *getstk* and *getmem*?

8.3 Allocating and deallocating blocks of varying size can *fragment* memory, leaving many small pieces on the free list. Investigate schemes other than "first-fit" for choosing a block of memory from the free list.

8.4 Xinu applies the "first-fit" method from two ends of the free list, one for *getmem* and one for *getstk*. Will Xinu fragment memory faster or slower than if it applied the first-fit method from one end?

8.5 Xinu merely reports an error when no block of memory exists that can satisfy the request. Consider an alternative in which the calling process is merely delayed (say, by placing it on a queue) until a sufficiently large piece of memory has been returned to the free list. Explain how all processes might eventually be enqueued waiting for memory, even though no process requests more memory than exists.

8.6 Carefully consider a program that allocates a large block of memory, frees half of it, frees the other half, and then repeats the actions. Under what circumstances will the program fail? Do you consider this a problem?

8.7 Modify the memory management routines to allow allocation of arbitrarily small blocks of memory.

8.8 Investigate the buddy system for memory allocation. Would it be wise to use it in Xinu?

8.9 Find out how the LSI 11/23 processor manages memory. Design software support routines to take advantage of the hardware.

8.10 Examine the Motorola 68000-style memory management scheme. What layers of software are needed at the lowest level of the system to implement demand paging?

8.11 Explore *segmentation* as an alternative to paging. What are its advantages? Does paging a segmented memory make sense?

9

Interrupt Processing

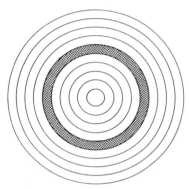

The hardware interrupt is a powerful mechanism that provides support for many of the services the operating system supplies. As described in Chapter 2, a device requests interrupt service by sending the CPU a signal using a bus line. Before executing an instruction, the CPU checks the interrupt line, and "calls" a procedure to handle the interrupt if it finds one pending. When the called routine "returns", control passes back to the process that was executing, as if nothing had happened. Without an interrupt mechanism, the operating system could not guarantee that it would ever regain control once it started executing a user process.

Before looking at devices in detail to see why they interrupt and how the system responds, we will explore, in this chapter, the routines Xinu uses to field interrupts and pass control to the appropriate routine. Later chapters explain more about the clock and other devices, showing how interrupt processing routines are designed.

9.1 Dispatching Interrupts

We said that the hardware calls the interrupt handler when it finds an interrupt pending. The terms *call* and *return* have special meaning when applied to interrupts. First, there is no procedure call instruction in the interrupted program — the processor simulates a call to the appropriate interrupt routine "in between" the execution of normal instructions in the user's program. Second, the processor automatically saves the current PC and PS by pushing them on the stack when an interrupt occurs (the interrupt routine must save and restore any other registers that it needs to use). Third, the interrupt routine must use a special return instruction to pop the old PS and PC off the stack in a single step.

Because interrupt routines manipulate hardware registers and use special call/return sequences, they cannot usually be written in high-level languages like C. The temptation is to write all the code related to interrupt processing, a significant portion of the operating system, in assembler language. But writing in a low-level language makes the software difficult to understand or modify. So, to keep the system code as readable as possible, our design employs a two-level strategy for processing interrupts. Interrupts branch to small, low-level *interrupt dispatch* routines that are written in assembler language. Dispatchers handle tasks like saving and restoring registers, identifying the interrupting device, and returning from the interrupt when it has been processed. However, they do little else — they call high-level routines to do the real work of interrupt processing, passing them enough information to identify the interrupting device.

Xinu contains three different interrupt dispatchers: one to handle clock interrupts, one to handle input interrupts, and one to handle output interrupts. The decision to divide dispatchers this way was made for convenience and efficiency: input and output interrupts were separated to make dispatching easier, and a special clock interrupt dispatcher was devised to make processing clock interrupts more efficient. This chapter concentrates on the input and output dispatchers, deferring a discussion of the special clock interrupt dispatcher until the next chapter.

9.2 Input And Output Interrupt Dispatchers

Devices connect to the computer system through hardware mechanisms called controllers. Controllers, which may be as simple as a few chips or as complicated as a microprocessor system, reside on boards plugged into the system bus. They have hardware that converts digital data into the waveforms and signals necessary to control peripheral devices like terminals and disks, as described in Chapter 2.

Terminal devices that allow simultaneous transfer of data in both directions consist of two independently controlled devices, one for input and one for output. Controllers for such devices group the input and output paths together in a pair, making it easier to associate the output of a device with its input. Pairing is natural because most systems allow user programs to view each terminal as a single device. For example, Xinu allows both input and output operations to the device *CONSOLE*, where output to the console is displayed on the screen, while input is read from the keyboard.

Although the operating system must recognize device pairing, hardware operations on the two devices proceed simultaneously and independently. In particular, input interrupts for characters typed on a terminal's keyboard trap to a different vector than output interrupts for characters sent to the terminal's display. Thus, at the lowest level, the system must operate as if the devices were independent. Figure 9.1 shows the logical organization.

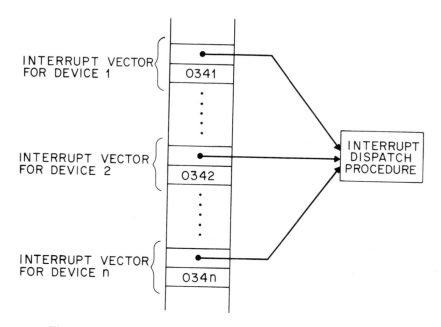

Figure 9.1 Input interrupt vectors pointing to the dispatch routine

If all input interrupts branch to the same dispatch routine, how does the dispatcher know which high-level interrupt routine to call? The choice of interrupt handler is determined by the type and address of the interrupting device, but the details of how a dispatcher identifies the interrupting device vary from machine to machine. Some have special instructions so the dispatcher can access the device address or determine the interrupt vector address through which it was called. On others, the dispatcher polls devices until it finds one with an interrupt pending. The 11/2 has no special instructions to help the operating system identify the interrupting device — if a single interrupt dispatch routine is used, the software must handle device identification.

To identify the interrupting device, the 11/2 version of Xinu employs a technique common to other operating systems for the same architecture — it encodes device identifiers in the second word of each interrupt vector location. Recall that the second word of an interrupt vector gives a value that the hardware loads into the processor status register, PS. The most important field of this new PS consists of the processor mask bits that can be set to disable further interrupts while the CPU processes the interrupt. However, the hardware loads all bits of the PS when an interrupt occurs, making it possible for the dispatch routine to determine which of several devices caused the interrupt. Xinu uses the low-order 4 bits of the PS entries to encode a device identifier from 0 through 15. When an interrupt occurs,

the processor loads the PC and PS from the interrupt vector, and begins executing
the interrupt dispatch routine. Immediately upon entry, the interrupt dispatcher
saves a copy of the PS by pushing it on the stack because instructions that set condition codes change the low-order bits of the PS register. To select an appropriate
high-level interrupt routine, the dispatcher fetches the saved value, masks off all
but the low-order 4 bits, and uses the result as an index into an interrupt dispatch
table. The dispatch table contains the addresses of high-level interrupt handlers,
which the dispatcher calls.

A look at the code will clarify the details. The interrupt dispatch table is defined in file *io.h*; its name is *intmap*.

```
/* io.h -  fgetc, fputc, getchar, isbaddev, putchar */



#define INTVECI inint           /* input interrupt dispatch routine   */
#define INTVECO outint          /* output interrupt dispatch routine  */
extern  int     INTVECI();
extern  int     INTVECO();

struct  intmap  {               /* device-to-interrupt routine mapping */
        int     (*iin)();       /* address of input interrupt routine  */
        int     icode;          /* argument passed to input routine    */
        int     (*iout)();      /* address of output interrupt routine */
        int     ocode;          /* argument passed to output routine   */
        };

#ifdef  NDEVS
extern  struct  intmap intmap[NDEVS];
#define isbaddev(f)     ( (f)<0 || (f)>=NDEVS )
#endif

/* In-line I/O procedures */

#define getchar()       getc(CONSOLE)
#define putchar(ch)     putc(CONSOLE,(ch))
#define fgetc(unit)     getc((unit))
#define fputc(unit,ch)  putc((unit),(ch))

struct  vector  {
        char    *vproc;         /* address of interrupt procedure      */
        int     vps;            /* saved process status word           */
        };
```

Each entry in *intmap* corresponds to one device. It contains the addresses of a high-level input interrupt routine, a high-level output interrupt routine, and an integer argument for each routine. These integer arguments can be anything that the high-level interrupt routines need (e.g., the device number). When the dispatcher calls an interrupt handler, it passes the appropriate argument from *intmap* in place of the encoded device identifier, eliminating the need for the high-level routine to again index *intmap*.

Because both input and output interrupt dispatchers perform essentially the same function, they set up pointers into the interrupt dispatch table and then both execute the same code to save registers, call the high-level interrupt routine, restore registers, and return from the interrupt. The code is found in file *ioint.s*. Input interrupts trap to *inint*, while output interrupts trap to *outint*.

```
/* ioint.s - inint, outint */


/* I/O interrupts trap here.  Original PC and PS are on top of the    */
/* stack upon entry.  Low order 4 bits of the current PS contain the  */
/* device descriptor.  Interrupts are disabled.                       */

        .globl   _inint,_outint,_intmap
_outint:                                / Output interrupt entry point
        mfps     -(sp)                  / Save device descriptor from PS
        mov      r0,-(sp)               / Save r0 (csv does not)
        mov      $_intmap+4,r0          / point r0 to output in intmap
        br       ioint                  / Go do common part of code
_inint:                                 / Input interrupt entry point
        mfps     -(sp)                  / Save device code from PS
        mov      r0,-(sp)               / Save r0 (csv does not)
        mov      $_intmap,r0            / point r0 to input in intmap
ioint:                                  / Code common to input & output
        mov      r1,-(sp)               / Save r1 (csv does not)
        mov      4(sp),r1               / Get saved PS in r1
        bic      $177760,r1             / Mask off device descriptor
        ash      $3,r1                  / pick correct entry in intmap
        add      r1,r0                  / Form pointer to intmap entry
        mov      2(r0),-(sp)            / Push "code" from intmap as arg
        jsr      pc,*(r0)               / Call interrupt routine
        mov      2(sp),r1               / Restore r1 and R0 from stack
        mov      4(sp),r0
        add      $8,sp                  / Pop arg, saved r0, r1, and PS
        rtt                             / Return from interrupt
```

The shared code starts at label *ioint*.

9.3 The Rules For Interrupt Processing

Because interrupt routines examine and modify global data structures like I/O buffers, the system must be designed to prevent other processes from interfering with them. Generally, noninterference is guaranteed by making the interrupt routines uninterruptable. For example, the LSI 11 version of Xinu disables interrupts by setting the processor mask bits in the second word of each interrupt vector location. When the interrupt occurs and this word is loaded into the PS, further interrupts are disabled. Interrupts remain disabled even if an interrupt routine calls other procedures. When the high-level interrupt procedure returns, control passes back to the interrupt dispatcher, which restores the PS and returns to the place at which processing was originally interrupted. Only after the dispatcher returns are interrupts enabled again.

Interrupt routines may also enable interrupts by calling *resched*, if it switches to a process that has interrupts enabled. An output interrupt routine, for example, might *signal* a semaphore to allow another process to write into the buffer space that it makes available, or an input interrupt routine might *send* data it obtains from the device to a process. In each case, if the call reaches *resched*, it might allow a process to execute that had interrupts enabled. So, shared data structures must be left in a valid state before calling any routines that switch context. To sum up:

> *Interrupts will be disabled when the dispatcher calls a high-level interrupt routine; the high-level routine must be designed to keep further interrupts disabled until it completes changes to global data structures.*

There are several other issues to consider when building interrupt routines. For one, interrupt routines cannot keep interrupts disabled too long. If they do, devices will fail to perform correctly. For example, if the processor does not accept a character from an input device before another arrives, data will be lost. So, interrupt routines must be designed to enable further interrupts as quickly as possible.

Another constraint arises because interrupt code is executed by whichever process happens to be running when the interrupt occurs. In particular, the interrupt routines must be designed so they work correctly even if executed by the null process. Recall that *resched* blindly assumes at least one process remains ready to run, so the null process must always be *current* or *ready*. The most important consequence is:

> *Interrupt routines can only call procedures that leave the executing process in the current or ready states.*

So, interrupt routines may use primitives like *send* or *signal*, but they may not use primitives like *wait*.

9.4 Rescheduling While Processing An Interrupt

Should interrupt routines be allowed to reschedule? We already stated that interrupt routines cannot explicitly enable further interrupts while processing an interrupt, and that they must leave global data structures in a valid state before rescheduling. It might seem that they should not be allowed to reschedule either, because switching to a process that had interrupts enabled would start a sequence of interrupts piling up until the stack overflowed. Rescheduling is important, however, because it provides the only way that interrupt routines can affect the running process. We must convince ourselves that rescheduling from an interrupt is safe as long as global data structures are valid.

To understand why rescheduling is safe, consider the series of events leading to a call of *resched* from an interrupt handler. Suppose a process P was running with interrupts enabled when the interrupt occurred. The hardware uses P's stack to save the PC and PS registers, and leaves process P running the interrupt dispatcher. Because the new PS loaded from the interrupt vector disables interrupts, P executes the dispatch routine with interrupts disabled. Interrupts remained disabled when the dispatcher calls the high-level interrupt routine. Suppose now that the high level interrupt routine calls *resched* which switches to another process, say Q. If Q happens to enable interrupts (e.g., by returning from a system call), another interrupt may occur. What prevents an infinite loop where unfinished interrupts pile up until the run-time stack overflows with interrupt procedure calls? Recall that each process has its own stack. Process P had one interrupt on its stack when it was stopped by the context switch. The new interrupt occurs while the processor is using Q's stack. Before another interrupt can pile up on P's stack, it must regain control of the CPU and enable interrupts. But P was running with interrupts disabled when it called the scheduler and context switch. The context switch saved P with interrupts disabled, so when it eventually switches back to P, it will restore the processor status register, and P will continue execution with interrupts disabled.

Interrupts remain disabled as *resched* returns to the high level interrupt routine, and as the high-level interrupt routine returns to the dispatcher. Interrupts only become enabled again when the dispatcher returns to the spot at which the original interrupt occurred. So, interrupts cannot occur while process P is executing interrupt code (even though they can occur to another process while P is not executing). Only a finite number of processes exist at any time, and each, in turn, can be processing at most one interrupt. Looking at this a different way, we can say that:

> *Rescheduling during interrupt processing is safe provided that (1) interrupt routines leave global data in a valid state before rescheduling, and (2) no procedure enables interrupts unless it disabled them.*

If you recall, you will see that we have used this rule in all the procedures built so far: a procedure that disables interrupts upon entry always restores them before returning to its caller; no routine ever enables interrupts explicitly. Because interrupts are disabled upon entry to the interrupt dispatcher, they are restored when it returns. The only exception to our rule about disabling and restoring interrupts is found in the initialization procedure which enables interrupts at system startup.

9.5 Summary

High-level languages like C cannot always manipulate the machine registers or execute special instructions to handle interrupts. To avoid writing all interrupt code in assembler language, we have divided the work into two parts. Small, assembler language dispatchers permit the bulk of interrupt handlers to be written in a high-level language. The dispatchers field interrupts, save machine registers, and pass control to an appropriate high-level interrupt handler based on entries in a dispatch table. When the high-level handler returns, control passes back to the dispatcher which reloads registers and executes special instructions that restore that state and return to the interrupted program.

A few rules simplify the design of interrupt handlers. First, the interrupt handler must not enable interrupts explicitly; it may, however, reschedule to allow other processes to execute. (Of course, the interrupt routine must insure that global data structures are in a valid state before rescheduling). Second, because an interrupt routine may be executed by the null process, it must never call a procedure that will move the calling process out of the *current* or *ready* states. Third, interrupt routines must not leave interrupts disabled "too long" or devices will fail to operate correctly. The length of time an interrupt can be delayed depends on the device hardware; the console input device, for example, need only be serviced before the user types another character.

FOR FURTHER STUDY

Tanenbaum [1976] and Stone [1972] describe interrupt mechanisms on various machines. Madnick and Donovan [1974], consider the details on an IBM 360 architecture. More information on the details of the LSI 11 can be found in the vendor's manual *Microprocessor Handbook*.

Information on interrupt processing in general can be found in Watson [1970]. Lister [1979] describes dispatching.

EXERCISES

9.1 Rewrite the I/O interrupt dispatchers, minimizing the number of instructions executed by building a different copy for each device. How many instructions can you save per interrupt?

9.2 What might happen if the new PS loaded from an interrupt vector did not disable interrupts?

9.3 Experiment with Xinu by setting PS values in the interrupt vectors to allow further interrupts. Try it on a system that does not have a clock (see the next chapter for information on clock interrupts). Are you surprised at how long the system runs before crashing? Determine *exactly* why it crashes.

9.4 Suppose the hardware automatically switched context to a process that handled interrupts whenever one occurred. Would the system be easier or more difficult to design? Would that process be permitted to reschedule?

9.5 Hardware with a separate interrupt vector for each device works best if the software has one interrupt routine per device. Why does Xinu use a central interrupt dispatcher? Modify the code to use multiple dispatchers.

9.6 Calculate how many milliseconds can be spent per interrupt assuming four devices each receive characters at 19.2 Kbaud (19.2 thousand bits per second, or approximately 1920 characters per second). Roughly how many LSI 11/2 instructions can be executed per interrupt at this rate?

10

Real-Time Clock Management

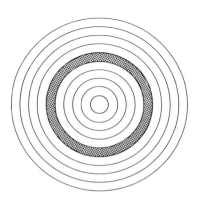

A *clock* is a hardware device that emits pulses, usually square waves, at regular intervals with high precision. Besides the central system clock that controls the rate at which the CPU executes instructions, computer systems may have a *real-time clock* and a *time-of-day clock*, the two being related, but not identical.

Like a digital wristwatch, a time-of-day clock is a chronometer. It consists of an accurate clock that pulses an integral number of times per second, and a counter to tally the pulses. Programs read the counter to determine the current time and date, and privileged programs write into the counter to set the time. Resetting is rarely needed because time-of-day clocks continue counting correctly as long as they receive power, independent of whether the CPU is heavily loaded or halted. (Stories abound about the confusion introduced by computer operators who set the time-of-day clock inaccurately after a power failure.)

10.1 The Real-Time Clock Mechanism

Unlike the time-of-day clock, a real-time clock does not tally pulses or keep track of the date. Instead, it pulses regularly an integral number of times each second, signalling the CPU each time a pulse occurs, by posting an interrupt. Thus, one distinction between the two clocks is based on whether the clock controls the CPU or the CPU controls the clock:

> *The CPU reads the time-of-day clock whenever it wants to obtain*
> *the current date and time; the real-time clock forces the CPU to*
> *process an interrupt each time it pulses.*

The two clocks are further distinguished by whether they count pulses. The real-time clock does not contain a counter, and it does not accumulate interrupts. Responsibility for counting interrupts falls on the system:

> *If the CPU takes too long to service a real-time clock interrupt,*
> *or if it operates with interrupts disabled for more than one clock*
> *cycle, it will miss the interrupt.*

Obviously, systems must be designed to service clock interrupts quickly. The hardware helps by giving highest priority to clock interrupts. Some clock hardware buffer a few interrupts allowing the CPU to delay more than one cycle. Even so, slow processors like the 11/2 cannot afford to call a C procedure on each clock interrupt, or they would spend most of their time handling clock interrupts. (Typical clock rates are 10Hz, 60Hz, 100Hz, and 1000Hz.)

10.2 Optimization Of Clock Interrupt Processing

How can a system avoid spending all its time processing real-time clock interrupts? The answer is that the clock rate must be adjusted to match the system. Slowing the clock is a significant optimization because it permits the designer to build richer functionality by sacrificing some precision.

Ideally, the hardware clock should be slowed, but this is usually inconvenient or impossible. Instead, a clock interrupt handler can be designed to simulate a slower-rate clock. The easiest way to simulate a slow clock consists of dividing the clock rate. For example, the real-time clock on the LSI 11/2 generates 60 pulses per second, a rate that would require much time to handle. To simulate a slower clock, the interrupt dispatcher ignores five clock interrupts before processing one, effectively dividing the rate by 6. In practice, the dispatcher must accept all clock interrupts, but it merely decrements a counter and returns quickly on five out of six. As a result, the main body of interrupt handling code is executed only 10 times per second, a rate affectionately known as the *tick rate*. It is important to distinguish the hardware clock interrupt rate, 60 Hertz, from the slower tick rate, 10 Hertz, because all of the clock procedures discussed below assume a 10 Hertz tick rate implicitly.

10.3 The Use Of A Real-Time Clock

Operating systems use real-time clocks internally, to limit the amount of time a process can execute, as well as externally, to provide user programs with services like timed delays. Usually, the system maintains a list of "events", ordered by the time at which they should occur. Whenever the real-time clock interrupts, it examines the event list and initiates any events for which the delay has expired.

Our design allows two kinds of events to be scheduled for the future. When granting CPU service to a process, the system schedules a *preemption* event to prevent the process from running forever. When a process requests a timed delay, it removes the process from the current state, and schedules a *wakeup* event to restart it at the correct time.

The system uses *preemption* to guarantee that equal priority processes receive service round-robin (specified by the scheduling policy in Chapter 4). Recall that whenever *resched* switches context, it resets the variable *preempt* to *QUANTUM* (*QUANTUM* is a symbolic constant defined in file *kernel.h*). The clock interrupt dispatcher decrements *preempt* on each clock tick, calling *resched* when it reaches zero. The currently executing process is always the highest priority process that is eligible for CPU service, but others of equal priority may be waiting on the ready list. If they are, *resched* places the current process on the ready list behind other processes with equal priority, and switches to the first process on the list. Thus, if k equal-priority processes all need CPU service, all k execute for at most *QUANTUM* clock ticks before any of them receive more service.

The value of symbolic constant *QUANTUM* gives the *granularity of preemption*; it can be changed before the system is compiled. Setting *QUANTUM* small, say 2 or 3, makes the granularity small, by rescheduling every few tenths of a second. Small granularity tends to keep all equal priority processes proceeding at approximately the same pace. But a small granularity introduces much overhead because it forces the clock interrupt routine to call *resched* often. Setting *QUANTUM* to a large value, say 100, reduces the overhead of context switching, but makes the granularity of switching large. The potential disadvantage of large granularity is that a process may execute many seconds before switching to another of equal priority.

As it turns out, processes seldom use the CPU long enough to warrant preemption. A process voluntarily calls *resched* by executing system routines like *wait* or doing I/O. It turns out that because input and output are slow compared to processing, processes spend most of their time waiting for devices. However, the system could never regain control from a process that executed an infinite loop without a preemptive capability, so it is important to include it in any system that supports multiprogramming.

Systems also use the real-time clock to honor requests for timed delays. For example, when the currently executing process requests a delay, Xinu moves it to a list of "sleeping" processes, arranging to have it awakened after the appropriate number of clock ticks. On each clock tick, the clock interrupt routine checks sleeping processes, moving those that have delayed the specified time back onto the ready list. Routines to handle such delays will be considered next.

10.4 Delta List Processing

Because it cannot afford to search through arbitrarily long lists of sleeping processes to find those that should awaken on each clock tick, the system keeps sleeping processes in a data structure called a *delta list*. Like other lists of processes, the sleeping process delta list resides in the *q* structure. Variable *clockq* contains the *q* index of its head. On each clock tick, the clock interrupt dispatcher examines the first process in *clockq*, and calls the high-level interrupt routine *wakeup* to awaken processes if their time delay has expired.

Unlike other lists in the *q* structure, *the delta list* is neither ordered by increasing key, nor FIFO. Instead, keys record successive deltas (differences) in delay:

> *Processes on clockq are ordered by the time at which they will awaken; each key tells the number of clock ticks that the process must delay beyond the preceding one on the list.*

The first process on the list is the one with least delay, and its key gives the remaining delay in clock ticks until it must awaken. The delta organization permits the clock interrupt routine to decrement the first key on each clock tick without scanning the list because the remaining delays are relative to it. For example, if four processes need to delay 17, 27, 28, and 32 ticks, then their keys on the delta list contain 17, 10, 1, and 4. Given only the delta list, partial sums of keys give the total delay before processes awaken. The total delay before the first process awakens is 17, the total for the second is 17+10, the total for the third is 17+10+1, and the total for the last is 17+10+1+4.

Routines to manipulate delta lists are easy to design, but the details can be tricky; close scrutiny of the code is worthwhile. Procedure *insertd*, shown below, inserts a process *pid* in *clockq*, given its delay in parameter *key*. As with priority queues, the *qkey* field of each node on the list records the key value for that node. In the code, variable *next* scans the list searching for the place to insert the new process.

Keys in the delta list specify delays relative to their predecessor; they cannot be compared directly to the initial value of *key*, which specifies a delay relative to the current time. To keep the delays comparable, *insertd* subtracts the relative delays from *key* as the search proceeds, maintaining the following invariant:

> *At any time during the search, both key and q[next].qkey specify a delay relative to the time at which the predecessor of the "next" awakens.*

Insertd inserts the new process at the point where its relative delay is less than the relative delay of those left on the list. Note that *insertd* does not have to explicitly check for the end of the list, because the key value in the tail forces an insertion. After linking process *pid* into the list, *insertd* subtracts the extra delay that it introduces from the delay of the next process.

```
/* insertd.c - insertd */

#include <conf.h>
#include <kernel.h>
#include <q.h>

/*------------------------------------------------------------------------
 *  insertd  --  insert process pid in delta list "head", given its key
 *------------------------------------------------------------------------
 */
insertd(pid, head, key)
        int     pid;
        int     head;
        int     key;
{
        int     next;                   /* runs through list       */
        int     prev;                   /* follows next through list  */

        for(prev=head,next=q[head].qnext ;
            q[next].qkey < key ; prev=next,next=q[next].qnext)
                key -= q[next].qkey;
        q[pid].qnext = next;
        q[pid].qprev = prev;
        q[pid].qkey  = key;
        q[prev].qnext = pid;
        q[next].qprev = pid;
        if (next < NPROC)
                q[next].qkey -= key;
        return(OK);
}
```

10.5 Putting A Process To Sleep

User programs do not usually access the real-time clock queue directly; they call system routines that provide delays. System call *sleep10(n)* delays the calling process *n* tenths of a second. It does so by inserting the process into the delta list of sleeping processes.

When a process is moved to the list of sleeping processes, it is no longer *ready* or *current*. In what state should it be placed? Sleeping processes differ from processes that are suspended, waiting to receive messages, or waiting for semaphores, so none of these states suffices. It is time to add a new process state to the design; we will call it *sleeping* and denote it with symbolic constant *PRSLEEP*. The new diagram of process state transitions is shown in Figure 10.1.

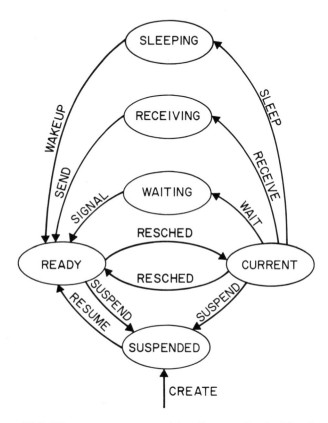

Figure 10.1 The process state transition diagram for the 'sleep' state

The implementation of *sleep10* is straightforward. As shown below, it uses *insertd* to move the current process to the sleeping process list, changes its state to *sleeping*, and then calls *resched* to allow other processes to execute.

```
/* sleep10.c - sleep10 */

#include <conf.h>
#include <kernel.h>
#include <proc.h>
#include <q.h>
#include <sleep.h>

/*------------------------------------------------------------------------
 * sleep10  --  delay the caller for a time specified in tenths of seconds
 *------------------------------------------------------------------------
 */
SYSCALL sleep10(n)
        int n;
{
        char ps;

        if (n < 0  || clkruns==0)
                return(SYSERR);
        if (n == 0) {
                resched();                      /* sleep10(0) -> end time slice */
                return(OK);
        }
        disable(ps);
        insertd(currpid,clockq,n);
        slnempty = TRUE;
        sltop = & q[q[clockq].qnext].qkey;
        proctab[currpid].pstate = PRSLEEP;
        resched();
        restore(ps);
        return(OK);
}
```

Sleep10 references four external variables defined in file *sleep.h* (below): *clockq*, *clkruns*, *sltop*, and *slnempty*. *Clockq* contains the *q* index of the list of sleeping processes, and *clkruns* indicates whether the hardware includes a real-time clock.

```
/* sleep.h */

#define CVECTOR 0100                /* location of clock interrupt vector  */

extern  int     clkruns;            /* 1 iff clock exists; 0 otherwise     */
                                    /* Set at system startup.              */
extern  int     clockq;             /* q index of sleeping process list    */
extern  int     count6;             /* used to ignore 5 of 6 interrupts    */
extern  int     *sltop;             /* address of first key on clockq      */
extern  int     slnempty;           /* 1 iff clockq is nonempty            */

extern  int     defclk;             /* >0 iff clock interrupts are deferred */
extern  int     clkdiff;            /* number of clock ticks deferred      */
extern  int     clkint();           /* clock interrupt handler             */
```

If the system configuration specifies no clock, the loader sets *clkruns FALSE*
without testing for the clock; otherwise, it calls *setclkr*, an assembler language routine shown below, to set *clkruns* at system startup. In any case, *Sleep10* refuses to
put a process to sleep if there is no clock to awaken it.

```
/* setclkr.s - setclkr */

CVECTPC =       100                 / clock interrupt vector address
CVECTPS =       102                 /  "       "          "      "
DISABLE =       340                 / PS that disables interrupts
ENABLE  =       000                 / PS that enables interrupts
COUNT   =       30000.              / Times to loop (in decimal)


/*------------------------------------------------------------------
/* setclkr  --  set cklruns to 1 iff real-time clock exists, 0 otherwise
/*------------------------------------------------------------------
        .globl  _setclkr
_setclkr:
        mov     r1,-(sp)            / save register used
        clr     _clkruns            / initialize for no clock
        mov     *$CVECTPS,-(sp)     / save clock interrupt vector
        mov     *$CVECTPC,-(sp)     /   on caller's stack
        mov     $DISABLE,*$CVECTPS  / set up new interrupt vector
        mov     $setint,*$CVECTPC
        mov     $COUNT,r1           / initialize counter for loop
        reset                       / clear other interrupts, if any
        mtps    $ENABLE             / allow interrupts
setloop:
        dec     r1                  / loop COUNT times waiting for
```

```
        bpl     setloop                 /   a clock interrupt
        mtps    $DISABLE                / no interrupt occurred, so quit
        br      setdone
setint:
        inc     _clkruns                / clock interrupt jumps here
        add     $4,sp                   / pop pc/ps pushed by interrupt
setdone:
        mov     (sp)+,*$CVECTPC         / restore old interrupt vector
        mov     (sp)+,*$CVECTPS
        mov     (sp)+,r1                / restore register
        rts     pc                      / return to caller
```

Even though the clock dispatcher simulates a slow tick rate, processing clock interrupts is expensive. Variables *sltop* and *slnempty* help optimize interrupt processing by making it easy to determine whether sleeping processes should be awakened. *Slnempty* tells whether the list *clockq* is currently nonempty. If any processes remain on *clockq*, *sltop* gives the address of the key in the first one. The interrupt routine completely skips the code for sleeping processes when *slnempty* is zero, and uses *sltop* to quickly locate the delta-key of the first sleeping process when *slnempty* is nonzero.

10.6 Delays Measured In Seconds

The size of an integer, 16 bits, limits the delay allowed by *sleep10* to $2**15 - 1$ tenths of seconds, which is 3276.7 seconds, or about 55 minutes. System call *sleep* provides a way for processes to delay up to 9 hours because its argument specifies a delay measured in seconds rather than tenths of seconds. *Sleep* uses *sleep10* repeatedly to schedule shorter delays until the total delay time has elapsed:

```
/* sleep.c - sleep */

#include <conf.h>
#include <kernel.h>
#include <proc.h>
#include <q.h>
#include <sleep.h>


/*------------------------------------------------------------------
 * sleep  --  delay the calling process n seconds
 *------------------------------------------------------------------
 */
SYSCALL sleep(n)
        int     n;
{
        if (n<0 || clkruns==0)
                return(SYSERR);
        if (n == 0) {
                resched();
                return(OK);
        }
        while (n >= 1000) {
                sleep10(10000);
                n -= 1000;
        }
        if (n > 0)
                sleep10(10*n);
        return(OK);
}
```

10.7 Awakening Sleeping Processes

The clock interrupt dispatcher decrements the count of the first key on *clockq* on each clock tick, calling *wakeup* to actually awaken processes when the delay reaches zero. *Wakeup* removes all processes from *clockq* whose delay time has elapsed, using *ready* to make them eligible for CPU service again. Because it has been called from an interrupt dispatcher, *wakeup* assumes that interrupts have been disabled upon entry; the keyword *INTPROC* reminds the reader of this assumption. It resets *sltop* and *slnempty* to reflect the new queue status before calling *resched*, because rescheduling may allow another process to run (and the clock to interrupt).

```
/* wakeup.c - wakeup */

#include <conf.h>
#include <kernel.h>
#include <proc.h>
#include <q.h>
#include <sleep.h>


/*------------------------------------------------------------------------
 * wakeup  --  called by clock interrupt dispatcher to awaken processes
 *------------------------------------------------------------------------
 */
INTPROC wakeup()
{
        while (nonempty(clockq) && firstkey(clockq) <= 0)
                ready(getfirst(clockq),RESCHNO);
        if ( slnempty = nonempty(clockq) )
                sltop = & q[q[clockq].qnext].qkey;
        resched();
}
```

10.8 Deferred Clock Processing

The clock dispatcher includes an additional feature that complicates it: deferred clock processing. In essence, deferred mode allows the system to accumulate clock ticks without initiating events. The difference between ignoring clock interrupts and deferring them is that the clock handler can schedule events that "should have occurred" when it leaves deferred mode and returns to normal mode. If the clock only remains deferred for a few ticks at a time, the system will appear to operate correctly. For the time being, we will postpone discussing the motivation for deferred processing, and concentrate on how it works.

10.8.1 Procedures For Changing To And From Deferred Mode

A process can place the clock in *deferred mode* by calling *stopclk*, and return the clock to *real-time* mode by calling *strtclk*. Any number of processes can request that the clock be deferred — it remains deferred until they have all called *strtclk*. *Stopclk* counts deferral requests by incrementing *defclk*, and *strtclk* counts restart requests by decrementing it. As long as *defclk* remains positive, the interrupt handler counts clock ticks in *clkdiff* without processing them.

Strtclk "makes up for lost time" when *defclk* reaches zero again, by catching up on all events that should have occurred while the clock remained deferred. To do so, *strtclk* updates the preemption counter, and subtracts the accumulated ticks from the delay of sleeping processes.

The code for both *strtclk* and *stopclk* is contained in file *ssclock.c*, shown below.

```c
/* ssclock.c - stopclk, strtclk */

#include <conf.h>
#include <kernel.h>
#include <proc.h>
#include <q.h>
#include <sleep.h>


/*------------------------------------------------------------------------
 *  stopclk  --  put the clock in defer mode
 *------------------------------------------------------------------------
 */
stopclk()
{
        defclk++;
}


/*------------------------------------------------------------------------
 *  strtclk  --  take the clock out of defer mode
 *------------------------------------------------------------------------
 */
strtclk()
{
        char ps;
        int makeup;
        int next;

        disable(ps);
        if ( defclk<=0 || --defclk>0 ) {
                restore(ps);
                return;
        }
        makeup = clkdiff;
        preempt -= makeup;
        clkdiff = 0;
        if ( slnempty ) {
                for (next=firstid(clockq) ;
                    next < NPROC && q[next].qkey < makeup ;
                    next=q[next].qnext) {
                        makeup -= q[next].qkey;
                        q[next].qkey = 0;
```

```
                }
                if (next < NPROC)
                        q[next].qkey -= makeup;
                wakeup();
        }
        if ( preempt <= 0 )
                resched();
        restore(ps);
}
```

10.9 Clock Interrupt Processing

We are finally ready to look at *clkint*, the assembly language routine that dispatches clock interrupts. File *clkint.s* contains the source code.

```
/* clkint.s -  clkint */


/*----------------------------------------------------------------------
/* clkint  --  real-time clock interrupt service routine
/*----------------------------------------------------------------------
         .globl  _clkint
_clkint:
         dec     _count6               / Is this the 6th interrupt?
         bgt     clret                 /  no => return
         mov     $6,_count6            /  yes=> reset counter&continue
         tst     _defclk               / Are clock ticks deferred?
         beq     notdef                /  no => go process this tick
         inc     _clkdiff              /  yes=> count in clkdiff and
         rtt                           /           return quickly
notdef:
         tst     _slnempty             / Is sleep queue nonempty?
         beq     clpreem               /  no => go process preemption
         dec     *_sltop               /  yes=> decrement delta key
         bgt     clpreem               /          on first process,
         mov     r0,-(sp)              /          calling wakeup if
         mov     r1,-(sp)              /          it reaches zero
         jsr     pc,_wakeup            /          (interrupt routine
         mov     (sp)+,r1              /           saves & restores r0
         mov     (sp)+,r0              /           and r1; C doesn't)
clpreem:
         dec     _preempt              / Decrement preemption counter
         bgt     clret                 /   and call resched if it
         mov     r0,-(sp)              /   reaches zero
         mov     r1,-(sp)              /      (As before, interrupt
         jsr     pc,_resched           /       routine must save &
         mov     (sp)+,r1              /       restore r0 and r1
         mov     (sp)+,r0              /       because C doesn't)
clret:
         rtt                           / Return from interrupt
```

Clkint uses *count6* to convert interrupts to one-tenth second ticks by decrementing it from 6 to 0 before processing an interrupt. On each tick, it decrements the time remaining on the first process in *clockq* (provided *clockq* is nonempty). When the time remaining reaches zero, *clkint* calls *wakeup* to remove processes and make them *ready*. Note how *slnempty* and *sltop* eliminate the computation of subscripts at interrupt time. Finally, *clkint* decrements the preemption counter, calling *resched* when it is time for preemption.

10.10 Clock Initialization

The clock interrupt vector must be initialized at system startup, before clock interrupts occur and before user processes request delays with *sleep*. Procedure *clkinit*, shown below, performs the necessary initialization.

```
/* clkinit.c - clkinit */

#include <conf.h>
#include <kernel.h>
#include <sleep.h>

/*
 *------------------------------------------------------------------------
 * clkinit - initialize the clock and sleep queue (called at startup)
 *------------------------------------------------------------------------
 */
clkinit()
{
        int *vector;

        vector = (int *) CVECTOR;       /* set up interrupt vector      */
        *vector++ = clkint;
        *vector = DISABLE;
        setclkr();
        preempt = QUANTUM;              /* initial time quantum         */
        count6 = 6;                     /* 60ths of a sec. counter      */
        slnempty = FALSE;               /* initially, no process asleep */
        clkdiff = 0;                    /* zero deferred ticks          */
        defclk = 0;                     /* clock is not deferred        */
        clockq = newqueue();            /* allocate clock queue in q    */
}
```

10.11 Summary

A real-time clock interrupts the CPU at regular intervals. Because the clock interrupts frequently, the interrupt routine must be designed to operate efficiently. The design described here optimizes interrupt processing by converting the hardware clock rate into a slower tick rate, and performing simple computation in the dispatcher to avoid calling a C procedure.

The real-time clock manager uses clock interrupts to schedule events in the future, and then to initiate the events at the appropriate time. A preemption event, scheduled every time the system switches context, forces a call to the scheduler after *QUANTUM* clock ticks pass. Preemption guarantees that no process uses the CPU forever. Wakeup events, scheduled when user processes request timed delays cause the running process to enqueue itself on a list of sleeping processes, and pass control to another process. The interrupt handler awakens sleeping processes when their delay expires by moving them back to the ready list.

FOR FURTHER STUDY

Because timing and clock processing rely on the hardware available, most books describe how the operating system uses timed delays without giving much detail about the clock routines. Examples of the use of clocks in virtual memory management, process management (e.g., time slicing) and distributed systems can be found in Calingaert [1982], Peterson and Silberschatz [1983], and Habermann [1976].

EXERCISES

10.1   The 11/2 does not have a hardware time-of-day clock. Rewrite the real-time clock routines to simulate a time-of-day clock.

10.2   Rewrite the Xinu clock routines to use a tick rate of 60 per second. Compare their performance with those using a rate of 10 per second.

10.3   Build a hardware clock with pulse rate equal to the desired tick rate, and modify the clock interrupt handler accordingly. Measure the difference it makes in the execution of CPU intensive programs.

10.4   Conduct an experiment to determine whether the system ever misses clock interrupts. Before beginning, estimate the number of instructions executed during an interrupt when a sleeping process awakens, and the time it will take to execute them.

10.5   Trace the series of calls starting with a clock interrupt that awakens two sleeping processes, one of which has higher priority than the currently executing process.

10.6   What goes wrong if *QUANTUM* is set to 1? Hint: consider switching back to a process that was suspended by *resched* while processing an interrupt.

10.7   Speculate about the usefulness of deferring clock interrupts. Compare its effect when the deferral lasts only a few clock ticks to cases where it lasts many seconds.

10.8   Does *sleep*(3) guarantee a minimum delay of 3 seconds, an exact delay of 3 seconds, or a maximum delay of 3 seconds?

10.9   Identify a problem in the way that *kill* removes processes from the queue of sleeping processes. Rewrite *kill* to correct the problem.

10.10   What might happen if *wakeup* called *wait*?

10.11   Systems that charge processes for CPU time face the following problem: when an interrupt occurs, it is most convenient to let the current process execute the interrupt routine even if the interrupt has nothing to do with the current process. Investigate how such systems charge the cost of executing interrupt routines like *wakeup* to the processes that are affected.

10.12 Rewrite *sleep* to avoid the overhead of calling *sleep10*.

10.13 Design an experiment to see if preemption ever causes the system to reschedule. Be careful: awakening a sleeping process to test a variable, or using normal output will affect the results of the experiment by forcing calls to *resched*.

10.14 Some machines have programmable *interval timer* hardware. The interval timer is set by specifying a delay; it interrupts when the delay has completed. Redesign the clock routines assuming that you have three independent interval timers available.

11

Device Independent Input and Output

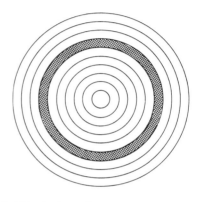

Operating systems control input and output (I/O) devices for three reasons. First, the hardware interface to most devices is relatively crude, requiring complex software to control and use them. The operating system hides these details in routines called *device drivers* through which programs transfer data and control the device. Second, devices are shared resources, protected and allocated by the operating system according to policies that make access fair and safe. Third, the operating system provides a consistent, uniform, and flexible interface to all devices, allowing users to write programs that reference devices by name and perform high-level operations without knowing about the machine configuration. This chapter begins by looking at how a set of high-level primitives might be selected, and proceeds to describe the data structures used to relate them to specific devices.

The choice of abstract input and output operations is not easy because goals like flexibility, simplicity, and generality tend to dictate contradictory designs. Any design will be an iterative process in which the designer chooses a set of primitives, maps device operations into them, and revises the choice as problems arise. However, the design process can be organized into roughly three steps that can be followed without many iterations. First: generate a list of desirable properties. Second: derive a set of high-level primitives, and explain the purpose of each by giving their meaning with respect to specific classes of devices (e.g., terminals, disks, etc.). Third: build software that maps an abstract device onto some particular instance of that device.

11.1 Properties Of The Input And Output Interface

What properties should I/O systems exhibit? Perhaps the most important design issue is synchrony: should processes block while performing I/O operations, or should they continue executing and be notified (somehow) when the operation completes. I/O systems that allow processes to initiate an operation and then to continue execution are called *asynchronous*; they are useful in a concurrent programming environment, especially when the user wants to control the overlap of computation and I/O. Those systems that delay input operations until the data arrives and delay output operations until the data has been consumed are called *synchronous*; they follow the pattern established in most high-level languages, and users generally prefer them. Synchronous I/O systems guarantee that the user can depend on data immediately after an input operation, and change data immediately after an output operation. Because it is easier to use, and because it seems to suffice for most applications, our design will use synchronous I/O.

The format of data and size of transfers is another issue that affects I/O system design. The question to ask is: "will data be transferred in blocks or bytes, and if in blocks, of what size and what form?" These questions are difficult to answer because some devices work with single bytes while others operate on blocks of data — it may depend on the hardware that the system uses. A general purpose system, one that may be connected to a variety of I/O devices in a variety of configurations, will probably need both single-byte transfers as well as block transfers. Thus, our design will include both.

Finally, issues like efficiency, generality, portability, and simplicity arise. These can be ignored for now, but may ultimately force changes in the design. We will see in Chapter 17, for example, that lower-levels of the disk I/O software operate asynchronously.

11.2 Abstract Operations

Once a basic set of properties has been developed, a set of abstract I/O operations can be derived. Experience with other systems may be as important in helping to choose abstract operations as anything else. The author's own bias can be observed in the nine abstract operations designed for Xinu. They are: *getc, putc, read, write, control, seek, open, close,* and *init*. Throughout the rest of the book, we will refer to them as the I/O *primitives*.

Each primitive has a meaning, loosely defined as follows. *Getc* and *putc* deal with single character transfers, receiving from the device or sending to it. *Read* and *write* do the same for one or more characters transferred to a contiguous block of memory. *Control* allows a user to control the device or the device driver, with *seek* being a special case of *control* that applies to randomly accessible storage devices. *Open* and *close* allow the user to inform the device that data transfer will begin or that it has ended. These may be useful, for example, to return the device to an idle state when it is not needed. Finally, *init* initializes the device and driver at system startup.

Consider, for example, how these abstract routines apply to the "console terminal". *Getc* reads the next character from the keyboard, and *putc* displays one character on the terminal. *Write* displays several characters with one call, and *read* reads a specified number of characters (or all that have been typed, depending on its arguments). Finally, *control* allows the program to change parameters in the driver to control such things as whether the system echoes each character as it is typed.

11.3 Binding Abstract Operations To Real Devices

The system maps high-level I/O operations like those described above into calls to specific device drivers. In so doing, it hides hardware and device driver details (e.g., that the keyboard and display on a terminal are actually independent devices), making programs independent of the hardware configuration. In one sense, these high-level calls comprise the environment that the system presents to running programs — the programs only perceive peripheral devices through these abstract primitives.

In addition to mapping abstract I/O operations onto driver routines, the system must map abstract names like *CONSOLE* onto real devices. Each system has its own mapping scheme; uniformity is not the rule. Some require the programmer to know about devices when writing the program. Others require the command interpreter to link names used in the program with real devices. Still others perform the linkage dynamically, allowing a running process to change the correspondence.

As a general rule, the later a system binds the names of abstract devices and abstract operations to real devices and device drivers, the more flexible it is. Programs that have device addresses and driver calls bound at compile-time are obviously impractical because they must be changed whenever the hardware device or address is altered, no matter how minor the change. At the other extreme, programs that bind names late usually incur more computational overhead — they are not as practical in small systems. So, the essence of the design problem consists of synthesizing a binding mechanism that allows maximum flexibility within the required performance bounds.

This chapter suggests a design which compromises between late binding and efficiency in a manner typical of many existing systems. Coded into the system is a description of each abstract device, the device driver routines it uses, and the address of a real device to which it corresponds. The system must be altered and recompiled when a new device is added or when existing device addresses are modified. User's programs, however, contain no direct calls to device drivers, and no device addresses; they need not be recompiled as long as the abstract device descriptors do not change. As a consequence, simple programs that only execute I/O operations on the *CONSOLE* work on almost any Xinu configuration, independent of the physical console device, its hardware interface, or its hardware address.

11.4 Binding I/O Calls To Device Drivers At Run-Time

At some point, routines like *read* must map abstract device descriptors like *CONSOLE* to device driver routines and specific device addresses. Both the technicalities of how the mapping is performed as well as the source of information about which devices the system contains are important.

In Xinu, each abstract device is assigned an integer *device descriptor* when the system is configured. By convention, devices like *CONSOLE* have the same device descriptor in all Xinu systems. Based on the results of configuration, device descriptors are bound into the system when it is compiled and placed in the library. The system need not be recompiled unless the configuration changes (e.g., a new device is added). Once the system has been configured, any number of programs can be compiled. These programs address devices by name, and the compiler is able to map names to the correct device descriptors based on the configuration information.

At run-time the program calls high-level I/O routines like *read* or *putc*, passing the device descriptor as an argument. The high-level I/O routines use the device descriptor as an index into a table called the *device switch table*. The device switch maps each device descriptor into a real device address and appropriate driver routines. The high-level routine then calls the driver to carry out the operation.

A look at the definition of the device switch table, *devtab*, should clarify the details. It can be found in file *conf.h*. Structure *devsw*, declared in the same file, defines the format of entries in the device switch table.

```
/* conf.h (GENERATED FILE; DO NOT EDIT) */

#define NULLPTR (char *)0

/* Device table declarations */
struct   devsw   {                      /* device table entry */
         int      dvnum;
         int      (*dvinit)();
         int      (*dvopen)();
         int      (*dvclose)();
         int      (*dvread)();
         int      (*dvwrite)();
         int      (*dvseek)();
         int      (*dvgetc)();
         int      (*dvputc)();
         int      (*dvcntl)();
         int      dvcsr;
         int      dvivec;
         int      dvovec;
```

```
                int     (*dviint)();
                int     (*dvoint)();
                char    *dvioblk;
                int     dvminor;
                };


extern  struct  devsw devtab[];              /* one entry per device */


/* Device name definitions */

#define CONSOLE    0                 /* type tty      */
#define OTHER      1                 /* type tty      */
#define RING0IN    2                 /* type dlc      */
#define RING0OUT   3                 /* type dlc      */
#define DISK0      4                 /* type dsk      */
#define FILE1      5                 /* type df       */
#define FILE2      6                 /* type df       */
#define FILE3      7                 /* type df       */
#define FILE4      8                 /* type df       */


/* Control block sizes */

#define Ntty    2
#define Ndlc    2
#define Ndsk    1
#define Ndf     4


#define NDEVS   9


/* Declarations of I/O routines referenced */

extern  int     ttyinit();
extern  int     ionull();
extern  int     ttyread();
extern  int     ttywrite();
extern  int     ioerr();
extern  int     ttycntl();
extern  int     ttygetc();
extern  int     ttyputc();
extern  int     ttyiin();
extern  int     ttyoin();
extern  int     dlcinit();
extern  int     dlcread();
extern  int     dlcwrite();
```

```
extern   int    dlccntl();
extern   int    dlcputc();
extern   int    dlciin();
extern   int    dlcoin();
extern   int    dsinit();
extern   int    dsopen();
extern   int    dsread();
extern   int    dswrite();
extern   int    dsseek();
extern   int    dscntl();
extern   int    dsinter();
extern   int    lfinit();
extern   int    lfclose();
extern   int    lfread();
extern   int    lfwrite();
extern   int    lfseek();
extern   int    lfgetc();
extern   int    lfputc();
```

```
/* Configuration and Size Constants */

#define MEMMARK                         /* define if memory marking used*/
#define NNETS    1                      /* number of Xinu ring networks */
                                        /*   (remove if there are zero)  */
#define NPROC    10                     /* number of user processes      */
#define NSEM     50                     /* total number of semaphores    */
#define RTCLOCK                         /* system has a real-time clock  */
#define VERSION "6.1b (05/22/84)"       /* label printed at startup      */
```

Each entry in *devtab* corresponds to a single device; it contains the address of
the device driver routines for that device, the device address, and miscellaneous other information used by the drivers. Fields *dvgetc, dvputc, dvread, dvwrite, dvcntl,
dvseek,* and *dvinit* hold the addresses of driver routines corresponding to the high-
level operations. Knowing the addresses of driver routines is not enough, however,
because more than one device can use the same driver routine. So, the device
switch table contains fields for the hardware device address (*dvcsr*), interrupt vector addresses (*dvivec* and *dvovec*), and interrupt dispatch routines (*dviint* and
dvoint), as well as a buffer pointer (*dvioblk*), and an integer to distinguish among
multiple copies of a device (*dvminor*). The minor device number is especially important for multiplexors that control a set of identical devices through a single
hardware interface.

11.5 The Implementation Of High-Level I/O Operations

Because the device switch table isolates high-level I/O operations from underlying details, it allows high-level procedures to be completed before device drivers. One of the chief benefits of such a strategy is that it allows the designer to build and test subsets of the I/O system.

There is a procedure for each of the abstract operations *getc*, *putc*, *read*, and so on. This section describes the C implementation of these high-level routines, and shows how they call low-level device drivers indirectly through the device switch table. For example, the C code in file *read.c* implements the *read* operation.

```
/* read.c - read */

#include <conf.h>
#include <kernel.h>
#include <io.h>

/*------------------------------------------------------------------------
 *  read  -  read one or more bytes from a device
 *------------------------------------------------------------------------
 */
read(descrp, buff, count)
int descrp, count;
char *buff;
{
        struct  devsw   *devptr;

        if (isbaddev(descrp) )
                return(SYSERR);
        devptr = &devtab[descrp];
        return( (*devptr->dvread)(devptr,buff,count) );
}
```

A program calls *read*, passing as arguments the device descriptor, the address of a buffer into which data should be read, and a count of the number of characters to read. Procedure *read* uses the device descriptor *descrp*, as an index into *devtab*, and calls the driver routine given by field *dvread*. It passes the driver three arguments: the address of the *devtab* entry (*dvptr*), the buffer address (*buff*) and a count of characters to read (*count*).

The remaining high-level routines operate in the same way as *read*. They are shown below.

```
/* control.c - control */

#include <conf.h>
#include <kernel.h>
#include <io.h>

/*------------------------------------------------------------------------
 *  control  -  control a device (e.g., set the mode)
 *------------------------------------------------------------------------
 */
control(descrp, func, addr, addr2)
int descrp, func;
char *addr,*addr2;
{
        struct  devsw   *devptr;

        if (isbaddev(descrp) )
                return(SYSERR);
        devptr = &devtab[descrp];
        return( (*devptr->dvcntl)(devptr, func, addr, addr2) );
}


/* getc.c - getc */

#include <conf.h>
#include <kernel.h>
#include <io.h>

/*------------------------------------------------------------------------
 *  getc  -  get one character from a device
 *------------------------------------------------------------------------
 */
getc(descrp)
int descrp;
{
        struct  devsw   *devptr;

        if (isbaddev(descrp) )
                return(SYSERR);
        devptr = &devtab[descrp];
        return( (*devptr->dvgetc)(devptr) );
}
```

```
/* init.c - init */

#include <conf.h>
#include <kernel.h>
#include <io.h>

/*------------------------------------------------------------------------
 *  init  -  initialize a device
 *------------------------------------------------------------------------
 */
init(descrp)
int descrp;
{
        struct  devsw   *devptr;

        if (isbaddev(descrp) )
                return(SYSERR);
        devptr = &devtab[descrp];
        return( (*devptr->dvinit)(devptr) );
}


/* putc.c - putc */

#include <conf.h>
#include <kernel.h>
#include <io.h>

/*------------------------------------------------------------------------
 *  putc  -  write a single character to a device
 *------------------------------------------------------------------------
 */
putc(descrp, ch)
int descrp;
char ch;
{
        struct  devsw   *devptr;

        if (isbaddev    (descrp) )
                return(SYSERR);
        devptr = &devtab[descrp];
        return( (*devptr->dvputc)(devptr,ch) );
}
```

```
/* seek.c seek */

#include <conf.h>
#include <kernel.h>
#include <io.h>

/*------------------------------------------------------------------------
 *  seek  --  position a device (very common special case of control)
 *------------------------------------------------------------------------
 */
seek(descrp, pos)
int descrp;
long pos;
{
        struct  devsw   *devptr;

        if (isbaddev(descrp) )
                return(SYSERR);
        devptr = &devtab[descrp];
        return( (*devptr->dvseek)(devptr,pos) );
}


/* write.c - write */

#include <conf.h>
#include <kernel.h>
#include <io.h>

/*------------------------------------------------------------------------
 *  write  -  write 1 or more bytes to a device
 *------------------------------------------------------------------------
 */
write(descrp, buff, count)
        int descrp, count;
        char *buff;
{
        struct  devsw   *devptr;

        if (isbaddev(descrp) )
                return(SYSERR);
        devptr = &devtab[descrp];
        return( (*devptr->dvwrite)(devptr,buff,count) );
}
```

11.6 Opening And Closing Devices

Some disk devices require the programs to start them before performing a transfer operation, and to stop them when the transfer completes. Although *control* can be used in such situations, it is sometimes helpful to have more meaningfully named procedures to start up and shut down a device. *Open* and *close* serve this purpose. The code is again similar to that of the other high-level I/O routines:

```c
/* close.c - close */

#include <conf.h>
#include <kernel.h>
#include <io.h>

/*------------------------------------------------------------------------
 *  close  -  close a device
 *------------------------------------------------------------------------
 */
close(descrp)
int descrp;
{
        struct  devsw   *devptr;

        if (isbaddev(descrp) )
                return(SYSERR);
        devptr = &devtab[descrp];
        return( (*devptr->dvclose)(devptr));
}
```

```
/* open.c - open */

#include <conf.h>
#include <kernel.h>
#include <io.h>


/*------------------------------------------------------------------------
 *  open  -  open a connection to a device/file (parms 2 &3 are optional)
 *------------------------------------------------------------------------
 */
open(descrp, nam, mode)
int     descrp;
char    *nam;
char    *mode;
{
        struct devsw    *devptr;

        if ( isbaddev(descrp) )
                return(SYSERR);
        devptr = &devtab[descrp];
        return( (*devptr->dvopen)(devptr, nam, mode) );
}
```

11.7 Null And Error Entries In Devtab

High level routines like *read* and *write* use the entries in *devtab* without checking to see that they are valid. Thus, a driver address must be supplied for every
operation and every device or catastrophe may result (e.g., branch to zero). However, not all combinations of operations and devices are meaningful. For example,
seek is not an operation that can be performed on terminal devices. How can such
devtab entries be filled in?

Two routines, *ioerr* and *ionull*, serve to fill in otherwise empty entries of
devtab . Procedure *ioerr* simply returns *SYSERR* whenever it is called; procedure
ionull always returns *OK*. By convention, entries filled with *ioerr* should never be
called; they signify an illegal operation. Entries for unnecessary, but otherwise innocuous operations (like *open* for a terminal device), point to procedure *ionull*.
The code for these routines is trivial.


```
/* ioerr.c - ioerr */

#include <conf.h>
#include <kernel.h>
```

```
/*------------------------------------------------------------------------
 *  ioerr  -  return an error (used for "error" entries in devtab)
 *------------------------------------------------------------------------
 */
ioerr()
{
        return(SYSERR);
}



/* ionull.c - ionull */

#include <conf.h>
#include <kernel.h>

/*------------------------------------------------------------------------
 *  ionull  -  do nothing (used for "don't care" entries in devtab)
 *------------------------------------------------------------------------
 */
ionull()
{
        return(OK);
}
```

11.8 Initialization Of The I/O System

We have seen how the hardware uses the address in an interrupt vector location to locate the interrupt dispatch routine, and how the interrupt dispatch routines use the interrupt dispatch table, *intmap*, to locate the appropriate high-level interrupt routine. We have also seen how I/O system calls like *read* use *devtab* to map device descriptors into drivers when programs perform I/O operations. The question that remains is how these tables and interrupt vectors are initialized in the first place.

Devtab is actually generated when the system is configured, so it is completely filled in by the time the system is compiled. The values in *devtab* vary from configuration to configuration, but a sample can be found in file *conf.c*:

```
/* conf.c (GENERATED FILE; DO NOT EDIT) */

#include <conf.h>

/* device independent I/O switch */

struct  devsw   devtab[NDEVS] = {

/*  Format of entries is:
device-number,
init, open, close,
read, write, seek,
getc, putc, cntl,
device-csr-address, input-vector, output-vector,
iint-handler, oint-handler, control-block, minor-device,
*/

/*  CONSOLE */
0,
ttyinit, ionull, ionull,
ttyread, ttywrite, ioerr,
ttygetc, ttyputc, ttycntl,
0177560, 0060, 0064,
ttyiin, ttyoin, NULLPTR, 0,

/*  OTHER */
1,
ttyinit, ionull, ionull,
ttyread, ttywrite, ioerr,
ttygetc, ttyputc, ttycntl,
0176500, 0300, 0304,
ttyiin, ttyoin, NULLPTR, 1,

/*  RING0IN */
2,
dlcinit, ioerr, ioerr,
dlcread, dlcwrite, ioerr,
ioerr, dlcputc, dlccntl,
0176510, 0310, 0314,
dlciin, dlcoin, NULLPTR, 0,

/*  RING0OUT */
3,
dlcinit, ioerr, ioerr,
dlcread, dlcwrite, ioerr,
```

```
ioerr, dlcputc, dlccntl,
0176520, 0320, 0324,
dlciin, dlcoin, NULLPTR, 1,

/*  DISK0 */
4,
dsinit, dsopen, ioerr,
dsread, dswrite, dsseek,
ioerr, ioerr, dscntl,
0177460, 0134, 0134,
dsinter, dsinter, NULLPTR, 0,

/*  FILE1 */
5,
lfinit, ioerr, lfclose,
lfread, lfwrite, lfseek,
lfgetc, lfputc, ioerr,
0000000, 0000, 0000,
ioerr, ioerr, NULLPTR, 0,

/*  FILE2 */
6,
lfinit, ioerr, lfclose,
lfread, lfwrite, lfseek,
lfgetc, lfputc, ioerr,
0000000, 0000, 0000,
ioerr, ioerr, NULLPTR, 1,

/*  FILE3 */
7,
lfinit, ioerr, lfclose,
lfread, lfwrite, lfseek,
lfgetc, lfputc, ioerr,
0000000, 0000, 0000,
ioerr, ioerr, NULLPTR, 2,

/*  FILE4 */
8,
lfinit, ioerr, lfclose,
lfread, lfwrite, lfseek,
lfgetc, lfputc, ioerr,
0000000, 0000, 0000,
ioerr, ioerr, NULLPTR, 3
        };
```

Do not despair — *conf.c* comes from a program; it was not typed by a programmer. For now, it is sufficient to glance through the entries of *devtab* and compare them to the declarations shown earlier in this chapter. We will discuss how *conf.c* is generated in Chapter 20.

11.9 Interrupt Vector Initialization

The interrupt vectors and interrupt dispatch table are initialized at run-time, based on information in *devtab*. The system calls *init(k)* for each device *k* at startup, before it starts executing the user's program. The device initialization routine, thought of as part of the device driver, usually initializes the interrupt vector, fills in the entry of the interrupt dispatch table, *intmap*, and initializes any control blocks or buffers associated with the device. It may also test the device, enable interrupts, or reset the hardware in other ways as required. Part of this initialization depends on the driver and the device, but because so many devices initialize the interrupt vectors and dispatch table, building a standard initialization routine is worthwhile.

Procedure *ioinit* is the initialization procedure that fills in the interrupt vectors and dispatch table. Recall that *intmap* specifies the addresses of the high-level input and output interrupt routines and an argument to be passed to each. *Ioinit* uses the minor device number *dvminor* as that argument. It calls procedure *iosetvec* to fill in the dispatch table.

```
/* ioinit.c - ioinit, iosetvec */

#include <conf.h>
#include <kernel.h>
#include <io.h>

/*------------------------------------------------------------------------
 * ioinit -- standard interrupt vector and dispatch initialization
 *------------------------------------------------------------------------
 */
ioinit(descrp)
int     descrp;
{
        int     minor;

        if (isbaddev(descrp) )
                return(SYSERR);
        minor = devtab[descrp].dvminor;
        iosetvec(descrp, minor, minor);
        return(OK);
```

```
}


/*-------------------------------------------------------------------
 * iosetvec  -  fill in interrupt vectors and dispatch table entries
 *-------------------------------------------------------------------
 */
iosetvec(descrp, incode, outcode)
int     descrp;
int     incode;
int     outcode;
{
        struct  devsw   *devptr;
        struct  intmap  *map;
        struct  vector  *vptr;

        if (isbaddev(descrp))
                return(SYSERR);
        devptr = &devtab[descrp];
        map = &intmap[devptr->dvnum];     /* fill in interrupt dispatch  */
        map->iin =  devptr->dviint;       /*   map with addresses of high-*/
        map->icode = incode;              /*   level input and output    */
        map->iout = devptr->dvoint;       /*   interrupt handlers and    */
        map->ocode = outcode;             /*   minor device numbers      */
        vptr = (struct vector *)devptr->dvivec;
        vptr->vproc = (char *)INTVECI;    /* fill in input interrupt     */
        vptr->vps = descrp | DISABLE;     /*   vector PC and PS values    */
        vptr = (struct vector *)devptr->dvovec;
        vptr->vproc = (char *)INTVECO;    /* fill in output interrupt    */
        vptr->vps = descrp | DISABLE;     /*   vector PC and PS values    */
        return(OK);
}
```

11.10 Summary

The operating system provides a high-level environment to user programs by hiding the details of peripheral devices under a layer of device-independent I/O routines. User programs access devices by name using the high-level operations *getc, putc, read, write, control, seek, open,* and *close.* In our design, the I/O system operates *synchronously,* delaying the calling process until data has been transferred.

To keep device information in user's programs independent of hardware devices and addresses, the system binds abstract names like *CONSOLE* to integer device descriptors. It binds descriptors to specific devices at run-time using a device switch table. The device switch table contains one entry for each device; the entry includes information like the device's hardware address as well as the set of driver routines that control the device. High level I/O operations like *read* or *write* access the device switch table to determine the driver routine that performs the operation on the specified device. Individual drivers interpret these calls in a way meaningful to the particular device; if an operation makes no sense when applied to a particular device, the system calls a routine that returns an error code.

One field of the device switch table specifies an initialization routine that the system calls at startup. Usually this initialization fills in the device control block, establishes interrupt vectors, and fills in the interrupt dispatch table.

FOR FURTHER STUDY

The ideas of blocking I/O, most of the general I/O primitives, and the device switch table are not new. Although pieces can be found in several systems, the set described here came mostly from UNIX (Ritchie and Thompson [1974]). Two earlier systems that contributed to these ideas are Multics (Corbato [1972]), and CTSS (Crisman [1965]).

EXERCISES

11.1   Identify the set of I/O operations available on various operating systems.

11.2   Find a system that uses *asynchronous* I/O, and identify the mechanism by which a running program is notified when the operation completes. Which system would you rather use?

11.3   There is a difference between the binding of device names (e.g., *CONSOLE*) to device descriptors and the binding of device descriptors (e.g., 0) to real hardware devices. Compare the two bindings in Xinu with bindings in other operating systems.

11.4   Consider the relationship between device names and device descriptors. How easy is it to write a program that will read a device name, like *CONSOLE*, and perform I/O to that device?

11.5   Assume that in the course of debugging you begin to suspect that a program is incorrectly calling high-level routines like *open* and *seek* on devices for which they make no sense. Make a quick change to catch I/O errors, printing the process id of the offending process. (Do not recompile the I/O system calls until you have tried other approaches.)

11.6   Modify *ioinit* to eliminate *iosetvec*. Why are they separate?

11.7   In one version of Xinu *ioinit*, *ionull*, *ioerr*, and *iosetvec* were bound together in the same object file, making it impossible to load one without the others. Explain why separating them is a good idea.

12

An Example Device Driver

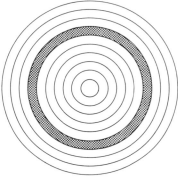

The previous chapter discussed high-level I/O operations and the device switch table, *devtab*, which forms the general framework linking interrupts, devices, and device driver routines. This chapter explores device driver routines for one particular device, a standard computer terminal with a keyboard. From the computer's point of view, of course, the "device" consists of an asynchronous line unit attached to the system bus. Seeing an example will help the reader both understand how device drivers operate and appreciate how the device switch framework eases the task of configuring devices and device drivers into the system.

12.1 The Device Type Tty

Xinu uses the name *tty* to refer to conventional "computer terminals" that connect to the system over asynchronous communication lines; the terminology was borrowed from older systems that used Teletype devices as terminals. Each tty device has a keyboard capable of transmitting characters to the computer, and an output device capable of displaying characters received from the computer.

In broad terms, the task of the tty device driver is to map operations like reading or writing characters to hardware operations that transmit characters to the display and receive characters from the keyboard. In practice, the driver communicates with a serial line unit controller, requesting it to send characters or receive them; the controller hardware transforms characters to and from electrical impulses on the lines that connect to the terminal. To minimize interference between I/O and running processes, the driver uses interrupt-driven processing, transmitting characters when the device is idle, and reading characters as they are received. In addition, it handles details like receiver errors, and coordinates requests for I/O with the speed of the device. The latter task is especially important because character transmission times are often several orders of magnitude slower than processing speed, something few programmers appreciate until they write device drivers.

Instead of operating a particular brand of terminal in a particular way, the tty drivers operate from parameters so they can be used with a variety of terminals in a variety of configurations. Several of the parameters control character "echo". Terminals that operate in what is known as *full-duplex mode* do not display characters as the user types them. Such terminals require the computer system to transmit back to the display every character received from the keyboard so the user can see what has been typed. However, not all terminals need character echo. Those that operate in *half-duplex mode* display keystrokes automatically. If the computer system echoes the characters received from a half-duplex terminal, two copies appear on the display. So, the tty driver keeps a parameter for each serial line that tells whether that line uses character echo or not. It keeps other parameters that tell it such things as whether or not to echo unprintable characters as a printable combination.

Most of the tty parameters will be obvious to anyone who has used a terminal, but readers who are unfamiliar with terminal hardware may puzzle over those that deal with moving onto new lines. The display unit of a terminal recognizes two unprintable characters that control cursor movement. *RETURN*, commonly called *carriage return*, moves the cursor left to the beginning of the current line (without spacing vertically). *NEWLINE*, sometimes called *line feed*, moves the cursor vertically downward one line (without moving horizontally). A terminal must receive both *NEWLINE* and *RETURN* to move to the start of the next line. Keyboards have separate keys that generate *RETURN* and *NEWLINE*, but naming is nonstandard so they might be labelled "return", "line feed", "enter", "newline", or "end line".

Although terminals send and interpret *NEWLINE* and *RETURN* separately, programs like to deal with a single end-of-line character for both input and output. In Xinu, *NEWLINE* is the favored end-of-line character, denoted "\n" in string and character constants. To simplify programming, the tty driver recognizes both *RETURN* and *NEWLINE* according to several parameters. A parameter denoted *icrlf* controls whether the driver maps *RETURN* to *NEWLINE* when received from the keyboard. Another parameter, *ocrlf*, controls whether the driver inserts *RETURN* in the output stream whenever a program writes *NEWLINE*.

12.2 Upper And Lower Halves Of The Device Driver

Like most device drivers, the tty driver routines can be partitioned into two sets: the *upper-half* and the *lower-half*. User processes call upper-half routines (indirectly through *devtab*) to read or write characters. Upper-half routines do not manipulate devices directly. Instead, they enqueue requests for transfer, and rely on routines in the lower-half to perform transfers later. This partition, difficult to appreciate at first, lies at the heart of driver design — it is fundamental because it decouples normal processing from hardware interrupts.

The queue of transfer requests is the primary data structure that connects high-level calls to actions on the device. Each device has its own queue of requests, and the contents of elements on the queue depends on the device characteristics. Requests for devices like disks must specify the direction of transfer (read or write), the location of the data, and its length. Requests for character transfer are much simpler; usually, they only consist of the character itself.

Besides the queue of requests, the driver may need space for a *buffer*. Drivers use buffer space to record outgoing data from the time the user requests it be sent until the time the device receives it. They also use buffer space to record incoming data from the time the device deposits it until a user program requests it.

Buffers are important for several reasons. First, the driver can accept incoming data and place it in a buffer before a user process reads it. This is important for devices like a terminal where the user may start to type at any time. Second, devices like disks often transfer data in large blocks. The system must have a buffer large enough to hold all that the device transfers, even if the user only needs one character. Third, buffering permits the driver to perform I/O concurrently with user processes. When a user process writes data, the driver copies it into a buffer, and allows the user process to continue executing while it transfers the data from the buffer to the device.

The tty driver described here uses two circular character buffers per terminal, one for input and the other for output. Output operations deposit characters to be written in the output buffer, and return to their caller. Meanwhile, the SLU transmitter interrupts whenever it is idle, calling an interrupt processing routine in the lower-half of the tty driver. On each interrupt, the lower-half routine picks up the next character from the output buffer and starts the transmitter sending it.

Input works the other way around. Whenever the SLU receiver interrupts, signalling that it has received a character, the interrupt dispatcher calls the tty input interrupt routine in the lower-half. The input interrupt handler reads the waiting character and deposits it in the circular input buffer. When a process calls an upper-half routine to read characters, the upper-half routine takes them from the queue, waiting for more input only if insufficient characters remain enqueued.

Ideally, the two halves of a driver communicate only through the shared buffers:

> *Upper-half routines enqueue requests for data transfer or device control; they do not interact with devices directly. Lower-half routines transfer data from buffers or control devices; they do not interact with user programs directly.*

In practice, the two halves of the driver may need to do more than manipulate the shared data. For example, the upper-half may need to start the lower-half when it deposits output in the buffer. It may also happen that nothing has been typed when a process tries to read, or the available buffer space has been filled when a process tries to write. In such cases, the upper and lower halves must coordinate, stopping a process that is trying to write until space becomes available, or starting a process that is waiting for input as soon as the next character arrives.

12.3 Synchronization Of The Upper And Lower Halves

At first glance, synchronization between the upper and lower halves of a driver appears to be an instance of "producer/consumer" coordination that can be solved nicely with semaphores. The upper-half output routines produce characters that the lower-half output routines consume, while the lower-half input routines produce characters that the upper-half input routines consume. But there is an added twist. Input poses no problem because user processes that call the upper-half can *wait* for the lower-half to "produce" an input character, and lower-half routines can *signal* each time they read ("produce") a character. Output is not as simple, however, because lower-half routines, which operate at interrupt time, cannot *wait* for an upper-half routine to "produce" an output character. (This restriction, you will recall, is a consequence of the interrupt structure: calling *wait* at interrupt time might lead to a situation in which no process remains ready to run.)

How can the lower and upper halves coordinate if the lower-half cannot *wait* for output characters? Surprisingly, semaphores can easily solve the problem. The trick is to turn around the call to *wait* by changing the purpose of the semaphore. Instead of having a lower-half routine *wait* for the upper-half to produce characters, our design has the upper-half *wait* for space in the buffer. Thus, the lower-half never "consumes" anything: the lower-half input routine "produces" characters, and the lower-half output routine "produces" space in the buffer.

12.4 Control Block And Buffer Declarations

Each SLU device being used as a tty must have its own pair of input and output semaphores, and its own input and output buffers. All of this data is kept in a structure commonly called a *control block*; there is a tty control block for each tty device. Along with the buffers and semaphores, the control block also contains the parameters mentioned earlier. Although these may seem confusing, they are similar to the parameters provided on other systems.

The code in file *tty.h* contains the C code for defining the tty control block. In the code, the definition is given in the structure named *tty*.

```
/* tty.h */

#define IOCHERR        0200        /* bit set on when an error       */
                                   /* occurred reading the char.     */
#define OBMINSP        20          /* min space in buffer before     */
                                   /* processes awakened to write    */
#define EBUFLEN        20          /* size of echo queue             */

/* size constants */

#ifndef Ntty
#define Ntty           1           /* number of serial tty lines     */
#endif
#ifndef IBUFLEN
#define IBUFLEN        128         /* num. chars in input queue      */
#endif
#ifndef OBUFLEN
#define OBUFLEN        64          /* num. chars in output queue     */
#endif

/* mode constants */

#define IMRAW          'R'         /* raw mode => nothing done       */
#define IMCOOKED       'C'         /* cooked mode => line editing    */
#define IMCBREAK       'K'         /* honor echo, etc, no line edit  */
#define OMRAW          'R'         /* raw mode => normal processing  */

struct  tty     {                  /* tty line control block         */
        int     ihead;             /* head of input queue            */
        int     itail;             /* tail of input queue            */
        char    ibuff[IBUFLEN];    /* input buffer for this line     */
        int     isem;              /* input semaphore                */
        int     ohead;             /* head of output queue           */
        int     otail;             /* tail of output queue           */
        char    obuff[OBUFLEN];    /* output buffer for this line    */
        int     osem;              /* output semaphore               */
        int     odsend;            /* sends delayed for space        */
        int     ehead;             /* head of echo queue             */
        int     etail;             /* tail of echo queue             */
        char    ebuff[EBUFLEN];    /* echo queue                     */
        char    imode;             /* IMRAW, IMCBREAK, IMCOOKED      */
        Bool    iecho;             /* is input echoed?               */
        Bool    ieback;            /* do erasing backspace on echo?  */
        Bool    evis;              /* echo control chars as ^X ?     */
        Bool    ecrlf;             /* echo CR-LF for newline?        */
```

```
        Bool    icrlf;              /* map '\r' to '\n' on input?    */
        Bool    ierase;             /* honor erase character?        */
        char    ierasec;            /* erase character (backspace)   */
        Bool    ikill;              /* honor line kill character?    */
        char    ikillc;             /* line kill character           */
        int     icursor;            /* current cursor position       */
        Bool    oflow;              /* honor ostop/ostart?           */
        Bool    oheld;              /* output currently being held?  */
        char    ostop;              /* character that stops output   */
        char    ostart;             /* character that starts output  */
        Bool    ocrlf;              /* echo CR/LF for LF ?           */
        char    ifullc;             /* char to send when input full  */
        struct  csr     *ioaddr;    /* device address of this unit   */
};
extern  struct  tty tty[];

#define BACKSP  '\b'
#define BELL    '\07'
#define ATSIGN  '@'
#define BLANK   ' '
#define NEWLINE '\n'
#define RETURN  '\r'
#define STOPCH  '\023'              /* control-S stops output        */
#define STRTCH  '\021'              /* control-Q restarts output     */
#define UPARROW '^'

/* ttycontrol function codes */

#define TCSETBRK    1               /* turn on BREAK in transmitter */
#define TCRSTBRK    2               /* turn off BREAK "         "   */
#define TCNEXTC     3               /* look ahead 1 character       */
#define TCMODER     4               /* set input mode to raw        */
#define TCMODEC     5               /* set input mode to cooked     */
#define TCMODEK     6               /* set input mode to cbreak     */
#define TCICHARS    8               /* return number of input chars */
#define TCECHO      9               /* turn on echo                 */
#define TCNOECHO    10              /* turn off echo                */
#define TFULLC      BELL            /* char to echo when buffer full*/
```

The key components of the *tty* structure are an input buffer, *ibuff*, an output buffer, *obuff*, and an echo buffer *ebuff*. Each buffer is an array (the exercises discuss this choice). Head and tail pointers point to the next location in the array to fill, and the next location in the array to empty, respectively. Characters are always inserted at the head, and taken from the tail, independent of whether they flow from the upper-half to the lower-half or vice versa. The driver treats each buffer as a circular list, with location zero following the last location. Initially, the head and tail both point to location zero, but there is never any confusion about whether the buffer is completely empty or completely full because the count of characters is controlled by semaphores, *isem* and *osem*, as discussed above.

There is one tty control block per device; they are kept in an array *tty*, which is indexed by the minor device number. The system configuration program sets constant *Ntty* to the number of tty devices. It also assigns each tty device a minor device number from 0 through *Ntty*-1, and places the minor device number in the device switch table. Both interrupt-driven routines in the lower-half and driver routines in the upper-half use the minor device number as an index into the array *tty*. Thus, the minor device number forms a crucial link between the device id and the control block associated with that device.

12.5 Upper-Half Tty Input Routines

The routines *ttygetc*, *ttyputc*, *ttyread*, and *ttywrite* form the basis of the upper-half of the tty driver. They correspond to the operations *getc*, *putc*, *read*, and *write* described in Chapter 9. The simplest driver routine is *ttygetc*.

```
/* ttygetc.c - ttygetc */

#include <conf.h>
#include <kernel.h>
#include <tty.h>
#include <io.h>
#include <slu.h>


/*------------------------------------------------------------------------
 *  ttygetc - read one character from a tty device
 *------------------------------------------------------------------------
 */
ttygetc(devptr)
struct  devsw   *devptr;
{
        char    ps;
        char    ch;
        struct  tty     *iptr;

        disable(ps);
        iptr = &tty[devptr->dvminor];
        wait(iptr->isem);                       /* wait for a character in buff */
        ch = iptr->ibuff[iptr->itail++];
        if (iptr->itail == IBUFLEN)
                iptr->itail = 0;
        restore(ps);
        return(ch);
}
```

When called, *ttygetc* first retrieves the minor device number from the device switch table, and uses it as an index into array *tty* to locate the correct control block. It then executes *wait* on the input semaphore, *isem*, until the lower-half deposits a character in the buffer. When *wait* returns, *ttygetc* extracts the next character from the input buffer, updates the tail pointer to make it ready for subsequent extractions, and returns.

Recall that the *read* operation is used to obtain more than one character in a single operation. The tty driver routine that implements *read* is called *ttyread*; it is shown below. *Ttyread* is not conceptually more difficult than *ttygetc* — only the programming details make it appear complex.

```
/* ttyread.c - ttyread, readcopy */

#include <conf.h>
#include <kernel.h>
#include <tty.h>
#include <io.h>
#include <slu.h>

/*------------------------------------------------------------------------
 *  ttyread - read one or more characters from a tty device
 *------------------------------------------------------------------------
 */
ttyread(devptr, buff, count)
struct  devsw   *devptr;
int count;
char *buff;
{
        char ps;
        register struct tty *iptr;
        int avail, nread;

        if (count < 0)
                return(SYSERR);
        disable(ps);

        avail = scount( (iptr= &tty[devptr->dvminor])->isem );
        if ( (count = (count==0 ? avail : count)) == 0) {
                restore(ps);
                return(0);
        }
        nread = count;
        if (count <= avail)
                readcopy(buff, iptr, count);
        else {
                if (avail > 0) {
                        readcopy(buff, iptr, avail);
                        buff += avail;
                        count -= avail;
                }
                for ( ; count>0 ; count--)
                        *buff++ = ttygetc(devptr);
        }
        restore(ps);
        return(nread);
}
```

```
/*------------------------------------------------------------------------
 *  readcopy - high speed copy procedure used by ttyread
 *------------------------------------------------------------------------
 */
LOCAL readcopy(buff,iptr,count)
register char *buff;
struct tty *iptr;
int count;
{
        register char *qtail, *qend, *uend;        /* copy loop variables */

        qtail = &iptr->ibuff[iptr->itail];
        qend  = &iptr->ibuff[IBUFLEN];
        uend = buff + count;
        while ( buff < uend ) {
                *buff++ = *qtail++;
                if ( qtail >= qend )
                        qtail = iptr->ibuff;
        }
        iptr->itail = qtail-iptr->ibuff;
        sreset(iptr->isem, scount(iptr->isem)-count);
}
```

The semantics of how *read* operates on terminals illustrates how the I/O primitives can be adapted to a variety of devices. Often, it is useful to read all the characters waiting in the input queue, even though the calling program does not know
how many (if any) are waiting. To permit such an operation without introducing
additional I/O primitives, the tty driver applies an unusual interpretation to what
might otherwise be considered an illegal operation: it interprets requests to *read*
zero characters as requests to "read all characters that are waiting".

The code in *ttyread* shows how the zero length requests are changed upon entry into requests for exactly the number of character that are waiting based on the
current count of the input semaphore, *isem*. After the special case has been handled, *ttyread* proceeds to obtain characters and move them to the specified location.
If enough characters are available to satisfy the request, *ttyread* copies them directly to the user's buffer with *readcopy*, and returns. If the user requests more characters than are waiting, *ttyread* copies out those that are available, and calls *ttygetc*
repeatedly to get one additional character at a time until the request has been satisfied.

12.6 Upper-Half Tty Output Routines

The upper-half output routines are almost as simple as the upper-half input routines. *Ttyputc* waits for space in the output buffer, deposits the character in the output queue, *obuff*, and increments the head pointer, *ohead*.

```
/* ttyputc.c - ttyputc */

#include <conf.h>
#include <kernel.h>
#include <tty.h>
#include <io.h>
#include <slu.h>


/*------------------------------------------------------------------------
 *  ttyputc - write one character to a tty device
 *------------------------------------------------------------------------
 */
ttyputc(devptr, ch )
struct  devsw   *devptr;
char    ch;
{
        struct  tty     *iptr;
        char    ps;

        iptr = &tty[devptr->dvminor];
        if ( ch==NEWLINE && iptr->ocrlf )
                ttyputc(devptr,RETURN);
        wait(iptr->osem);                       /* wait for space in queue        */
        disable(ps);
        iptr->obuff[iptr->ohead++] = ch;
        if (iptr->ohead >= OBUFLEN)
                iptr->ohead = 0;
        (iptr->ioaddr)->ctstat = SLUENABLE;
        restore(ps);
        return(OK);
}
```

In addition to the processing mentioned above, *ttyputc* honors one of the tty parameters, *ocrlf*, and starts device interrupts. When *ocrlf* is nonzero, it indicates that *NEWLINE* should map to the combination *RETURN* plus *NEWLINE*. To write the extra character, *ttyputc* calls itself recursively.

Just before it returns, *ttyputc* enables transmitter interrupts in the SLU to guarantee that the lower-half will transfer the character just inserted in the buffer. If the device is currently operating, it will interrupt whenever it finishes its current operation; if it is idle, it will interrupt as soon as interrupts are enabled again (probably when *ttyputc* restores interrupts before it returns). Device output interrupts remain enabled as long as the lower-half is sending characters, so it may not be necessary to turn them on every time a character is added to the buffer. Enabling device interrupts when they are already enabled is innocuous, so blindly enabling them for every character is less expensive than testing whether it is necessary.

To understand the code in *ttyputc* that references the device to enable interrupts, it is necessary to look at the declarations of SLU device registers contained in file *slu.h*:

```
/* slu.h */

/* standard serial line unit device constants */

#define SLUENABLE       0100            /* device interrupt enable bit  */
#define SLUREADY        0200            /* device ready bit             */
#define SLUDISABLE      0000            /* device interrupt disable mask*/
#define SLUTBREAK       0001            /* transmitter break-mode bit   */
#define SLUERMASK       0170000         /* mask for error flags on input*/
#define SLUCHMASK       0377            /* mask for input character      */


/* SLU device register layout and correspondence to vendor's names      */

struct   csr     {
         int     crstat;                /* receiver control and status  (RCSR) */
         int     crbuf;                 /* receiver data buffer         (RBUF) */
         int     ctstat;                /* transmitter control & status (XCSR) */
         int     ctbuf;                 /* transmitter data buffer      (XBUF) */
};
```

Structure *csr* defines the layout of the four SLU device registers in the address space. The transmitter control and status register, *ctstat*, resides two words from the beginning of the *csr* structure. (Refer to Chapter 2 for more details.)

To move data into the SLU device register, *ttyputc* needs to determine the address assigned to the SLU when the hardware was installed. This address is given to the system configuration program which stores it in the device's *devtab* entry. During device initialization, the address is copied into the tty control block field *ioaddr*, which is where *ttyputc* obtains it. Using the device register address as a pointer, *ttyputc* writes into the *ctstat* field of the structure it "points to". Although this appears to be an assignment to the field of a structure, the address computed at run-time is that of the transmitter control and status device register, beyond the end of real memory. By assigning that register constant *SLUENABLE*, *ttyputc* turns "on" the device interrupt enable bit (bit 7), causing the device to interrupt whenever it becomes ready to transmit.

Starting interrupts is the only way upper-half output routines awaken lower-half output routines to initiate transfers. They do not call them directly, nor do they initiate character transmission. Once the interrupt bit is set on, the SLU will post an interrupt as soon as the transmitter becomes idle; the interrupt dispatcher will call the lower-half output routine; and the lower-half output routine will find the character in the buffer and transmit it.

The *tty* driver also supports multiple-byte transfers (*write*s). The appropriate driver routine is *ttywrite*. *Ttywrite* copies characters into the output buffer and starts the device, allowing the lower-half to transmit characters when the device is idle. To eliminate overhead, *ttywrite* determines how much space is available in the output buffer. If enough space remains, *ttywrite* copies the specified data into the buffer and returns. Otherwise, it fills the available space and then calls *ttyputc* to add the remaining characters one-by-one. File *ttywrite.c* contains the code.

```
/* ttywrite.c - ttywrite, writcopy */

#include <conf.h>
#include <kernel.h>
#include <tty.h>
#include <io.h>
#include <slu.h>

/*------------------------------------------------------------------------
 *  ttywrite - write one or more characters to a tty device
 *------------------------------------------------------------------------
 */
ttywrite(devptr, buff, count)
struct   devsw   *devptr;
char     *buff;
int      count;
{
        register struct tty *ttyp;
        int avail;
        char ps;

        if (count < 0)
                return(SYSERR);
        if (count == 0)
                return(OK);
        disable(ps);
        ttyp = &tty[devptr->dvminor];
        if ( (avail=scount(ttyp->osem)) >= count) {
                writcopy(buff, ttyp, count);
                (ttyp->ioaddr)->ctstat = SLUENABLE;
        } else {
                if (avail > 0) {
                        writcopy(buff, ttyp, avail);
                        buff += avail;
                        count -= avail;
                }
                for (; count>0 ; count--)
                        ttyputc(devptr, *buff++);
        }
        restore(ps);
        return(OK);
}


/*------------------------------------------------------------------------
 *  writcopy - high-speed copy from user's buffer into system buffer
```

```
*-------------------------------------------------------------------------
*/
LOCAL writcopy(buff, ttyp, count)
register char *buff;
struct  tty *ttyp;
int     count;
{
        register char   *qhead, *qend, *uend;

        qhead = &ttyp->obuff[ttyp->ohead];
        qend  = &ttyp->obuff[OBUFLEN];
        uend  = buff + count;
        while (buff < uend) {
                *qhead++ = *buff++;
                if ( qhead >= qend )
                        qhead = ttyp->obuff;
        }
        ttyp->ohead = qhead - ttyp->obuff;
        sreset(ttyp->osem, scount(ttyp->osem)-count);
}
```

12.7 Lower-Half Tty Driver Routines

The lower-half of the tty driver performs the real work of operating the device and fielding interrupts. It consists of two procedures: the input interrupt routine, *ttyiin*, and the output interrupt routine, *ttyoin*. First, we will consider the output interrupt routine, found in file *ttyoin.c*:

```
/* ttyoin.c - ttyoin */

#include <conf.h>
#include <kernel.h>
#include <tty.h>
#include <io.h>
#include <slu.h>


/*------------------------------------------------------------------------
 *  ttyoin  --  lower-half tty device driver for output interrupts
 *------------------------------------------------------------------------
 */
INTPROC ttyoin(iptr)
        register struct tty    *iptr;
{
        register struct csr      *cptr;
        int     ct;

        cptr = iptr->ioaddr;
        if (iptr->ehead != iptr->etail) {
                cptr->ctbuf = iptr->ebuff[iptr->etail++];
                if (iptr->etail >= EBUFLEN)
                        iptr->etail = 0;
                return;
        }
        if (iptr->oheld) {                              /* honor flow control  */
                cptr->ctstat = SLUDISABLE;
                return;
        }
        if ((ct=scount(iptr->osem)) < OBUFLEN) {
                cptr->ctbuf = iptr->obuff[iptr->otail++];
                if (iptr->otail >= OBUFLEN)
                        iptr->otail = 0;
                if (ct > OBMINSP)
                        signal(iptr->osem);
                else if ( ++(iptr->odsend) == OBMINSP) {
                        iptr->odsend = 0;
                        signaln(iptr->osem, OBMINSP);
                }
        } else
                cptr->ctstat = SLUDISABLE;
}
```

Remember while you read the code that the interrupt dispatcher calls *ttyoin* with interrupts disabled whenever the output device is idle. The initialization routine arranges to have the dispatcher pass *ttyoin* one argument when it is called, namely, the address of the tty control block for the interrupting device.

Processing an output interrupt is straight-forward. The driver either transmits a character from the echo buffer, a character from the output buffer, or does nothing at all. *Ttyoin* gives priority to characters waiting in the echo buffer, *ebuff*. If *ebuff* is nonempty, *ttyoin* takes a character from it and deposits the character in the device transmitter buffer register; otherwise, *ttyoin* proceeds with normal processing.

Normal output processing consists of selecting a character from the output buffer, *obuff*, and depositing it in the device transmitter buffer register. Before doing so, *ttyoin* checks the tty parameter *oheld* to see whether output has been stopped. As we will see, the input interrupt handler sets *oheld* when it detects the "stop" character, and clears *oheld* when it detects a "start" character. By convention, the stop and start characters are Control-S and Control-Q; the user types them to suspend output and restart it (e.g., to read something before it moves off the screen). When *ttyoin* finds *oheld* set, it turns off interrupts without sending more characters. Because *ttyoin* will not be called again until the device interrupts, some other routine (probably *ttyiin*) must eventually clear *oheld* and enable device interrupts.

The lower-half may find the buffer empty when an interrupt occurs if it has sent the last waiting character to the device already. This is not an error, just an indication that the device can stop interrupting until more output has been generated. So when it finds nothing to send, *ttyoin* clears the device interrupt and returns, depending on upper-half driver routines to enable interrupts again when they deposit more characters in the output buffer.

12.7.1 Watermarks And Delayed Signals

Ttyoin uses a technique called *watermark processing* to minimize overhead in the interaction between upper and lower halves of the driver. The technique is worthy of comment because it is both fundamental and popular.

To understand the motivation for watermark processing, suppose for a moment that the lower-half called *signal* each time it removed a character from the buffer. Because the processor can generate characters much faster than the SLU can transmit them, the output buffer usually remains full with a process waiting for the output semaphore. When *ttyoin* removes a character, it signals the semaphore, causing the first waiting process to deposit a character and continue processing. Because programs often write more than one character at a time, the process that was waiting has a high probability of producing another character quickly and ending up waiting for the semaphore again before the transmitter has time to transmit a single character and interrupt again. The problem is that rescheduling is relatively expensive; executing it on every character interrupt deprives other ready processes of CPU time.

To lower the rescheduling overhead, *ttyoin* runs in two modes. It continues processing normally until it finds the buffer filled beyond the high watermark at which time it switches to delayed mode and stops signalling the output semaphore. While in delayed mode, it accumulates the count of times it should have called *signal*. Finally, when the buffer has drained to the low watermark, *ttyoin* calls *signal* to make up for the signals it has skipped. Delaying when the buffer is nearly full introduces hysteresis, because it does not reschedule until some minimum number of buffer positions are available. Thus, the process that was generating output can run for a while before the buffer fills and the upper-half forces rescheduling.

In the code, constant *OBMINSP* determines the high and low watermarks. When less than *OBMINSP* space remains, *ttyoin* switches to delayed mode, and delays exactly *OBMINSP* times before switching back to normal mode.

12.7.2 Lower-Half Input Processing

Input interrupt processing is the most complex part of the tty device driver because it includes code for character echo and line editing. The input routine operates in one of three modes: *raw*, *cbreak*, and *cooked*, as specified by the *imode* field in the tty control block. Raw mode, the simplest of the three, accumulates characters in the input buffer *ibuff* without further processing. At the opposite extreme, cooked mode does character echo; honors suspend or restart output; and accumulates complete lines before giving them to the upper-half routines. Cooked mode is the usual mode in which computer systems operate — it honors special characters that permit the typist to edit input by erasing the previous character, or killing the entire line. Cbreak mode, something in between, honors all control characters except those related to line editing; like raw mode, it delivers characters to the upper-half routines without waiting for a complete line.

```
/* ttyiin.c ttyiin, erase1, eputc, echoch */


#include <conf.h>
#include <kernel.h>
#include <tty.h>
#include <io.h>
#include <slu.h>


/*------------------------------------------------------------------------
 * ttyiin  --  lower-half tty device driver for input interrupts
 *------------------------------------------------------------------------
 */
INTPROC ttyiin(iptr)
        register struct tty     *iptr;  /* pointer to tty block         */
{
        register struct csr *cptr;
```

```
register int    ch;
Bool    cerr;
int     ct;

cptr = iptr->ioaddr;
if (iptr->imode == IMRAW) {
        if (scount(iptr->isem) >= IBUFLEN){
                ch = cptr->crbuf;
                return;
        }
        if ((ch=cptr->crbuf)&SLUERMASK) /* character error     */
                iptr->ibuff[iptr->ihead++]=(ch&SLUCHMASK)|IOCHERR;
        else                            /* normal read complete */
                iptr->ibuff[iptr->ihead++] = ch & SLUCHMASK;
        if (iptr->ihead >= IBUFLEN)     /* wrap buffer pointer  */
                iptr->ihead = 0;
        signal(iptr->isem);
} else {                                /* cbreak | cooked mode */
        cerr = ((ch=cptr->crbuf)&SLUERMASK) ? IOCHERR : 0;
        ch &= SLUCHMASK;
        if ( ch == RETURN && iptr->icrlf )
                ch = NEWLINE;
        if (iptr->oflow) {
                if (ch == iptr->ostart) {
                        iptr->oheld = FALSE;
                        cptr->ctstat = SLUENABLE;
                        return;
                }
                if (ch == iptr->ostop) {
                        iptr->oheld = TRUE;
                        return;
                }
        }
        iptr->oheld = FALSE;
        if (iptr->imode == IMCBREAK) {            /* cbreak mode */
                if (scount(iptr->isem) >= IBUFLEN) {
                        eputc(iptr->ifullc,iptr,cptr);
                        return;
                }
                iptr->ibuff[iptr->ihead++] = ch | cerr;
                if (iptr->ihead >= IBUFLEN)
                        iptr->ihead = 0;
                if (iptr->iecho)
                        echoch(ch,iptr,cptr);
                if (scount(iptr->isem) < IBUFLEN)
```

```
                                        signal(iptr->isem);
                }  else  {                                         /* cooked mode  */
                        if (ch == iptr->ikillc && iptr->ikill) {
                                iptr->ihead -= iptr->icursor;
                                if (iptr->ihead < 0)
                                        iptr->ihead += IBUFLEN;
                                iptr->icursor = 0;
                                eputc(RETURN,iptr,cptr);
                                eputc(NEWLINE,iptr,cptr);
                                return;
                        }
                        if (ch == iptr->ierasec && iptr->ierase) {
                                if (iptr->icursor > 0) {
                                        iptr->icursor--;
                                        erase1(iptr,cptr);
                                }
                                return;
                        }
                        if (ch == NEWLINE || ch == RETURN) {
                                if (iptr->iecho)
                                        echoch(ch,iptr,cptr);
                                iptr->ibuff[iptr->ihead++] = ch | cerr;
                                if (iptr->ihead >= IBUFLEN)
                                        iptr->ihead = 0;
                                ct = iptr->icursor+1; /* +1 for \n or \r*/
                                iptr->icursor = 0;
                                signaln(iptr->isem,ct);
                                return;
                        }
                        ct = scount(iptr->isem);
                        ct = ct < 0 ? 0 : ct;
                        if ((ct + iptr->icursor) >= IBUFLEN-1) {
                                eputc(iptr->ifullc,iptr,cptr);
                                return;
                        }
                        if (iptr->iecho)
                                echoch(ch,iptr,cptr);
                        iptr->icursor++;
                        iptr->ibuff[iptr->ihead++] = ch | cerr;
                        if (iptr->ihead >= IBUFLEN)
                                iptr->ihead = 0;
                }
        }
}
```

```
/*------------------------------------------------------------------
 *  erase1  --  erase one character honoring erasing backspace
 *------------------------------------------------------------------
 */
LOCAL erase1(iptr,cptr)
        struct  tty     *iptr;
        struct  csr     *cptr;
{
        char    ch;

        if (--(iptr->ihead) < 0)
                iptr->ihead += IBUFLEN;
        ch = iptr->ibuff[iptr->ihead];
        if (iptr->iecho) {
                if (ch < BLANK || ch == 0177) {
                        if (iptr->evis) {
                                eputc(BACKSP,iptr,cptr);
                                if (iptr->ieback) {
                                        eputc(BLANK,iptr,cptr);
                                        eputc(BACKSP,iptr,cptr);
                                }
                        }
                        eputc(BACKSP,iptr,cptr);
                        if (iptr->ieback) {
                                eputc(BLANK,iptr,cptr);
                                eputc(BACKSP,iptr,cptr);
                        }
                } else {
                        eputc(BACKSP,iptr,cptr);
                        if (iptr->ieback) {
                                eputc(BLANK,iptr,cptr);
                                eputc(BACKSP,iptr,cptr);
                        }
                }
        } else
                cptr->ctstat = SLUENABLE;
}


/*------------------------------------------------------------------
 *  echoch  --  echo a character with visual and ocrlf options
 *------------------------------------------------------------------
 */
LOCAL echoch(ch, iptr, cptr)
        char    ch;             /* character to echo                  */
        struct  tty     *iptr;  /* pointer to I/O block for this devptr */
```

```
        struct  csr      *cptr;  /* csr address for this devptr        */
{
        if ((ch==NEWLINE||ch==RETURN)&&iptr->ecrlf) {
                eputc(RETURN,iptr,cptr);
                eputc(NEWLINE,iptr,cptr);
        } else if ((ch<BLANK||ch==0177) && iptr->evis) {
                eputc(UPARROW,iptr,cptr);
                eputc(ch+0100,iptr,cptr);          /* make it printable   */
        } else {
                eputc(ch,iptr,cptr);
        }
}


/*-------------------------------------------------------------------------
 *  eputc - put one character in the echo queue
 *-------------------------------------------------------------------------
 */
LOCAL eputc(ch,iptr,cptr)
        char    ch;
        struct  tty    *iptr;
        struct  csr      *cptr;
{
        iptr->ebuff[iptr->ehead++] = ch;
        if (iptr->ehead >= EBUFLEN)
                iptr->ehead = 0;
        cptr->ctstat = SLUENABLE;
}
```

Raw mode is the simplest to implement, and accounts for only a dozen lines of code as shown in file *ttyiin.c.* In raw mode, *ttyiin* obtains the input character from the SLU receiver, deposits it in the input buffer, and signals the input semaphore *isem.* If no space remains in the buffer, *ttyiin* extracts the character from the device and throws it away. If the receiver reports an error (as indicated by bits in *SLUER-MASK*), *ttyiin* sets the high-order bit of the character in the input buffer. (This is an unreliable, but economical way of reporting errors to the upper-level; the exercises discuss alternatives.)

12.7.3 Cooked Mode And Cbreak Mode Processing

Cooked and cbreak mode share code that obtains the input character from the SLU, maps *RETURN* to *NEWLINE*, and handles output flow control. Field *oflow* of the tty control block determines whether the driver honors flow control at all. If it does, the driver suspends output by setting *oheld* when it receives character *os-top*, and restarts output when it receives character *ostart*. Characters *ostart* and *ostop* are considered "control" characters, so the driver does not place them in the buffer for the upper-half to receive.

Cbreak mode performs character echo and reports buffer overflow. It sends *ifullc* if the input buffer *ibuff* cannot hold more characters. Normally, *ifullc* is a "bell" that causes the terminal to sound an audible alarm; the idea is that a human who is typing characters before they have been read will hear the alarm and stop typing until characters have been read. Cbreak calls local routines *eputc*, to place *ifullc* in the echo buffer, and *echoch*, to echo the character that has been received.

Cooked mode operates much like cbreak mode except that it also performs line editing. It accumulates lines in the input buffer, using variable *icursor* to keep a count of the characters on the current line. When the erase character, *ierasec*, arrives, *ttyiin* decrements *icursor* by one, backing up over the previous character. When the line kill character, *ikillc*, arrives, *ttyiin* backs over all characters on the current line by decrementing *icursor* to zero. In either case, it calls procedure *erase1* to obliterate the characters from the display. Finally, when a *NEWLINE* or *RETURN* character arrives, *ttyiin* makes the line available to the upper-half routines by signalling the input semaphore *icursor* times.

12.8 Tty Control Block Initialization

Procedure *ttyinit*, shown below, initializes the tty control block and interrupt vectors given a pointer to the *devtab* entry for the device:

```
/* ttyinit.c - ttyinit */

#include <conf.h>
#include <kernel.h>
#include <tty.h>
#include <io.h>
#include <slu.h>


/*------------------------------------------------------------------------
 *  ttyinit - initialize buffers and modes for a tty line
 *------------------------------------------------------------------------
 */
ttyinit(devptr)
        struct  devsw    *devptr;
{
        register struct tty *iptr;
        register struct csr *cptr;
        int     junk, isconsole;

        /* set up interrupt vector and interrupt dispatch table */

        iptr = &tty[devptr->dvminor];
        iosetvec(devptr->dvnum, iptr, iptr);

        devptr->dvioblk = iptr;                 /* fill tty control blk */
        isconsole = (devptr->dvnum == CONSOLE); /* make console cooked  */
        iptr->ioaddr = devptr->dvcsr;           /* copy in csr address  */
        iptr->ihead = iptr->itail = 0;          /* empty input queue    */
        iptr->isem = screate(0);                /* chars. read so far=0 */
        iptr->osem = screate(OBUFLEN);          /* buffer available=all */
        iptr->odsend = 0;                       /* sends delayed so far */
        iptr->ohead = iptr->otail = 0;          /* output queue empty   */
        iptr->ehead = iptr->etail = 0;          /* echo queue empty     */
        iptr->imode = (isconsole ? IMCOOKED : IMRAW);
        iptr->iecho = iptr->evis = isconsole;   /* echo console input   */
        iptr->ierase = iptr->ieback = isconsole;/* console honors erase */
        iptr->ierasec = BACKSP;                 /*  using ^h            */
        iptr->ecrlf = iptr->icrlf = isconsole;  /* map RETURN on input  */
        iptr->ocrlf = iptr->oflow = isconsole;
        iptr->ikill = isconsole;                /* set line kill == @   */
        iptr->ikillc = ATSIGN;
        iptr->oheld = FALSE;
        iptr->ostart = STRTCH;
        iptr->ostop = STOPCH;
        iptr->icursor = 0;
```

```
        iptr->ifullc = TFULLC;
        cptr = (struct csr *)devptr->dvcsr;
        junk = cptr->crbuf;                      /* clear receiver and    */
        cptr->crstat = SLUENABLE;                /* enable in. interrupts*/
        cptr->ctstat = SLUDISABLE;               /* disable out.   "      */
}
```

ttyinit calls *iosetvec* to set the interrupt vector and fill in the interrupt dispatch table. It then initializes the control block for raw or cooked mode, depending on whether or not the line corresponds to the console terminal. *Ttyinit* creates the input and output semaphores, and resets the buffer head and tail pointers. After parameters, buffers, and interrupt vectors have been set, it clears the receiver buffer in the hardware, enables receiver interrupts, and disables transmitter interrupts.

Ttyinit initializes the *CONSOLE* terminal line to cooked mode, assuming it connects to a terminal that a human will use. The parameters chosen work best for a CRT-like device that can backspace over characters on the display and erase them. In particular, the parameter *ieback* causes the driver to echo three characters, backspace-space-backspace, when it receives the erase character, *ierasec*. On a CRT screen this gives the effect of erasing characters as the user backs over them. If you look again at *ttyin* you will see that it carefully backs up the correct number of spaces, even if the user erases a control character that is displayed as two printable characters.

12.9 Device Driver Control

So far we have discussed the upper-half data transfer operations like *read* and *write*. Another operation, *control* provides a way for user programs to control devices and device drivers. For example, the file *ttycntl.c* contains a sample set of control functions for the tty device driver:

```
/* ttycntl.c - ttycntl */

#include <conf.h>
#include <kernel.h>
#include <tty.h>
#include <io.h>
#include <slu.h>


/*------------------------------------------------------------------------
 *  ttycntl  -  control a tty device by setting modes
 *------------------------------------------------------------------------
 */
ttycntl(devptr, func, addr)
struct  devsw   *devptr;
int func;
char *addr;
{
        register struct tty *ttyp;
        char    ch;
        char    ps;

        ttyp = &tty[devptr->dvminor];
        switch ( func ) {
        case TCSETBRK:
                ttyp->ioaddr->ctstat |= SLUTBREAK;
                break;
        case TCRSTBRK:
                ttyp->ioaddr->ctstat &= ~SLUTBREAK;
                break;
        case TCNEXTC:
                disable(ps);
                wait(ttyp->isem);
                ch = ttyp->ibuff[ttyp->itail];
                restore(ps);
                signal(ttyp->isem);
                return(ch);
        case TCMODER:
                ttyp->imode = IMRAW;
                break;
        case TCMODEC:
                ttyp->imode = IMCOOKED;
                break;
        case TCMODEK:
                ttyp->imode = IMCBREAK;
                break;
```

```
        case TCECHO:
                ttyp->iecho = TRUE;
                break;
        case TCNOECHO:
                ttyp->iecho = FALSE;
                break;
        case TCICHARS:
                return(scount(ttyp->isem));
        default:
                return(SYSERR);
        }
        return(OK);
}
```

Consider the control functions given by symbolic constants *TCSETBRK* and *TCRSTBRK*. Passing *ttycntl* function code *TCSETBRK* causes it to set the "break" bit in the SLU transmitter, placing the line in a break state. Calling *ttycntl* with function code *TCRSTBRK* turns off the break bit in the SLU transmitter and returns the line to normal processing. Setting and resetting break mode provides a good example of why control functions are necessary — they handle device control operations that data transfer routines like *ttywrite* and *ttyputc* cannot.

Some tty control functions change parameters in the tty control block. For example, function codes *TCMODER* and *TCMODEC* switch between raw and cooked modes; *TCECHO* and *TCECHONO* control character echo. Other functions like *TCICHARS* allow the user to query the driver, in this case to find how many characters are waiting in the input queue.

Observant readers may have noticed that parameter *addr* is not used by procedure *ttycntl*. It has been declared, however, because the device-independent I/O routine *control* always provides three arguments when calling *ttycntl*. Omitting the argument declaration would make the code less portable and more difficult to understand.

12.10 Summary

A device driver consists of a set of procedures that control a peripheral hardware device. The driver routines are partitioned into two halves: an upper-half that contains the routines called from user programs, and a lower-half that contains routines that handle device interrupts. The two halves communicate through a shared data structure called the device control block.

The example device driver examined in this chapter is referred to as a tty driver. It manages output to a display screen and input from a keyboard using an asynchronous serial line interface. The tty driver upper-half contains routines that implement *read*, *write*, *getc*, *putc*, and *control* operations; a user calls them indirectly with the device-independent I/O procedures. The lower-half output procedure, called whenever the transmitter interrupts, sends characters from the queue of those waiting to be sent. When an input character arrives, the lower-half input procedure deposits it in the queue of incoming characters where it can be retrieved by the upper-half. The driver also contains an initialization procedure that fills in the device control block and interrupt vectors when the system starts.

FOR FURTHER STUDY

Device drivers are seldom described in detail because they depend on the hardware and higher-levels of the operating system. A general discussion of device management can be found in Freeman [1975], Calingaert [1982], and Habermann [1976]. Watson [1970] focuses on drivers for terminal devices.

The basic style of the terminal interface used here, as well as the name "tty" have been taken from the UNIX system (Ritchie and Thompson [1974]).

EXERCISES

12.1 Predict what would happen if two processes executed *ttyread* concurrently when both requested a large number of characters. Experiment and see what happens.

12.2 Making the input and output buffers arrays simplifies programming but may introduce additional overhead at run-time. Rewrite the tty driver routines to use pointers instead of array subscripts. Can you measure a change in performance?

12.3 The lower-half tty output interrupt routine stops signalling the output semaphore when less than *OBMINSP* remains. Can the buffer ever be filled completely?

12.4 Explain how more than *OBMINSP* positions can be free in the output buffer immediately after *ttyoin* switches back to normal mode from delayed mode. What is the maximum number of free positions? The minimum?

12.5 *Ttyoin* uses "relative" high and low watermarks. Suppose it used absolute counts of characters in the buffer instead, switching to delayed mode when the buffer was full and switching back to normal mode when it contained less than *OBMINSP*. Would the change result in more or fewer reschedules?

12.6 Some systems partition asynchronous device drivers into three levels: interrupt level to do nothing but transfer characters to and from the device, upper level to transfer characters to and from the user, and a middle level to implement a *line discipline* that handles details like character echo, flow control, special processing, and out of band signals. Convert the Xinu tty driver to a 3-level scheme. What processes execute code in the middle layer?

12.7 Multi-level drivers are often needed on systems that have more than one type of asynchronous serial line device, all of which connect to terminals that should act identically. Explore the code for a system that uses heterogeneous serial line hardware. Identify the low-level and middle-level drivers.

12.8 A user observes that his process, which uses *ttywrite*, writes a different sequence of characters when run on a system with a low output baud rate than when run on a system with a high output baud rate. The problem occurs at high baud rates when other processes call *ttywrite* concurrently. Can you explain the problem?

12.9 Rewrite *ttywrite* to correct the error referred to in the previous question.

12.10 Conduct an experiment to find out whether an output interrupt ever occurs before *ttyputc* returns (it must occur after *ttyputc* restores the PS).

12.11 The tty driver turns on the high-order bit in each character to indicate that a receiver error occurred. This is unreliable when the sending device uses all 8 bits. Rewrite the tty driver to keep all 16 bits received from the SLU receiver device buffer register and return them to the upper-half routines.

12.12 *Ttycntl* handles changes of mode poorly because it does not reset the cursor or buffer pointers. Rewrite the code to improve it. What happens to partially entered lines when changing from cooked to raw mode?

12.13 Consider the following deadlock: processes are waiting for space in the output buffer; *ttyoin* is in delayed mode so although space remains it has not signalled the output semaphore; and device output interrupts are disabled so the driver will not awaken to signal the output semaphore. If the processes waiting for buffer space could execute, they would restart interrupts. If the device interrupts were enabled, they would start output and signal the semaphore. Can this occur?

12.14 When connecting two computers, it is useful to have flow control in both directions. Modify the tty driver to include "tandem" flow control.

13

System Initialization

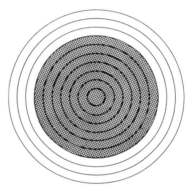

Initialization is the last step of the design process. Designers should create a system by thinking about it in the executing state, postponing the details of how to get the system started. Thinking about initialization early has the same bad effect as worrying about optimization early: it tends to impose unnecessary constraints on the design, and divert the designer's attention from important issues to trivial ones.

If initialization is the last step of design, why should this chapter take it up? We have chosen to introduce it here to show how the pieces discussed so far fit together before the reader loses sight of the fundamental system components. The most important thing to realize is that many microcomputer applications require no more than what we have at hand — a process manager to support concurrent computation, and the means to transmit information to and from running programs. In fact, several applications have been built on top of the "minimal" system we have already put together; the rest is just icing on the (layered) cake. So, it makes sense to take a look at how one might start such a system running. It also makes sense to consider initialization now because subsequent chapters describe pieces of the system that are more or less optional; this chapter will help explain why they can be included or ignored without affecting the lower-layer software. The discussion of initialization begins with a consideration of system termination.

13.1 Starting From Scratch

Everyone who has worked with a computer system knows that errant programs or malfunctions in the hardware lead to catastrophic failures popularly called *crashes*. A crash occurs when the hardware attempts an invalid operation caused because code or data in the operating system has been destroyed. Users also know that a crash means the contents of memory have been corrupted or lost, and that it will take considerable time (and perhaps a wizard) to restart the operating system. But users often do not understand or appreciate the restart mechanisms.

How can a machine, devoid of programs, spring into action and begin executing again? It cannot. Somehow a program must be deposited in memory before the machine can start. On the oldest machines, restarting was a painful process because a human operator entered the initial program through switches on the front panel. (Some microcomputer systems still use this method.) Switches were replaced by standard keyboards, and later by special terminals that could feed in restart programs from paper tape. Now, large machines have attached micro- or mini-computer systems that load the initial program from tape or disk storage attached to the micro. (The microcomputer itself often has its initial program in Read-Only Memory so it can restart without help from another machine.)

Using switches, keyboards, paper tape, or a microcomputer to load memory is a slow and tedious process; these techniques are only used to load the smallest possible startup program. Once a program has been loaded, the main CPU can execute the startup program which reads a larger program, usually from a specific location on a specific disk storage device. The CPU then branches to the larger program which reads the entire operating system into memory, and branches to its beginning. Programs in the sequence that load ever larger programs are often called *bootstraps*, and the entire process is called *rebooting* the system. The terminology comes from the phrase "pulling one's self up by one's bootstraps", a seemingly impossible task. Other names for the process are *Initial Program Load* (IPL), and *cold start*.

The work of initialization does not end when the CPU begins executing operating system code. The system must initialize devices and system data structures like the semaphore table. It must also check for, and repair, damage to the linked lists and disk pointers in the file system. Most importantly, it must undergo metamorphosis, changing itself from a single program into an operating system capable of running multiple processes concurrently.

After a brief sketch of how Xinu gets started, this chapter concentrates on explaining exactly what happens after the system begins execution. The main goal is to explain the steps necessary to transform the single, sequential program into an operating system that can support concurrent execution.

13.2 Booting Xinu

Xinu is not a stand-alone system that resides on disk. In fact, it can run on machines with no disk storage at all because it is *downloaded* from another computer called the *host*. Despite its origin, the procedure for booting Xinu is similar to the procedure for booting other systems. The details are informative, especially to readers who have used Xinu:

1. Communicating over the console terminal line, the host generates a break condition to halt the 11/2 processor.

2. The 11/2 responds in a mode called *Octal Debugging Technique* (ODT). In a sense, ODT is the modern equivalent of front-panel switches: it sends a prompt and recognizes a handful of commands to display and change memory locations and general purpose registers. (The host may even change the PC and PS because the 11/2 is not running).

3. The host loads an initial boot program in the 11/2 memory starting at location zero, and starts the 11/2 executing it. Loading with ODT is slow because it is designed for humans working at a terminal, so the initial boot program is kept as short as possible (about 30 words).

4. The initial boot program reads characters, using polled I/O, and deposits them in memory starting at the highest location and moving downward. The host sends a second boot program to the 11/2, trusting that the initial boot program is transferring it to high memory.

5. After the last byte of the second boot program has been loaded, the host again sends a break, forcing the 11/2 into ODT mode.

6. When ODT responds, the host starts the 11/2 executing the second boot program in high memory.

7. The host and the second boot program communicate, with the host sending a "packet" of bytes, and the boot program acknowledging receipt or requesting retransmission. The host continues sending until the entire memory image has been loaded (the memory image containing Xinu must be smaller than the size of real memory minus the size of the second bootstrap program).

8. The host either tells the second bootstrap to branch to the start of Xinu or to halt and await further ODT commands.

9. In most cases, the host directs the second bootstrap to branch to Xinu; when it does, the CPU begins executing Xinu at entry point *start* (location 01000 octal).

The bootstrap loader described above is independent of Xinu; it is a parameterized, general-purpose tool that can download any memory image and start at any location. The exercises suggest some ways to optimize bootstrapping if one is willing to settle for less generality.

13.3 System Startup

When Xinu first begins, the CPU starts executing at the location labelled *start* shown in file *startup.s*:

```
/* startup.s - start */

DISABLE =        340                    / PS to disable interrupts


/*---------------------------------------------------------------------
/*  Xinu system entry point -- first location beyond interrupt vectors
/*---------------------------------------------------------------------
        .globl  start
start:
        mtps    $DISABLE                / Disable interrupts
        mov     $kernstk,sp             / set up temporary stack pointer
        jsr     pc,sizmem               / _maxaddr set to max address
        mov     _maxaddr,sp             / switch stack to high memory
        reset                           / reset bus
        clr     r5                      / clear initial r5 for debugging
        clr     r4
        jmp     _nulluser               / Jump to C startup routine
```

The startup program performs the minimum number of instructions necessary to create the environment that a C program expects, and then jumps to the C procedure *nulluser*. Basically, it must disable interrupts and establish a valid stack. By convention, stack space is allocated starting at the highest location in memory; the stack will grow downward. The startup routine calls procedure *sizmem* to find the size of real memory, and then sets the stack pointer to the highest memory address. Procedure *sizmem* needs a little stack space because it saves and restores a handful of values. To guarantee that the stack pointer is valid while *sizmem* runs, the startup routine sets it to the address of *kernstk*. *Kernstk* consists of a few locations in the data area that are used by utility programs like *startup* when the usual stack cannot be used; its declaration can be found in file *panic.s*, shown in Chapter 19.

13.4 Finding The Size Of Memory

Procedure *sizmem*, shown below, determines the size of real memory on the machine. It employs no magic; the highest valid memory address is found by referencing successively smaller addresses until one does not cause an exception.

```
/* sizmem.s - sizmem */

MAXADDR =       157776                  / Maximum possible mem. address
DISABLE =       340                     / PS to disable interrupts
ENABLE  =       000                     / PS to enable interrupts
EXCPPC  =       4                       / exception vector address for
EXCPPS  =       6                       / "memory out of range" errors


/*------------------------------------------------------------------------
/*  sizmem  --  size memory, placing highest valid address in _maxaddr
/*------------------------------------------------------------------------
        .globl  sizmem
sizmem:
        mfps    -(sp)                   / save incoming PS
        mtps    $DISABLE                / disable interrupts
        mov     r0,-(sp)                / save registers used
        mov     *$EXCPPC,-(sp)          / save old contents of
        mov     *$EXCPPS,-(sp)          /  exception vector
        mov     $siztrap,*$EXCPPC       / set up vector to catch memory
        mov     $DISABLE,*$EXCPPS       / exceptions; disable interrupts
        mov     $MAXADDR,r0             / set r0 to highest possible loc
sizloop:
        mov     (r0),(r0)               / reference what r0 points to
        mov     r0,_maxaddr             / no interrupt - memory exists.
        mov     (sp)+,*$EXCPPS          / restore exception vector
        mov     (sp)+,*$EXCPPC
        mov     (sp)+,r0                / restore r0
        mtps    (sp)+                   / restore PS
        rts     pc                      / return to caller
siztrap:
        add     $4,sp                   / pop interrupted PC and PS
        sub     $2,r0                   / move to next lower address
        jbr     sizloop                 / try again
```

To detect an invalid address, *sizmem* relies on the hardware — when nonexistent memory is referenced, the resulting error causes the CPU to trap through the exception vector at location four in memory (the exception is called a *bus exception*). *Sizmem* places an address in the exception vector so each time it references an illegal address the hardware will branch to location *siztrap*. Of course, *sizmem* cannot destroy the original data in the bus exception vector, so it saves the contents upon entry by pushing them on the stack, and restores them before it returns.

In the code, the label *sizloop* marks the point at which *sizmem* tests a memory location. An exception trap occurs on each reference, causing a branch to *siztrap*, until a valid address has been reached. When a reference succeeds, *sizmem* saves the address in global variable _maxaddr_, making it available to other system routines.

13.5 Initializing System Data Structures

The assembler language startup routines in *startup.s* and *sizmem.s* do nothing more than create a valid run-time environment for a C program by setting the stack pointer to a high memory address. A single program, not an operating system, is running when the CPU jumps to the C procedure *nulluser*, and begins executing it. It is this program that initializes important data structures, devices, semaphores, and processes. The code is found in file *initialize.c*. If there is drama in the system, it lies here, where the transformation from program to system takes place.

```
/* initialize.c - nulluser, sysinit */

#include <conf.h>
#include <kernel.h>
#include <proc.h>
#include <sem.h>
#include <mem.h>
#include <tty.h>
#include <q.h>
#include <io.h>
#include <disk.h>


extern  int     main();                  /* address of user's main prog  */

/* Declarations of major kernel variables */

struct  pentry  proctab[NPROC]; /* process table                        */
int     nextproc;               /* next process slot to use in create   */
struct  sentry  semaph[NSEM];   /* semaphore table                      */
int     nextsem;                /* next semaphore slot to use in screate*/
struct  qent    q[NQENT];       /* q table (see queue.c)                */
int     nextqueue;              /* next slot in q structure to use      */
int     *maxaddr;               /* max memory address (set by sizmem)   */
#ifdef  NDEVS
struct  intmap  intmap[NDEVS];  /* interrupt dispatch table             */
#endif
struct  mblock  memlist;        /* list of free memory blocks           */
#ifdef  Ntty
struct  tty     tty[Ntty];      /* SLU buffers and mode control         */
```

```
#endif

/* active system status */

int      numproc;                    /* number of live user processes       */
int      currpid;                    /* id of currently running process     */
int      reboot = 0;                 /* non-zero after first boot           */

/* real-time clock variables and sleeping process queue pointers            */

#ifdef   RTCLOCK
int      count6;                     /* counts in 60ths of a second 6-0     */
int      defclk;                     /* non-zero, then deferring clock count */
int      clkdiff;                    /* deferred clock ticks                */
int      slnempty;                   /* FALSE if the sleep queue is empty   */
int      *sltop;                     /* address of key part of top entry in */
                                     /* the sleep queue if slnonempty==TRUE */
int      clockq;                     /* head of queue of sleeping processes */
int      preempt;                    /* preemption counter.  Current process */
                                     /* is preempted when it reaches zero;  */
                                     /* set in resched; counts in ticks     */
int      clkruns;                    /* set TRUE iff clock exists by setclkr */
#else
int      clkruns = FALSE;            /* no clock configured; be sure sleep  */
#endif                               /*   doesn't wait forever              */
int      rdyhead,rdytail;            /* head/tail of ready list (q indexes) */


/************************************************************************/
/***                          NOTE:                                 ***/
/***                                                                ***/
/***    This is where the system begins after the C environment has ***/
/***    been established.  Interrupts are initially DISABLED, and    ***/
/***    must eventually be enabled explicitly.  This routine turns   ***/
/***    itself into the null process after initialization.  Because  ***/
/***    the null process must always remain ready to run, it cannot  ***/
/***    execute code that might cause it to be suspended, wait for a  ***/
/***    semaphore, or put to sleep, or exit.  In particular, it must ***/
/***    not do I/O unless it uses kprintf for polled output.         ***/
/***                                                                ***/
/************************************************************************/


/*------------------------------------------------------------------
 * nulluser -- initialize system and become the null process (id==0)
 *------------------------------------------------------------------
```

```
*/
nulluser()                                          /* babysit CPU when no one home */
{
        char    ps;

        kprintf("\n\nXinu Version %s", VERSION);
        if (reboot++ < 1)
                kprintf("\n");
        else
                kprintf("    (reboot %d)\n", reboot);
        sysinit();                                  /* initialize all of Xinu */
        kprintf("%u real mem\n",(unsigned)maxaddr+(unsigned)sizeof(int));
        kprintf("%u avail mem\n",
                (unsigned)maxaddr-(unsigned)(&end)+(unsigned)sizeof(int));
        kprintf("clock %sabled\n\n", clkruns==1?"en":"dis");
        enable();                                   /* enable interrupts */

        /* start a process executing the user's main program */

        resume(
          create(main,INITSTK,INITPRIO,INITNAME,1,0)
        );
        while (TRUE) {                              /* run forever without actually */
                pause();                            /*  executing instructions      */
        }
}

/*------------------------------------------------------------------------
 *  sysinit  --  initialize all Xinu data structures and devices
 *------------------------------------------------------------------------
 */
LOCAL   sysinit()
{
        int     i,j;
        struct  pentry  *pptr;
        struct  sentry  *sptr;
        struct  mblock  *mptr;

        numproc = 0;                                /* initialize system variables */
        nextproc = NPROC-1;
        nextsem = NSEM-1;
        nextqueue = NPROC;                          /* q[0..NPROC-1] are processes */

        memlist.mnext = mptr =                      /* initialize free memory list */
          (struct mblock *) roundew(&end);
```

```
        mptr->mnext = (struct mblock *)NULL;
        mptr->mlen = truncew((unsigned)maxaddr-NULLSTK-(unsigned)&end);

        for (i=0 ; i<NPROC ; i++)        /* initialize process table */
                proctab[i].pstate = PRFREE;

        pptr = &proctab[NULLPROC];       /* initialize null process entry */
        pptr->pstate = PRCURR;
        for (j=0; j<7; j++)
                pptr->pname[j] = "prnull"[j];
        pptr->plimit = ( (int)maxaddr ) - NULLSTK;
        pptr->pbase = maxaddr;
        pptr->paddr = nulluser;
        pptr->pargs = 0;
        currpid = NULLPROC;

        for (i=0 ; i<NSEM ; i++) {        /* initialize semaphores */
                (sptr = &semaph[i])->sstate = SFREE;
                sptr->sqtail = 1 + (sptr->sqhead = newqueue());
        }

        rdytail = 1 + (rdyhead=newqueue());/* initialize ready list */

#ifdef  MEMMARK
        _mkinit();                        /* initialize memory marking */
#endif
#ifdef  RTCLOCK
        clkinit();                        /* initialize r.t.clock */
#endif
#ifdef  Ndsk
        dskdbp= mkpool(DBUFSIZ,NDBUFF); /* initialize disk buffers */
        dskrbp= mkpool(DREQSIZ,NDREQ);
#endif
        for ( i=0 ; i<NDEVS ; i++ )       /* initialize devices */
                init(i);
#ifdef  NNETS
        netinit();                        /* initialize networks */
#endif
        return(OK);
}
```

Nulluser itself is exceedingly simple. It calls procedure *sysinit* to do the initialization. When *sysinit* returns, it has made the running program into process 0, but interrupts remain disabled and no other processes exist. After printing a few introductory messages, *nulluser* enables interrupts, and calls *create* to start a process running the user's main program.

Because the process executing *nulluser* has become the null process, it cannot exit, sleep, wait for a semaphore, or suspend itself. If the initialization routine needed to perform any of these actions, it would have created another process to be the null process, but that seems unnecessary. Once initialization is complete and a process has been created to execute the user's program, the null process just falls into an infinite loop, giving *resched* a process to schedule when no user processes are ready to run.

The null process is slightly more sophisticated than it may seem. Conceptually, it executes an infinite loop. Actually, the loop invokes a special machine instruction (*pause*). *Pause* stops the processor but leaves interrupts enabled. After an interrupt has been processed, the CPU starts executing at the instruction immediately following the *pause*, and continues around the loop until it encounters the *pause* again. Pausing the CPU when there are no computations to perform minimizes interference between the CPU and other devices using the system bus because it prevents the CPU from fetching instructions from memory. Such minimization is important when devices like disks are performing direct transfer from the device to memory because it means the transfer will take less time.

13.6 Transforming The Program Into A Process

Procedure *sysinit* performs the tough part of system initialization. It initializes the system data structures like the semaphore table, the process table, and the free memory list. It also initializes the clock routines by calling *clkinit*. Finally, *sysinit* calls *init* once for each device in the system. Procedure *init*, in turn, calls the device initialization routines indirectly through *devtab*.

The most interesting piece of initialization code occurs about half-way through *sysinit* when it fills in the process table entry for process zero. Most of the process table fields, like the process name field, are merely dressing to make debugging easier. The real work is done by only two lines that assign the process state field *PRCURR*, and the current process id variable, *currpid*, the index of the null process. Until these two values are in place, rescheduling would be impossible. Once they have been assigned, however, the program becomes a currently running process that *resched* can identify as process 0. All that remains is to initialize the other pieces of the system so that all services are available before *nulluser* starts a process executing the user's program.

13.7 The Map Of Low Core

Located at memory address 01000 (octal), *start* lies just beyond the interrupt vectors that occupy locations 0 through 0777. It may seem wasteful to leave the unused parts of the vector area idle, but doing so makes Xinu able to run on any LSI 11 configuration, independent of the hardware devices or their vector addresses. It also makes Xinu better able to detect mismatches between the hardware vector addresses and the vector addresses that the software expects. The interrupt vectors are all initialized to a default value before the interrupt vectors for specific devices are filled in. Unexpected interrupts trap to procedure *panic* which prints a message on the console and halts the 11/2. Xinu also uses procedure *panic* to print a message whenever hardware-detected errors like illegal instruction execution cause traps through the *exception vectors*.

None of the initialization code we have seen fills in exception or interrupt vector locations other than the clock vector and the I/O vectors specified in the device switch table. How are these locations initialized? The remaining vector addresses are initialized statically, before execution begins, to an appropriate entry point in *panic*. File *lowcore.s* contains the code.

```
/* lowcore.s - (map of interupt vectors in low part of memory) */

DISABLE =        340                 / PS to disable interrupts
ENABLE  =        000                 / PS to enable interrupts


/*-----------------------------------------------------------------------
/*  absolute location 0  -- fixed interrupt and exception vectors
/*-----------------------------------------------------------------------
    .      =       000^.             / panic because something jumped
           jmp     panic0            /      to location zero
    .      =       004^.             / bus error (e.g., malfunction)
           panic;  DISABLE+0
    .      =       010^.             / illegal/reserved instruction
           panic;  DISABLE+1
    .      =       014^.             / BPT instruction and T bit
           panic;  DISABLE+2
    .      =       020^.             / Input/Output trap
           panic;  DISABLE+3
    .      =       024^.             / Power fail
           panic;  DISABLE+4
    .      =       030^.             / EMT instruction, emulator trap
           panic;  DISABLE+5
    .      =       034^.             / TRAP instruction
           panic;  DISABLE+6
    .      =       040^.
           panic;  DISABLE+7
    .      =       044^.
           panic;  DISABLE+7
    (repeated for all locations through 774)
```

The first 30 lines of *lowcore.s* contain interesting code; remaining lines are not shown because they repeat the same assignment for all device vector locations through location 0777. Location 0 is not used as an exception vector address, but programs sometimes fail by branching to it. So, location 0 contains an instruction that branches to address *panic0*; other interrupt vector locations contain the address of the *panic* routine.

Exception vectors start at location 4, and device interrupt vectors start at location 040 (octal). *Lowcore.s* initializes all these exception and interrupt vectors with the address of *panic*, another error reporting routine. To distinguish among the various types of exceptions and traps caused by unexpected interrupts, it places a code in the low-order 4 bits of the stored PS, just as the device interrupt dispatcher does.

The routines *panic0* and *panic* need not be complex. They could, for example, be as simple as a single *halt* instruction. Chapter 19 shows a set of panic routines that are quite sophisticated. The code beginning at *panic0* prints the message "Panic: branch to location 0" on the console, and halts the processor. *Panic* does more. It prints a message giving the cause of the exception or interrupt along with a message giving the contents of all registers and the top few locations of the stack. To determine the type of exception, it saves the PS immediately upon entry and retrieves it later to recover the code stored in the low-order bits.

13.8 Summary

Initialization is the last step of system design; it should be postponed to avoid changing the design simply to make it easier. We have discussed initialization here because it shows how the components designed so far can form a usable system.

FOR FURTHER STUDY

Many books comment on system startup. Both Habermann [1976] and Calingaert [1982] touch on the subject. One of the few detailed examples of system startup can be found in Madnick and Donovan [1974], which describes the IBM System/360 "cold start" procedure.

EXERCISES

13.1   Obtain the Xinu distribution tape and modify the Xinu downloader to use the LSI 11/2 ODT "load" command.

13.2   The second part of the Xinu bootstrap loader divides the file into packets and requests an acknowledgement for each packet so it will not have to retransmit the entire file if an error occurs. Instrument the code to see if retransmission ever occurs. If it does, experiment with various packet sizes to find one that minimizes the traffic (transmissions plus retransmissions).

13.3   Move the bootstrap loader code into Read-Only-Memory (ROM). How much time/space can you save?

13.4   Is the order of initialization important for the process table, semaphore table, memory free list, devices, and ready list?

13.5   Why does *sysinit* perform initialization at run-time that could be done by the loader? Speculate on why Xinu allows the loader to initialize interrupt vectors (i.e. why the values are statically bound in *lowcore*).

13.6   Rewrite *sizmem* to find the highest memory address faster, assuming memory comes in 512-byte increments. Can you improve the code even without the assumption?

13.7   Can you write *sizmem* in C?

13.8   Explain, by tracing through the procedures involved, what would go wrong if *nulluser* enabled interrupts before calling *sysinit*.

14

A Data Link Communication Driver

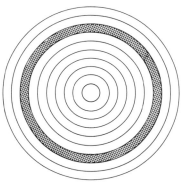

The question of how to distribute computing over many systems is an important operating system design issue. Part of the motivation for distributed computing comes from advances in technology that have lowered the cost of small systems and the cost of communication. As a result, several small computers connected with a packet-switched computer communication network can provide more cost effective computing than a single large mainframe. A small computer connected to such networks is often called a *workstation*. Usually, workstations have little or no local storage; they send and receive data over the network from machines called *servers*.

To show how network communication fits into the operating system, we will design software for a simple network that connects multiple, independent Xinu systems. This chapter describes the lowest layer of this communication software, a device driver that controls transmission of data from one machine to another over an asynchronous serial line. The next two chapters show how higher levels of the communication software build on top of it.

The level at which the designer embeds communication in an operating system determines which objects can be shared across the network. For example, if the communication layer lies below the process manager, the process manager can be designed to create processes on foreign machines. If the communication layer lies above the process manager (as it will in our system), the process manager cannot be designed to switch processes onto other machines. Similarly, a memory manager

203

can only be designed to treat the memories on individual machines as part of one large address space if it is built on top of the network communication layer.

We have chosen to place communication above the process manager but below the file system for three reasons. First, placing it above the process manager allows a clean subset of our hierarchy to run on a single machine (the single-machine subset consists of the layers described in Chapters 1 through 13). Second, adding communication to the minimal subset produces a system appropriate for a network of "diskless" workstations. Third, placing the communication layer below the file system means that files can be shared by all machines on the network. Before discussing how a file system can be added on top of the communication layer, we will look at the design of the network software in detail.

14.1 The Difficult Problem Of Communication

Inter-machine communication can be extremely tricky because the software cannot rely on operating system primitives to synchronize or coordinate processes on separate machines. Problems occur when the receiving process cannot consume data as quickly as the sending process transmits it, or when one of the systems crashes during the exchange. In essence, one machine can never quite be sure what another is doing. To further complicate matters, connections between machines are prone to interference, so the software may have to contend with errors introduced by unreliable communication channels.

Fortunately, the machine-to-machine communication problems can be divided into smaller subproblems. The software can be written in layers so that each layer solves some of the subproblems, while relying on layers beneath it to solve others. Network software layers are somewhat different than other layers in our design because data passes through all of them on its way from the network to the rest of the system. Nevertheless, the two layering schemes fit well together.

14.2 Nomenclature For The Network Software Layers

This chapter deals with the lowest layer of the network communication software, the piece that lies farthest from the user program and closest to the network hardware interface. It is called the *data link communication* (*dlc*) layer. To help explain the motivation behind *dlc*, this section summarizes each of the layers and explains their purpose.

Data Link Communication. The *dlc* layer consists of a device driver that operates the network interface device. Its purpose is to move blocks of data to or from the hardware device. The device may be a simple asynchronous serial line (as in our network), or a complicated processor. *Dlc* software provides *unreliable* transmission because it does not verify that the data arrived at its ultimate destination, or that the transmission required a reasonable amount of time. *Dlc* only sends or receives data in the simplest way. In our implementation, *dlc* receives no verification whatsoever. If no machine is waiting to receive input when *dlc* transmits a block of data, the transmitted data is lost. When asked for input *dlc* waits for data to arrive; if no input comes, *dlc* waits forever.

Frame Layer. Implemented directly above the data link driver, the *frame level layer* is responsible for reliable transmission over a single link. It must verify that the data moves correctly and quickly across the hardware link to the next machine (which is not necessarily its final destination). To guarantee correctness, the frame handling routines sequence each block of data and ask the receiving machine to acknowledge blocks in order. They may also compute and send a *checksum* value that the receiver can use to verify that the data arrived intact. To guarantee quick delivery, frame level procedures time *acknowledgements*. If the receiving machine fails to acknowledge receipt or to request retransmission in the allotted time, the frame routines assume the block was lost and resend it.

Higher layers. Data may have to pass through several machines to reach its final destination. The layers above the frame handler have responsibility for routing (choosing a path to a target machine given its address), and end-to-end acknowledgements (acknowledgements from the ultimate destination back to the sender). These higher levels also use timers, reporting that the path to the ultimate destination is unavailable if an acknowledgement is not received before the specified time runs out.

14.3 A Dlc Driver Design

Consider how to design *dlc* software that communicates between two machines over an asynchronous serial line unit. We have chosen serial hardware not because it provides the best available network, but because it is easily available, easy to understand, and illustrates most of the problems involved in data link driver design. Because the *dlc* driver runs on the same hardware as the *tty* driver described in Chapter 12, a comparison of the two may illuminate the design.

Like the *tty* driver, *dlc* will use the high-level procedures *read*, *write*, *init*, *control*, and *putc* to invoke upper-half driver routines indirectly through the device switch table. Also like the *tty* driver, *dlc* will need procedures to handle input and output interrupts.

Our *dlc* differs from the *tty* routines, however, in the way it manages the line and coordinates the upper and lower halves of the driver. To reduce the overhead of copying data to and from buffers, *dlc* does not use semaphores or buffer the data that passes between the upper and lower parts of the driver, nor does it allow multiple processes to read and write concurrently. Instead, it dedicates the driver to exactly one process at a time. While that process *writes* to a *dlc* device, concurrent output operations by other processes are prohibited (they return *SYSERR*). Similarly, while one process executes an input operation, concurrent input operations on that device fail.

These basic differences between the *tty* and *dlc* drivers arise because the high level I/O operations on a *tty* involve one character at a time, while the high-level operations on a *dlc* device always involve a block of characters. This so-called *block mode* is the natural choice for packet-style communication because data flowing from one machine to another does so in blocks.

14.3.1 Transmission Paradigm

In our design, data flowing from one machine to another does so over asynchronous lines. Although asynchronous hardware can carry data in both directions, we assume that a given *dlc* line carries blocks of data only in one direction, using the reverse direction to carry single-character responses, called *acknowledgements*. To further simplify the design we will assume that the communicating systems know the direction of data flow before communication begins. For example, in a ring of Xinu machines each machine might have two *dlc* lines as shown in Figure 14.1. Data flows *away from* the machine on one and *toward* the machine on the other. The "from" line of one machine is connected to the "to" line of another, giving rise to the term *ring-shaped network*.

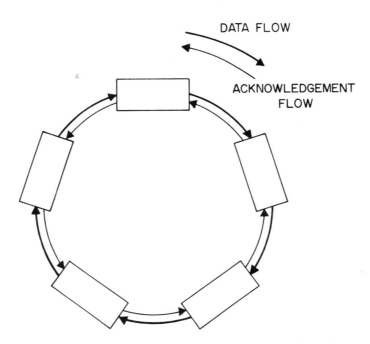

Figure 14.1 A Ring Network of Xinu Systems

Probably the most difficult part of communication system design involves the invention of protocols — agreements on how the machines send messages, test for their correctness, and assure timely delivery. To simplify *dlc* protocols, we adopt the following viewpoint:

> *The dlc transmitter initiates transfer; the dlc receiver passively waits for data to arrive.*

This design rule will be apparent throughout the discussion of both *dlc* and the frame level software. Although assuming passive reception greatly simplifies design, readers should be aware that this optimization is only useful on a one-way transmission path; an additional layer of software (or better network hardware) would be needed before *dlc* could operate over a two-way transmission path.

14.3.2 High-Level I/O Operations With Dlc Devices

A process initiates block-mode transmission by calling *write* on a *dlc* device, passing as arguments the address and size of the data block. *Write* calls the upper-half driver routine, *dlcwrite* indirectly through the device switch table. Rather than copy data into a buffer and return to the caller, *dlcwrite* obtains access to the channel, suspends the calling process, and enables device interrupts to start the lower-half. When the lower-half finishes sending the block of characters, it resumes the process that called the upper-half, allowing *dlcwrite* to return to its caller.

Transmission of characters occurs during interrupt processing, with *dlc* adding special characters to delineate block boundaries. The first interrupt causes the lower-half to transmit *DLSTART*, a special character to tell the receiver that a block follows. Successive interrupts cause the handler to transmit data characters from the user's buffer. After it has transmitted all data characters, the interrupt handler transmits *DLEOB*, a special character interpreted as "end-of-block". Once the end of block character has been sent, block transmission is complete; the lower-half resumes the process that initiated the *write*.

Block-mode input proceeds like block mode output. To initiate reading, a process calls *read*, passing as arguments the address of a buffer into which data should be read along with the maximum acceptable block size. *Read* calls *dlcread* indirectly through the device switch table, passing these arguments. *Dlcread* initiates the lower-half, and then suspends the calling process to wait for a block of data to arrive. As input interrupts occur, the lower-half routine retrieves characters, counts them, and stores them in successive locations of the user's data area. When it receives an end-of-block character or when the count of characters exceeds the buffer size, the lower-half input routine resumes the process that initiated the *read* operation.

14.3.3 Acknowledgement Traffic

Block transmission only accounts for data traveling from a *dlc* driver doing block-mode output to a *dlc* driver doing block-mode input. The hardware also carries acknowledgement traffic back from the machine receiving data blocks to the machine sending them. Upper-levels of the communication software use this "backward" data path to carry synchronization requests and acknowledgements from the block-mode receiver back to the block-mode transmitter.

How can the driver distinguish block mode transmission from the single-character transmission used for acknowledgements? One possibility is to have two *modes* of operation analogous to the *tty* modes "raw" and "cooked". Our design illustrates another solution in which the high-level primitive *putc* is used for acknowledgement traffic and the high-level primitive *write* for block-mode traffic. The detail to keep in mind is:

> *Only the machine receiving blocks uses putc to send responses; the machine sending blocks uses write.*

Because acknowledgements consist of single characters that occur infrequently, the non-blockmode parts of *dlc* are much simpler than their counterparts in the *tty* driver. In particular, the upper-half driver for *putc* does not maintain a queue of input or output characters — it merely starts the device transmitting and returns to its caller.

Like the acknowledgement output driver, the acknowledgement input driver does not buffer characters. As a consequence, the receiving process cannot read characters after they arrive. Instead, it must arrange to have the non-blockmode input driver pass incoming characters to it immediately as they arrive. This is an excellent opportunity to exploit existing machinery in our design. If we think of incoming acknowledgements as messages, we can use the message passing primitive *send* to deliver them to the correct process.

How does the driver know which process should receive incoming acknowledgements? To initiate reception, the process must correspond with the device driver, passing its process id. The high-level I/O operation *control* was designed for just such tasks; all we need do is construct an upper-half control routine with functions to initiate and stop acknowledgement reception.

14.3.4 Optimizing With Deferred Processing

In theory, transmitting characters from one machine to another is simple. In practice, however, many things go wrong: interference may distort signals, the receiving machine may not be ready when the sender transmits the block, or incoming characters may overrun the receiver. Most communication problems have been studied in detail, so much is known about how to build software that detects and recovers from transmission errors.

In Xinu, however, some errors arise from our design rather than from the communication network. The operating system keeps interrupts disabled while it switches context. Disabling interrupts poses no problem when input comes from a keyboard because humans type slowly compared to the speed at which computers consume data. But *dlc* receives data sent at high speed by another computer. If a context switch happens to occur while it is receiving a block of characters, at least some of the characters will be lost. This problem could be solved with more sophisticated network interface hardware, but it serves to illustrate how such constraints can be accommodated without compromising our clean design.

In essence, the I/O system needs to prohibit context switches for short periods of time even though interrupts remain enabled. Ideally, the system should be able to "make up for lost time" when context switching is reenabled again. Even though it is impossible to prevent context switching without changing the system behavior, the idea is to find a solution that has minimal impact without corrupting the basic design. The solution, called *deferred processing*, consists of postponing, but not ignoring, context switches. During a deferred period, general processing is suspended by deferring clock interrupts and giving the null process the highest possible priority. Only interrupt routines in the lower-halves of device drivers operate freely. When the deferral ends, normal processing resumes.

You might ask how the system can switch to and from deferred mode, especially if only the null process runs. The answer is that routines in the lower-half of the *dlc* can switch to deferred mode when they receive the start of a block, and they can switch back when they receive the end of a block. Deferring the clock consists of incrementing the global variable *defclk*, as described in Chapter 10. Deferring processing consists of setting the priority of the null process to the highest in the system, and rescheduling if necessary, to guarantee that no other processes run. When the block has been received, or reception terminated due to an error, the driver restores the null process priority, restarts the clock, and allows normal processing to continue.

14.3.5 Efficient Error Correction

What should a block-mode receiver do if it detects an error (e.g., from a character overrun)? It could ignore the error and allow a higher layer to request retransmission. Doing so could be extremely inefficient, however, especially if the error occurred near the beginning of the block. *Dlc* attempts to abort transmission and resend the block. The sequence of events leading to a retransmission proceeds as follows. When an error occurs, the block-mode receiver sends a *restart request* back to the block-mode transmitter over the acknowledgement line. It cannot know whether the block-mode transmitter will receive the restart request before it finishes transmission, so the receiver continues to read input, waiting for the block to be sent again. If the block-mode transmitter receives the restart request before it finishes transmitting the block, it aborts and starts again, sending a new start-of-block character to delineate the block. After transmitting a block, however, the *dlc* output routine returns to its caller, so the restart request may arrive too late. If the *dlc* transmitter misses the restart request, responsibility for retransmission falls to the higher levels of protocol.

14.4 The Important Details Of Dlc

Most programmers underestimate the effort needed to design and debug correct communication software. Great care must be taken with such software because failures can occur in extremely subtle ways. The most difficult failures to anticipate and understand are those that arise from the interaction of two or more systems; what makes them difficult is that the failure is not a result of a coding error, but a fundamental error in the design. One such failure, called a *deadlock*, occurs when two or more systems all end up waiting for each other to respond. Another quite similar failure, called an *intrigue*, occurs when a set of machines is busy trying to resynchronize but the resynchronization never converges. For example, if an acknowledgement is lost, two machines may end up in a situation where one keeps resending the block because it did not receive the acknowledgement, but the other keeps rejecting the block because it is expecting the next one. More insidious forms of these problems arise when several machines communicate. Many times they only surface under transient conditions (e.g., when one system stops and restarts while all others remain running).

The key to a good data link level design lies in knowing exactly which problems it must solve, and understanding in detail the interaction between a transmitter/receiver pair. To reason about their interaction, the designer must document the actions performed by dlc routines precisely. An effective way of doing so involves identifying the possible "states" of the driver and the conditions that cause transitions between states. The diagram in Figure 14.2 shows the six states of a *dlc* input driver.

Descriptions such as these are referred to as *finite state machines* or *finite state automata*. In the figure, each circle represents a state, and arcs show transitions between states. The automata is designed so that each incoming character (i.e., each interrupt) forces a transition; when the driver makes a transition from one state to another it performs an appropriate action.

Labels on the arcs leaving a state determine which transition is taken out of that state. A label of the form *c/a* indicates that if condition *c* is true, action *a* should be performed and the transition should be made. In most cases conditions merely list a character, meaning "take the transition if the character was just received." When used in place of a condition, an asterisk indicates "take this transition only if no other condition holds."

The choice of transitions leaving each state must be unambiguous. For example, consider the possible transitions taken when an interrupt occurs while the driver is in state *IWAIT*. Receiving the end-of-block character causes the driver to transfer to state *IREADY*; receiving the start-of-block character causes the driver to transfer to state *IREAD*; and receiving any other character causes the driver to stay in state *IWAIT*.

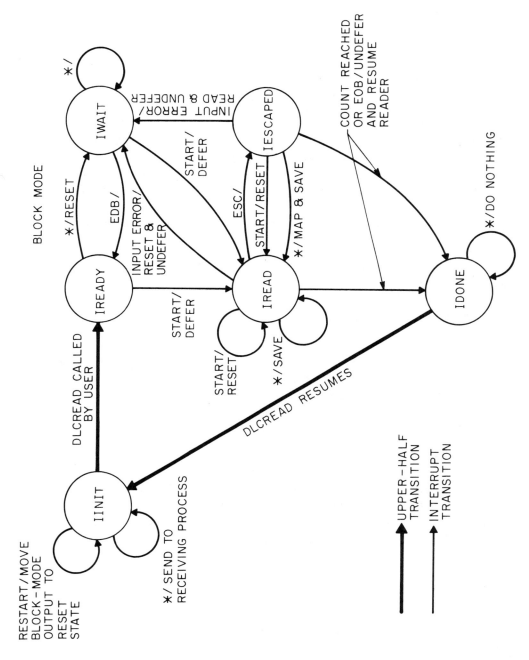

Figure 14.2 The dlc Finite State Machine for Block Reception

211

Follow through the automata for this normal sequence of operations:

1. The driver is idle in state *IINIT* when a process calls *dlcread*.
2. *Dlcread* transfers the driver to state *IREADY*, enabling it to receive characters in block mode.
3. The start-of-block character arrives, causing the driver to transfer from state *IREADY* to state *IREAD*. (The character itself is discarded, but the new state records its arrival.)
4. As data characters arrive, the driver remains in state *IREAD*, saving each one in successive positions of the data area designated by the user.
5. The end-of-block character arrives, causing the driver to transfer to state *IDONE*. When making the transition, the driver resumes the process that called *dlcread*.
6. When resumed, the process that called *dlcread* transfers the driver out of state *IDONE* back into state *IINIT*.

We will discuss the abnormal conditions under which the driver enters the remaining state (*IWAIT*) later.

14.4.1 Escaped Characters

Characters like the start-of-block character that control transmission are called *special characters*. Special characters cannot be transferred directly by *dlc*, as other characters are, because they control processing. To allow the user to transfer them, *dlc* uses an *escape* mechanism. Whenever a "special" character must be sent, the output driver converts it into a sequence of two characters: *DLESC* followed by a transliteration of the special character. In practice, all special characters have the high-order bit turned on; the transliteration has it turned off. Escape mechanisms that insert extra characters are sometimes called *character stuffing* escapes.

In the receiving machine, escaping must be reversed. Upon receipt of the special character *DLESC*, the driver changes from state *IREAD* to state *IESCAPED*, throwing away the special escape character itself. When it receives a character while in state *IESCAPED*, the driver maps the character back into its original form, stores it in the user's buffer, and transfers back from state *IESCAPED* to state *IREAD*. (The exercises discuss some of the motivation behind this particular escape mechanism).

14.5 Dlc Finite State Output Machine

Like the block-mode input driver, the operation of the *dlc* block-mode output driver can be specified with a finite state machine. Figure 14.3 shows the details.

As in the input driver, we assume that an upper-half output routine transfers the finite state machine to and from block mode. While in block-mode, a state transition occurs on each interrupt. Once *dlcwrite* places the driver in state *OREADY*, the sequence of transitions through *OSTALL*, *OWRITE*, and *ODONE* is straight-forward.

Transitions to state *ORESTART* are not expected; they occur when a restart request from the receiving machine arrives back at the transmitting machine before the block-mode driver has finished transmission. Upon detecting a restart request the input side of the driver checks its companion output driver, transferring it to state *ORESTART* if block-mode transmission is still in progress.

14.6 Deferred Input And Stalled Output

The output state *OSTALL* performs a curious function — it introduces delay between the start-of-block character and the rest of the block. Both its purpose and implementation need explanation. The original version of *dlc* did not delay block transmission. It worked correctly at low baud rates (e.g. 300 baud), but never at higher speeds (9.6K baud and higher). The reason was simple: the receiving machine defers processing upon receipt of the start-of-block character. Deferring is meant to prohibit context switches, but the act of deferring may cause a context switch if the driver reschedules to force the CPU to run the null process. In the early implementation the third character in the block would always overrun the receiving machine's input device during this switch.

To give the receiving machine sufficient time to defer processing, the sender delays between the time it sends the start-of-block character and the time it sends the data. Why not use the clock routines to delay? Interrupt handlers cannot delay by calling *sleep* because the null process may be executing them. They could delay by performing a CPU-intensive operation like counting, but doing so would prevent other interrupts from being serviced. Ironically, a *dlc* transmitter that delayed with interrupts disabled would interfere with any *dlc* drivers on the same machine that happened to be receiving characters. The solution chosen, though not the most elegant, uses the device interrupt mechanism to delay.

To delay, the driver disables and then reenables interrupts on the SLU without sending a character. The SLU hardware is designed such that toggling interrupts causes it to interrupt the CPU again, even though no character was sent. As long as the lower-half is in state *OSTALL* it counts interrupts without sending characters, moving to the normal output state after it has stalled *DLNSTALL* times. By placing the *dlc* output device farthest from the CPU, a designer can guarantee that these interrupts have lower priority than input interrupts. Thus, block-mode input interrupts on one device can be serviced while the block mode transmitter stalls on another device.

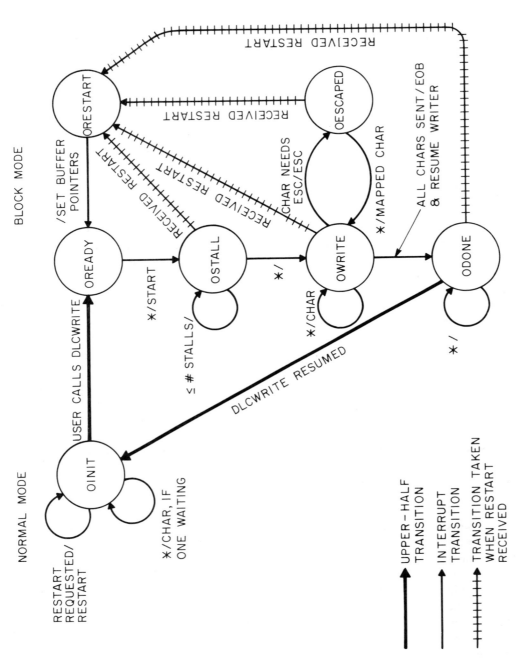

Figure 14.3 The dlc Finite State Machine for Block Output

214

14.7 Implementation Of The Dlc Driver

The chief advantage of finite state machine specifications is that they can be translated into efficient programs. In fact, the finite machine specifications discussed earlier form the basis for the *dlc* driver. Before examining the procedures that form the upper and lower halves of the driver, look at the control block through which they communicate. File *dlc.h* contains its declaration.

```
/* dlc.h */

/* driver states */

#define DLIINIT       0        /* initial input=not block mode */
#define DLIREAD       1        /* doing block input            */
#define DLIREADY      2        /* ready to begin block mode    */
#define DLIWAIT       3        /* waiting for start of block    */
#define DLIDONE       4        /* block mode read completed     */
#define DLOINIT       0        /* initial output=not block mode*/
#define DLOREADY      1        /* ready to begin block mode    */
#define DLOWRITE      2        /* doing block mode write        */
#define DLOSTALL      3        /* stall before sending frame    */
#define DLODONE       4        /* blockmode write completed     */
#define DLORESTART    5        /* reset and resend block        */

/* character stuffing constants */

#define DLESC        '\251'    /* block mode ESCape character   */
#define DLRESTART    '\257'    /* RESTART character: sent from  */
                               /*  blockmode receiver BACK TO   */
                               /*  blockmode transmitter        */
#define DLSTART      '\253'    /* START of frame character      */
#define DLEOB        '\252'    /* End Of Block (frame) char.    */
#define DLESCPED     0250      /* char escaped if it's 025x     */
#define DLESCMASK    0770      /* mask of bits to test for esc  */
#define DLESCBIT     0200      /* bit that is masked on escape  */
#define DLEBMASK     0177      /* mask for other 7 bits         */
#define DLNSTALL     3         /* number of times to stall      */

/* dlc control function codes */

#define DCSETREC      1        /* set normal mode process id    */
#define DCCLRREC      2        /* clear normal mode process id  */
```

```
struct  dlblk   {                       /* dlc control block             */
        struct  csr     *dioaddr;       /* csr address                   */
        char    distate, dostate;       /* input and output states       */
        int     dicount;                /* current number of chars read */
        int     docount;                /* number of chars left to write*/
        int     diproc;                 /* process to resume after read */
        int     doproc;                 /* process to resume after write*/
        char    *dinext;                /* next input buffer location    */
        char    *donext;                /* next output buffer location   */
        char    *distart;               /* addr of start of input buffer*/
        char    *dostart;               /* addr of start of output "     */
        int     dimax;                  /* maximum characters to read    */
        int     dotot;                  /* total characters to write     */
        Bool    diesc;                  /* true iff next input escaped   */
        Bool    doesc;                  /* true iff DLESC just sent and */
                                        /* next char should be escaped   */
        int     dostall;                /* num. of times output stalled */
        int     dpid;                   /* non-blockmode input process   */
        char    dochar;                 /* non-blockmode output char.    */
        Bool    dovalid;                /* true iff dochar valid         */
        };

#ifndef Ndlc
#define Ndlc    1
#endif

extern  struct  dlblk   dlc[];
```

Each device has two variables in the control block that record its input and output driver states. Variable *distate*, for example, takes on a numeric value corresponding to one of the six states in the input automaton. Other fields provide little more than a global data structure used to pass arguments from the upper-half to the lower-half, and pointers to record the current position in the user's data area.

14.8 Upper-Half Dlc Driver Routines

The upper-half of the input side of the driver consists of procedure *dlcread*, shown below:

```
/* dlcread.c - dlcread */

#include <conf.h>
#include <kernel.h>
#include <slu.h>
#include <proc.h>
#include <sleep.h>
#include <dlc.h>


/*------------------------------------------------------------------------
 * dlcread  --  read a block (frame) to user's buffer, unstuffing chars
 *------------------------------------------------------------------------
 */
dlcread(devptr, buf, maxchars)
struct   devsw   *devptr;
char     *buf;
int      maxchars;
{
        char     ps;
        int      nread;
        struct   dlblk   *dptr;

        disable(ps);
        if (maxchars<=0 || (dptr=devptr->dvioblk)->distate != DLIINIT) {
                restore(ps);
                return(SYSERR);
        }
        dptr->distate = DLIREADY;
        dptr->dinext = dptr->distart = buf;
        dptr->dimax = maxchars;
        dptr->dicount = 0;
        dptr->diesc = FALSE;
        dptr->diproc = currpid;
        suspend(currpid);
        nread = dptr->dicount;
        dptr->distate = DLIINIT;
        restore(ps);
        return(nread);
}
```

After recording its arguments in the control block and initializing appropriate counters, *dlcread* moves the input driver to state *DLIREADY* and suspends itself. When resumed, the upper-half assumes that interrupt routines in the lower-half have successfully read a block of data. The driver merely accesses the number of

characters read, and returns to its caller. Note that the upper-half changes the
state back to *DLIINIT* where it remains while no reception is in progress. While
the state is not *DLIINIT*, concurrent calls to *read* for that device fail. The lower-
half cannot move back to state *DLIINIT* because the upper-half has not finished
accessing the control block.

Upper-half output, procedure *dlcwrite*, is similar to upper-half input. It checks
its arguments and records them in the control block so the lower-half can access
them. It then changes the driver output state to *DLOREADY*, enables interrupts,
and suspends itself.

```
/* dlcwrite.c - dlcwrite */

#include <conf.h>
#include <kernel.h>
#include <slu.h>
#include <proc.h>
#include <sleep.h>
#include <dlc.h>


/*------------------------------------------------------------------------
 * dlcwrite  --  write a block (frame) with byte-stuffing and EOB
 *------------------------------------------------------------------------
 */
dlcwrite(devptr, buff, count)
struct  devsw   *devptr;
char    *buff;
int     count;
{
        char    ps;
        struct  dlblk   *dptr;
        struct  csr     *cptr;

        if (count < 0)
                return(SYSERR);
        else if (count == 0)
                return(OK);
        disable(ps);
        dptr = devptr->dvioblk;
        if (dptr->dostate != DLOINIT) {
                restore(ps);
                return(SYSERR);
        }
        dptr->dostate = DLOREADY;
        dptr->dostart = dptr->donext = buff;
```

```
        dptr->dotot = dptr->docount = count;
        dptr->doesc = FALSE;
        (dptr->dioaddr)->ctstat = SLUENABLE;
        dptr->doproc = currpid;
        suspend(currpid);
        dptr->dostate = DLOINIT;
        restore(ps);
        return(OK);
}
```

When resumed, the process that initiated output assumes the transmission has taken place. It changes the driver back to state *DLOINIT* and returns to its caller.

The only other upper-half transfer routine, *dlcputc*, sends acknowledgements back to the block-mode transmitter. Its implementation is straightforward, *dlcputc* records the character to be sent and enables interrupts.

```
/* dlcputc.c - dlcputc */

#include <conf.h>
#include <kernel.h>
#include <slu.h>
#include <proc.h>
#include <sleep.h>
#include <dlc.h>


/*------------------------------------------------------------------------
 *  dlcputc  --  write non-blockmode character (used for acks & resets)
 *------------------------------------------------------------------------
 */
dlcputc(devptr, ch)
struct  devsw   *devptr;
char    ch;
{
        char    ps;
        struct  dlblk   *dptr;
        struct  csr     *cptr;

        disable(ps);
        if ( (dptr = devptr->dvioblk)->dostate != DLOINIT) {
                restore(ps);
                return(SYSERR);
        }
        dptr->dochar = ch;
        dptr->dovalid = TRUE;
        (dptr->dioaddr)->ctstat = SLUENABLE;
        restore(ps);
        return(OK);
}
```

14.9 Lower-Half Dlc Driver Routines

14.9.1 The Lower-Half Of The Output Driver

File *dlcoin.c* contains the output interrupt handler. Code for the driver comes directly from the machine diagram in Figure 14.3. The reader should compare each state of the machine to the *case* in the code corresponding to that state. Notice that state *OESCAPED* has been combined with state *OWRITE* because they share so many transitions. Such combination is merely an optimization; it would not be worthwhile to combine states if the code became unreadable.

```
/* dlcoin.c - dlcoin */

#include <conf.h>
#include <kernel.h>
#include <slu.h>
#include <proc.h>
#include <sleep.h>
#include <dlc.h>

/*------------------------------------------------------------------
 *  dlcoin  --  dlc output interrupt handler
 *------------------------------------------------------------------
 */
INTPROC dlcoin(dptr)
register struct dlblk    *dptr;
{
        struct  csr      *cptr;
        char    ch;

        cptr = dptr->dioaddr;

        switch (dptr->dostate) {

        case DLOINIT:                                   /* non-blockmode output */
                if (dptr->dovalid) {
                        cptr->ctbuf = dptr->dochar;
                        dptr->dovalid = FALSE;
                } else
                        cptr->ctstat = SLUDISABLE;
                return;

        case DLOREADY:                                  /* ready to write block */
                cptr->ctbuf = DLSTART;
                dptr->dostate = DLOSTALL;
                dptr->dostall = DLNSTALL;
                dptr->doesc = FALSE;
                return;

        case DLOSTALL:                                  /* stalling a while    */
                cptr->ctstat = SLUDISABLE;
                cptr->ctstat = SLUENABLE;
                if (dptr->dostall-- > 0)
                        return;
                dptr->dostate = DLOWRITE;
                return;
```

```
        case DLOWRITE:                              /* writing a block      */
                    if (dptr->docount-- <= 0) {
                            dptr->dostate = DLODONE;
                            cptr->ctbuf = DLEOB;
                            return;
                    }
                    if (((ch= *dptr->donext++)&DLESCMASK)==DLESCPED){
                            if (dptr->doesc) {
                                    dptr->doesc = FALSE;
                                    cptr->ctbuf = ch & DLEBMASK;
                            } else {
                                    dptr->donext--;
                                    dptr->docount++;
                                    dptr->doesc = TRUE;
                                    cptr->ctbuf = DLESC;
                            }
                            return;
                    }
                    cptr->ctbuf = ch;
                    return;

        case DLODONE:                               /* finished writing     */
                    if (dptr->docount < 0) {
                            ready(dptr->doproc, RESCHYES);
                            dptr->docount = 0;
                    }
                    cptr->ctstat = SLUDISABLE;
                    return;

        case DLORESTART:                              /* restart transmission */
                    dptr->dostate = DLOREADY;
                    dptr->donext = dptr->dostart;
                    dptr->docount = dptr->dotot;
                    cptr->ctstat = SLUDISABLE;
                    cptr->ctstat = SLUENABLE;
                    return;

        default:
                    panic("impossible dlc output state");
        }
}
```

14.9.2 The Lower-Half Of The Input Driver

Interrupt procedure *dlciin* processes input interrupts. Again, it has been created directly from the finite state machine description. States *IESCAPED* and
IREAD have been merged to reduce the amount of code. *Dlciin* calls procedure
sendf, the modified form of *send* described in Exercise 7.9. *Sendf* forces delivery of
the latest message, discarding any messages that happen to be waiting.

```
/* dlciin.c - dlciin */

#include <conf.h>
#include <kernel.h>
#include <slu.h>
#include <proc.h>
#include <sleep.h>
#include <dlc.h>


/*------------------------------------------------------------------------
 *  dlciin  --  dlc input interrupt handler (block + normal modes)
 *------------------------------------------------------------------------
 */
INTPROC dlciin(dptr)
register struct dlblk  *dptr;
{
        struct  csr *cptr;
        register char   ch;
        int     icode;

        ch = ( (icode = ((cptr=dptr->dioaddr)->crbuf)) ) & SLUCHMASK;

        switch (dptr->distate) {

        case DLIINIT:                                   /* non-blockmode read */
                        if (ch == DLRESTART && dptr->dostate!=DLOINIT) {
                                dptr->dostate = DLORESTART;
                                return;
                        }
                        if (dptr->dpid)
                                sendf(dptr->dpid, (ch&0377) );
                        return;

        case DLIREADY:                                  /* ready for block */
                        if (ch == DLSTART) {
                                dptr->distate = DLIREAD;
                                defclk++;
```

```
                            if (currpid == NULLPROC)
                                    proctab[NULLPROC].pprio = MAXINT;
                            else {
                                    insert(dequeue(NULLPROC),rdyhead,
                                    proctab[NULLPROC].pprio=MAXINT);
                                    resched();
                            }
                    } else {                    /* unexpected character */
                            dptr->dochar = DLRESTART;
                            dptr->dovalid = TRUE;
                            cptr->ctstat = SLUENABLE;
                            dptr->distate = DLIWAIT;
                    }
                    return;

        case DLIREAD:                           /* doing blockmode read */
                    if (icode & SLUERMASK) {          /* input error  */
                            dptr->distate = DLIWAIT;
                            dptr->dicount = 0;
                            dptr->dinext = dptr->distart;
                            dptr->diesc = FALSE;
                            dptr->dochar = DLRESTART;
                            dptr->dovalid = TRUE;
                            cptr->ctstat = SLUENABLE;
                            proctab[NULLPROC].pprio = 0;
                            strtclk();
                            return;
                    }
                    if (ch == DLEOB) {        /* end of block */
                            dptr->distate = DLIDONE;
                            ready(dptr->diproc, RESCHNO);
                            proctab[NULLPROC].pprio = 0;
                            strtclk();
                            resched();
                            return;
                    }
                    if (ch == DLSTART) {              /* restart read */
                            dptr->diesc = FALSE;
                            dptr->dinext = dptr->distart;
                            dptr->dicount = 0;
                            return;
                    }
                    if (dptr->diesc) {               /* map escapes  */
                            dptr->diesc = FALSE;
                            if ( ch & DLESCBIT) {   /* impossible   */
                                    dptr->distate = DLIWAIT;
```

```
                                        dptr->dicount = 0;
                                        dptr->dinext = dptr->distart;
                                        dptr->dochar = DLRESTART;
                                        dptr->dovalid = TRUE;
                                        cptr->ctstat = SLUENABLE;
                                        proctab[NULLPROC].pprio = 0;
                                        strtclk();
                                        return;
                                } else
                                        ch |= DLESCBIT;
                        } else if (ch == DLESC) {              /* escape next */
                                dptr->diesc = TRUE;
                                return;
                        }
                        *dptr->dinext++ = ch;
                        if ( ++(dptr->dicount) >= dptr->dimax ) {
                                dptr->distate = DLIDONE;
                                ready(dptr->diproc, RESCHNO);
                                proctab[NULLPROC].pprio = 0;
                                strtclk();
                                resched();
                        }
                        return;

        case DLIWAIT:

                        if (ch == DLSTART) {
                                dptr->distate = DLIREAD;
                                defclk++;
                                if (currpid == NULLPROC)
                                        proctab[NULLPROC].pprio = MAXINT;
                                else {
                                        insert(dequeue(NULLPROC),rdyhead,
                                        proctab[NULLPROC].pprio=MAXINT);
                                        resched();
                                }
                        } else if (ch == DLEOB)
                                dptr->distate = DLIREADY;
                        return;

        case DLIDONE:
                        return;

        default:

                        panic("impossible dlc input state");
        }
}
```

14.10 Dlc Driver Initialization

The main pieces of the driver have been designed; now we can consider initialization. There is little to do at system startup, except to fill in entries in the control
block and initialize the device. As a practical matter, it helps with debugging if
driver initialization routines fill in the entire control block even though it may not
be necessary.

Procedure *dlcinit* contains initialization code for *dlc* devices. It initializes devices so they can be used for either block-mode input or block-mode output, allowing
the upper-level software to decide how they will be used. *Dlcinit* starts the input
and output drivers in states *DLIINIT* and *DLOINIT*, with output interrupts disabled and input interrupts enabled. Thus, they are ready for either *dlcread* or
dlcwrite to use.

```
/* dlcinit.c - dlcinit */

#include <conf.h>
#include <kernel.h>
#include <slu.h>
#include <proc.h>
#include <sleep.h>
#include <dlc.h>

struct  dlblk   dlc[Ndlc];

/*------------------------------------------------------------------------
 *  dlcinit  --  initialize dlc control block and device
 *------------------------------------------------------------------------
 */
dlcinit(devptr)
struct  devsw   *devptr;
{
        struct  dlblk   *dptr;
        struct  csr     *cptr;
        char    ps;
        int     junk;

        disable(ps);
        dptr = &dlc[devptr->dvminor];
        devptr->dvioblk = dptr;
        iosetvec(devptr->dvnum, dptr, dptr);
        dptr->dioaddr = devptr->dvcsr;
```

```
        dptr->dostall = 0;
        dptr->distate = DLIINIT;
        dptr->dostate = DLOINIT;
        dptr->donext = dptr->dinext = NULL;
        dptr->doesc = dptr->diesc = 0;
        dptr->dpid = 0;
        dptr->dovalid = FALSE;
        dptr->diproc = dptr->doproc = -1;
        dptr->dotot = dptr->docount = 0;
        dptr->dimax = dptr->dicount = 0;
        cptr = dptr->dioaddr;           /* get device CSR address        */
        junk = cptr->crbuf;             /* clear device receiver and     */
        cptr->crstat = SLUENABLE;       /*   enable read interrupts       */
        cptr->ctstat = SLUDISABLE;      /* disable write interrupts      */
}
```

14.11 Control Over Non-Blockmode Reception

The network software passes acknowledgements in the opposite direction than it sends blocks of characters. The "non-blockmode" portion of the *dlc* handles transmission and reception of acknowledgements, using the message passing primitive *send* to deliver them to a designated process. Because *send* can only deliver messages to one process at a time, only one process can receive each acknowledgement. Procedure *dlcntl* controls which process, if any, will receive the acknowledgement by recording the process id in field *dpid* of the *dlc* control block. Its code is found in file *dlcntl.c*.

```
/* dlccntl.c - dlccntl */

#include <conf.h>
#include <kernel.h>
#include <slu.h>
#include <proc.h>
#include <sleep.h>
#include <dlc.h>


/*------------------------------------------------------------------
 *  dlccntl  --  perform control operations on dlc devices and driver
 *------------------------------------------------------------------
 */
dlccntl(devptr, opcode, parm1)
struct  devsw   *devptr;
int     opcode;
int     parm1;
{
        struct dlblk   *dptr;

        dptr = devptr->dvioblk;
        if (opcode == DCSETREC) {
                dptr->dpid = parm1;
                return(OK);
        } else if (opcode == DCCLRREC) {
                dptr->dpid = 0;
                return(OK);
        } else
                return(SYSERR);
}
```

14.12 Summary

Network communication is an important part of the operating system; its place in the design determines which objects the system can share globally across the network and which are local. Machine-to-machine communication is an especially tricky problem because it requires the designer to accommodate unreliable communication systems and synchronization between independent systems. Subtle design errors may allow deadlocks and intrigues to surface under unusual conditions in systems that normally function well.

The lowest level of communication software is called the *data link communication* level. It consists of a device driver that transmits blocks of characters from one machine to the next. Specified as a finite state machine, the simple *dlc* mechanism described here transfers blocks of data across asynchronous serial lines.

Another piece of the *dlc* driver transfers single-character acknowledgements "backward" from the machine receiving data blocks to the machine sending them. The message passing facility from Chapter 7 is used to deliver acknowledgements to the destination process. The protocol between transmitter and receiver has been simplified by making the receiver passive. Once called, the passive receiver waits until a block arrives; it depends on the sending machine to timeout acknowledgements and retransmit the data if no acknowledgement is received.

FOR FURTHER STUDY

Computer communication networks have been studied extensively outside the domain of operating systems. Books by Tanenbaum [1981] and Ahuja [1982] survey the field, describing the basic hardware as well as the purpose of such systems. McNamara [1977] covers the electrical and logical conventions used to transfer bits over various transmission media.

General-purpose protocols like IBM's SNA (Gray [1977], SNA [1975]), Xerox's NS (Xerox [1981]), and DARPA's NCP (Cerf and Kahn [1974]) and newer TCP/IP (Postel [1981]), have been developed to allow arbitrary machines and networks to be interconnected. Public carriers support other computer communication protocols (e.g., CCITT's X.25 [1978]).

EXERCISES

14.1   Design a protocol that two machines can use to verify that they are both operating. Document the protocol with finite state machine diagrams that indicate how characters are to be passed back and forth. Can you prove that neither machine assumes the other is operational unless it is? Can you prove that transmission failures will not produce deadlocks or intrigues?

14.2   The block-mode transmitter sends two characters whenever it finds one of the reserved control characters in the user's data. Why does it change the second character before sending it?

14.3   Make a list of all characters that must be escaped. Does *dlc* escape any others?

14.4   Why are "escape" states combined with normal ones in the code?

14.5   Can *dlcread* return without receiving an end-of-block character? a start-of-block character?

14.6   Consider transitions through a pair of *dlc* input and output automata. Assume they both start in their initial states, and find a sequence of events in which the output automaton reaches state *ODONE* but the input automaton does not (you may assume transmission errors).

14.7   Construct a sequence of events in which the lower-half resumes *dlcwrite*, but *dlcwrite* finds the driver in a state other than *DLODONE*.

14.8   Both *dlcread* and *dlcwrite* malfunction if another process accidentally *resumes* them during a block-mode transfer. Rewrite the code to repair the problem (be careful of the problem described in the previous exercise).

14.9   Is *dlc* more complex than it needs to be? If you have never designed a protocol, try to build a simpler one.

14.10   Much of the code in *dlc* could be eliminated if the network interface device transmitted entire blocks of data to or from memory without interrupting the CPU for each character. Redesign *dlc* for such an environment. How much smaller is the resulting code?

14.11   Without reading ahead, design the next level of communication software for a set of workstations connected in a ring. Each machine on the net has two connections — one for incoming blocks, the other for outgoing blocks. Assume that each block transmitted contains an integer "machine address." If the address matches the machine's id, enqueue the block for processing locally; otherwise, add it to the list of blocks waiting to be sent out. To make the system reliable, either the sending machine, receiving machine, or both must time transmission and restart it if something goes wrong.

14.12   Generalize *dlc* to allow two-way communication. Notice that both sides must now be equally active in that they must both be allowed to initiate transfer.

14.13   Under what circumstances can *dlc* deliver the same block twice?

15

High-Level Memory Management and Message Passing

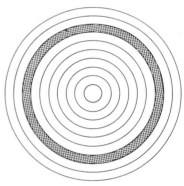

This chapter describes the design of high-level memory management and message passing facilities. The motivation comes from the network software that uses these facilities to allocate fixed-size buffers, pass them among processes freely, and release them. To prevent the network software from exhausting memory resources, the high level memory manager must be able to limit the amount of memory used for a given function. It must coordinate processes by blocking them until their requests can be satisfied. To allow the network software to pass data among the layers efficiently, the high-level message passing facility must provide buffered message exchange through named rendevous points.

Instead of building these primitives directly into the network software, we have chosen to design general-purpose routines that can be used in a variety of ways. One advantage of designing general-purpose primitives is that they become available to user programs. Another advantage is that they can be implemented and tested independent of the specific routines that use them. In the case of the primitives described in this chapter, testing can be carried out even before the network software has been designed. While we have said little about testing up to this point, it should be obvious that systems as complicated as Xinu must be built and tested in small pieces; designs that attempt to integrate functions into large subsystems are doomed to failure.

15.1 Self-Initializing Modules

Lower layers of the operating system, like the process manager, must be present whenever a program runs. Higher layers like the network software need not be included, however, unless a program uses them. In the LSI 11 implementation of Xinu, optional software is stored in libraries, from which the cross-loader selects the routines that are referenced when it constructs a memory image. It is convenient to think of a set of related library routines as a *module* that implements operations on some abstract data object. For example, one can imagine a set of procedures *push*, *pop*, and *makestack* that push an element onto a stack, pop an element from a stack, and create a stack.

In C, procedures that form a module can be combined into a single source file along with the static data upon which they operate. When a program references one of the procedures in the file, the entire file is loaded. (Alternatively, the procedures can reside in separate files and use shared external data structures.)

This chapter describes two modules — one that implements a mechanism for data exchange (called *ports*), and one that implements a mechanism for frame storage allocation (called *buffer pools*). Before describing the routines themselves, we address the issue of how to initialize the static data associated with a module.

15.1.1 Specifying Initialization

The designer could arrange for the operating system to initialize each module when it first starts. This solution has three drawbacks. First, if the system initialization procedure explicitly references an object the loader would include that object (and all other objects defined in the same file) in the memory image. Thus, every procedure and variable from every library module would be present in memory — something that is clearly undesirable on a small machine. Second, adding a module to a library would involve changing the operating system initialization procedure. Third, users could not have their modules initialized automatically because they could not change the system initialization routine.

Forcing the programmers to initialize modules explicitly is equally undesirable, because they would have to know which primitives go with each module, and remember to change the way their programs performed initialization when they add or remove calls to library procedures. Ideally, the routines that comprise a module should be *self-initializing*; they should perform initialization automatically (and exactly once) as they are called.

15.1.2 Automatic Initialization

In most environments, self-initialization is not difficult. Modules include a Boolean variable that is set to *false* when the program is loaded. Each procedure in the module checks the module's Boolean variable when called, performing initialization if it is zero. The initialization code assigns the Boolean variable the value *true* so subsequent uses of the module can proceed without calling the initialization procedure.

Loader-defined Boolean variables do not suffice for self-initialization in a Xinu-like environment because the system can be restarted without being reloaded. There are two ways to overcome the problem: the system could be changed to set all static memory to zero at startup, or a new operating system primitive could be added that tests whether something has been initialized independent of the values in static memory. We have chosen the latter option; the next section describes such a primitive.

15.2 Memory Marking

This section introduces a technique called *memory marking* that enables modules to correctly initialize themselves. Memory marking does not perform initialization, it is merely a service supplied by the system that reliably determines whether a memory location has been "marked" since the system started. The essential idea is this: the system maintains a set S of "marked" memory locations. When the system starts running, it sets S to empty. As execution proceeds, processes call system procedure *mark(k)*, to add memory location k to set S; they call Boolean function *unmarked(k)*, to test whether the location of integer k is currently in set S.

The implementation of memory marking is surprising because the operations are extremely efficient. Initializing S to empty at startup requires one instruction. Testing whether a location has been marked, or marking a location each require only a few instructions; their execution cost does not depend on the number of locations that have been marked. The trick required to achieve this efficiency comes from a clever use of pointers — the "marked" location contains an index that lets the system verify whether it is in S without searching the entire set.

15.3 Implementation Of Memory Marking

The memory marking routines maintain a set of addresses of "marked" locations in array *marks*. Each marked location contains the integer index in *marks* corresponding to that location's mark. To test whether the location of integer L has been marked, *unmarked* checks whether *marks[L]* contains the address of L. The code for predicate *unmarked* is found in file *mark.h*.

```
/* mark.h - unmarked */


#ifndef MAXMARK
#define MAXMARK 20              /* maximum number of marked locations   */
#endif
#ifdef   MEMMARK
extern   int      *(marks[]);
extern   int      nmarks;
extern   int      mkmutex;
typedef int       MARKER[1];    /* by declaring it to be an array, the  */
                                /* name provides an address so forgotten*/
                                /* &'s don't become a problem           */


#define unmarked(L)             (L[0]<0 || L[0]>=nmarks || marks[L[0]]!=L)
#endif
```

Marking requires the system to add a new element to the *marks* array and to place the appropriate index in the "marked" location. The code is found in file *mark.c.*

```
/* mark.c - _mkinit, mark */

#include <conf.h>
#include <kernel.h>
#include <mark.h>


#ifdef   MEMMARK
int      *marks[MAXMARK];
int      nmarks;
int      mkmutex;

/*------------------------------------------------------------------------
 *  _mkinit -- called once at system startup
 *------------------------------------------------------------------------
 */
_mkinit()
{
        mkmutex = screate(1);
        nmarks = 0;
}
```

```
/*------------------------------------------------------------------
 * mark  --  mark a location if it hasn't been marked
 *------------------------------------------------------------------
 */
mark(loc)
int *loc;
{
        if ( *loc>=0 && *loc<nmarks && marks[*loc]==loc )
                return(0);
        if (nmarks>=MAXMARK)
                return(SYSERR);
        wait(mkmutex);
        marks[ (*loc) = nmarks++] = loc;
        signal(mkmutex);
        return(OK);
}
#endif
```

The buffer pool routines, found in the next section, show how modules use these memory marking primitives for self-initialization.

15.4 Partitioned Space Allocation

Routines *getmem* and *freemem* that were described in Chapter 8 constitute the basic memory manager. They place no limit on the amount that a given process can allocate, nor do they attempt to divide free space "fairly" — they merely honor requests on a first-come-first-served basis until no free memory remains. Once free memory has been exhausted, these routines reject further requests without waiting for memory to be released. Such global allocation strategies are relatively efficient, but because they force all processes to contend for the same memory they permit deprivation, a situation in which a process or processes cannot obtain memory because it has been consumed.

Global memory allocation schemes do not work well for communication software because the time required to process messages is often longer than the time required to read them. Exhaustive allocation can lead to disaster. Consider, for example, the situation where a receiver process repeatedly obtains a buffer, reads data into it from the network, and then enqueues the buffer for processing. As incoming messages pile up waiting to be processed, the process reading input keeps allocating space for new messages from the free memory. In the worst case, it will use up all the available space. One might expect that the process consuming messages would eventually release space, allowing the reader to continue, but this may not happen. The process that consumes incoming messages must also allocate space to perform such tasks as reassembling long messages or forwarding copies of messages to other machines. If no space remains, the system can deadlock with the consumer process waiting for space so it can process existing messages, and the reader process waiting for space before it can read more messages.

To prevent deadlocks in the communication software, higher-level memory management must be designed to partition free memory, and control the allocation and deallocation independently within each partition. By limiting the amount of memory that processes use for a particular function the system can guarantee that excessive requests will not lead to global deprivation. Furthermore, the system can assume that memory allocated for a particular function will always be returned, so it can arrange to suspend processes until their memory request can be satisfied, eliminating the overhead introduced by busy waiting. The mechanism we have chosen to handle these tasks is a *buffer pool* manager.

15.5 Buffer Pools

Each buffer pool consists of a fixed number of memory blocks, where all blocks in a given pool are the same length. The term *buffer* was chosen to reflect the intended use in I/O routines and communication software.

The memory space for a particular set of buffers is allocated all at once, when the pool is created. Each pool is identified by an integer *pool identifier* though which processes refer to it. After initialization, a process can request a buffer from a pool (by giving its identifier) or release a buffer back to a pool. There is no need to specify a buffer length in these requests because the size of memory blocks allocated to the pool is fixed when the pool is created.

The buffer pool mechanism differs from the low-level memory manager in another way: processes that request buffers will block until one is available. As usual, semaphores are used to control the resource. A process requesting a buffer from a pool *waits* on that pool's semaphore; the call returns immediately if buffers remain in the pool. If no buffers remain, the process blocks. Eventually, when another process returns a buffer to a pool, it signals the pool's semaphore, allowing a blocked process to obtain the buffer and resume execution.

The pool data structures consist of a table that contains a semaphore and a linked list of buffers for each pool. Pertinent declarations can be found in file bufpool.h:

```
/* bufpool.h */

#ifndef NBPOOLS
#define NBPOOLS 5                    /* Maximum number of pools      */
#endif
#ifndef BPMAXB
#define BPMAXB  512                  /* Maximum buffer length        */
#endif
```

```
#define BPMINB   2                    /* Minimum buffer length          */
#ifndef BPMAXN
#define BPMAXN   100                  /* Maximum buffers in any pool */
#endif
struct  bpool   {                     /* Description of a single pool */
        int     bpsize;               /* size of buffers in this pool */
        char    *bpnext;              /* pointer to next free buffer  */
        int     bpsem                 /* semaphore that counts buffers*/
        };                            /*  currently in THIS pool      */

extern  struct  bpool bptab[];        /* Buffer pool table            */
extern  int     nbpools;              /* current number of pools      */
#ifdef  MEMMARK
extern  MARKER  bpmark;
#endif
```

Structure *bpool* defines the contents of entries in the buffer pool table, *bptab*. The buffers for a given pool are linked into a list, with head *bpnext*. Semaphore *bpsem* controls allocation from the pool, and integer *bpsize* gives the length of buffers in the pool.

Processes call procedure *getbuf* to obtain a buffer, passing the pool identifier as an argument. *Getbuf* works as expected, waiting until a buffer is available and then unlinking it from the list:

```
/* getbuf.c - getbuf */

#include <conf.h>
#include <kernel.h>
#include <mark.h>
#include <bufpool.h>

/*------------------------------------------------------------------------
 *  getbuf  --  get a buffer from a preestablished buffer pool
 *------------------------------------------------------------------------
 */
SYSCALL *getbuf(poolid)
int poolid;
{
        char    ps;
        int     *buf;

#ifdef  MEMMARK
        if ( unmarked(bpmark) )
                return((int *)SYSERR);
#endif
        if (poolid<0 || poolid>=nbpools)
                return((int *)SYSERR);
        wait(bptab[poolid].bpsem);
        disable(ps);
        buf = bptab[poolid].bpnext;
        bptab[poolid].bpnext = *buf;
        restore(ps);
        *buf++ = poolid;
        return(buf);
}
```

The conditional code at the beginning of *getbuf* contains an if statement that determines whether the buffer pool routines have been initialized, and returns *SYSERR* if they have not. The statement is valid only if memory marking is available on the system, so it has been made into conditional code that will be compiled only if constant *MEMMARK* is defined.

Observant readers may have noticed that *getbuf* does not return the address of the buffer to its caller. Instead, it stores the pool id in the first integer location, and returns the address just beyond the id. A user need not worry that the first location in the buffer holds the pool id — the initialization routine actually allocates extra space in each buffer to hold the id when it creates the pool. As we will see, the procedure *freebuf* uses this pool id when it returns the buffer to free storage, making it unnecessary to specify the pool id when returning buffers. The technique of identifying a buffer automatically turns out to be useful when buffers are returned by processes other than the one that allocated them.

15.6 Returning Buffers To The Buffer Pool

Procedure *freebuf* returns a buffer to the correct pool given its address. The code is located in file freebuf.c:

```
/* freebuf.c - freebuf */

#include <conf.h>
#include <kernel.h>
#include <mark.h>
#include <bufpool.h>


/*------------------------------------------------------------------
 * freebuf  --  free a buffer that was allocated from a pool by getbuf
 *------------------------------------------------------------------
 */
SYSCALL freebuf(buf)
int *buf;
{
        char    ps;
        int     poolid;

#ifdef  MEMMARK
        if ( unmarked(bpmark) )
                return(SYSERR);
#endif
        poolid = *(--buf);
        if (poolid<0 || poolid>=nbpools)
                return(SYSERR);
        disable(ps);
        *buf = bptab[poolid].bpnext;
        bptab[poolid].bpnext = buf;
        restore(ps);
        signal(bptab[poolid].bpsem);
        return(OK);
}
```

Freebuf obtains the pool id that *getbuf* stored in the block when it was allocated, links the buffer back into the appropriate pool, and signals the pool semaphore *bpsem*, allowing a process to use the buffer.

15.7 Creating A Buffer Pool

Procedure *mkpool* creates a new buffer pool and returns its id. Like most other identifiers in Xinu, the pool id is merely an index into the global buffer pool table. *Mkpool* computes the size of memory required and calls *getmem* to allocate it. It then divides up the memory into buffers, and links them together into a free list. Enough space is allocated for each buffer so the integer pool id can be stored in the buffer along with user data. After the free list has been formed, *mkpool* returns its id to the caller:

```
/* mkpool.c - mkpool */

#include <conf.h>
#include <kernel.h>
#include <mark.h>
#include <bufpool.h>

/*------------------------------------------------------------------------
 * mkpool  --  allocate memory for a buffer pool and link together
 *------------------------------------------------------------------------
 */
SYSCALL mkpool(bufsiz, numbufs)
int     bufsiz, numbufs;
{
        char    ps;
        int     poolid;
        char    *where;

#ifdef  MEMMARK
        if ( unmarked(bpmark) )
                poolinit();
#endif
        disable(ps);
        if (bufsiz<BPMINB || bufsiz>BPMAXB
            || numbufs<1 || numbufs>BPMAXN
            || nbpools >= NBPOOLS
            || (where=getmem((bufsiz+sizeof(int))*numbufs)) == SYSERR) {
                restore(ps);
                return(SYSERR);
        }
        poolid = nbpools++;
        bptab[poolid].bpnext = where;
        bptab[poolid].bpsize = bufsiz;
```

```
        bptab[poolid].bpsem = screate(numbufs);
        bufsiz+=sizeof(int);
        for (numbufs-- ; numbufs>0 ; numbufs--,where+=bufsiz)
                *( (int *) where ) = (int)(where+bufsiz);
        *( (int *) where) = (int) NULL;
        restore(ps);
        return(poolid);
}
```

15.8 Initializing The Buffer Pool Table

Procedure *poolinit* initializes the buffer pool table, *bptab*. The code, found in file *poolinit.c* uses conditional compilation to select one of two versions. If memory marking is available, *poolinit* and the other buffer pool routines use it to self-initialize. If it is not, they require the user to call *poolinit* explicitly.

Refer to the conditional code in *mkpool* to see how it calls *poolinit*. When compiled to use memory marking, *mkpool* performs an extra test at the beginning: it invokes *unmarked* to test whether the module's memory marker, *bpmark*, has been marked. If it has not, then *mkpool* needs to initialize the module, so it calls *poolinit* and marks *bpmark*. When *mkpool* is compiled without memory marking, the user must call *poolinit* explicitly before creating any buffer pools.

```
/* poolinit.c - poolinit */

#include <conf.h>
#include <kernel.h>
#include <mark.h>
#include <bufpool.h>

struct   bpool   bptab[NBPOOLS];
int      nbpools;
#ifdef  MEMMARK
MARKER  bpmark;                              /* self initializing mark      */
#endif

/*------------------------------------------------------------------------
 * poolinit  --  initialize the buffer pool routines
 *------------------------------------------------------------------------
 */
poolinit()
{
#ifdef  MEMMARK
        int     status;
        char    ps;

        disable(ps);
        if ( (status=mark(bpmark)) == OK) {
                nbpools = 0;
        }
        restore(ps);
        return( (status==OK) ? OK : SYSERR );
#else
        nbpools = 0;
        return(OK);
#endif
}
```

15.9 Communication Ports

Communication ports are rendevous points through which processes exchange messages. They differ from process-to-process message passing described in Chapter 7 because ports allow multiple outstanding messages, and processes accessing them are blocked until requests can be satisfied. Each port, which holds a fixed set of (one-word) messages, consists of a finite length message queue. Processes producing messages send them to the port with primitive *psend* (messages are deposited in FIFO order). The sending process can continue to execute after depositing its message as long as space remains in the port. If no space remains in the port, however, the sending process is blocked until messages have been removed and space becomes available.

Processes invoke primitive *preceive* to remove the next message from a port. Like *psend*, *preceive* operates synchronously, blocking the caller until a message is available.

15.10 The Implementation Of Ports

Each port consists of a queue to hold messages and two semaphores. One of the semaphores controls producers, blocking any process that attempts to add messages to a full port (i.e., one in which the current count of messages fills its quota). The other semaphore controls consumers, blocking any process that attempts to remove a message from an empty port.

Because ports are created at run-time, it is impossible to know the total count of items that will be enqueued at all ports at any given time. Although each message is small (one word), the total space required for port queues must be limited to prevent the port procedures from using all the free space. To guarantee a limit on the total space used, the port procedures allocate a fixed number of queue nodes and share them among all ports. Initially, these nodes are linked into a free list given by variable *ptfree*. Procedure *psend* takes a node from the free list and adds it to the queue at a specified port when sending a message; procedure *preceive* returns a node to the free list after the message has been received.

In file *ports.h*, structure *pt* defines the contents of an entry in the port table, and structure *ptnode* defines the contents of a message node. Most of the fields in *ptnode* are expected. We will comment on the sequence field *ptseq* in structure *pt* later.

```
/* ports.h - isbadport */

#define NPORTS          30          /* maximum number of ports      */
#define MAXMSGS         100         /* maximum messages on all ports*/
#define PTFREE          '\01'       /* port is Free                 */
#define PTLIMBO         '\02'       /* port is being deleted/reset  */
#define PTALLOC         '\03'       /* port is allocated            */
#define PTEMPTY         -1          /* initial semaphore entries    */

struct  ptnode  {                   /* node on list of message ptrs */
        int     ptmsg;              /* a one-word message           */
        int     *ptnext;            /* address of next node on list */
};

struct  pt      {                   /* entry in the port table      */
        char    ptstate;            /* port state (FREE/LIMBO/ALLOC)*/
        int     ptssem;             /* sender semaphore             */
        int     ptrsem;             /* receiver semaphore           */
        int     ptmaxcnt;           /* max messages to be queued    */
        int     ptseq;              /* sequence changed at creation */
        struct  ptnode  *pthead;    /* list of message pointers     */
        struct  ptnode  *pttail;    /* tail of message list         */
};

extern  struct  ptnode  *ptfree;    /* list of free nodes           */
extern  struct  pt      ports[];    /* port table                   */
extern  int     ptnextp;            /* next port to examine when    */
                                    /*    looking for a free one    */

#ifdef  MEMMARK
extern  MARKER  ptmark;
#endif

#define isbadport(portid)       ( (portid)<0 || (portid)>=NPORTS )
```

Because initialization routines are designed after basic operations have been implemented, we have been discussing them after other routines. In the case of ports, we will discuss initialization first, because it may make the remaining routines easier to understand. File *pinit.c* contains the code to initialize ports and the declaration of the port table as well. Global variable *ptnextp* gives the index in array *ports* at which to start when searching for a free port. Initialization consists of marking each port free, and forming the linked list of free nodes. *Pinit* first allocates a block of memory using *getmem*, and then moves through it, linking the individual nodes together.

```
/* pinit.c - pinit */

#include <conf.h>
#include <kernel.h>
#include <mark.h>
#include <ports.h>

#ifdef   MEMMARK
MARKER   ptmark;
#endif
struct   ptnode    *ptfree;                    /* list of free queue nodes    */
struct   pt        ports[NPORTS];
int      ptnextp;

/*------------------------------------------------------------------------
 *  pinit  --  initialize all ports
 *------------------------------------------------------------------------
 */
SYSCALL pinit(maxmsgs)
int maxmsgs;
{
        int     i;
        struct  ptnode  *next, *prev;

        if ( (ptfree=getmem(maxmsgs*sizeof(struct ptnode)))==SYSERR )
                panic("pinit - insufficient memory");
        for (i=0 ; i<NPORTS ; i++) {
                ports[i].ptstate = PTFREE;
                ports[i].ptseq = 0;
        }
        ptnextp = NPORTS - 1;

        /* link up free list of message pointer nodes */

        for ( prev=next=ptfree ;   --maxmsgs > 0  ; prev=next )
                prev->ptnext = ++next;
        prev->ptnext = NULL;
        return(OK);
}
```

Port creation consists of allocating an entry in the port table from among those that are free; procedure *pcreate* contains the code. After *pinit* establishes the list of free message nodes and fills in the port table, procedure *pcreate* creates a port and returns its table index to serve as a port identifier. It takes as an argument the maximum count of outstanding messages that the port should allow, permitting the caller to determine how many messages can be enqueued at a port before the

sender blocks. Note that, like the buffer pool routines, the port procedures are
self-initializing if memory marking is available.

```
/* pcreate.c - pcreate */

#include <conf.h>
#include <kernel.h>
#include <mark.h>
#include <ports.h>

/*------------------------------------------------------------------------
 *  pcreate  --  create a port that allows "count" outstanding messages
 *------------------------------------------------------------------------
 */
SYSCALL pcreate(count)
int     count;
{
        char    ps;
        int     i, p;
        struct  pt      *ptptr;

        if (count < 0)
                return(SYSERR);
        disable(ps);
#ifdef  MEMMARK
        if (mark(ptmark) == OK)
                pinit(MAXMSGS);
#endif
        for (i=0 ; i<NPORTS ; i++) {
                if ( (p=ptnextp--) <= 0)
                        ptnextp = NPORTS - 1;
                if ( (ptptr= &ports[p])->ptstate == PTFREE) {
                        ptptr->ptstate = PTALLOC;
                        ptptr->ptssem = screate(count);
                        ptptr->ptrsem = screate(0);
                        ptptr->pthead = ptptr->pttail = NULL;
                        ptptr->ptseq++;
                        ptptr->ptmaxcnt = count;
                        restore(ps);
                        return(p);
                }
        }
        restore(ps);
        return(SYSERR);
}
```

The basic operations on ports, sending and receiving messages, are handled by routines *psend* and *preceive*. They each require the caller to specify the port on which the operation is to be performed by passing the port identifier as an argument. Procedure *psend* adds a message to those that are waiting at the port. It waits for space in the port, enqueues the message given by its argument, signals the receiver semaphore to indicate another message is available, and returns.

```
/* psend.c - psend */

#include <conf.h>
#include <kernel.h>
#include <mark.h>
#include <ports.h>


/*------------------------------------------------------------------------
 *  psend  --  send a message to a port by enqueuing it
 *------------------------------------------------------------------------
 */
SYSCALL psend(portid, msg)
int     portid;
int     msg;
{
        char    ps;
        struct  pt      *ptptr;
        int     seq;
        struct  ptnode  *freenode;


        disable(ps);
        if ( isbadport(portid) ||
#ifdef  MEMMARK
                unmarked(ptmark) ||
#endif
                (ptptr= &ports[portid])->ptstate != PTALLOC ) {
                        restore(ps);
                        return(SYSERR);
        }

        /* wait for space and verify port is still allocated */

        seq = ptptr->ptseq;
        if (wait(ptptr->ptssem) == SYSERR
            || ptptr->ptstate != PTALLOC
            || ptptr->ptseq != seq) {
```

```
                  restore(ps);
                  return(SYSERR);
        }
        if (ptfree == NULL)
                  panic("Ports  -  out of nodes");
        freenode = ptfree;
        ptfree  = freenode->ptnext;
        freenode->ptnext = NULL;
        freenode->ptmsg  = msg;
        if (ptptr->pttail == NULL)                    /* empty queue */
                  ptptr->pttail = ptptr->pthead = freenode;
        else {
                  (ptptr->pttail)->ptnext = freenode;
                  ptptr->pttail = freenode;
        }
        signal(ptptr->ptrsem);
        restore(ps);
        return(OK);
}
```

The initial code in *psend* merely verifies that the argument is valid. What happens next is more interesting. *Psend* waits on the "sender" semaphore. The call returns immediately if the port is not full, but it delays if the number of messages already enqueued equals the maximum allowed. What may seem odd is that *psend* records the value of *ptseq* before the call to *wait*, and then verifies that it remained the same after the call. The code has been introduced because ports may be deleted (and even recreated) while processes remain enqueued waiting to send to them. When this happens, the port sequence number changes and the waiting processes are resumed. The idea is to have waiting processes verify that the *wait* did not terminate because the port was deleted. If it did, and the sequence number changed, *psend* reports an error to its caller.

The implementation of *psend* enqueues messages in FIFO order. It relies on *pttail* to point to the last node if the queue is nonempty, and it leaves *pttail* pointing to the new node after adding it to the list. It signals semaphore *ptrsem* once the new message has been added to the queue, allowing a receiver to consume it. The invariant being maintained is:

> Semaphore *ptrsem* has nonnegative count *n* if *n* messages are waiting in the port; it has negative count −*n* if *n* processes are waiting for messages.

The call to *panic* also deserves comment because this is its first occurrence. In our design, running out of message nodes is a catastrophe from which the system cannot recover. It means that the arbitrary limit on message nodes, set to prevent ports from using all the free memory, is insufficient. Perhaps the programs using ports are operating incorrectly. Perhaps, through no fault of the user, the system cannot honor a valid request; there is no way to know. Under such circumstances it is often better to announce failure and stop rather than attempt to go on. *Panic* is designed for just such situations; it prints the specified error message and halts processing. If the user chooses to continue execution, the call to panic may return, but often the user will restart the system or change the program instead. (The exercises suggest alternative ways of handling the problem.)

Procedure *preceive* implements the basic consumer operation. It removes a message from a port and returns it to the caller.

```
/* preceive.c - preceive */

#include <conf.h>
#include <kernel.h>
#include <mark.h>
#include <ports.h>

/*------------------------------------------------------------------
 * preceive  --  receive a message from a port, blocking if port empty
 *------------------------------------------------------------------
 */
SYSCALL preceive(portid)
int portid;
{
        char    ps;
        struct  pt      *ptptr;
        int     seq;
        int     msg;
        struct  ptnode  *nxtnode;

        disable(ps);
        if ( isbadport(portid) ||
#ifdef  MEMMARK
                unmarked(ptmark) ||
#endif
                (ptptr= &ports[portid])->ptstate != PTALLOC ) {
                    restore(ps);
                    return(SYSERR);
        }

        /* wait for message and verify that the port is still allocated */

        seq = ptptr->ptseq;
        if (wait(ptptr->ptrsem) == SYSERR || ptptr->ptstate != PTALLOC
            || ptptr->ptseq != seq) {
                    restore(ps);
                    return(SYSERR);
        }

        /* dequeue first message that is waiting in the port */

        nxtnode = ptptr->pthead;
        msg = nxtnode->ptmsg;
        if (ptptr->pthead == ptptr->pttail)     /* delete last item     */
                    ptptr->pthead = ptptr->pttail = NULL;
```

```
        else
                ptptr->pthead = nxtnode->ptnext;
        nxtnode->ptnext = ptfree;                    /* return to free list */
        ptfree = nxtnode;
        signal(ptptr->ptssem);
        restore(ps);
        return(msg);
}
```

Preceive waits until a message is available, verifies that the port was not deleted, and dequeues the message node. It records the message in local variable *msg* before returning the message node to the free list.

15.11 Other Operations On Ports

It is sometimes useful to delete a port, or to reset it. In both cases, the system must dispose of waiting messages, return message nodes to the free list, and permit waiting processes to continue execution. How should the port mechanism dispose of waiting messages? It could choose to throw them away, or it might return them to the processes that sent them. Often, the user can describe a more meaningful disposition, so the design presented here allows the user to specify disposition. Procedures *pdelete* and *preset* perform port deletion and reset operations. Both take as an argument a function that will be called to dispose of each waiting message. The code is found in files *pdelete.c* and *preset.c*:

```
/* pdelete.c - pdelete */

#include <conf.h>
#include <kernel.h>
#include <mark.h>
#include <ports.h>

/*------------------------------------------------------------------------
 *  pdelete  --  delete a port, freeing waiting processes and messages
 *------------------------------------------------------------------------
 */
SYSCALL pdelete(portid, dispose)
        int     portid;
        int     (*dispose)();
{
        char    ps;
        struct  pt *ptptr;

        disable(ps);
        if ( isbadport(portid) ||
#ifdef  MEMMARK
                unmarked(ptmark) ||
#endif
                (ptptr= &ports[portid])->ptstate != PTALLOC ) {
                restore(ps);
                return(SYSERR);
        }
        _ptclear(ptptr, PTFREE, dispose);
        restore(ps);
        return(OK);
}


/* preset.c - preset */

#include <conf.h>
#include <kernel.h>
#include <mark.h>
#include <ports.h>

/*------------------------------------------------------------------------
 *  preset  --  reset a port, freeing waiting processes and messages
 *------------------------------------------------------------------------
 */
SYSCALL preset(portid, dispose)
```

```
        int       portid;
        int       (*dispose)();
{
        char      ps;
        struct    pt *ptptr;

        disable(ps);
        if ( isbadport(portid) ||
#ifdef  MEMMARK
                unmarked(ptmark) ||
#endif
                (ptptr= &ports[portid])->ptstate != PTALLOC ) {
                    restore(ps);
                    return(SYSERR);
        }
        _ptclear(ptptr, PTALLOC, dispose);
        restore(ps);
        return(OK);
}
```

Both *pdelete* and *preset* verify that their arguments are correct, and then call *_ptclear* to perform the work of clearing messages and waiting processes.

_Ptclear places the port in a "limbo" state while clearing it. The limbo state guarantees that no other processes can use the port — procedures like *psend* and *preceive* will refuse to operate on a port that is not allocated, and *pcreate* will not allocate the port unless it is free. Thus, *_ptclear* can allow rescheduling while it clears the port.

Before declaring a port eligible for use again, *_ptclear* calls *dispose* repeatedly, passing it each waiting message. Finally, after all messages have been removed, *_ptclear* deletes or resets the semaphores as specified by its second argument. Before disposing of messages, *_ptclear* increments the port sequence number so that waiting processes can tell that the port has changed when they awaken.

```
/* ptclear.c - _ptclear */

#include <conf.h>
#include <kernel.h>
#include <mark.h>
#include <ports.h>


/*------------------------------------------------------------------------
 * _ptclear -- used by pdelete and preset to clear a port
 *------------------------------------------------------------------------
 */
_ptclear(ptptr, newstate, dispose)
        struct  pt      *ptptr;
        int     newstate;
        int     (*dispose)();
{
        struct  ptnode  *p;


        /* put port in limbo until done freeing processes */

        ptptr->ptstate = PTLIMBO;
        ptptr->ptseq++;
        if ( (p=ptptr->pthead) != NULL ) {
                for(; p != NULL ; p=p->ptnext)
                        (*dispose)( p->ptmsg );
                (ptptr->pttail)->ptnext = ptfree;
                ptfree = ptptr->pthead;
        }
        if (newstate == PTALLOC) {
                ptptr->pttail = ptptr->pthead = NULL;
                sreset(ptptr->ptssem, ptptr->ptmaxcnt);
                sreset(ptptr->ptrsem, 0);
        } else {
                sdelete(ptptr->ptssem);
                sdelete(ptptr->ptrsem);
        }
        ptptr->ptstate = newstate;
}
```

15.12 Summary

High-level memory management and message passing primitives are needed to build network communication software. The memory manager must prevent global exhaustion, and the message passing facility must provide buffered rendevous points for message exchange. This chapter introduced two sets of primitives that satisfy these needs. Instead of building these primitives into the network software we have chosen to design and build them separately. Such separation makes the primitives available to other system software and to user programs. It also makes them easier to test.

The high-level memory manager consists of buffer pool routines. Buffer pools permit memory to be partitioned such that the number of buffers in a given pool is fixed. Once a pool has been created, processes can allocate and deallocate buffers from the pool without affecting other free memory. A process that attempts to allocate a buffer from an empty pool is blocked until another process returns a buffer to the pool.

The high level message passing mechanism, called communication ports, permits processes to exchange messages efficiently. Each port consists of a fixed length queue of messages. The basic operations *psend* and *preceive* deposit a message at the tail of the queue, and extract a message from the head of the queue. Processes that attempt to receive from an empty port are blocked until a message arrives, and processes that attempt to send to a full port are blocked until space becomes available.

Both buffer pools and communication ports use another mechanism introduced in this chapter, namely memory marking. Memory marking provides an efficient way to determine whether a memory location has been "marked" since system startup, or to "mark" a given location. As demonstrated by the buffer pool and port routines, memory marking can be used to make a set of procedures self-initializing.

FOR FURTHER STUDY

Calingaert [1982] discusses allocation from a pool as well as alternative methods of recovering storage. Knuth [1968] describes in detail two such recovery methods: the "buddy system" and garbage collection. Memory marking is akin to the constant-time array initialization problem in exercise 2.12 of Aho et. al. [1974].

EXERCISES

15.1   The chief advantage of combining procedures into a single file is that they can share static data structures. Consider, for example, the memory marking routines. Recode them so that *marks* is protected from access except through *mark* and *un-*

mark.

15.2   The implementation of memory marking described here does not provide adequate mutual exclusion for two or more processes that attempt to access self-initializing routines concurrently. Redesign the primitives by introducing a third primitive, *marking*, so a process can declare that a cell is "being marked" during module initialization. Have concurrent calls to *mark* and *unmarked* block until the caller declares that the cell is "marked".

15.3   Can you envision an alternative to the three state marking scheme described above?

15.4   Design a new *getmem* that subsumes *getbuf.* Hint: allow the user to suballocate from a previously allocated block of memory.

15.5   Explain how to modify *getbuf* so it does not allocate buffers until they are needed even though it still limits the number of buffers that can be simultaneously allocated from a pool at a given time.

15.6   Why is *freebuf* more efficient than *freemem*?

15.7   Consider the primitives *send—receive* and *psend—preceive.* Design a single message passing scheme that encompasses both.

15.8   An important distinction is made between statically allocated and dynamically allocated resources. For example, *ports* are dynamically allocated while inter-process message slots are statically allocated. What is the key problem with dynamic allocation in a multi-process environment?

15.9   Change the message node allocation scheme so that a semaphore controls nodes on the free list. Have *psend* wait for a free node if none exists. What potential problems, if any, does the new scheme introduce?

15.10   Panic is used for conditions like internal inconsistency or potential deadlock. Often the conditions causing a panic are irreproducible, so their cause is difficult to pinpoint. Discuss what you might do to trace the cause of the panic in *psend*.

15.11   As alternatives to the panic in *psend*, consider allocating more nodes or retrying the operation. What are the liabilities of each?

15.12   Rewrite *psend* and *preceive* to return a special value when the port is deleted while they are waiting.

15.13   Modify the routines in previous chapters that allocate, use, and delete objects so they use sequence numbers to detect deletion as the communication ports routines do.

15.14   *Psend* and *preceive* cannot transmit a message with value equal to *SYSERR* because *preceive* cannot distinguish between a message with that value and an error. Redesign them to transmit any value.

16

Frame-Level Network Communication

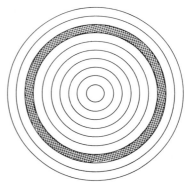

This chapter explores the design of a *frame manager*. The frame management routines comprise the layer of communication software that provides *reliable* transmission from one machine to another. Frame routines accept requests from higher level routines to send datagrams, encapsulate each in a frame, and call the data link communication driver described in Chapter 14 to transfer the frame onto the network. The frame manager also accepts incoming frames from the data link layer, and enqueues them for processing in the local machine or for forwarding to other machines.

Designing a frame manager is interesting because it involves a seemingly impossible task: provide a mechanism that guarantees reliable delivery of messages over an unreliable communication channel. How can the frame layer be more reliable than lower layers it uses or the raw hardware? The frame routines do not just send data and hope it arrives — they keep trying until the frame manager on the receiving machine acknowledges successful transmission. The tradeoff is that messages arrive reliably, but may take a long time to do so.

This chapter discusses how two communicating machines agree that a frame has been transferred successfully and how they recover from errors by retransmitting lost frames. It also illustrates how the buffer pool and communication port mechanisms can be used to make frame processing and the interface between the frame software and other software efficient.

16.1 Operation Of The Frame Manager

To control transmission and help detect errors, the frame procedures add control information to each block of data being sent. Frame procedures on the receiving system use the control information to decide whether a block has been transferred successfully, or whether it should be sent again. The two systems also use the control information to resynchronize after catastrophic failures (e.g., a broken connection).

The rules that frame routines follow when they exchange messages and control information are referred to as the *frame protocol*. Protocols specify the format of the data and control information, and give the procedures that the sender and receiver follow. For example, protocols specify that when data arrives mutilated or out of sequence, the receiving machine must request retransmission by returning a *negative acknowledgement* (*NACK*); they specify that the receiver should send back a *positive acknowledgement* (*ACK*) to indicate a successful transfer. In most protocols, after the sender transmits a block, it waits for an acknowledgement from the receiver, retransmitting the block if a negative acknowledgement arrives, and sending the next block if the acknowledgement is positive.

Forcing the sender to wait for a positive or negative acknowledgement from the receiver is not sufficient to guarantee trouble-free communication because acknowledgements may also be lost. If the receiver only responds to messages from the sender and the sender always waits for acknowledgements from the receiver, losing a single acknowledgement can produce a deadlock in which the sender waits for an acknowledgement that will never arrive and the receiver waits for the next frame. To avoid such deadlocks protocols arrange for the sender, receiver, or both to retry the operation after a fixed time interval. (In our design, responsibility for timing transfers will be assigned to the sender.) Protocols that use acknowledgements and timers to provide reliable delivery are generally called *positive-acknowledgement-with-retransmission* (*PAR*) protocols — they are the basis for reliable computer communication network software.

16.2 Details Of The Frame-Level Protocol

We want the frame-level protocol to guarantee that when two systems transfer blocks of data, the blocks arrive in order, and that none are missing. These details are handled by adding sequence numbers to the protocol: the sending machine attaches a sequence number to each block, and the receiving machine checks the sequence numbers on blocks that arrive to make sure they follow in sequence. To prevent sequence numbers from growing arbitrarily large, they are computed modulo some constant M; in most sequenced protocols, M is small (e.g., three or seven). The protocol specifies how the two systems synchronize their sequence numbers, and how they agree whether a block should be retransmitted. In practice, the receiving machine sends the next sequence number it expects along with each positive or negative acknowledgement, so no confusion can arise about which acknowledgement matches which block.

Protocols that acknowledge blocks in sequence can be difficult to design because they must be able to recover from the loss of an acknowledgement as well as from the loss of a data block. Suppose, for example, that a positive acknowledgement of block 5 is lost. Having sent an acknowledgement, the receiver increments its sequence number, and begins rejecting all but block number 6. Having never received the acknowledgement for block 5, the sender eventually times out and retransmits it. Unless something more is added to the protocol, the receiver will again reply with a negative acknowledgement, causing the sender to retransmit it, and the cycle to repeat. Sequencing mismatches are especially important when the machines first begin to communicate or when one restarts while the other continues to execute.

Our frame manager uses a simple method of resynchronizing sequence numbers. The receiving machine counts the number of times it receives an incorrectly sequenced block that is otherwise undamaged. When the count of incorrectly sequenced frames reaches a predefined threshold, the receiver sends a *startup acknowledgement (SACK)* and resets its sequence number to zero. The sending machine resets its sequence to zero upon receiving SACK, and retransmits the block with the new sequence. The important detail here is that the receiver initiates the change, while the sender makes the change. The following property is a consequence of this asymmetry:

> *Lost acknowledgements can result in duplicate frames being received, but it never results in frames being lost or delivered out of sequence.*

Thus, higher levels of communication software must detect and eliminate duplicate frames.

16.3 The Xinu Ring Network

The frame level routines designed in this chapter assume the communicating systems are connected in a ring network, as depicted in Figure 14.1. To distinguish our ring network from others, we will call it a *Xinu ring*. Each machine on the Xinu ring, called a *node*, has connections to exactly two other systems. As the term "ring" implies, we think of the machines arranged in a circle with the network passing through them. Although the hardware connections allow traffic to flow in either direction, the frame manager creates a *one-way* ring, in which messages flow in only one direction around the circle, and acknowledgements flow in the opposite direction.

To make it possible for all machines on a ring to communicate, each node must accept all incoming messages, *forwarding* messages not destined for that machine by sending them on around the ring. This *store-and-forward* mechanism makes it possible for N machines to communicate even though each has only two connections. In the worst case, a message must pass through $N-2$ intermediate machines on the ring as it travels from its source to its final destination.

In order to know whether to keep a message or to forward it, the frame manager must be able to identify the message's destination. It does so by passing the destination along with each message (the transmitted message contains the address of the machine that sent the message as well). The next sections review the exact format of messages and frames, showing how the source and destination addresses are stored.

16.4 Messages, Packets, Frames, Blocks, And The Network Layers

We have used the terms *message*, *frame*, and *block* to describe the data exchanged between machines. To understand how the frame manager operates, and the format of the data with which it deals, we need to define the terms more precisely, and to discover how the frame manager interacts with other network software. This section provides a brief overview of the communication subsystem, explaining the purpose of each layer. Although a brief outline cannot explain all the details of network communication, it will help the reader appreciate how the role of the frame manager influences its design.

Figure 16.1 shows how communication software can be partitioned into four conceptual layers. The topmost, called the *transport layer*, provides reliable connections between a process on one machine and a process on another. It divides an arbitrarily long *message* into *packets* (typically of from 100 to 2000 bytes). Each packet consists of data to be delivered as well as a header that identifies the processes on the two machines that are communicating. The transport layer passes the packets, one at a time, to the internet layer along with the address of the ultimate destination.

The *internet* layer prepends the ultimate destination address onto the packet to form a *datagram*. From the ultimate destination address, the internet layer computes a pair (n,f), where n is the correct network over which the datagram should be sent, and f the frame-level address of a machine on that network. If the sending machine connects directly with the same network as the ultimate destination, computing n is easy. In cases where the sending machine does not connect directly to the destination network, the internet layer must select an intermediate stop on one of the networks to which it holds a direct connection. Intermediate machines capable of forwarding a datagram from one network to another are called *gateways*. Once the internet layer selects a gateway, it sets n and f to the address of the gateway, and passes the datagram to the frame level routines. Remember that the ultimate destination address has been placed in the datagram, and that it may not be the machine specified by n and f.

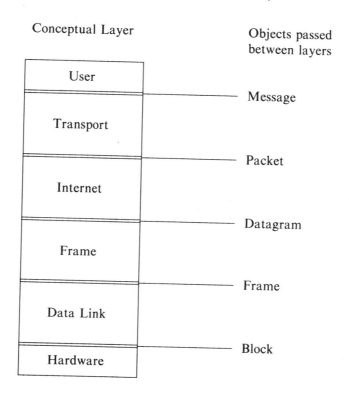

Figure 16.1 The four layers of network software that stand between user programs and the hardware

The *frame* layer accepts a datagram along with its destination address, (*n* and *f*). It encapsulates the datagram in a frame by prepending a frame header that contains, among other things, the frame-level destination address, *f*. Finally, the frame layer passes the result to the *data link* layer for transfer. The data link layer treats each frame like a block of data, adding its own header (the start-of-block character) before sending it.

16.5 An Example Of Packet Transfer Across An Internet

An example may provide further insight into the role of each layer of network software. Consider a configuration of five machines and two networks, interconnected as shown in Figure 16.2. The term *internet* is often used to refer to such interconnections. (Thus, we have chosen the same name for the layer of software that selects a gateway).

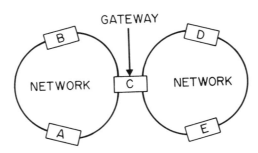

Figure 16.2 An example internet consisting of two Xinu ring networks

In the example, ring network 0 connects machines *A*, *B*, and *C*; and ring network 1 connects machines *C*, *D*, and *E*. Machine *C*, common to both networks is the *gateway* that can be used to pass messages from one network to another.

Suppose a process on machine *A* wants to send a file to a process on machine *E*. It calls the transport layer software on machine *A* which divides the file into packets. Figure 16.3 shows the form of each packet:

| header | zero or more bytes of data |

Figure 16.3 The packet format.

The header, which is formatted according to the transport protocol rules, contains control information used by the transport layer on the receiving machine (e.g., the process id of the destination process).

After creating a packet, the transport layer on machine *A* passes it to the internet layer, specifying the ultimate destination to be machine *E* on network 1. The internet layer encapsulates the packet in a datagram by prepending the ultimate address to the packet. Figure 16.4 shows the result.

| internet header | complete packet treated as data |

Figure 16.4 The datagram format.

The internet layer determines that machine *A* has no direct connection to network 1, so the packet must be sent to an intermediate machine that can forward the packet on toward its destination. It selects, probably by looking up the network in a table, gateway *C*. It then passes the datagram to the frame layer, specifying that it should be sent to machine *C* on network 0.

The frame-level routines encapsulate each datagram in a frame by adding a header that contains such things as the frame-level address of *C* and control information like the frame-level sequence numbers. Figure 16.5 shows how the datagram appears after it has been embedded in a frame.

frame header	complete datagram treated as data

Figure 16.5 The frame format.

The frame-level header format may be completely different than the packet or datagram headers because frame-level protocols are usually chosen to match the hardware. A single machine that connects to several networks may use a different frame format with each.

To send the frame, the frame-level routines call the data link layer. Because the network is a store-and-forward ring network, the data link layer software (*dlc*) always transfers outgoing packets to the adjacent machine, *B*. As we have seen in Chapter 14, the data link layer encapsulates the frame before transmission by adding a header (the start-of-block character), and a trailer (the end-of-block character). It also escapes any characters in the frame that coincide with its control characters. Thus, when the block travels across the communication link, it has the form shown in Figure 16.6.

SOB	complete frame treated as data with dlc characters escaped	EOB

Figure 16.6 The block format.

Dlc is a transparent communication mechanism. As it reads the incoming block on machine *B*, dlc removes the header and trailer, and translates escaped characters back to their original form. It passes up to the frame layer on machine *B* exactly the same frame that was passed down from the frame layer on machine *A*.

The frame routines on *B* route the incoming frame based on its frame-level address. Because the address specifies machine *C*, the frame routines on *B* forward the frame without passing it up to the internet layer and without examining the ultimate address of the packet.

When the frame reaches machine *C*, the frame layer recognizes that its frame-level address matches *C*'s frame-level address. They remove the datagram contained inside (that is, the data portion of the frame), and pass it up to the internet layer. Like the dlc software, the frame layer software has provided a transparent transfer: the internet layer on machine *C* receives exactly the data sent by the internet layer on machine *A*.

Gateway C connects two networks. When the internet layer in C receives the datagram, it extracts the ultimate destination address, and computes a new route for the packet. Routing that occurs at machine C differs from the routing at machine A because C connects to different networks than A; in the example, C decides to send the datagram to machine E on network 1. Having selected a new frame-level address, the internet layer on C passes the datagram down to the frame layer, which encapsulates it in a new frame and sends it out on network 1.

Only when the data reaches its destination machine, E do the lower layers pass the packet up to the transport layer. Dlc receives the block, removes escape characters, and passes the resulting frame up to the frame layer. Because the frame-level address matches E's frame-level address, the frame layer removes the frame header and passes the resulting datagram to the internet layer. The internet layer removes the packet, and passes it up to the transport layer. When the packet finally arrives at the transport layer, it is exactly the same as when the transport layer on machine A sent it, even though it has been encapsulated in a datagram and several different frames during its journey.

16.6 Frame-Level Processing

Having sketched the flow of data across a network, we turn to the details of frame level processing. As the reader may have observed, it is important that such processing operate independent of activity on the local machine because forwarding must continue or activity across the network will cease.

To insure that machines accept and send frames independent of other processing, the frame manager contains independent processes that run at higher priority than user processes. Each network needs three frame processes: an input process, an output process, and a timer process. The input process reads and acknowledges incoming frames, enqueuing them for local processing (presumably by the internet layer) or for forwarding. The output process selects outbound frames from the local output queue or from the forwarding queue, and transmits them onto the network until receiving a positive acknowledgement.

The code in the output process that selects a frame from the local output queue or the forwarding queue implements the *frame selection policy* that determines how the network is multiplexed among machines. Selecting frames from the forwarding queue gives priority to other machines; selecting them from the local queue gives priority to local processes. The selection policy is important because a poor choice can jam the network with more frames than it can absorb. To avoid such congestion, we adopt the following policy:

> *Forwarded frames always take precedence over locally produced outbound frames.*

Selection policies are not easy to decide upon because they have subtle, and often unexpected side-effects. The exercises discuss some interesting ramifications.

16.7 The Frame Format

It is time to choose a frame format in our network. Knowing that almost no transmission errors will occur, and that the network hardware is relatively slow, we chose a design that minimizes the size of the frame header. File *frame.h* contains the C declarations of structure *frame* that defines the frame format, and structure *fglob* that defines the global data structures shared by all three frame processes. Structure *frame* includes fields for the frame's address, sequence number, length, and data.

```
/* frame.h - getfto, getfrom, getflen, setfto, setfa, setfrom */

#define FRACK           '\030'   /* frame ACK/NACK/SACK codes -- frame   */
#define FRNACK          '\060'   /*    sequence number appears in low-   */
#define FRSACK          '\070'   /*    order 3 bits of each              */
#define FRCODE          070      /* mask for "code" part of ACK/NACK     */
#define FRSEQ           07       /* mask for sequence part of ACK/NACK   */
#define FRBCAST         0        /* broadcast address                    */
#define FRTIME          4        /* number of seconds to timeout a frame */
#define FRFAIL          2        /* number of failures for sack          */
#define FRMINLEN        3        /* minimum legal frame length           */
#define FRMAXLEN        128      /* maximum bytes in a frame             */
#define FRMAXSEQ        3        /* maximum sequence number for frames   */
#define FRSTACK         500      /* words of stack needed by frame proc. */
#define FRLEN           sizeof(struct frame)
#define NFRAMES         40       /* total number of frame buffers        */
#define FRIPRIO         30       /* input process priority               */
#define FROPRIO         25       /* output process priority              */
#define FRTPRIO         100      /* priority of timer process            */
#define FIPORTS         20       /* size of input port queue             */
#define FOPORTS         8        /* size of output port queue            */
#define FFPORTS         10       /* size of forwarding queue             */
#define FRTMSG          8191     /* timeout message for transmitter      */


#define getfto(x)       ( ((x)&070) >>3)
#define getfrom(x)      ( (x) & 07 )
#define getflen(fptr)   ( fptr->frlen & 0377 )
#define setfto(fptr, x) fptr->fraddr = (fptr->fraddr & ~070) | ((x&07)<<3)
#define setfrom(fptr,x) fptr->fraddr = (fptr->fraddr & ~07)  | (x&07)
#define setfa(fptr,t,f) fptr->fraddr = ( (t&07)<<3 ) | ( f&07 )


/* frame structure */

struct  frame   {
        char    fraddr;         /* from/to addresses, each 3 bits       */
        char    frseq;          /* frame sequence number                */
        char    frlen;          /* length of frame including fraddr     */
                                /* through all data.  Does not count    */
                                /* characters added by dlc              */
        char    frdata[FRMAXLEN];
};

struct  fglob   {               /* global frame-level data              */
        int     fiport;         /* local machine input port             */
        int     foport;         /* local machine output port            */
```

```
        int     ffport;         /* forwarded frame port                */
        int     fosem;          /* output waiting semaphore            */
        int     findev;         /* input device id for this network    */
        int     foutdev;        /* output device id for this network   */
        int     ftfuse;         /* timer fuse for send on this net     */
        int     ftpid;          /* id of process to signal for timeout */
        int     fmachid;        /* id of this machine on this network   */
        int     ftimproc;       /* timer process for this network      */
        int     fiseq;          /* next input sequence to expect       */
        int     foseq;          /* next output sequence number to write */
        int     fifails;        /* number of input failures            */
        int     fofails;        /* number of output failures           */
};

extern  struct  fglob    fdata[];
extern  int     frbpool;
```

File *frame.h* contains a set of in-line procedures that set and extract the length and address fields of a frame. The version shown squeezes two machine addresses into one byte, assuming that only a few machines connect to a given network. To change frame format, it is only necessary to change the definition of the *frame* structure and the inline address routines.

16.8 The Interface Between The Frame And Internet Layers

The frame layer passes incoming datagrams to, and accepts outgoing datagrams from, the internet layer above it. The interface through which the internet and frame layers communicate consists of two communication ports per network, one for datagrams traveling in each direction. To receive a datagram from network *n*, the upper layer routine calls procedure *freceive*, passing *n* as an argument. The code for *freceive* is found in file *freceive.c*.

```
/* freceive.c - freceive */

#include <conf.h>
#include <kernel.h>
#include <frame.h>

#ifndef NNETS
#define NNETS 0
#endif

/*------------------------------------------------------------------------
 *  freceive  --  receive the next frame that arrives from a net.
 *------------------------------------------------------------------------
 */
SYSCALL freceive(netid)
        int     netid;
{
        if (netid < 0 || netid >= NNETS)
                return(SYSERR);
        return( preceive(fdata[netid].fiport) );
}
```

Freceive obtains the local input port id for the specified network from field *fiport* of
the global data structure *fdata*, and returns the message it retrieves from that port.

Passing a datagram down to the frame layer for transmission is only slightly
more complex. The code can be found in procedure *fsend*.

```
/* fsend.c - fsend */

#include <conf.h>
#include <kernel.h>
#include <frame.h>
#ifndef NNETS
#define NNETS   0
#endif

/*------------------------------------------------------------------------
 *  fsend  --  enqueue a message for transmission to another machine
 *------------------------------------------------------------------------
 */
SYSCALL fsend(netid, toaddr, fptr)
        int     netid;
        int     toaddr;
        char    *fptr;
```

```
{
        struct   fglob   *fgptr;

        if (netid < 0 |¦ netid >= NNETS)
                return(SYSERR);
        fgptr = &fdata[netid];
        setfa(fptr, toaddr, fgptr->fmachid);
        psend(fgptr->foport, fptr);
        signal(fgptr->fosem);
        return(OK);
}
```

Like *freceive*, *fsend* accesses the global data structure *fdata*, taking the output
port id from field *foport*. Passing a datagram to the frame layer consists of sending
it to that port id. Although the upper layer routines deal with datagrams, the
software has been designed to store them in the "data" area of the frame buffers,
so entire frame buffers can be passed between the layers. A later section in this
chapter comments on the importance and consequences of this convention; for now,
we ignore the motivation and concentrate on building the interface procedures.

When it receives a frame to be sent, the frame layer must fill in the header.
Procedure *fsend* fills in the frame header "to" and "from" addresses before it deposits the frame in the local output port. After the frame has been added to the output port, *fsend* signals the output semaphore, allowing the frame output process to
retrieve the frame from the port and send it over the network. Before transmitting
the frame, the output process completes the header by filling in the sequence
number.

16.9 The Frame-Level Input Process

Each network has a frame-level input process that receives frames and decides
whether to enqueue them for upper layers of the network software or to forward
them to another machine. The frame input process executes procedure *finput*,
which is shown in file *finput.c*.

```
/* finput.c - finput, sendack, sendnack, sendsack */


#include <conf.h>
#include <kernel.h>
#include <frame.h>


/*------------------------------------------------------------------
 * finput  -- read frames and enqueue for local machine or forwarding
 *------------------------------------------------------------------
 */
PROCESS finput(netid)
        int     netid;
{
        int     len;                    /* length of actual data     */
        int     to, from;               /* "to" and "from" addresses */
        struct  fglob   *fgptr;
        struct  frame   *fptr, *fptr2;
        char    *t, *f;                 /* used to copy broadcast frames*/

        fgptr = &fdata[netid];
        fptr = getbuf(frbpool);
        for (fgptr->fiseq = fgptr->fifails = 0 ; TRUE ; ) {
                len = read(fgptr->findev, fptr, FRMAXLEN);
                if (len < FRMINLEN || len != getflen(fptr))
                        sendnack(fgptr);
                else if ( (int)fptr->frseq != fgptr->fiseq)
                        sendsack(fgptr);
                else {
                        to = getfto(fptr->fraddr);
                        from = getfrom(fptr->fraddr);
                        if (to == FRBCAST) {    /* broadcast */
                                if (from == fgptr->fmachid) {
                                        psend(fgptr->fiport, fptr);
                                        fptr = getbuf(frbpool);
                                } else {
                                        fptr2 = getbuf(frbpool);
                                        for (f=fptr,t=fptr2; len-->0; )
                                                *t++ = *f++;
                                        psend(fgptr->fiport, fptr);
                                        psend(fgptr->ffport, fptr2);
                                        signal(fgptr->fosem);
                                        fptr = getbuf(frbpool);
                                }
                        } else if (to == fgptr->fmachid) {
                                psend(fgptr->fiport, fptr);
```

```
                                        fptr = getbuf(frbpool);
                        } else if (from == fgptr->fmachid) {
                                printf("Can't deliver to %d\n", to);
                        } else {
                                psend(fgptr->ffport, fptr);
                                fptr = getbuf(frbpool);
                        }
                        sendack(fgptr);
                }
        }
}


/*------------------------------------------------------------------------
 *   sendack  --   send a positive acknowledgement with sequence number
 *------------------------------------------------------------------------
 */
LOCAL   sendack(fgptr)
        struct  fglob   *fgptr;
{
        fgptr->fifails = 0;
        if (++fgptr->fiseq > FRMAXSEQ)
                fgptr->fiseq = 0;
        putc(fgptr->findev, FRACK | fgptr->fiseq);
}


/*------------------------------------------------------------------------
 *   sendnack  --   send a negative acknowledgement with sequence number
 *------------------------------------------------------------------------
 */
LOCAL   sendnack(fgptr)
        struct  fglob   *fgptr;
{
        putc(fgptr->findev, FRNACK | fgptr->fiseq);
}


/*------------------------------------------------------------------------
 *   sendsack  --   send a negative acknowledgement and restart sequence
 *------------------------------------------------------------------------
 */
LOCAL   sendsack(fgptr)
        struct  fglob   *fgptr;
{
        if (++fgptr->fifails >= FRFAIL) {
                fgptr->fiseq = 0;
                fgptr->fifails = 0;
```

```
                    putc(fgptr->findev, FRSACK);
        } else
                    putc(fgptr->findev, FRNACK);

}
```

Finput implements the receiver's side of the frame-level protocol. It is relatively easy to understand. *Finput* begins by initializing the frame sequence counter to zero, and allocating a frame buffer. It then executes an infinite loop that reads a frame, acknowledges it, disposes of it if necessary, allocates another buffer if necessary, and returns to the top of the loop to read another.

After reading a frame *finput* compares the length field with the actual length, and verifies that the sequence is the one expected before further processing. (The exercises discuss adding further tests for correctness). If the frame is deemed correct, *finput* extracts the source and destination addresses, (*to* and *from*), using in-line procedures *getfto* and *getfrom*. Based on the source and destination address, it decides how to dispose of the frame. It may add the frame to the local input port, add it to the forwarding port, duplicate it for both ports (in case of broadcast), or destroy it (if it is an undelivered frame received back at the machine from which it was sent).

In any case, *finput* acknowledges receipt of the frame using one of the acknowledgement procedures: *sendack*, *sendnack*, or *sendsack*. Besides transmitting the positive acknowledgement, *sendack* increments the frame sequence count, modulo *FRMAXSEQ*, and resets the count of badly sequenced frames to zero, making the receiver ready for the next frame. Procedure *sendnack* is called to acknowledge frames that were mangled during transfer; it merely transmits the negative acknowledgement along with the frame sequence number that was expected. Procedure *sendsack* is called to acknowledge receipt of a frame that contains a bad sequence number. If the count of badly sequenced frames reaches *FRFAIL*, *sendsack* sends a startup acknowledgement to request that the transmitter resynchronize its sequence number; otherwise, *sendsack* sends a negative acknowledgement, assuming the sequence number was damaged by a transmission error.

16.10 The Frame-Level Output Process

Each machine has two processes per network that manage the frame-level output. One of these does the work of transmitting frames; the other is used only for timing. The output process executing procedure *foutput* selects frames from the local output port or forwarding port, and sends them. The code can be found in file *foutput.c*.

```
/* foutput.c - foutput */

#include <conf.h>
#include <kernel.h>
#include <frame.h>
#include <dlc.h>


/*------------------------------------------------------------------
 * foutput  --  select a frame from local or forward ports and send it
 *------------------------------------------------------------------
 */
PROCESS foutput(netid)
        int     netid;
{
        struct  frame   *fptr;
        struct  fglob   *fgptr;

        fgptr = &fdata[netid];
        control(fgptr->foutdev, DCSETREC, getpid());
        for (fgptr->fofails = fgptr->foseq = 0 ; TRUE ; ) {
                wait(fgptr->fosem);
                if (pcount(fgptr->ffport) > 0)
                        fptr = (struct frame *)preceive(fgptr->ffport);
                else
                        fptr = (struct frame *)preceive(fgptr->foport);
                _frsend(fptr, fgptr);
                freebuf(fptr);
        }
}
```

As the code shows, this process selects a frame from the forward port, *ffport* or the local output port, *foport*, and calls procedure *_frsend* to send it out. Once the frame has been sent, *foutput* frees the buffer and continues processing with the next frame. Before beginning its work, the process executing *foutput* calls *control* to inform the *dlc* driver that it should receive non-blockmode input (acknowledgments) from the network.

Like other network processes, the output process runs at higher priority than user processes. Thus, it cannot poll the output ports to know when a frame is ready or it would starve user programs of the CPU resource. To coordinate without "busy waiting", the frame process uses semaphore *fosem*. Each time a frame is added to the output or forward ports, semaphore *fosem* must be signalled. *Foutput* waits on the semaphore before extracting a frame and sending it.

When *foutput* obtains a frame, it calls procedure *_frsend*, shown below, to transfer it onto the network and await the acknowledgement. *_frsend* does not re-

turn to its caller until the frame has been transmitted and a positive acknowledgement has been received. If it receives a negative acknowledgement, or the timer expires before an acknowledgement has been received, _frsend_ transmits the frame
again. If the connection between machines is broken or the receiving machine is
not operating, _frsend_ continues sending forever.

```
/* frsend.c - _frsend */

#include <conf.h>
#include <kernel.h>
#include <frame.h>
#include <dlc.h>

/*-------------------------------------------------------------------------
 * _frsend  --  transmit one frame until receipt acknowledged
 *-------------------------------------------------------------------------
 */
_frsend(fptr, fgptr)
        struct  frame   *fptr;
        struct  fglob   *fgptr;
{
        int     len;
        int     seq, nextseq;
        int     msg;            /* response from receiver or timeout   */
        int     msgcode;        /* ack code without sequence number    */

        len = getflen(fptr);
        fgptr->fofails = 0;
        fptr->frseq = seq = fgptr->foseq;
        nextseq = seq >= FRMAXSEQ ? 0 : seq+1;
        while ( TRUE ) {
                recvclr();
                write(fgptr->foutdev, fptr, len);

                /* schedule timeout message */

                fgptr->ftfuse = FRTIME;
                fgptr->ftpid = getpid();
                resume(fgptr->ftimproc);
                if ( (msg=receive()) != FRTMSG) {
                        fgptr->ftfuse = -1;
                        switch (msg & FRCODE) {

                        case FRACK:
```

```
                            if ( (msg&FRSEQ) == nextseq) {
                                    fgptr->foseq = nextseq;
                                    return;
                            }
                            break;

                    case FRSACK:
                            fptr->frseq = fgptr->foseq = 0;
                            nextseq = 1;
                            sleep10(1);
                    }
            }
            sleep10(1);
    }
}
```

16.11 Using The Acknowledgement Timer

In the system we have designed so far, a given process can only perform one operation at a time. Adding a frame output process to this design presents a challenge, because it performs two operations at once. After sending a frame, it simultaneously waits for an acknowledgement and times the wait (because it has responsibility for retransmission in case the frame or acknowledgement is lost). There are several approaches to the problem. New primitives could be invented to provide *timed operations* (e.g., *read-with-timeout*); an *event* mechanism could be added to allow a process to wait for one of several events; or existing primitives could be used by starting a second process to perform the timing. Although timed operations provide the cleanest interface, they would require redesign of lower layers. Thus, we have chosen to use existing primitives.

How can a process know whether the timer expires or an acknowledgement arrives first? It arranges to have both acknowledgements and timeout signals sent to it, and uses *receive* to await the first message. The timer sends a message different from any that dlc sends, so the receiving process can always distinguish the "time's up" message from acknowledgements, even if they arrive mutilated. Arranging to receive acknowledgements is straightforward because the dlc driver passes acknowledgements with *send* (now you understand why it was designed to do so).

The frame-level output process (the one executing *frsend*) needs to start the timer just before it calls *receive* to wait for an acknowledgement. Creating and killing a timer process for each frame is too expensive. So, the frame initialization routine creates the timer process, and the output process merely controls it to start and stop timing as needed. The mechanics are simple: first, the output process sets variable *ftfuse* in the network structure to the number of seconds it wishes to delay. The value it uses, given by symbolic constant *FRTIME*, is usually around five seconds. Second, the output process leaves its process id in field *ftpid* of the global data structure so the timer knows which process to awaken. Third, it *resumes* the timer process to start it counting. When the fuse reaches zero, the timer sends message *FRTMSG* to the output process. If the timer runs out before an acknowledgement arrives, *receive* will return *FRTMSG*. If an acknowledgement arrives first, the timer is cancelled by making the fuse negative.

16.12 Implementation Of The Timer

Designing the timer process is not difficult, but it must be constructed carefully because the details are important. (Two earlier versions of the frame timer contained flaws in the way they terminated when the timer was cancelled). The goals are to use as little CPU time as necessary, to keep the timer from executing when nothing needs to be timed, and to make it efficient to cancel the timer before it expires. The latter is important because most acknowledgements, whether positive or negative, arrive without being lost, so cancellation is performed frequently. Our design consists of a process that executes procedure *frtimer*. The code is found in file *frtimer.c*.

```
/* frtimer.c - frtimer */

#include <conf.h>
#include <kernel.h>
#include <frame.h>


/*-------------------------------------------------------------------
 * frtimer  --  countdown and send timeout message to output process
 *-------------------------------------------------------------------
 */
frtimer(netid)
int     netid;
{
        struct  fglob   *fgptr;

        for (fgptr = &fdata[netid]; TRUE ; ) {
                for (fgptr->ftfuse++ ; --fgptr->ftfuse > 0 ; )
                        sleep10( 10);
                if (fgptr->ftfuse == 0)
                        send(fgptr->ftpid, FRTMSG);
                suspend(getpid());
        }
}
```

When not in use, the timer process calls *suspend*. Thus, when not being used, it takes no CPU time. After *ftfuse* and *ftpid* have been set, the process that wants to be timed *resume*s the timer allowing it to execute the *for* loop. While in this loop, it awakens once per second and decrements the "fuse" variable, *ftfuse*, sending message *FRTMSG* to process *ftpid* if the fuse reaches zero. The timer can be cancelled by setting the fuse to any negative value — when it awakens to decrement the fuse, the loop will cease and the timer will return to the suspended state without sending the timeout message.

16.13 Initialization Of The Frame Layer

Now that the frame level processing has been designed, the initialization procedure can be considered. The initialization routine must create the needed communication ports, a buffer pool for frame buffers, and the three frame-level processes. All this is straightforward, as procedure *frinit* shows.

```
/* frinit.c - frinit */

#include <conf.h>
#include <kernel.h>
#include <frame.h>

#ifdef NNETS
struct  fglob    fdata[NNETS];
int     frbpool;
#endif

/*------------------------------------------------------------------------
 * frinit  --  initialize frame-level network input and output processes
 *------------------------------------------------------------------------
 */
SYSCALL frinit(netid, indev, outdev)
        int     netid;
        int     indev, outdev;
{
#ifdef NNETS
        struct  fglob   *fgptr;
        int     frtimer(), finput(), foutput();

        if (netid < 0 || netid >= NNETS)
                return(SYSERR);
        fgptr = &fdata[netid];
        fgptr->findev = indev;
        fgptr->foutdev = outdev;
        fgptr->fiport = pcreate(FIPORTS);
        fgptr->foport = pcreate(FOPORTS);
        fgptr->ffport = pcreate(FFPORTS);
        fgptr->fosem = screate(0);
        fgptr->ftfuse = -1;
        fgptr->ftpid = 0;
        fgptr->fmachid = getmid(netid);
        fgptr->ftimproc =
                create(frtimer, FRSTACK, FRTPRIO, "frtimer", 1, netid);
        resume( create(finput, FRSTACK, FRIPRIO, "finput", 1, netid) );
        resume( create(foutput,FRSTACK, FROPRIO, "foutpt", 1, netid) );
        return(OK);
 #else
        return(SYSERR);
 #endif
 }
```

Frinit is called with three arguments: the id of the network to initialize, the network input device, and the network output device. It creates three communication ports, one for incoming frames, one for outgoing frames, and one for forwarded frames; makes a pool of frame buffers; and starts the input, output, and timer processes. Note that it leaves the timer process suspended. The timer code has been carefully designed to operate the same way when resumed at the beginning or from the call of *suspend*. *Frinit* records information like the port ids in the global data structure *fdata[netid]* so all three processes can access it.

16.14 Optimizing The Transfer Of Datagrams To Frames

At the beginning of this chapter, we said that the internet layer of communication software deals in datagrams, and that the frame layer must encapsulate each datagram into a frame by adding a header. The reader might have expected the interface procedures *fsend* and *freceive* to accept and deliver datagrams, copying them to and from frames as needed. Yet *fsend* and *freceive* do not copy datagrams into or out of frames at all. *Fsend* expects the caller to allocate a frame from the appropriate buffer pool and place the data to be sent (i.e. the datagram) in the correct location, beyond the area used for the frame header. Similarly, *freceive* passes the entire frame to the internet software and allows it to access the datagram directly in the frame buffer. We assume that after the upper-level routines consume the data in a frame they must return it to the buffer pool by calling *freebuf*.

Why does the network software pass entire frames around? For efficiency. Passing pointers to entire frames throughout the communication software turns out to be an extremely important optimization because frame copying consumes much CPU time. If the internet layer copied packets to datagrams, the frame layer copied datagrams to frames, and the data link layer copied frames to buffers, the overhead would swamp the processor. So, to avoid unnecessary overhead, the communication software avoids copying by allocating the frame once and using it at all layers. The software is also careful to pass pointers, not actual frames through the communication ports and among the procedures of a given layer. There are some consequences of not copying, but these are minimal. For example, the transport layer must leave space at the beginning of the frame for the internet header and frame header; the consequence is that these headers must have fixed maximum size.

16.15 Summary

The frame manager software provides reliable communication between pairs of machines on a network. It achieves this reliability by using a positive-acknowledgement-with-retransmission protocol that repeatedly sends each block of data until it has been received correctly.

In the frame manager shown here, each network requires three processes. The first process accepts incoming frames and enqueues each in a communication port to be processed locally or forwarded to another machine. The second process accepts frames from the local output queue or the forwarding queue, and sends them out to the next machine. The third process, a timer, cooperates with the output process to time acknowledgements; it prevents deadlocks by enabling the output process to wake up and resend frames even if the acknowledgement is lost.

To make the communication system efficient, the frame layer uses buffer pools and communication ports. The frame routines accept and return pointers to frames, even though the upper layers only deal with datagrams or packets. Because buffers are large enough to hold a complete frame, lower layers of the network software never need to copy packets into datagrams or datagrams into frames.

FOR FURTHER STUDY

The general scheme for network layers presented here comes from Postel [1981]. Although the details of frame layout differ from those used on other networks, the same basic frame components can be found in most. An alternative, designed for commercial carriers can be found in CCITT [1978]. Tanenbaum [1981] surveys many networks and compares some of the layering schemes.

EXERCISES

16.1   Many systems add a *checksum* to the header of each frame so that the receiver has higher probability of finding errors. Modify the frame header to contain a 16-bit checksum as well as a length and sequence number. Compute a value for the checksum so that adding all 16-bit words in the frame to the checksum (ignoring overflows) produces zero. (Note: you may decide to transmit an even number of bytes, but be sure to somehow recover the "correct" length of the frame).

16.2   Investigate error correcting codes other than simple checksums that can be used to verify that frames arrive intact.

16.3   Procedure *frsend* is "blocking" in the sense that it does not return to its caller until the frame has been transferred and a positive acknowledgement received. Modify *frsend* to stop trying after some fixed number of attempts fail, and report the problem to its caller.

16.4   Identify at least three advantages of dividing communication into packets or frames instead of transferring arbitrarily long messages. (Hint: see next problem).

16.5   The packet length can be changed to minimize the number of bytes transferred. Assume that characters arrive scrambled with probability $1/c$, and that the entire packet must be retransmitted if any character in it is scrambled. Characters in retransmitted packets have the same probability of being scrambled. Ignoring the number of header bytes and acknowledgements, derive a formula for optimum packet length for a message of size M.

16.6 A network traffic policy is "fair" if any pair of machines has equal chance to exchange packets. The Xinu frame selection policy always chooses forwarded frames over those being sent from higher levels. Show that this policy is not "fair".

16.7 Argue that priority should be given to outbound frames carrying packets to gateways (i.e., packets intended for networks other than the local one).

16.8 Consider traffic flow on a Xinu ring network plagued by interference. Suppose the line carrying acknowledgements from machine B back to A works intermittently and describe the flow of frames.

16.9 The procedure *frinit* creates a different frame buffer pool for each network. Under what circumstances is this better than having a single frame buffer pool for all networks? When is the latter method better? (You may assume that all networks use roughly the same size frames.)

16.10 Play detective with these clues: One of the machines on a Xinu ring crashes after being squashed by an irate student who could not solve this problem. The remaining students disconnect the dead machine and rewire the ring to exclude it, leaving the remaining machines running. Communication continues. During lunch that day a single wire breaks, and the students return to find that they cannot send frames across the network. When the wire is reconnected the network does not seem to recover — none of the frames being generated reach their destination even though a hardware monitor reveals that the machines are all busy sending frames and ACKS (not NACKS). What happened? How can the frame routines be changed to stop this problem?

16.11 Modify the frame-level routines to collect statistics on the number of errors (frame sequence errors, length errors, etc).

16.12 Design a two-way ring network. Start with the frame-level layer, and determine what primitives the lower layer should provide.

16.13 Design the internet layer for a Xinu ring.

17

A Disk Driver

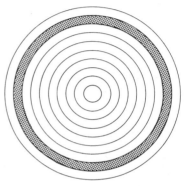

This chapter describes the design of device driver routines for secondary storage devices called *disks*. At this level, the disk is viewed as a randomly accessible array of blocks. The next chapter describes how higher layers of the file system software build on this driver to provide named files and directories.

Disk drivers differ from the single-character device drivers covered earlier in several ways. Because disk devices are more complex than asynchronous serial line units, the interaction between the driver software and the device is more complicated. The disk is a *random access* device. Therefore, the driver must position the disk arm as well as transfer data. Even the basic hardware differs. Disk hardware uses *direct-memory-access* mode (*DMA*), so it does not interrupt the CPU for every character transfer. Instead, the driver must arrange to transfer data in large blocks.

17.1 Operations Supplied By The Disk Driver

When users think of secondary storage devices like disks, they visualize programs or textual material organized into files, with files further organized into directories. It is the file system software that provides such facilities, not the hardware. At the device driver level, a disk is nothing more than a large array of data blocks that can be accessed randomly using three basic operations: select a block, copy the contents of the selected block from disk to memory, or copy the contents of memory to the selected block on disk. The data blocks, which correspond to *sectors* on the disk, are all the same size. (The disk used with Xinu has 512 bytes per sector, a typical size).

Because the raw hardware provides block transfer, it makes sense to design a disk driver that *read*s and *write*s entire blocks. The question becomes how to include the notion of "block selection" in the existing high-level I/O operations. The high-level operation *seek* might be appropriate, because it was designed to move to a specified position in a file. Requiring a user to first call *seek* to position the disk arm and then *read* or *write* to transfer data would be clumsy and inconvenient. To keep the driver interface simple, we will design the driver to always transfer exactly one block, and to use the "length" argument of *read* or *write* to specify a position. For example, the call

read(DISKDEV, buff, 5)

requests the driver to read all of block five into memory starting at location *buff*.

As long as calls to *read* and *write* include a block position, a separate *seek* operation is unnecessary. In many systems, however, disk controller hardware does not permit simultaneous transfer from two disks even though it does allow simultaneous motion of all disk arms. Operating systems using such hardware can significantly reduce disk access times by moving one disk arm to the desired position while reading a block from another disk. Arm movement is the most costly part of disk access, so overlapping *seeks* with computation (and transfer operations on other disks) is an important optimization. To ensure that higher layers of software can perform such optimization, a *seek* operation will be included in the design.

Thus, the driver will supply three operations to higher level routines: *read*, which copies a single block from the disk into memory; *write*, which copies data from memory onto a specified disk block; and *seek*, which positions the disk head over a specified block without transferring data. Having decided on the interface, we are ready to begin writing the driver. Before discussing the three driver routines that correspond to the high-level operations, we consider the hardware interface, and describe how the driver manages requests internally.

17.2 Controller Request And Interface Register Descriptions

Chapter 2 described the controller request block format and interface device registers. Files *xebec.h* and *dtc.h* give the C declarations for these structures:

```
/* xebec.h */

/* Xebec S1410 5.25 inch Winchester Disk Controller */

struct  xbdcb   {                       /* Xebec disk controller regs.  */
        char    xop;                    /* command class/opcode         */
```

```
        char    xunit;          /* unit/high-order address bits */
        char    xmaddr;         /* middle-order address bits    */
        char    xladdr;         /* low-order address bits       */
        char    xcount;         /* block count                  */
        char    xcnt1;          /* control field                */
        char    xres1;          /* reserved field #1            */
        char    xres2;          /* reserved field #2            */
};


/* Xebec controller operation codes */


#define XOTDR    0              /* Test Drive Ready             */
#define XORCAL   1              /* Recalibrate                  */
#define XONONO   2              /* Reserved (is a no-no)        */
#define XORSS    3              /* Request Sense Status         */
#define XOFMTD   4              /* Format Drive                 */
#define XOCTF    5              /* Check Track Format           */
#define XOFMTT   6              /* Format Track                 */
#define XOFMTBT  7              /* Format Bad Track             */
#define XOREAD   8              /* Read                         */
#define XONO2    9              /* Reserved (is also a no-no)   */
#define XOWRITE 10              /* Write                        */
#define XOSEEK  11              /* Seek                         */
#define XOINIT  12              /* Initialize Drive Character.  */
#define XOREBEL 13              /* Read ECC Burst Error Length  */
#define XORAMD  14              /* Perform RAM Diagnostic Test  */


#define XRETRY   0              /* retry control byte           */
```

In file *xebec.h*, structure *xbdcb* specifies the format of controller request records. Field *xop* contains an operation code. Symbolic constants beginning with "XO" define some of the possible operations — *XOREAD*, *XOWRITE*, and *XOSEEK* have the obvious meanings. Details like the values of specific operation codes and the format of the request record vary from vendor to vendor, so they are not worth remembering. It is sufficient to observe the general contents of the controller request and how it has been declared in C.

File *dtc.h* defines the C structures and symbolic constants used with the host interface device. Again, details are unimportant; refer to Chapter 2 for a description.

```
/* dtc.h */

/* Digital Technology Corp. DTC-11-1 disk controller host interface */

struct  dtc     {                       /* controller interface regs.  */
        int     dt_ccsr;                /* command completion status   */
        int     dt_csr;                 /* control and status register */
        char    *dt_dar;                /* data address register       */
        struct  xbdcb   *dt_car;        /* command address register    */
        int     dt_xdar;                /* extension of dar (not used)  */
        int     dt_xcar;                /* extension of car (not used)  */
};

/* bits in the dtc csr register */

#define DTGO     0000001                /* "go" bit - start interface   */
#define DTRESET 0000002                 /* "force reset" bit            */
#define DTINTR  0000100                 /* enable interface interrupt   */
#define DTDONE  0000200                 /* command done                 */
#define DTERROR 0100000                 /* some error occurred          */
```

Structure *dtc* specifies the layout of the interface device control registers. The most striking difference between these and the serial line unit device registers is that the control and status register does not occupy the lowest address location; a completion status register precedes it. Symbolic constants beginning "DT" specify particular bits in the device *csr* register as explained in Chapter 2.

17.3 The List Of Pending Disk Requests

Like other device drivers, disk driver routines are partitioned into two sets, the upper-half and the lower-half, that communicate through a shared data structure. The shared structure includes a list of pending requests. Upper-half routines enqueue a request for an operation, start the device if it is idle, and then *wait* for it to complete. The lower-half, an interrupt handler that is called when an operation completes, starts the next operation and awakens the process waiting for the request that just completed.

Before considering the upper and lower-half driver procedures, we need to decide on the content and format of the data area that they share. Following the terminology used with previous drivers, the shared structure is called a *control block*. The list of pending operations forms the centerpiece of this control block. In practice, the designer only adds fields to the control block structure as the driver routines are built, but we will examine all the fields now and see how the driver uses them later in the chapter.

Structure *dsblk*, found in file *disk.h*, defines the disk control block in C.

```
/* disk.h - dssync, dsdirec */

#include <xebec.h>                  /* disk controller constants    */
#include <dtc.h>                    /* disk interface constants     */

typedef unsigned int    DBADDR;     /* disk data block addresses    */
#define DBNULL          (DBADDR)0177777 /* null disk block address  */

struct  dsblk   {                   /* disk driver control block    */
        struct  dtc     *dcsr;      /* disk interface csr address   */
        struct  dreq    *dreqlst;   /* list of pending requests     */
        int     dnum;               /* device number of this disk   */
        int     dibsem;             /* i-block mutual exclusion sem.*/
        int     dflsem;             /* free list    "        "    " */
        int     ddirsem;            /* directory    "        "    " */
        int     dnfiles;            /* num. of currently open files */
        char    *ddir;              /* address of in-core directory */
        struct  xbdcb   ddcb;       /* holds command that interface */
                                    /*   sends to disk controller   */
};
extern  struct  dsblk   dstab[];

struct  dreq    {                   /* node in list of requests     */
        DBADDR  drdba;              /* disk block address to use    */
        int     drpid;              /* process id making request    */
        char    *drbuff;            /* buffer address for read/write*/
        char    drop;               /* operation: READ/WRITE/SEEK   */
        int     drstat;             /* returned status OK/SYSERR     */
        struct  dreq    *drnext;    /* ptr to next node on req. list*/
};

#define DRNULL  (struct dreq *) 0   /* null pointer in request list */
#define DIRBLK  0                   /* block used to hold directory */
#define DONQ    2                   /* status if request enqueued   */
#define DBUFSIZ 512                 /* size of disk data block      */
#define DREQSIZ sizeof(struct dreq) /* size of disk request node    */
#ifndef NDBUFF
#define NDBUFF  10                  /* number of disk data buffers  */
#endif
#define NDREQ   10                  /* number of disk request buf.  */
#define DREAD   XOREAD              /* read command in dreq.drop    */
#define DWRITE  XOWRITE             /* write     "                  */
```

```
#define DSEEK    XOSEEK                /* seek     "                      */
#define DSYNC    XOTDR                 /* sync     "   (test-disk-ready) */

extern   int     dskrbp;               /* disk request node buffer pool*/
extern   int     dskdbp;               /* disk data block buffer pool  */

/* disk control function codes */

#define DSKSYNC 0                      /* synchronize (flush all I/O)  */
#define dssync(ddev)     control((ddev),DSKSYNC);

#define dsdirec(ddev)    ((struct dir *)devtab[ddev].dvioblk->ddir)
```

Fields *dcsr* and *dnum* in structure *dsblk* should look familiar because they occur in all driver control blocks: *dcsr* gives the address of the device registers, and *dnum* gives the device id for the disk. Other fields present no surprises. The driver uses field *ddcb* to store the 6-byte controller request record that it passes to the controller when starting an operation. Field *dreqlst* points to the list of requested operations (or equals *DRNULL* if the list is empty). The driver follows an important invariant:

> *The first request on the list is always the one that the hardware is performing; if the list is empty, the hardware is idle.*

The list of pending requests, headed by field *dreqlst*, is a singly linked list where each node on the list has the form given by structure *dreq*. In a given node, field *drdba* specifies the number of the disk block that the operation will affect, and field *drop* specifies the operation to be performed. If the operation transfers data, field *drbuff* gives the memory address for the transfer. This address is assumed to be the start of a 512-byte block. The remaining field, *drstat* is used to communicate status information from the lower-half to the upper-half. The lower-half records information about errors that occur during the operation, and the upper-half extracts the information and passes it to the caller.

17.4 Enqueuing Disk Requests

To reduce the time needed to restart a disk operation after one completes, the disk driver routines follow this rule:

> *The disk driver processes I/O requests in the order that they occur on the request list. When one completes, it is removed from the list and the next one is started.*

Thus, the responsibility for ordering requests in a sensible way falls to the upper-half routines that enqueue requests.

Why is the order of requests important? Remember that disk accesses are slow compared to the processor and memory speed. Most of the time is expended moving the disk arm; the time required is approximately proportional to the distance moved. If all accesses refer to a small locality, the time per access is lower than if the requests refer to blocks scattered over the disk. Unfortunately, the driver receives requests from all processes, so the sequence of blocks specified are not usually restricted to a small locality even if each individual process accesses blocks sequentially. Honoring these requests in a first-in-first-out (FIFO) order usually means moving the arm back and forth across the disk frequently. To reduce the arm motion, disk drivers reorder requests in an attempt to group together requests that access blocks in a small area. (Recall from Chapter 2 that the driver can afford to spend much time organizing requests, even if it only eliminates one or two sweeps of the arm.)

Given a set of outstanding requests, the driver must decide which one to satisfy next. Ideally, it should move the disk arm as little as possible, but postponing requests for outlying blocks indefinitely would be unfair because it would always favor requests in the current locality. Furthermore, the amount of time the driver spends reordering requests should be minimized. What is the best way to satisfy the goals of efficiency and fairness? There is no "best" way; it depends largely on the order in which requests arrive, the mixture of processes that are executing, and the characteristics of the hardware. Fortunately, compromises are possible. With only a small amount of CPU time, the driver can produce an order of requests that takes far less time than honoring requests first-come-first-serve.

Most drivers use rule-of-thumb, or *heuristic* procedures, to help optimize disk accesses. The heuristics, which are easy to compute, usually group requests by locality. For example, we will adopt the following heuristic which orders requests by block position.

> *When adding a request for block B to the existing list of requests, schedule it to be performed between requests i and i+1 if the disk arm will pass over block B on its way from i to i+1. If no such pair i and i+1 exist, add the new request to the end of the list.*

The general idea is to force the disk arm to "sweep" back and forth across the surface, going from low numbered blocks to high numbered ones and back again. Inserting blocks in the existing list optimizes arm movement because it accesses blocks when the arm passes over them. Inserting outlying requests at the end of the list either extends the sweep in one direction or starts it moving in the other.

Implementing the request ordering heuristic is straightforward; as procedure *dskenq* demonstrates.

```
/* dskenq.c - dskenq */

#include <conf.h>
#include <kernel.h>
#include <disk.h>


/*------------------------------------------------------------------
 * dskenq -- enqueue a disk request and start I/O if disk not busy
 *------------------------------------------------------------------
 */
dskenq(drptr, dsptr)
        struct  dreq    *drptr;
        struct  dsblk   *dsptr;
{
        struct  dreq    *p, *q;        /* q follows p through requests */
        DBADDR  block;
        int     st;

        if ( (q=dsptr->dreqlst) == DRNULL ) {
                dsptr->dreqlst = drptr;
                drptr->drnext = DRNULL;
                dskstrt(dsptr);
                return(DONQ);
        }
        block = drptr->drdba;
        for (p = q->drnext ; p != DRNULL ; q=p,p=p->drnext) {
                if (p->drdba==block && (st=dskqopt(p, q, drptr)!=SYSERR))
                                return(st);
                if ( (q->drdba <= block && block < p->drdba) ||
                     (q->drdba >= block && block > p->drdba)  ) {
                        drptr->drnext = p;
                        q->drnext = drptr;
                        return(DONQ);
                }
        }
        drptr->drnext = DRNULL;
        q->drnext = drptr;
        return(DONQ);
}
```

Dskenq first examines the request list to see if it is empty because an empty list means that the device is idle. If the list is empty, it adds the new request, and calls *dskstrt* to start the device. Otherwise, it searches the existing list.

During the search of the request list *dskenq* keeps two pointers, *p* and *q*, because the list is singly linked. As the search proceeds, p and q always point to adjacent nodes; initially, q points to the first node; p points to the node beyond that (or is empty if the list contains one node). Ignore for the moment the first "if" statement in the loop, and consider only the second one. If the request specifies a disk block that lies between the blocks specified in the requests given by p and q, the new request is inserted between them in the list. Otherwise, p and q move down the list. Testing whether the new request lies between two existing requests is done with four comparisons because adjacent blocks on the list may be in either ascending or descending order. Look carefully at the comparisons — *dskenq* takes care to ensure that multiple requests for the same block are handled in FIFO order; overlooking this detail can lead to totally unexpected results.

17.5 Optimizing the Request Queue

Because disk operations take much longer than CPU operations, the driver has been constructed to minimize arm movement. In special cases, further optimization is possible. Consider the situation in which a process attempts to *read* a block for which there is a pending *write* request already in the queue. The driver can copy the data from the buffer associated with the *write* request into the buffer associated with the *read* request, and allow the reading process to continue. Another special case occurs when a second *write* request arrives for a given block before an existing request has been serviced (the driver can discard the first request).

To handle these special cases, *dskenq* uses procedure *dskqopt* as shown below. Look again at the loop in *dskenq* to see how *dskqopt* is called whenever the request being inserted in the list specifies a block number identical to one already in the list. If the "optimization" succeeds, *dskenq* returns to its caller. Otherwise, *dskenq* continues the usual insertion algorithm.

```
/* dskqopt.c - dskqopt */

#include <conf.h>
#include <kernel.h>
#include <disk.h>

/*------------------------------------------------------------------------
 * dskqopt  --  optimize requests to read/write/seek to the same block
 *------------------------------------------------------------------------
 */
dskqopt(p, q, drptr)
struct  dreq    *p, *q, *drptr;
{
        char    *to, *from;
        int     i;
        DBADDR  block;

        /* By definition, sync requests cannot be optimized.  Also,   */
        /* cannot optimize read requests if already reading.          */

        if (drptr->drop==DSYNC || (drptr->drop==DREAD && p->drop==DREAD))
                return(SYSERR);

        if (drptr->drop == DSEEK) {      /* ignore extraneous seeks    */
                freebuf(drptr);
                return(OK);
        }

        if (p->drop == DSEEK) {          /* replace existing seeks     */
                drptr->drnext = p->drnext;
                q->drnext = drptr;
                freebuf(p);
                return(OK);
        }

        if (p->drop==DWRITE && drptr->drop==DWRITE) {   /* dup write   */
                drptr->drnext = p->drnext;
                q->drnext = drptr;
                freebuf(p->drbuff);
                freebuf(p);
                return(OK);
        }

        if (drptr->drop==DREAD && p->drop==DWRITE) {    /* satisfy read */
                to = drptr->drbuff;
```

```
                    from = p->drbuff;
                    for (i=0 ; i<DBUFSIZ ; i++)
                            *to++ = *from++;
                    return(OK);
            }

        if (drptr->drop==DWRITE && p->drop==DREAD) {      /* sat. old read*/
                block = drptr->drdba;
                from = drptr->drbuff;
                for (; p!=DRNULL && p->drdba==block ; p=p->drnext) {
                        q->drnext = p->drnext;
                        to = p->drbuff;
                        for (i=0 ; i<DBUFSIZ ; i++)
                                *to++ = *from++;
                        p->drstat = OK;
                        ready(p->drpid, RESCHNO);
                }
                drptr->drnext = p;
                q->drnext = drptr;
                resched();
                return(OK);
        }
    }
    return(SYSERR);
}
```

17.6 Starting A Disk Operation

Procedure *dskstrt* does the work of starting a disk operation. It builds a controller request in the *ddcb* field of the disk control block. Although the disk block address is an unsigned integer, the controller hardware requires the bytes to be swapped from their usual order. Thus, *dskstrt* uses separate statements to store the two parts of the disk block address.

```
/* dskstrt.c - dskstrt */

#include <conf.h>
#include <kernel.h>
#include <disk.h>


/*------------------------------------------------------------------
 *  dskstrt  --  start an I/O operation on a disk device
 *------------------------------------------------------------------
 */
dskstrt(dsptr)
        struct  dsblk    *dsptr;
{
        struct  xbdcb    *xptr;
        struct  dtc      *dtptr;
        struct  dreq     *drptr;

        /* build command for controller */

        drptr = dsptr->dreqlst;
        xptr = & dsptr->ddcb;
        xptr->xop    = (char) drptr->drop;                /* opcode        */
        xptr->xunit  = (char) 0;                          /* top addr bits*/
        xptr->xmaddr = (char) ((drptr->drdba>>8)&0377);   /* mid addr bits*/
        xptr->xladdr = (char) (drptr->drdba & 0377);      /* low addr bits*/
        xptr->xcount = (char) 1;                          /* num of blocks*/
        xptr->xcntl  = (char) XRETRY;                     /* retry code    */

        /* feed command to controller through interface */

        dtptr = dsptr->dcsr;
        dtptr->dt_dar = drptr->drbuff;
        dtptr->dt_car = xptr;
        dtptr->dt_xdar = dtptr->dt_xcar = 0;
        dtptr->dt_csr = DTINTR | DTGO;
}
```

Once the request block has been filled in, *dskstrt* passes its address to the device interface. It also passes the address of the data buffer and clears the extended
address registers. To initiate the operation it sets the interrupt enable bit and "go"
bits of the interface control and status register. These details are all hardware-
specific; they have been isolated in one place to make them easy to change.

17.7 Driver Initialization

Although the driver initialization is designed after the other parts, we have chosen to examine it now because it also controls the hardware directly. At start-up, the system calls *init* for each disk device; *init* uses the device switch table to transfer control to the corresponding driver routine *dsinit*. Procedure *dsinit* fills in the disk control block and resets the disk.

```
/* dsinit.c - dsinit */

#include <conf.h>
#include <kernel.h>
#include <disk.h>

#ifdef   Ndsk
struct   dsblk    dstab[Ndsk];
#endif
int      dskdbp, dskrbp;

/*------------------------------------------------------------------
 * dsinit  --  initialize disk drive device
 *------------------------------------------------------------------
 */
dsinit(devptr)
        struct   devsw    *devptr;
{
        struct   dsblk    *dsptr;
        struct   dtc      *dtptr;
        int      status;
        char     ps;

        disable(ps);
        devptr->dvioblk = dsptr = &dstab[ devptr->dvminor ];
        dsptr->dcsr     = devptr->dvcsr;
        dsptr->dreqlst  = DRNULL;
        dsptr->dnum     = devptr->dvnum;
        dsptr->dibsem   = screate(1);
        dsptr->dflsem   = screate(1);
        dsptr->ddirsem  = screate(1);
        dsptr->dnfiles  = 0;
        dsptr->ddir     = getbuf(dskdbp);
        iosetvec(devptr->dvnum, dsptr, dsptr);
```

```
                /* read directory block: setup read command then start interface */

        dsptr->ddcb.xop    = (char) XOREAD;
        dsptr->ddcb.xunit  = (char) 0;
        dsptr->ddcb.xcntl  = (char) XRETRY;
        dsptr->ddcb.xmaddr = (char) ((DIRBLK>>8)&(0377));
        dsptr->ddcb.xladdr = (char) (DIRBLK&0377);
        dsptr->ddcb.xcount = (char) 1;
        dtptr = dsptr->dcsr;
        dtptr->dt_dar   = dsptr->ddir;
        dtptr->dt_car   = &dsptr->ddcb;
        dtptr->dt_xdar  = dtptr->dt_xcar = NULL;
        dtptr->dt_csr   = DTGO;
        while ( ( (status=dtptr->dt_csr) & DTDONE) == 0)
                ;
        if (status & DTERROR)
                panic("Disk error");
        restore(ps);
        return(OK);
}
```

Following the same conventions used by other drivers, *dsinit* assumes it will be called once, before other operations are attempted.

Initialization is surprisingly simple. It consists of allocating a buffer to hold block 0 and three semaphores. The file system software uses the buffer and semaphores; they are not part of the driver. After initializing fields in the disk control block, *dsinit* calls *iosetvec* to fill in the interrupt vectors and interrupt dispatch table.

To test the disk hardware, *dsinit* reads block 0 into memory. (The file system uses block 0 as a directory.) Because the system executes the initialization routine before interrupts are enabled, *dsinit* must poll to determine when the operation completes. Thus, the code in *dsinit* is an abbreviated form of that in *dskstrt* — it starts the operation and polls the device. After it builds the 6-byte controller request in the *ddcb* field of the *dsblk* structure, *dsinit* passes the address of the controller request to the host interface and sets the "go" bit in the interface CSR register; it does not set the "interrupt enable" bit.

Polling proceeds as it would with any device: *dsinit* executes a loop testing the "done" bit in the host interface CSR register again and again. When the operation finally completes, the done bit becomes 1, terminating the loop. Before returning to its caller, *dsinit* checks the error bit in the device CSR register to make sure that no error occurred during the operation.

17.8 The Upper-Half Read Routine

Having defined the request list and driver initialization routines we are ready
to design the upper-half routines that implement the operations *read*, *write*, and
seek; we begin with *read*. Basically, the upper-half input routine must build a request node, insert the request in the list of pending requests, and wait until the
lower-half routine indicates that the request has been honored. The code consists of
procedure *dsread*, shown below in file *dsread.c*.

```
/* dsread.c - dsread */

#include <conf.h>
#include <kernel.h>
#include <proc.h>
#include <disk.h>


/*------------------------------------------------------------------
 * dsread  --   read a block from a disk device
 *------------------------------------------------------------------
 */
dsread(devptr, buff, block)
        struct  devsw   *devptr;
        char    *buff;
        DBADDR  block;
{
        struct  dreq    *drptr;
        int     stat;
        char    ps;

        disable(ps);
        drptr = (struct dreq *) getbuf(dskrbp);
        drptr->drdba = block;
        drptr->drpid = currpid;
        drptr->drbuff = buff;
        drptr->drop = DREAD;
        if ( (stat=dskenq(drptr, devptr->dvioblk)) == DONQ) {
                suspend(currpid);
                stat = drptr->drstat;
        }
        freebuf(drptr);
        restore(ps);
        return(stat);
}
```

Dsread allocates a request node from the buffer pool that contains all request nodes, and then fills in the desired disk block address, memory buffer address, and the operation requested, "read". Once the request has been specified, *dsread* calls *dskenq* to enqueue the new request in the list of pending requests and to start the device if necessary. After the request has been enqueued, *dsread* suspends the calling process until the operation completes and the lower-half resumes it. When resumed by the lower-half, the upper-half deallocates the request block, extracts the exit status value left by the lower-half, and returns to its caller to indicate whether an error occurred.

It may seem odd that the driver is designed to allocate storage for request nodes from a single, global buffer pool (*dskrbp*). Keeping buffers in a single pool instead of dividing them among disk devices has benefits and liabilities. For example, it reduces the chance that a process will be blocked waiting for a request node, but allows activity on one disk to prevent activity on another. The exercises consider other ways in which keeping a separate set of request nodes for each disk device affect the behavior of the system.

17.9 The Upper-Half Output Routine

The upper-half output driver behaves quite differently from the upper-half input driver. Instead of waiting for a request to be honored, the output driver allocates and fills in a request node, enqueues it in the list of pending requests, and returns to its caller without waiting for the request to be honored. By doing so, it assumes that the data has been placed in a buffer, and that the caller will not change the buffer between the time it calls *write* and the time the data is written.

Returning to the caller before data has been written is a violation of the general principles for input and output laid down in Chapter 9. There, we said that the system should block processes until output has been consumed. Earlier drivers adhered to this principle either by copying data into an internal buffer or by suspending the process until the data had been written. Besides violating the general design guidelines and introducing inconsistency, arranging for the driver to return before the data has been written is dangerous because it leaves programmers susceptible to an error that is easy to make but difficult to diagnose. After a call to *write*, only the address of the buffer has been recorded; if the program continues to change the data, changes made between the call to *write* and the time the lower-half copies the data to disk will appear in the copy on disk.

If non-blocking output is so dangerous, why design the disk driver to use it? The answer is that the current design is a compromise. Suspending the caller until the operation completes will not work because disk operations are so slow that processes using disks would spend most of their time suspended. The upper-half could avoid waiting if it copied data into a buffer itself. An earlier version of the upper-half output routine did just that — it allocated a buffer and copied the data from the caller's area into the buffer before returning. It turned out, however, that the CPU spent most of its time copying data from one buffer to another. Closer examination of the code in the next layer of the file system revealed that routines calling the output driver usually deallocated the buffer immediately after writing data, so the driver was copying data from one system buffer to another needlessly. To avoid wasting time, the driver was changed to write directly from the specified address, leaving the responsibility of buffering to the upper layers of file system software.

Is there a better alternative to driver optimization? If users were expected to call the driver routines directly, nonblocking output routines would be unacceptable. As we will see in the next chapter, only Xinu file system routines call the disk driver, so we can be careful to ensure that they buffer output before calling the driver. In a system designed to support calls from both user programs and file system routines, the problem can be solved by building two upper-level interfaces for the disk driver. One interface, called only by other system routines, would provide unbuffered output like the current driver; the other, called by user programs, would copy data into buffers before returning to the caller.

17.10 Implementation Of The Upper-Half Output Routine

Procedure *dswrite*, found in file *dswrite.c*, implements the upper-half output routine described above.

```
/* dswrite.c - dswrite */

#include <conf.h>
#include <kernel.h>
#include <proc.h>
#include <disk.h>


/*------------------------------------------------------------------------
 * dswrite  --  write a block (system buffer) onto a disk device
 *------------------------------------------------------------------------
 */
dswrite(devptr, buff, block)
        struct  devsw   *devptr;
        char    *buff;
        DBADDR  block;
{
        struct  dreq    *drptr;
        char    ps;

        disable(ps);
        drptr = (struct dreq *) getbuf(dskrbp);
        drptr->drbuff = buff;
        drptr->drdba = block;
        drptr->drpid = currpid;
        drptr->drop = DWRITE;
        dskenq(drptr, devptr->dvioblk);
        restore(ps);
        return(OK);
}
```

Like the input routine, *dswrite* is straightforward. It allocates a request node from global buffer pools *dskrbp*, fills in the request block, and calls *dskenq* to add it to the list of requests.

17.11 The Upper-Half Seek Routine

The third upper-half routine, *dsseek*, implements the *seek* operation:

```
/* dsseek.c - dsseek */

#include <conf.h>
#include <kernel.h>
#include <proc.h>
#include <disk.h>

/*------------------------------------------------------------------
 *  dsseek  --  schedule a request to move the disk arm
 *------------------------------------------------------------------
 */
dsseek(devptr, block)
        struct  devsw   *devptr;
        DBADDR  block;
{
        struct  dreq    *drptr;
        char    ps;

        disable(ps);
        drptr = (struct dreq *) getbuf(dskrbp);
        drptr->drdba = block;
        drptr->drpid = currpid;
        drptr->drbuff = NULL;
        drptr->drop = DSEEK;

        /* enqueued with normal policy like other read/write requests */

        dskenq(drptr, devptr->dvioblk);
        restore(ps);
        return(OK);
}
```

Dsseek operates much like *dswrite*. It allocates a request block, fills in the operation and block address fields, and calls *dskenq* to enqueue the request in the list of pending requests. Like *dswrite*, *dsseek* returns to its caller as soon as the request has been enqueued, without waiting for the operation to complete.

17.12 The Lower-Half Of The Disk Driver

The lower-half of the disk driver is called whenever the interface device interrupts to signal that the controller has completed an operation. Its task is simple: remove the first request from the head of the list of pending requests (the operation that just finished), start the next operation if one exists, and dispose of the request

node just removed. If the request just satisfied was an input request, the lower-half
awakens the reading process, allowing it to return to its caller. Otherwise, the
lower-half deallocates the request node itself (the data buffer as well if the operation was a *write*) because the process that initiated the operation has already returned from the upper-half routines.

Procedure *dsinter* implements the lower-half.

```
/* dsinter.c - dsinter */

#include <conf.h>
#include <kernel.h>
#include <disk.h>


/*------------------------------------------------------------------------
 * dsinter -- process disk interrupt (DTC interface; XEBEC controller)
 *------------------------------------------------------------------------
 */
INTPROC dsinter(dsptr)
        struct  dsblk   *dsptr;
{
        struct  dtc     *dtptr;
        struct  dreq    *drptr;

        dtptr = dsptr->dcsr;
        drptr = dsptr->dreqlst;
        if (drptr == DRNULL) {
                panic("Disk interrupt when disk not busy");
                return;
        }
        if (dtptr->dt_csr & DTERROR)
                drptr->drstat = SYSERR;
        else
                drptr->drstat = OK;
        if ( (dsptr->dreqlst=drptr->drnext) != DRNULL)
                dskstrt(dsptr);
        switch (drptr->drop) {

                case DREAD:
                case DSYNC:
                        ready(drptr->drpid, RESCHYES);
                        return;

                case DWRITE:
                        freebuf(drptr->drbuff);
```

```
                              /* fall through */
                case DSEEK:
                          freebuf(drptr);
        }
}
```

The interrupt dispatcher calls *dsinter* whenever the disk interrupts to signal that an operation has completed. After recording the address of the first request node in *drptr*, *dsinter* detaches it from the request list, and calls procedure *dskstrt* to start the next operation if the list remains nonempty. Depending on the operation just completed, *dsinter* resumes the calling process or deallocates the request node. If the operation was a *read*, it resumes the process that requested input and returns. If the operation was a *write* or *seek*, *dsinter* deallocates the request node by calling *freebuf*; in the case of a *write* it deallocates the data buffer as well.

17.13 Flushing Pending Requests

Because *dswrite* does not wait for data transfer, a process cannot know when blocks have been written to disk. However, making sure that blocks have been written may be important. For example, the system may want to ensure that activity on all disk devices completes before shutdown.

To allow programs in higher layers to check that all disk transfers have occurred, the driver includes a primitive that will block the calling process until all existing requests have been performed. Because "synchronizing" the disk is not a data transfer operation, we will use the high-level operation *control*. To flush pending requests, a process calls

        control(device, DSKSYNC)

The driver suspends the caller until all existing requests have been satisfied on the specified device; then, the call returns.

Procedure *dscntl* implements the upper-half *control* function.

```
/* dscntl.c - dscntl */

#include <conf.h>
#include <kernel.h>
#include <proc.h>
#include <disk.h>

/*------------------------------------------------------------------
 *  dscntl  --  control disk driver/device
 *------------------------------------------------------------------
 */
dscntl(devptr, func)
        struct  devsw   *devptr;
{
        int     stat;
        char    ps;

        disable(ps);
        switch (func) {

                case DSKSYNC:
                        stat = dsksync(devptr);
                        break;

                default:
                        stat = SYSERR;
                        break;
        }
        restore(ps);
        return(stat);
}
```

Synchronization is specified with an argument given by symbolic constant *DSKSYNC*. *Dscntl* invokes procedure *dsksync* to synchronize the disk; its definition can be found in file *dsksync.c*.

```
/* dsksync.c - dsksync */

#include <conf.h>
#include <kernel.h>
#include <proc.h>
#include <disk.h>

/*------------------------------------------------------------------
```

```
*  dsksync  -- wait for all outstanding disk requests before returning
*-------------------------------------------------------------------
*/
dsksync(devptr)
struct  devsw   *devptr;
{
        struct  dreq    *drptr, *p, *q;
        int     stat;

        if ( (q=(devptr->dvioblk)->dreqlst) == DRNULL )
                return(OK);
        drptr = (struct dreq *) getbuf(dskrbp);
        drptr->drdba = 0;
        drptr->drpid = currpid;
        drptr->drbuff = NULL;
        drptr->drop = DSYNC;
        drptr->drnext = DRNULL;


        /* place at end of request list */

        for (p=q->drnext ; p!=DRNULL ; q=p,p=p->drnext)
                ;
        q->drnext = drptr;
        drptr->drstat = SYSERR;
        suspend(currpid);
        stat = drptr->drstat;
        freebuf(drptr);
        return(stat);
}
```

Like the other upper-half drivers, *dsksync* allocates a request node and fills it. Unlike the other drivers it does not use *dskenq* to insert the request in the list. Instead, it searches the list using pointers *p* and *q*, and inserts the request when *q* points to the last node. Because the block specified is 0, the request is guaranteed to go at the end of the list (the exercises discuss one of the shortcomings of this implementation). To avoid making synchronization a special case, *dsksync* requests an operation that tests the disk status. When the request reaches the front of the list, the driver passes it to the hardware exactly as it does for other operations.

When the "sync" operation completes, the lower-half receives an interrupt, and awakens the process executing *dsksync* as it awakens the process executing *dsread* when a *read* operation completes. After being awakened, the process that suspended itself returns to *dscntl*, and from there to its caller.

17.14 Summary

This chapter considers the design of a low-level disk driver that implements *read*, *write*, *seek*, and *control* operations. At this level, the disk is viewed as a large array of randomly accessible data blocks; there is no notion of named files, directories, or the index techniques used to speed searching. Reading consists of copying data from a specified block on disk into memory; writing consists of copying data from memory onto a specified disk block. Because the hardware can read and write directly into memory without interrupting the CPU, the upper-half routines merely enqueue requests for service. Whenever an operation completes, the lower-half routine takes the next pending request from the queue, and starts the hardware performing that operation.

The driver reduces the time required to honor requests by reordering them to minimize disk arm movement. When enqueuing a request, upper-half routines insert it between two adjacent existing requests if the arm will pass over the requested block while traveling from one block to the other. Otherwise, it adds the request to the end of the list. While this heuristic does not guarantee minimum access time for a set of requests, it works well in practice.

Because copying data for each transfer requires too much CPU time, the disk driver has been designed to accept output requests, and return to the caller without copying the data into system buffers. This strategy can be dangerous because it places all responsibility for buffering on the caller. Although unbuffered output forms an efficient foundation for file system routines, it should be rewritten before being used as a general-purpose disk interface.

FOR FURTHER STUDY

The treatment of disk scheduling heuristics in Denning [1967] compares First-Come-First-Served (FCFS) and Shortest-Seek-Time-First (SSTF) along with a heuristic similar to the one described here. Teorey [1972], Wilhelm [1976], and Hofri [1980] compare FCFS with SSTF, giving an in-depth analysis.

EXERCISES

17.1 Build a synchronous output driver that waits for I/O to complete before returning to the calling process.

17.2 The upper-half tries to minimize the amount of disk arm movement by keeping the list of requests ordered by block number. Show that the algorithm is not optimum by finding a sequence of requests for which the algorithm produces a list that requires more arm movement than necessary. What is the worst possible sequence of requests that can be presented to this algorithm?

17.3   Should requests from high-priority processes take precedence over requests from low-priority processes?

17.4   Verify that the driver honors all requests for a given block in FIFO order.

17.5   Investigate other algorithms like the "elevator" algorithm (mentioned in Knuth [1968]) that are used to order disk requests.

17.6   Verify that a request to "synchronize" will not return until all pending requests have been satisfied. Is there a bound on the time it can be delayed by new requests?

17.7   Describe a sequence of operations in which a call to *dssync* does not return even though all requests that were pending when it was inserted have completed. Redesign the synchronization routine to allow the caller to wait for a specific request.

17.8   Rewrite the driver routines so that "sync" requests do not control the hardware or generate interrupts.

17.9   Rewrite the driver routines so they allow each controller to control several physical disks.

18

File Systems

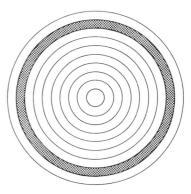

This chapter discusses the purpose of file systems, and the type of objects that can be kept in such systems, as well as the details of the software that manages data files on a local disk.

18.1 What Is A File System?

A *file system* consists of software that manages permanent data objects, objects whose values persist longer than the processes that create and use them. Permanent data is kept in *files* on secondary storage devices like disks. These files are organized into *directories*. Conceptually, each file consists of a sequence of data objects (e.g., a sequence of integers). The file system provides operations that *create* or *delete* a file, *open* a file given its name, *read* the next object from an open file, *write* an object onto an open file, or *close* a file. If the file system allows random access, it may also provide a way to *seek* to a specified location in a file.

File system software does much more than manipulate individual files on secondary storage — it provides an abstract name space and high-level operations to manipulate objects in that space. The abstract space consists of the set of valid file names. It can be as simple as "the set of strings formed from at least one but fewer than nine alphabetic characters", or as complex as "the set of strings that form a valid encoding of the network, machine, user, subdirectory, and file identifiers." In some systems, the syntax of names in the abstract space conveys information about their type (e.g., text files end in ".TXT"). In others, names give information about the organization of the file system (e.g., file names that begin with "M1_d0:" reside on disk 0 of machine 1).

Names in the abstract space need not correspond to conventional files on secondary storage. They may refer to devices, services that the system supplies, or files that reside on another machine. For example, the name *console* may correspond to the *CONSOLE* device; the name *printer* may correspond to a service that prints a copy of data written to it; and the name *foo:bar* may correspond to disk file *bar* accessed through network *foo*.

Allowing names to refer to devices and services is convenient because it permits programs to perform a variety of useful functions that depend only on the file names accessed. Consider, for example, a general-purpose utility program, *CP*, that reads data from one file and writes it to another (i.e. copies the contents of one file to another). If the abstract space contains names of devices and remote files, *CP* can be used: to print the contents of a file on the console terminal; to accept input from the console and write it on a disk file; to copy a file from a remote machine to the local one; or to copy the contents of one disk file to another.

What high-level operations should the file system support to make it possible to write programs like *CP*? The answer depends largely on the type of objects that the name space includes, and the structure of data files on the disk. If the file name space includes devices, the set of operations that programs perform on files must map into the set of operations they can perform on devices. If the file system treats data files as a sequence of bytes, operations that transfer bytes may suffice; but if data files have more structure, operations that transfer records may be required.

Our choice of high-level operations is motivated by a desire to make devices and files compatible, and to keep the software small. It uses the following principle:

> *The file system considers each object to be a sequence of zero or more bytes; any further structure must be enforced by user-level programs.*

Treating files as streams of bytes makes the file system primitives easier to implement and remember, keeps them applicable to devices and services as well as conventional files, and allows programs to impose whatever structure they desire on the file. For example, if integers are two bytes long, programs can create a file of integers by always transferring two bytes at a time.

Having decided to treat files as streams of bytes, we are ready to design a set of high-level operations for files. Our system will use exactly the same high-level operations that were used for devices. Thus, the file system will support *read*, *write*, *putc*, *getc*, *init*, *open*, *close*, *seek*, and *control* primitives. The semantics of these operations will depend on the type of file just as their interpretation depended on the type of device. (To be honest, we should admit that the set of device-independent operations were chosen with both devices and files in mind.)

When applied to conventional disk files, the high-level operations produce the following effects. *Open*ing a named file connects an executing process with the data on disk, and establishes a pointer to the first byte. Operations *getc* and *read* retrieve bytes of data from the file and advance the pointer. Operations *putc* and *write* change bytes in the file and move the pointer along, extending the file if new data is written beyond the end. The *seek* operation moves the pointer to a specified position in the file. Finally, *close* detaches the running process from the disk file.

18.2 Disk And File Servers

Machines that connect to a network can have a file system even if they do not have a local secondary storage device. File systems on diskless machines pass requests across the network to a *server* machine. The server contains special-purpose software that interprets the requests and sends data back as needed. The server may provide a *pseudo-disk* for each workstation, leaving most of the work of managing files and directories to the individual machine, or it may perform most of the file system services itself, relieving the individual workstations of that responsibility. Whether the server simulates a disk (i.e., provides a large array of disk blocks that must be accessed by number), or a complete file system (i.e., provides *read* and *write* operations on named files) is determined largely by the hardware environment and expected use of the system. The latter style is more popular because it means each individual machine needs less software.

Neither disk servers or file servers are difficult to implement given reliable network software and the software to manage local disk files. The questions of how to name and address the server, where to store directories, and what pieces of the file system name space are shared among all users are the most difficult to answer because they depend on the hardware configuration and intended use of the system. Rather than tackle the issues of how to assign names or how to access files over a network, we will turn our attention to the more fundamental piece of the file system, the efficient, general-purpose access mechanism that manages information on a local disk.

18.3 A Local File System

Files are called *local* to a given machine if they reside on a disk that is connected to the machine. The design of software that manages such files is nontrivial; it has been the subject of much research. Local file software must support the high-level operations as defined above: *read*, *write*, *putc*, *getc*, *seek*, *open*, and *close*. Although these operations seem simple, complexity arises from the details of buffer and index management, and concurrency control.

To what extent should the system support concurrent operations? Large systems usually allow arbitrary numbers of processes to read and write arbitrary numbers of files concurrently. The chief difficulty with multiple access lies in specifying exactly what it means to have multiple processes interacting on a single file. When will readers be able to access changed portions? If two processes attempt to write to the same disk block, which will be accepted? How can a process lock pieces of a file to avoid interference?

The generality of allowing multiple processes to read and write a file is usually not necessary on small systems. Thus, to limit the software complexity and make better use of disk space, small systems constrain the ways in which files can be accessed. Instead of allowing files to grow incrementally as needed, they may require the user to preallocate space for the file. They may also limit the number of files that a given process can access simultaneously, or the number of processes that can simultaneously access a given file.

Our goal is to design file system software that makes it convenient to create and extend files without making the system unnecessarily large or slow. As a compromise between generality and efficiency, we will allow multiple processes to access the file system concurrently, and we will allow a single process to access an arbitrary number of files concurrently; but we will restrict access of each file to at most one process. Finally, because preallocating space makes programming difficult, we will allow files to grow dynamically. The most significant consequence of this design is that good data structures will be needed to allocate disk space and access files.

18.4 Data Structures For The File System

To support concurrent file growth and random movement, the file system allocates disk blocks dynamically, and uses an *index* mechanism to locate them quickly. Our design partitions the disk into three separate areas as shown in Figure 18.1.

directory	index	data area

Figure 18.1 The disk partitioned into three areas

Physical disk blocks in the data area are referred to as *data blocks* because they hold all the data that has been written onto files. The file system allocates unused data blocks from a free list when they are needed, and returns them to the free list when a file is deleted. The data blocks allocated to a given file contain no pointers to link them together or to relate them to the file; such information resides only in the file's index.

Separate from the data area, the index area on each disk contains a set of *index blocks* or *i-blocks*. Each file on the disk has its own index, which consists of a singly-linked list of i-blocks. Each i-block contains pointers to a set of data blocks as shown in Figure 18.2.

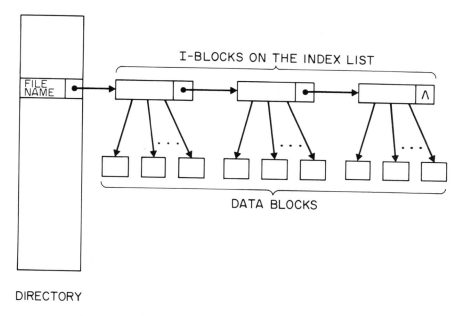

Figure 18.2 Part of a file's index with pointers to data blocks

Unlike data blocks, index blocks are smaller than physical disk blocks. Thus, there are several index blocks in each disk block. A layer of software handles the details of reading and writing index blocks, making it possible to think of them as randomly accessible items.

The third area of the disk holds a directory that contains pointers to the lists of free i-blocks and free disk blocks, the names of all files, and pointers to each file's index list. Each directory entry also contains an integer that gives the size of the file measured in bytes.

18.5 Implementation Of The Index Manager

Manipulation of the index area introduces a common problem with disk software. The index area contains a set of fixed-size i-blocks mapped onto a contiguous area of the disk. Because i-blocks are smaller than physical disk blocks, the system packs eight i-blocks into each physical block. The hardware transfers entire disk blocks, however, making it impossible to transfer a single i-block without transferring others that reside in the same block. So, to write an i-block, the software must read the entire physical disk block in which it resides, copy the new i-block into its correct place in the physical block, and write the resulting physical block back to disk. Similarly, reading an i-block requires the software to read the physical disk block in which it resides.

Before looking at the procedures that read and write i-blocks, we must understand a few more details. File *iblock.h* is a good place to start — it defines the contents of an i-block with structure *iblk*.

```
/* iblock.h - ibtodb, ibdisp */

typedef int             IBADDR;         /* iblocks addressed 0,1,2,... */

#define IBLEN           29              /* # d-block ptrs in an i-block */
#define IBNULL          -1              /* null pointer in i-block list */
#define IBAREA          1               /* start if iblocks on disk     */
#define IBWDIR          TRUE            /* ibnew: write directory       */
#define IBNWDIR         FALSE           /* ibnew: don't write directory */

struct  iblk            {               /* index block layout           */
        long            ib_byte;        /* first data byte indexed by   */
                                        /*  this index block            */
        IBADDR          ib_next;        /* address of next i-block      */
        DBADDR          ib_dba[IBLEN];  /* ptrs to data blocks indexed  */
};

#define ibtodb(ib)      (((ib)>>3)+IBAREA)/* iblock to disk block addr. */
#define ibdisp(ib)      (((ib)&07)*sizeof(struct iblk))
```

Each i-block contains an array of pointers to data blocks. The array contains addresses of 29 (*IBLEN*) data blocks, each of which is 512 bytes long. Thus, a single i-block indexes 29 X 512 or 14,848 bytes. An i-block also contains a value that specifies which bytes of the file it indexes, and a pointer to the next i-block on the index list. Pointers to i-blocks are given by integers starting at zero.

How does the software know where to find an i-block given its address? The answer is that it must know where the index area starts on the disk, and how many i-blocks are contained in each physical disk block. In our design, the directory occupies disk block zero, and the index area lies just beyond, so it starts at disk block one. Thus, i-blocks zero through seven lie in physical block one. In-line procedure *ibtodb* contains code that converts an i-block address into the correct physical disk block address. Procedure *ibdisp* converts an i-block address into the byte displacement within its physical block.

18.6 Operations On I-Blocks

18.6.1 Clearing An I-Block

The file system initialization routine links all i-blocks into the free list when it builds an empty file system. As the file system allocates i-blocks from the free list, it needs to clear out old information. Clearing is performed by procedure *ibclear*. It consists of making all data block pointers null, so they cannot be confused with valid pointers, and setting the offset field to the value specified. In the code, shown below, file *iblock.h* is not included explicitly. As we will see later, file *file.h* includes it.

```
/* ibclear.c - ibclear */

#include <conf.h>
#include <kernel.h>
#include <disk.h>
#include <file.h>
#include <dir.h>

/*------------------------------------------------------------
 * ibclear  --  clear in-core copy of an iblock
 *------------------------------------------------------------
 */
ibclear(ibptr, ibbyte)
struct  iblk    *ibptr;
long    ibbyte;
{
        int     i;

        ibptr->ib_byte = ibbyte;
        for (i=0 ; i<IBLEN ; i++)
                ibptr->ib_dba[i] = DBNULL;
        ibptr->ib_next = IBNULL;
}
```

18.6.2 Reading An I-Block

To read an i-block, the system maps its address to a physical disk block address, reads the physical disk block, and copies the appropriate area from the physical block into the desired location. File *ibget.c* contains the code.

```
/* ibget.c - ibget */

#include <conf.h>
#include <kernel.h>
#include <disk.h>
#include <file.h>
#include <dir.h>

/*------------------------------------------------------------------
 *  ibget  --  get an iblock from disk given its number
 *------------------------------------------------------------------
 */
ibget(diskdev, inum, loc)
int     diskdev;
IBADDR  inum;
struct  iblk    *loc;
{
        char    *from, *to;
        int     i;
        char    *buff;

        buff = getbuf(dskdbp);
        read(diskdev, buff, ibtodb(inum));
        from = buff + ibdisp(inum);
        to = (char *)loc;
        for (i=0 ; i<sizeof(struct iblk) ; i++)
                *to++ = *from++;
        freebuf(buff);
}
```

Ibget allocates space for the physical disk block from the system buffer pool,
dskdbp. After it reads the physical block and extracts the desired i-block, it
releases the storage with *freebuf*.

18.6.3 Writing An I-Block

I-blocks from several files may occupy the same physical disk block. Because
processes may try to write i-blocks into the same physical disk block concurrently,
writing an i-block is more complicated than reading one. To prevent interference,
writing processes must obtain exclusive use of the index area. File *ibput.c* shows
how the calling process waits for access using the exclusion semaphore that was
created at system startup by the disk driver initialization routine.

```
/* ibput.c - ibput */

#include <conf.h>
#include <kernel.h>
#include <io.h>
#include <disk.h>
#include <file.h>
#include <dir.h>


/*------------------------------------------------------------------------
 *  ibput  --  write an iblock back to disk given its number
 *------------------------------------------------------------------------
 */
ibput(diskdev, inum, loc)
int     diskdev;
IBADDR  inum;
struct  iblk    *loc;
{
        DBADDR  dba;
        char    *buff;
        char    *to, *from;
        int     i;
        int     ibsem;

        dba = ibtodb(inum);
        buff = getbuf(dskdbp);
        ibsem = ((struct dsblk *)devtab[diskdev].dvioblk)->dibsem;
        wait(ibsem);
        read(diskdev, buff, dba);
        to = buff + ibdisp(inum);
        from = (char *)loc;
        for (i=0 ; i<sizeof(struct iblk) ; i++)
                *to++ = *from++;
        write(diskdev, buff, dba);
        signal(ibsem);
        return(OK);
}
```

As expected, *ibput* allocates space for a physical disk block from the system buffer
pool, reads the appropriate physical block, copies in the changed i-block, and writes
the physical block back to disk. It need not free the buffer because the driver will
free it when the output operation completes.

18.6.4 Allocating I-Blocks From The Free List

The file system allocates an i-block from the free list whenever it needs one for
an index, and returns i-blocks to the free list when it deallocates a file. Procedure
ibnew obtains the next free i-block and returns its identifier. The code is found in
file *ibnew.c*.

```
/* ibnew.c - ibnew */

#include <conf.h>
#include <kernel.h>
#include <io.h>
#include <disk.h>
#include <file.h>
#include <dir.h>

/*------------------------------------------------------------------------
 * ibnew  --  allocate a new iblock from free list on disk
 *------------------------------------------------------------------------
 */
ibnew(diskdev, writedir)
int     diskdev;
Bool    writedir;
{
        struct  dir     *dirptr;
        struct  iblk    iblock;
        IBADDR  inum;
        int     i;
        int     sem;

        sem = ((struct dsblk *)devtab[diskdev].dvioblk)->dflsem;
        dirptr = dsdirec(diskdev);
        wait(sem);
        inum = dirptr->d_filst;
        ibget(diskdev, inum, &iblock);
        dirptr->d_filst = iblock.ib_next;
        if (writedir)
                write(diskdev, dskbcpy(dirptr), DIRBLK);
        signal(sem);
        ibclear(&iblock, 0L);
        ibput(diskdev, inum, &iblock);
        return(inum);
}
```

Concurrency control complicates what is otherwise a simple procedure. *Ibnew* first obtains exclusive use of the free list by waiting for the "free list" mutual exclusion semaphore. (Recall that the disk driver initialization routine, *dsinit*, created the semaphore and placed its id in *dflsem*.) After obtaining access, *ibnew* retrieves the id of the first free i-block from the directory. It must then update the free list by reading the first i-block and making the directory entry point to its successor. After changing the directory, *ibnew* writes a copy back to disk. Finally, *ibnew* clears the allocated i-block and writes it to disk.

18.6.5 Returning I-Blocks To The Free List

When a file is deleted, its index and data blocks must be returned to their appropriate free lists. Procedure *iblfree* performs this task. It takes an i-block address as an argument, and releases the i-blocks on that list. Thus, a single call to *iblfree* will release all the space used by a file.

```
/* iblfree.c - iblfree */

#include <conf.h>
#include <kernel.h>
#include <io.h>
#include <disk.h>
#include <file.h>
#include <dir.h>

/*------------------------------------------------------------------------
 * iblfree  --  free a list of iblocks given the number of the first
 *------------------------------------------------------------------------
 */
iblfree(diskdev, iblist)
int     diskdev;
IBADDR  iblist;
{
        IBADDR  ilast;
        struct  iblk    iblock;
        struct  dir     *dirptr;
        int     sem;
        DBADDR  dba;
        int     j;

        if (iblist == IBNULL)
                return(OK);
        dirptr = dsdirec(diskdev);
        ibget(diskdev, iblist, &iblock);
        for (ilast=iblist ; iblock.ib_next!=IBNULL ;) {
                for (j=0 ; j<IBLEN ; j++)
                        if ( (dba=iblock.ib_dba[j]) != DBNULL)
                                lfsdfree(diskdev, dba);
                ilast = iblock.ib_next;
                ibget(diskdev, ilast, &iblock);
        }
        for (j=0 ; j<IBLEN ; j++)
                if ( (dba=iblock.ib_dba[j]) != DBNULL)
                        lfsdfree(diskdev, dba);
        sem = ( (struct dsblk *)devtab[diskdev].dvioblk)->dflsem;
        wait(sem);
        iblock.ib_next = dirptr->d_filst;
        dirptr->d_filst = iblist;
        ibput(diskdev, ilast, &iblock);
        write(diskdev, dskbcpy(dirptr), DIRBLK);
        signal(sem);
```

```
        return(OK);
}
```

Iblfree moves along the list of i-blocks, calling procedure *lfsdfree* to free each data block. After all data blocks have been released, *iblfree* links the nodes on its argument list into the free list. To do so, it adds a pointer from the tail of the argument list to the head of the free list, and makes the free list point to the head of its argument list. After updating the free list pointer, *iblfree* writes a copy of the modified directory back to disk. Although these operations would be simpler if the lists resided in memory, the details are not difficult to follow.

18.7 The Directory Structure

Before plunging into the details of the file system software, we need to consider the format of data in the directory. Obviously, the directory must contain an entry for each file. The file entry includes the file's name and the address of the first i-block on the file's index list. The directory also contains the total number of i-blocks on the disk, as well as pointers to the lists of free blocks. Structure *dir*, found in file *dir.h*, defines the directory layout in detail.

```
/* dir.h */

#define FDNLEN   10                          /* length of file name + 1    */
#define NFDES    28                          /* number of files per directory*/

struct fdes     {                            /* description of each file   */
        long    fdlen;                       /* length in bytes            */
        IBADDR  fdiba;                       /* first index block          */
        char    fdname[FDNLEN];              /* zero-terminated file name  */
};

struct dir      {                            /* directory layout           */
        int     d_iblks;                     /* i-blocks on this disk      */
        DBADDR  d_fblst;                     /* pointer to list of free blks */
        IBADDR  d_filst;                     /* pointer to list of free iblks*/
        int     d_id;                        /* disk identification integer */
        int     d_nfiles;                    /* current number of files    */
        struct  fdes    d_files[NFDES];      /* descriptions of the files  */
};

struct freeblk {                             /* shape of block on free list */
        DBADDR  fbnext;                      /* address of next free block  */
};
```

Because index blocks each contain a "next" pointer field, linking them into the free list is easy. Normally, data blocks do not contain pointers, however, so linking them onto a free list is not as simple. We have chosen to link free data blocks together in a singly-linked list by storing pointers at the beginning of each. Structure *freeblk* in file *dir.h* documents this decision. Whenever the software manipulates data blocks on the free list, it assumes they have the shape declared by this structure. For example, if disk block addresses are two bytes long, data blocks on the free list will contain a pointer to the next block in the first two bytes.

18.8 Using The Device Switch Table For Files

The file system software must establish connections between running processes and disk files so that operations like *read* and *write* can be mapped onto the correct file. Exactly how the system performs this mapping depends on both the size and generality needed. To keep our system small, we will avoid introducing new software by using the device switch machinery already in place.

Imagine that a set of *pseudo-devices* have been added to the device switch table such that each pseudo-device can be used to control a file. Just like conventional devices, a pseudo-device has a set of driver routines that perform *read*, *write*, *getc*, *putc*, *seek*, and *close* operations. When a process opens a disk file, the file system searches for a currently unused pseudo-device, sets up the control block for that "device", and returns the device identifier to the caller. After the file has been opened, the process uses the device identifier to *read* or *write* it. The device switch maps high-level operations to driver routines for the pseudo-device exactly as they map high-level operations onto device drivers for other devices. Finally, the process finishes accessing the file and calls *close* to break the connection and make the pseudo-device available for use with another file. The details will become clear as we review the code.

Designing a pseudo-device driver is not unlike designing real device drivers. Just like other drivers, the pseudo-device driver keeps a control block for each pseudo-device. File *file.h* contains the pertinent declarations.

```
/* file.h */

/* Local disk layout: disk block 0 is directory, then index area, and    */
/* then data blocks.  Each disk block (512 bytes) in the index area       */
/* contains 8 iblocks, which are 64 bytes long.  Iblocks are referenced   */
/* relative to 0, so the disk block address of iblock k is given by        */
/* truncate(k/8)+1.  The offset of iblock k within its disk block is       */
/* given by 64*remainder(k,8).  The directory entry points to a linked     */
/* list of iblocks, and each iblock contains pointers to IBLEN (29) data   */
/* blocks. Index pointers contain a valid data block address or DBNULL.    */

#include <iblock.h>

#define EOF            -2              /* value returned on end-of-file*/
#define FLREAD         001             /* fl_mode bit for "read"        */
#define FLWRITE        002             /* fl_mode bit for "write"       */
#define FLRW           003             /* fl_mode bits for read+write   */
#define FLNEW          010             /* fl_mode bit for "new file"    */
#define FLOLD          020             /* fl_mode bit for "old file"    */

struct  flblk   {                      /* file "device" control block   */
        int     fl_id;                 /* file's "device id" in devtab  */
        int     fl_dev;                /* file is on this disk device   */
        int     fl_pid;                /* process id accessing the file */
        struct  fdes    *fl_dent;      /* file's in-core dir. entry      */
        int     fl_mode;               /* FLREAD, FLWRITE, or both       */
        IBADDR  fl_iba;                /* address of iblock in fl_iblk   */
        struct  iblk    fl_iblk;       /* current iblock for file        */
        int     fl_ipnum;              /* current iptr in fl_iblk        */
        long    fl_pos;                /* current file position (bytes)  */
        Bool    fl_dch;                /* has fl_buff been changed?       */
        char    *fl_bptr;              /* ptr to next char in fl_buff    */
        char    fl_buff[DBUFSIZ];      /* current data block for file     */
};

#ifdef  Ndf
extern  struct  flblk   fltab[];
#endif
```

Most of the fields in the control block make sense without explanation. Field *fl_id*, for example, contains the file's device id. Field *fl_mode* tells whether the file has been opened for reading, writing, or both. (Symbolic constants *FLREAD* and *FLWRITE* identify the individual mode bits.) Field *fl_dent* points to the file's directory entry; it is the only link between the control block and the file name.

Other fields of the file control block contain information that identifies a position in the file and the data found at that position. Opening a file establishes a "cursor" that points to the beginning of the file. As processes *read* or *write* data, the cursor moves along through the file. At any time, field *fl_pos* gives the *current cursor position*, measured in bytes from the beginning of the file.

The control block contains enough information to enable upper-half routines to easily retrieve or modify data found at the current cursor position. Field *fl_iblk* contains a copy of the i-block from the file's index list that indexes the current position. Field *fl_ipnum* identifies which pointer in the index block corresponds to the current position. The data block in buffer *fl_buff* is the data block that includes the current position. Finally, field *fl_bptr* points to the character in the buffer that is found at the current position.

18.9 Establishing A Pseudo-Device

Making a connection between a running program and a named file involves searching the directory to see if the name is valid, allocating a pseudo-device, and initializing the control block and cursor to the beginning of the file. We will examine procedures that perform each of these tasks.

In Xinu the user can specify, when opening a file, whether the file should be old or new (i.e., whether it must or must not exist), and whether it will be read or written. Such specifications are made by passing a *mode string* to the procedure that opens files. To parse the mode string and convert it to a single integer the open routine calls *dfckmd*, shown below. *Dfckmd* returns an integer with mode bits set according to the symbolic constants defined in *file.h*.

```
/* dfckmd.c - dfckmd */

#include <conf.h>
#include <kernel.h>
#include <disk.h>
#include <file.h>

/*------------------------------------------------------------------------
 *  dfckmd  --  parse file mode argument and generate actual mode bits
 *------------------------------------------------------------------------
 */
dfckmd(mode)
char    *mode;
{
        int     mbits;
        char    ch;

        mbits = 0;
        while (ch = *mode++)
                switch (ch) {

                    case 'r':   if (mbits&FLREAD) return(SYSERR);
                                mbits |= FLREAD;
                                break;

                    case 'w':   if (mbits&FLWRITE) return(SYSERR);
                                mbits |= FLWRITE;
                                break;

                    case 'o':   if (mbits&FLOLD || mbits&FLNEW)
                                        return(SYSERR);
                                mbits |= FLOLD;
                                break;

                    case 'n':   if (mbits&FLOLD || mbits&FLNEW)
                                        return(SYSERR);
                                mbits |= FLNEW;
                                break;

                    default:    return(SYSERR);
                }
        if ((mbits&FLREAD) == (mbits&FLWRITE))      /* default: allow R + W */
                mbits |= (FLREAD|FLWRITE);
        return(mbits);
}
```

Dfckmd scans the mode string looking for occurrences of the characters "n" (new), "o" (old), "r" (read), and "w" (write). As it finds each character it sets the appropriate bit of the mode integer. If it finishes without detecting an error, it returns the resulting integer. Note that the mode string may specify a new file or an old file, but not both. If neither new nor old is specified, *dfckmd* assumes that the user does not care whether the file currently exists or whether it must be created.

Once the mode string has been parsed, the directory can be searched. Procedure *dfdsrch* uses the mode integer created by *dfckmd*. It searches for the specified file name, creating a new file if the mode bits allow creation and the name does not exist. The code is shown below.

```
/* dfdsrch.c - dfdsrch */

#include <conf.h>
#include <kernel.h>
#include <disk.h>
#include <file.h>
#include <dir.h>

/*------------------------------------------------------------------------
 *  dfdsrch  --  search disk directory for position of given file name
 *------------------------------------------------------------------------
 */
struct  fdes    *dfdsrch(dsptr, filenam, mbits)
struct  dsblk   *dsptr;
char    *filenam;
int     mbits;
{
        struct  dir     *dirptr;
        struct  fdes    *fdptr;
        int     len;
        int     i;
        int     inum;

        if ( (len=strlen(filenam))<=0 || len>=FDNLEN)
                return((struct fdes *)SYSERR);
        dirptr = dsdirec(dsptr->dnum);
        for (i=0 ; i<dirptr->d_nfiles ; i++)
                if (strcmp(filenam, dirptr->d_files[i].fdname) == 0)
                        if ( (mbits&FLNEW) != 0)
                                return((struct fdes *)SYSERR);
                        else
                                return(&dirptr->d_files[i]);
        wait(dsptr->ddirsem);
        if ( (mbits&FLOLD) || dirptr->d_nfiles >= NFDES) {
                signal(dsptr->ddirsem);
                return((struct fdes *)SYSERR);
        }
        inum = ibnew(dsptr->dnum, IBNWDIR);
        fdptr = &(dirptr->d_files[dirptr->d_nfiles++]);
        fdptr->fdlen = 0L;
        strcpy(fdptr->fdname, filenam);
        fdptr->fdiba = inum;
        write(dsptr->dnum, dskbcpy(dirptr), DIRBLK);
        signal(dsptr->ddirsem);
        return(fdptr);
}
```

Although the code may seem confusing, it is easy to understand. *Dfdsrch* first checks to see that the name is valid. It then searches the directory. If a match is found, it uses the mode bits to determine whether an old file is allowed. If no match is found, *dfdsrch* uses the mode bits to determine whether a new file is allowed. If a new file is needed, *dfdsrch* creates one by adding the new name to the directory and allocating an i-block for the file from the free list.

Once a file has been found or created, a connection to it can be established by allocating a pseudo-device and initializing its control block. Procedure *dfalloc* allocates a pseudo-device:

```
/* dfalloc.c - dfalloc */

#include <conf.h>
#include <kernel.h>
#include <disk.h>
#include <file.h>

/*------------------------------------------------------------------------
 * dfalloc  --  allocate a device table entry for a disk file; return id
 *------------------------------------------------------------------------
 */
#ifdef  Ndf
dfalloc()                       /* assume exclusion for dir. provided by caller */
{
        int     i;

        for (i=0 ; i<Ndf ; i++)
                if (fltab[i].fl_pid == 0) {
                        fltab[i].fl_pid = getpid();
                        return(i);
                }
        return(SYSERR);
}
#endif
```

Allocation is straightforward. *Dfalloc* searches the array of pseudo-device control blocks looking for an unused device. It checks the process id field in each pseudo-device control block because the process id is nonzero whenever the device is in use. When it finds an unused device, *dfalloc* marks the device busy by storing the caller's process id in the process id field. It then returns the index of the file control block it reserved.

Procedure *dsopen* uses the three procedures described above to make a connec-

tion between a running program and a disk file. It calls *dfckmd* to check the mode
string and convert it to an integer, *dfdsrch* to search the directory, and *dfalloc* to
allocate a pseudo-device for the file. Finally, *dsopen* fills in the file control block
by setting the current position to zero and reading the first i-block from the file's
index list. It returns the file's device id to the caller so it can be used in operations
like *read* and *write*. File *dsopen.c* contains the code.

```
/* dsopen.c - dsopen */

#include <conf.h>
#include <kernel.h>
#include <disk.h>
#include <file.h>
#include <dir.h>

/*------------------------------------------------------------------------
 *  dsopen  --  open/create a file on the specified disk device
 *------------------------------------------------------------------------
 */
#ifdef  Ndf
dsopen(devptr, filenam, mode)
struct  devsw   *devptr;
char    *filenam;
char    *mode;
{
        struct  dir     *dirptr;
        struct  flblk   *flptr;
        struct  fdes    *fdptr;
        DBADDR  dba;
        int     mbits, findex;
        int     retcode;
        char    ps;

        disable(ps);
        dirptr = dsdirec(devptr->dvnum);
        if ( (mbits=dfckmd(mode)) == SYSERR)
                retcode = SYSERR;
        else if( (int)(fdptr=dfdsrch(devptr->dvioblk,filenam,mbits))
                == SYSERR)
                retcode = SYSERR;
        else if ( (findex=dfalloc()) == SYSERR)
                retcode = SYSERR;
        else {
                flptr = &fltab[findex];
```

```
                    flptr->fl_dev = devptr->dvnum;
                    flptr->fl_dent = fdptr;
                    flptr->fl_mode = mbits & FLRW;
                    flptr->fl_iba = fdptr->fdiba;
                    ibget(flptr->fl_dev, flptr->fl_iba, &(flptr->fl_iblk));
                    flptr->fl_pos = 0L;
                    flptr->fl_dch = FALSE;
                    dba = flptr->fl_iblk.ib_dba[flptr->fl_ipnum = 0];
                    if (dba != DBNULL) {
                            read(flptr->fl_dev, flptr->fl_buff, dba);
                            flptr->fl_bptr = flptr->fl_buff;
                    } else
                            flptr->fl_bptr = &flptr->fl_buff[DBUFSIZ];
                    retcode = flptr->fl_id;
            }
            restore(ps);
            return(retcode);
    }
    #endif
```

As the name *dsopen* implies, this procedures is associated with the disk driver.
This may seem confusing, but it will become clear once you understand the following:

> *Because the directory maps names to disk files, the open opera-*
> *tion is associated with the disk driver, not with the individual*
> *files.*

To connect to a file on disk device *i*, the user calls *open*, passing *i* as the device argument, the filename as the second argument, and the mode string as the third.
Open uses the device switch table to pass the call to *dsopen*.

18.10 Pseudo-Device Driver Routines

Like any device driver, pseudo-devices need routines that handle high-level
operations like *read* or *write*. Of course, there are no lower-half routines for
pseudo-devices because the driver never receives interrupts from a real hardware
device. Instead of starting hardware, the upper-half file routines carry out requests
by performing input and output operations on the disk device.

Although the pseudo-device drivers do not contend with real hardware, they
are quite complex because they deal with the details of buffer and index management. To help manage the complexity, some of the work has been pushed into
separate procedures; we will consider these first. Procedures *lfsnewd* and *lfsdfree*

allocate and release data blocks. Procedure *lfsnewd* allocates a data block from the
free list almost exactly the same way *ibnew* allocated an index block. The code,
found in file *lfsnewd.c*, needs little further explanation.

```
/* lfsnewd.c - lfsnewd */

#include <conf.h>
#include <kernel.h>
#include <disk.h>
#include <file.h>
#include <dir.h>

#define DFILLER  '+'

/*------------------------------------------------------------------------
 * lfsnewd  --  allocate a new data block from free list on disk
 *------------------------------------------------------------------------
 */
lfsnewd(diskdev, flptr)
int     diskdev;
struct  flblk   *flptr;
{
        struct  iblock  *ibptr;
        struct  dir     *dirptr;
        struct  freeblk *fbptr;
        char    *buf;
        int     sem;
        DBADDR  dba;
        int     i;

        dirptr = dsdirec(diskdev);
        fbptr = (struct freeblk *) (buf = flptr->fl_buff);
        sem = ((struct dsblk *)devtab[diskdev].dvioblk)->dflsem;
        wait(sem);
        dba = dirptr->d_fblst;
        read(diskdev, fbptr, dba);
        dirptr->d_fblst = fbptr->fbnext;
        write(diskdev, dskbcpy(dirptr), DIRBLK);
        signal(sem);
        for (i=0 ; i<DBUFSIZ ; i++)
                *buf++ = DFILLER;
        write(diskdev, dskbcpy(fbptr), dba);
        return(dba);
}
```

Companion procedure *lfsdfree* reverses the action of *lfsnewd* by returning a data block to the free list. As expected, it makes the data block point to the current list and makes the list head point to the block being deallocated. Again, the code is similar to the code used to deallocate i-blocks.

```
/* lfsdfree.c - lfsdfree */

#include <conf.h>
#include <kernel.h>
#include <disk.h>
#include <file.h>
#include <dir.h>


/*------------------------------------------------------------------------
 * lfsdfree  --  free a data block given its address
 *------------------------------------------------------------------------
 */
lfsdfree(diskdev, dba)
int     diskdev;
DBADDR  dba;
{
        struct dir      *dirptr;
        int     dirsem;
        struct  freeblk *buf;

        dirptr = dsdirec(diskdev);
        dirsem = devtab[diskdev].dvioblk->dflsem;
        buf = (struct freeblk *)getbuf(dskdbp);
        wait(dirsem);
        buf->fbnext = dirptr->d_fblst;
        dirptr->d_fblst = dba;
        write(diskdev, buf, dba);
        write(diskdev, dskbcpy(dirptr), DIRBLK);
        signal(dirsem);
        return(OK);
}
```

18.10.1 Index Management Routines

The file system cannot afford to write a data block every time the program changes one character. Instead, it waits until the block has been filled and a new one is needed before writing the block to disk. Changed blocks must also be writ-

ten when the user closes the file (even if the block has not been filled), and when
the user positions the file pointer outside the current block by calling *seek*. Of
course, the file system should not copy the buffer to disk unless it has been changed
because disk accesses require much time. To eliminate unnecessary writes, it uses a
Boolean variable (field *fl_dch* in the file control block), clearing the variable whenever a new block has been read, and setting it whenever the contents are changed.

Procedure *lfsflush* writes data from the buffer to disk if the data has been
changed. It computes the disk block address of the current buffer by looking in the
i-block (field *fl_iblk*), and writes a copy of the buffer to that address. The code is
found in file *lfsflush.c*.

```
/* lfsflush.c - lfsflush */

#include <conf.h>
#include <kernel.h>
#include <disk.h>
#include <file.h>
#include <dir.h>

/*------------------------------------------------------------------------
 *  lfsflush  --  flush data and i-block for a file
 *------------------------------------------------------------------------
 */
lfsflush(flptr)
struct  flblk   *flptr;
{
        DBADDR  dba;

        if (!flptr->fl_dch)
                return(SYSERR);
        dba = flptr->fl_iblk.ib_dba[flptr->fl_ipnum];
        write(flptr->fl_dev, dskbcpy(flptr->fl_buff), dba);
        flptr->fl_dch = FALSE;
        return(OK);
}
```

Another procedure that helps manage the index is named *lfsetup*. *Lfsetup* positions a file at a specified location by finding the correct index block and data
block. It starts with the current i-block, and moves along the index list until it
finds the correct i-block. The index list is singly-linked, so if the desired position
lies before the region covered by the current index block, *lfsetup* moves to the file's
first index block before it begins the search. Once the correct index block has been
read into memory, *lfsetup* determines which data block pointer to use by moving to
the correct entry in the i-block. After extracting the data block address, it reads a

copy of the data block into the buffer. Finally, it positions the buffer pointer to the desired byte within the buffer. The code is shown below.

```
/* lfsetup.c - lfsetup */

#include <conf.h>
#include <kernel.h>
#include <disk.h>
#include <file.h>
#include <dir.h>


/*------------------------------------------------------------------------
 *  lfsetup  --  set up appropriate iblock and data block in memory
 *------------------------------------------------------------------------
 */
lfsetup(diskdev, flptr)
int      diskdev;
struct   flblk    *flptr;
{
        struct  iblk     *ibptr;
        int      displ, i;
        long     ibrange;
        IBADDR   nextib;
        DBADDR   dba;

        ibrange = (long) (IBLEN * DBUFSIZ);
        ibptr = &flptr->fl_iblk;
        if (flptr->fl_pos < ibptr->ib_byte) {
                flptr->fl_iba = (flptr->fl_dent)->fdiba;
                ibget(diskdev, flptr->fl_iba, ibptr);
        }
        while (ibptr->ib_byte+ibrange <= flptr->fl_pos) {
                if (ibptr->ib_next == IBNULL) {
                        ibptr->ib_next = ibnew(diskdev, IBWDIR);
                        ibput(diskdev, flptr->fl_iba, ibptr);
                        flptr->fl_iba = ibptr->ib_next;
                        ibclear(ibptr, (long)ibptr->ib_byte+ibrange);
                        ibput(diskdev, flptr->fl_iba, ibptr);
                } else {
                        flptr->fl_iba = ibptr->ib_next;
                        ibget(diskdev, flptr->fl_iba, ibptr);
                }
        }
        displ = (int) (flptr->fl_pos - ibptr->ib_byte);
```

```
            for (flptr->fl_ipnum=0 ; displ>=DBUFSIZ ; displ-=DBUFSIZ)
                    flptr->fl_ipnum++;
            flptr->fl_bptr = flptr->fl_buff + displ;
            if ( (dba=ibptr->ib_dba[flptr->fl_ipnum]) == DBNULL) {
                    ibptr->ib_dba[flptr->fl_ipnum] = lfsnewd(diskdev,flptr);
                    ibput(diskdev, flptr->fl_iba, ibptr);
            } else
                    read(diskdev, flptr->fl_buff, dba);
            flptr->fl_dch = FALSE;
    }
}
```

18.10.2 The Pseudo-Device Seek Routine

The *seek* operation moves the current file position to a given location without
transferring data. Procedure *lfseek*, shown below, implements the *seek* operation.
First, it checks to see if the buffer has been modified, and writes a copy to disk if it
has been. It then verifies that the specified position is valid. If the request is valid,
lfseek updates the current file position (*fl_pos*), and calls *lfsetup* to locate the
correct i-block.

```
/* lfseek.c - lfseek */

#include <conf.h>
#include <kernel.h>
#include <disk.h>
#include <file.h>
#include <dir.h>


/*------------------------------------------------------------------------
 *  lfseek  --  seek to a specified position of a file
 *------------------------------------------------------------------------
 */
lfseek(devptr, offset)
struct  devsw    *devptr;
long    offset;
{
        struct  flblk    *flptr;
        int     retcode;
        char    ps;

        disable(ps);
        flptr = (struct flblk *)devptr->dvioblk;
        if (flptr->fl_mode & FLWRITE) {
                if (flptr->fl_dch)
```

```
                        lfsflush(flptr);
        } else if (offset > (flptr->fl_dent)->fdlen) {
                        restore(ps);
                        return(SYSERR);
        }
        flptr->fl_pos = offset;
        retcode = lfsetup(flptr->fl_dev, flptr);
        restore(ps);
        return(retcode);
}
```

18.10.3 The Pseudo-Device Getc Routine

Once a file has been opened and the index is in place, input from the file is trivial. It consists of extracting the next character from the buffer and advancing the buffer pointer. Procedure *lfgetc*, shown below, performs the operation.

```
/* lfgetc.c - lfgetc */

#include <conf.h>
#include <kernel.h>
#include <proc.h>
#include <disk.h>
#include <file.h>
#include <dir.h>

/*------------------------------------------------------------------------
 * lfgetc -- get next character from (buffered) disk file
 *------------------------------------------------------------------------
 */
lfgetc(devptr)
struct  devsw    *devptr;
{
        struct  flblk    *flptr;
        char    nextch;
        char    ps;

        disable(ps);
        flptr = (struct flblk *)devptr->dvioblk;
        if (flptr->fl_pid!=currpid || !(flptr->fl_mode&FLREAD)) {
                restore(ps);
                return(SYSERR);
        }
        if (flptr->fl_pos >= (flptr->fl_dent)->fdlen) {
                restore(ps);
                return(EOF);
        }
        if (flptr->fl_bptr >= &flptr->fl_buff[DBUFSIZ]) {
                if (flptr->fl_dch)
                        lfsflush(flptr);
                lfsetup(flptr->fl_dev, flptr);
        }
        nextch = *(flptr->fl_bptr)++;
        flptr->fl_pos++;
        restore(ps);
        return(nextch);
}
```

When called *lfgetc* checks to see that the invoking process owns the pseudo-
device, and that the file has been opened for reading. It then checks to see if the
current position lies beyond the end of the file, and returns a value indicating *end-*

of-file (*EOF*) if it does. If end of file has not been reached, *lfgetc* checks to see if the buffer pointer points beyond the current buffer, and moves to the next data block if necessary. Finally, after it has positioned the buffer pointer correctly, *lfgetc* returns the next character from the buffer.

18.10.4 The Pseudo-Device Putc Routine

Procedure *lfputc* writes a single character to an open file. Like *lfgetc*, it checks the file status and moves to a new buffer if the current one is full. It then deposits the character and sets *fl_dch* to indicate that the buffer has been changed. Note that *lfputc* merely accumulates characters in the buffer; it does not write the buffer to disk each time it changes. The buffer will only be copied to disk when the current position moves to another disk block.

```
/* lfputc.c - lfputc */

#include <conf.h>
#include <kernel.h>
#include <proc.h>
#include <disk.h>
#include <file.h>
#include <dir.h>


/*-----------------------------------------------------------------------
 *  lfputc  --  put a character onto a (buffered) disk file
 *-----------------------------------------------------------------------
 */
lfputc(devptr, ch)
struct  devsw   *devptr;
char    ch;
{
        struct  flblk   *flptr;
        char    ps;

        disable(ps);
        flptr = (struct flblk *) devptr->dvioblk;
        if (flptr->fl_pid != currpid || !(flptr->fl_mode&FLWRITE)) {
                restore(ps);
                return(SYSERR);
        }
        if (flptr->fl_bptr >= &flptr->fl_buff[DBUFSIZ]) {
                if (flptr->fl_dch)
                        lfsflush(flptr);
                lfsetup(flptr->fl_dev, flptr);
        }
        if (flptr->fl_pos >= (flptr->fl_dent)->fdlen)
                (flptr->fl_dent)->fdlen++;
        flptr->fl_pos++;
        *(flptr->fl_bptr)++ = ch;
        flptr->fl_dch = TRUE;
        restore(ps);
        return(OK);
}
```

18.10.5 The Pseudo-Device Read Routine

Procedure *lfread* implements the *read* operation. It reads zero or more characters into a specified buffer by calling *lfgetc* repeatedly, as shown below. This implementation was chosen because it was easy to code; the exercises suggest redesigning it to improve the efficiency.

```
/* lfread.c - lfread */

#include <conf.h>
#include <kernel.h>
#include <disk.h>
#include <file.h>
#include <dir.h>

/*------------------------------------------------------------------------
 * lfread  --  read from a previously opened disk file
 *------------------------------------------------------------------------
 */
lfread(devptr, buff, count)
struct  devsw    *devptr;
char    *buff;
int     count;
{
        int     done;
        int     ichar;

        if (count < 0)
                return(SYSERR);
        for (done=0 ; done < count ; done++)
                if ( (ichar=lfgetc(devptr)) == SYSERR)
                        return(SYSERR);
                else if (ichar == EOF ) {        /* EOF before finished */
                        if (done == 0)
                                return(EOF);
                        else
                                return(done);
                } else
                        *buff++ = (char) ichar;
        return(done);
}
```

18.10.6 The Pseudo-Device Write Routine

Procedure *lfwrite* implements the *write* operation by writing a sequence of zero
or more bytes. Like *lfread*, it calls a single-character (*lfputc*, in this case) routine
to perform the output operation. File *lfwrite.c* contains the code.

```
/* lfwrite.c - lfwrite */

#include <conf.h>
#include <kernel.h>

/*------------------------------------------------------------------------
 *  lfwrite  --  write 'count' bytes onto a local disk file
 *------------------------------------------------------------------------
 */
lfwrite(devptr, buff, count)
struct  devsw   *devptr;
char    *buff;
int     count;
{
        int     i;

        if (count < 0)
                return(SYSERR);
        for (i=count; i>0 ; i--)
                if (lfputc(devptr, *buff++) == SYSERR)
                        return(SYSERR);
        return(count);
}
```

18.10.7 The Pseudo-Device Close Routine

When a process finishes using a file, it must call *close* to flush unwritten
buffers out to disk, and detach the file from the process. Procedure *lfclose* implements the *close* operation. It performs exactly as expected, calling *lfsflush* to write
data from the buffer if necessary, and assigning the process id field in the file control block zero to indicate that the pseudo-device can be used again. After it writes
the data blocks to disk, *lfclose* writes a copy of the directory to disk in case the file
length recorded in the directory entry was changed. The details are shown below in
file *lfclose.c*.

```
/* lfclose.c - lfclose */

#include <conf.h>
#include <kernel.h>
#include <proc.h>
#include <disk.h>
#include <file.h>

/*------------------------------------------------------------------------
 * lfclose  --  close a file by flushing output and freeing device slot
 *------------------------------------------------------------------------
 */
lfclose(devptr)
struct  devsw   *devptr;
{
        struct  dsblk   *dsptr;
        struct  dir     *dirptr;
        struct  flblk   *flptr;
        int     diskdev;
        char    ps;

        disable(ps);
        flptr = (struct flblk *) devptr->dvioblk;
        if (flptr->fl_pid != currpid) {
                restore(ps);
                return(SYSERR);
        }
        diskdev = flptr->fl_dev;
        dsptr = (struct dsblk *)devtab[diskdev].dvioblk;
        dirptr = (struct dir *) dsptr->ddir;
        if ( (flptr->fl_mode & FLWRITE) && flptr->fl_dch)
                lfsflush(flptr);
        flptr->fl_pid = 0;
        dsptr->dnfiles--;
        write(diskdev, dskbcpy(dirptr), DIRBLK);
        restore(ps);
        return(OK);
}
```

18.10.8 The Pseudo-Device Initialization Routine

Although procedure *dsopen* initializes most of the entries in the file control block when it opens a file, some initialization is required at system startup. As in most drivers, the initialization routine assigns field *fl_id* in the file control block the device id that the high-level routines call to access the file. It also initializes field *fl_pid* to zero, indicating that the pseudo-device is not in use. The pseudo-device initialization routine also places a pointer to the file control block in the device switch table (field *dvioblk*) so the upper-half routines can find the correct control block. These details are all handled by procedure *lfinit*, as shown below.

```
/* lfinit.c - lfinit */

#include <conf.h>
#include <kernel.h>
#include <disk.h>
#include <file.h>

#ifndef Ndf
#define Ndf        1
#endif
struct  flblk   fltab[Ndf];

/*------------------------------------------------------------------------
 * lfinit  --  mark disk file 'device' available at system startup
 *------------------------------------------------------------------------
 */
lfinit(devptr)
struct  devsw   *devptr;
{
        struct  flblk   *flptr;

        devptr->dvioblk = flptr = &fltab[devptr->dvminor];
        flptr->fl_pid = 0;
        flptr->fl_id = devptr->dvnum;
        return(OK);
}
```

18.11 Summary

The file system manages an abstract name space in which objects correspond to disk files, devices, or operating system services. This chapter concentrated on the part of the file system software that manages data files on secondary storage. To keep the interface to files the same as the interface to devices, the software was organized into a pseudo-device driver that supported *read*, *write*, *getc*, *putc*, *seek* and *close* operations. When a process opened a file, the software established a connection to it through the device switch table, allowing the high-level I/O routines to access the file driver just as they access hardware device drivers.

Our design allows multiple files to grow concurrently by using an index to keep track of the data blocks associated with each file. The index for a file consists of a singly-linked list of nodes called i-blocks, where each i-block contains pointers to a set of data blocks. When a file is opened, the driver software reads its first index block into memory. It also reads a copy of the first data block if the file is nonempty. Subsequent accesses or changes affect the buffer in memory. Only when the file position moves outside the current buffer does the file system copy the buffer back to disk and read another.

Concurrency control, as well as the details of index and buffer management, make the file system software large and complex. The large volume of detail has been handled by dividing the driver into small pieces. We have also chosen to make the system simpler by limiting concurrent access to a file.

FOR FURTHER STUDY

Literature on file systems abounds. Knuth [1973] describes several data structures used for indexes. The search method described here is an *indexed sequential file* where the offset in the file is the key; it is a simplification of the UNIX file system described by Ritchie and Thompson [1974]. Broader descriptions of file system alternatives can be found in Calingaert [1982], Habermann [1976], and Peterson and Silberschatz [1983]. Some of these authors distinguish between the terms *file system*, using it to refer to the lowest layer of file manipulation software, and *directory system*, using it to refer to the mapping of names onto files.

EXERCISES

18.1   Implement a higher layer of file system software that accepts requests to open files and either maps them into local disk files or sends them across the network to a file server.

18.2   Redesign routines *lfread* and *lfwrite* to perform high-speed copies like the *tty read* and *write* routines.

18.3   Consider what happens when two processes open the same file and begin writing on it. Rewrite the code to prevent the problem.

18.4   Free data blocks are chained together on a singly-linked list. Redesign the software to use an index for them (i.e., link them into a giant "file" made up of free blocks).

18.5   What are the maximum number of disk accesses necessary to allocate/free a data block under the current scheme and the scheme suggested in the previous problem? The average number of accesses?

18.6   The number of index blocks is important because having too many wastes space that could be used for data, while having too few makes it impossible to allocate all space to files. Given that there are 29 data block pointers in an i-block, and that 8 i-blocks fill a disk block, how many index blocks might be needed for a disk of n total blocks if the directory can hold k files?

18.7   The size of index i-blocks is as important as the number of them. Does the distribution of file sizes on your local computer system suggest how the i-block size was chosen?

18.8   Rewrite the code that handles process termination so it closes all files associated with the terminating process.

18.9   Change the system to separate the file switch table from the device switch table. Make the directory contain a field for each name telling whether that name refers to a conventional file or a device.

18.10   Discuss the advantages and disadvantages of adopting the convention that all entries in the device switch table above position *NDEVS* are files.

18.11   Copying data among buffers can be expensive. Modify the disk driver and file system procedures to use *int* pointers in place of *char* pointers when copying data, and measure the resulting speed-up.

19

Exception Handling and Support Routines

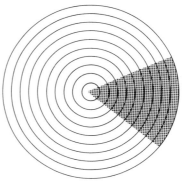

This chapter discusses the exception handling routines, and the support routines that have been used throughout the system (e.g., *kprintf*). It concentrates on engineering and programming techniques. Although such details may seem trivial, building a reasonable set of support routines early can ease debugging significantly. So, though this chapter has been placed at the end of the book, implementers would do well to establish such software before tackling the system proper.

19.1 Exceptions, Traps, And Illegal Interrupts.

Arranging an operating system to correctly associate device addresses, interrupt vector locations, and interrupt dispatchers is an annoying task that plagues most implementers. Often, mismatches between the wiring and coding cause devices to interrupt at vector locations other than those expected by the system. A similar problem occurs if a device is added to the bus without changing the operating system to accommodate it.

A related problem occurs when bugs in a program cause it to generate an exception. Recall that the hardware handles exceptions, events that occur when a program attempts an illegal operation, like interrupts. An exception might occur, for example, if a program generates an array subscript beyond the end of the array, or if it attempts to divide by zero.

To inform the programmer of exceptions and unexpected interrupts, Xinu captures them and prints a message on the console. Because so many hardware-specific details are involved, the routines, called *panic* routines, have been written in assembler language. It should be explained that early versions consisted of a series of *halt* statements — panic was expanded incrementally as the system was developed.

19.2 Initialization Of Interrupt Vectors

Chapter 13 explains how the exception and interrupt vectors are initialized statically by the code in file *lowcore.s*. Each interrupt vector is loaded with the address of procedure *panic*, and a code that indicates the type of interrupt. Exceptions each have their own code, 0-6; all device interrupts have code 7. Unless the initial interrupt vector values are overwritten before interrupts occur, the interrupt will trap to procedure *panic* which can extract the code from the low-order bits of the PS register just as standard interrupt dispatchers do.

Procedure *panic* prints information about the machine state, including the contents of registers and the top values on the stack, along with a message explaining the cause of the error. Commonly referred to as a *dump*, the machine state information is generally useless to programmers who work in high-level languages like C. However, it can give programmers trying to create a new operating system important clues about how the hardware is behaving, whether the stack is valid, and why the exception occurred.

To read and manipulate machine registers and the stack, the panic routine must be coded in assembler. When entered, it saves a copy of the exact machine state for later reference. Then, it proceeds to format and print a message giving the saved values of the registers and processor status word, along with a reason for the panic. If the stack pointer points to a valid memory location, the panic routine also prints the top few locations on the stack on the console. After printing the message, panic restores the exact machine state, and halts the processor. If the user continues execution with the ODT *P* command, processing will continue starting with the instruction immediately following the one that caused the panic.

19.3 Implementation Of Panic

Routines *panic0*, *_panic*, and *panic* comprise the panic handler, as shown in file *panic.s*. Although the routines may seem long, remember that they are written in assembler language and have to contend with many details.

```
/* panic.s - panic, panic0, _panic */

DISABLE  =        340                         / PS to disable interrupts
ENABLE   =        000                         / PS to enable interrupts


        .globl  panic, panic0, _panic, kernstk
/*-------------------------------------------------------------------
/*  panic0 -- entry point for "branch to zero" error; never called
/*-------------------------------------------------------------------
panic0:
        mfps    kernstk-2               / save old ps for message
        mtps    $DISABLE                / disable interrupts
        mov     sp,kernstk              / save old sp for message
        mov     $kernstk-2,sp           / use kernel stack for printing
        mov     $panmsg1,-(sp)          / push address of message
        jsr     pc,_kprintf             / print message
        halt
        jmp     start                   / restart system if user continues


/*-------------------------------------------------------------------
/*  _panic  --  entry point when called by user programs
/*-------------------------------------------------------------------
_panic:                                 / Note: "_panic" pushes the
                                        / PC/PS to simulate a trap so it
                                        / can flow into "panic" (the
                                        / trap entry point, below)
        mfps    pansav                  / save old PS
        mtps    $DISABLE                / disable interrupts
        mov     2(sp),pmsguser          / address of users message
        mov     (sp),-(sp)              / push ret. address and user's
        mov     pansav,2(sp)            /  PS for trap simulation
        mtps    $DISABLE+8              / put "user trap" code in PS


/*-------------------------------------------------------------------
/*  panic  -- entry point for traps and exceptions only; not called
/*-------------------------------------------------------------------
panic:
        mfps    pansav                  / save trap type code from ps
        mov     2(sp),kernstk           / push on kernel stack: old ps
        mov     (sp),kernstk-2          /       old pc
        mov     sp,kernstk-4            /       old sp (from before trap)
        add     $4,kernstk-4
        mov     $kernstk-4,sp
        mov     r5,-(sp)                /       old r5
        mov     r4,-(sp)                /       old r4
```

```
        mov     r3,-(sp)            /           old r3
        mov     r2,-(sp)            /           old r2
        mov     r1,-(sp)            /           old r1
        mov     r0,-(sp)            /           old r0
        jsr     pc,sizmem           / size up memory (needed later)
```

/ set up call to kprintf to print register and stack dump

```
        mov     kernstk,-(sp)       / user's ps
        mov     kernstk-2,-(sp)     / user's pc
        mov     pansav,-(sp)        / address of panic message
        bic     $177760,(sp)        /  (mask off type&use as index
        mov     (sp),-(sp)          / panic trap type
        asl     2(sp)               / compute message address from type
        add     $pmsglist,2(sp)
        mov     *2(sp),2(sp)        / go through vector to message
        mov     $panmsg2,-(sp)      / push format address
        jsr     pc,_kprintf         / print message
        add     $10.,sp             / pop off args to printf, leaving
                                    /   saved regs, even though printed
```

/ dump stack as long as sp was valid

```
        mov     kernstk-4,r3        / r3 = addr. user's stack before trap
        sub     $2,sp               / save space for arg to printf
        mov     $panmsg3,-(sp)      / format arg for printf
        mov     $6,r4               / count of stack items to print
panloop:
        cmp     r3,_maxaddr         / avoid references beyond valid
        bhi     pandone             /  memory addresses
        mov     (r3),2(sp)          / insert value to print as arg.
        jsr     pc,_kprintf         / print one value
        dec     r4                  / decrement counter of # to print
        ble     pandone             / stop if enough have been printed
        add     $2,r3               / otherwise, move along the stack
        jbr     panloop
```

/ clean up and restore the state so user can continue after halt

```
pandone:
        add     $4,sp               / pop off the printf args
        mov     (sp)+,r0            / restore registers
        mov     (sp)+,r1
        mov     (sp)+,r2
        mov     (sp)+,r3
```

```
          mov       (sp)+,r4
          mov       (sp)+,r5
          mov       (sp)+,sp              / restore user's stack pointer
          halt                            / user probably won't continue
          mov       kernstk,-(sp)         / but we should restore PS and PC
          mov       kernstk-2,-(sp)       / in case of ODT "P" command,
          rtt                             / especially for call to _panic
          .data
pansav:
.         =         .+2^.                 / word for saving state info.
panmsg1:
          .byte     12,12,'P,'a,'n,'i,'c,':,' ,'b,'r,'a,'n,'c,'h,' ,'t,'o
          .byte     ' ,'1,'o,'c,'.,' ,'0,',,' ,'p,'s,'=,'%,'o,' ,'s,'p,'=,'%
          .byte     'o,12,12,0
panmsg2:
          .byte     12,12,'P,'a,'n,'i,'c,':,' ,'t,'r,'a,'p,' ,'t,'y,'p,'e
          .byte     ' ,'%,'d,' ,'(,'%,'s,'),12
          .byte     'S,'t,'a,'t,'e,':,' ,'p,'c,'=,'%,'o,' ,'p,'s,'=,'%,'o
          .byte     ' ,'r,'0,'=,'%,'o
          .byte     ' ,'r,'1,'=,'%,'o
          .byte     ' ,'r,'2,'=,'%,'o
          .byte     ' ,'r,'3,'=,'%,'o
          .byte     ' ,'r,'4,'=,'%,'o
          .byte     ' ,'r,'5,'=,'%,'o,12
          .byte     'S,'t,'a,'c,'k,':,' ,'(,'t,'o,'p,' ,'a,'t,' ,'%,'o,'),12,0
panmsg3:
          .byte     '%,'o,12,0
          .even
pmsglist:
          pmsg0
          pmsg1
          pmsg2
          pmsg3
          pmsg4
          pmsg5
          pmsg6
          pmsg7
pmsguser:
          pmsg0                           / Gets overwritten on panic call
pmsg0:
          .byte     'B,'u,'s,' ,'e,'r,'r,'o,'r,0
pmsg1:
          .byte     'I,'1,'1,'e,'g,'a,'1,' ,'i,'n,'s,'t,'r,'u,'c,'t,'i,'o,'n,0
pmsg2:
          .byte     'B,'P,'T,' ,'o,'r,' ,'T,'-,'b,'i,'t,0
```

```
pmsg3:
        .byte    'I,'O,'T,0
pmsg4:
        .byte    'P,'o,'w,'e,'r,' ,'f,'a,'i,'l,0
pmsg5:
        .byte    'E,'M,'T,0
pmsg6:
        .byte    'T,'r,'a,'p,' ,'i,'n,'s,'t,'r,'u,'c,'t,'i,'o,'n,0
pmsg7:
        .byte    'U,'n,'k,'n,'o,'w,'n,' ,'d,'e,'v,'i,'c,'e,0

/* Stack used by kernel at startup and to handle panic messages.        */

        .       =       .+300.           / decimal bytes in kernel stack
kernstk:
        .       =       .+2              / Otherwise kernstk overlaps
                                         / next symbol
```

The system jumps to entry point *panic0* whenever a program branches to location 0; it enters at location *panic* in case of an exception or unexpected interrupt. Code in the system or in a user program calls entry point *_panic* (written in C without the underscore) like a procedure, passing it the address of a message when an irrecoverable error condition arises (e.g., running out of buffers in the frame level communication software).

The code at *Panic0* prints a message explaining that the program branched to location zero, and halts. It restarts at the system entry point if resumed, because it has no way of knowing where the program was executing when it branched to location zero.

Entry point *_panic* pushes data on the stack to simulate an interrupt/exception, and uses the code at location *panic* to print the message and a dump. If resumed, the machine will continue processing where it left off. Restarting after a panic is usually unwise, but it might make sense in some cases.

All three panic routines use *kprintf* to format and print the message. Although the assembler language details make the code that sets up the call seem complex, it is not. What happens is this: *kprintf* takes a variable number of arguments, with the first being a string that tells how to format the output — it knows how many arguments follow from the contents of the format string. The arguments must be pushed on the stack in reverse order (with the format string nearest the top of the stack). After the call to *kprintf*, they must be popped off again.

19.4 Formatted Output

Throughout the system, procedures have called *printf* or *kprintf* to format and write data on the console terminal. Procedure *fprintf*, available from a library, formats and writes a string on a specified file or device. This section shows how these three procedures use a common formatting routine to perform their task.

Printf, fprintf, and *kprintf* each require as arguments a *format specification string*, and a set of variables to be formatted. They convert the variables into a printable representation according to the format specification, and write the result to a device. At the heart of these routines is a common procedure, *doprnt*, that actually performs the formatting. We start by looking at it:

```
/* doprnt.c - _doprnt, _prt10, _prtl10, _prt8, _prtl8, _prt16, _prtl16 */

#define MAXSTR   80
#define LOCAL    static


/*-----------------------------------------------------------------------
 *   _doprnt -- format and write output using 'func' to write characters
 *-----------------------------------------------------------------------
 */
_doprnt(fmt, args, func, farg)  /* adapted by S. Salisbury, Purdue U.   */
        char    *fmt;           /* Format string for printf             */
        int     *args;          /* Arguments to printf                  */
        int     (*func)();      /* Function to put a character          */
        int     farg;           /* Argument to func                     */
{
        int     c;
        int     i;
        int     f;              /* The format character (comes after %) */
        char    *str;           /* Running pointer in string            */
        char    string[20];     /* The string str points to this output */
                                /*  from number conversion              */
        int     length;         /* Length of string "str"               */
        char    fill;           /* Fill character (' ' or '0')          */
        int     leftjust;       /* 0 = right-justified, else left-just. */
        int     longflag;       /* != 0 for long numerics - not used    */
        int     fmax,fmin;      /* Field specifications % MIN . MAX s   */
        int     leading;        /* No. of leading/trailing fill chars.  */
        char    sign;           /* Set to '-' for negative decimals     */
        char    digit1;         /* Offset to add to first numeric digit */

        for(;;) {
                /* Echo characters until '%' or end of fmt string */
                while( (c = *fmt++) != '%' ) {
                        if( c == '\0' )
                                return;
                        (*func)(farg,c);
                }
                /* Echo "...%%..." as '%' */
                if( *fmt == '%' ) {
                        (*func)(farg,*fmt++);
                        continue;
                }
                /* Check for "%-..." == Left-justified output */
                if (leftjust = ((*fmt=='-') ? 1 : 0) )
                        fmt++;
```

```
/* Allow for zero-filled numeric outputs ("%0...") */
fill = (*fmt=='0') ? *fmt++ : ' ';
/* Allow for minimum field width specifier for %d,u,x,o,c,s*/
/* Also allow %* for variable width (%0* as well)       */
fmin = 0;
if( *fmt == '*' ) {
        fmin = *args++;
        ++fmt;
}
else while( '0' <= *fmt && *fmt <= '9' ) {
        fmin = fmin * 10 + *fmt++ - '0';
}
/* Allow for maximum string width for %s */
fmax = 0;
if( *fmt == '.' ) {
        if( *(++fmt) == '*' ) {
                fmax = *args++;
                ++fmt;
        }
else while( '0' <= *fmt && *fmt <= '9' ) {
        fmax = fmax * 10 + *fmt++ - '0';
        }
}
/* Check for the 'l' option to force long numeric */
if( longflag = ((*fmt == 'l') ? 1 : 0) )
        fmt++;
str = string;
if( (f= *fmt++) == '\0' ) {
        (*func)(farg,'%');
        return;
}
sign = '\0';    /* sign == '-' for negative decimal */

switch( f ) {
    case 'c' :
        string[0] = (char) *args;
        string[1] = '\0';
        fmax = 0;
        fill = ' ';
        break;

    case 's' :
        str = (char *) *args;
        fill = ' ';
        break;
```

```
        case 'D' :
            longflag = 1;
        case 'd' :
            if (longflag) {
                    if ( *(long *)args < 0) {
                            sign = '-';
                            *(long *)args = -*(long *)args;
                    }
            } else {
                    if ( *args < 0 ) {
                            sign = '-';
                            *args = -*args;
                    }
            }
            longflag--;
        case 'U':
            longflag++;
        case 'u':
            if( longflag ) {
                    digit1 = '\0';
                    /* "negative" longs in unsigned format  */
                    /* can't be computed with long division */
                    /* convert *args to "positive", digit1  */
                    /* = how much to add back afterwards     */
                    while(*(long *)args < 0) {
                            *(long *)args -= 1000000000L;
                            ++digit1;
                    }
                    _prtl10(*(long *)args, str);
                    str[0] += digit1;
                    ++args;
            } else
                    _prt10(*args, str);
            fmax = 0;
            break;

        case 'O' :
            longflag++;
        case 'o' :
            if ( longflag ) {
                    _prtl8(*(long *)args, str);
                    ++args;
            } else
                    _prt8(*args, str);
```

```
                            fmax = 0;
                            break;

                    case 'X' :
                        longflag++;
                    case 'x' :
                        if( longflag ) {
                                _prt116(*(long *)args, str);
                                ++args;
                        } else
                                _prt16(*args, str);
                        fmax = 0;
                        break;

                default :
                    (*func)(farg,f);
                    break;
            }
            args++;
            for(length = 0; str[length] != '\0'; length++)
                    ;
            if ( fmin > MAXSTR || fmin < 0 )
                    fmin = 0;
            if ( fmax > MAXSTR || fmax < 0 )
                    fmax = 0;
            leading = 0;
            if ( fmax != 0 || fmin != 0 ) {
                    if ( fmax != 0 )
                            if ( length > fmax )
                                    length = fmax;
                    if ( fmin != 0 )
                            leading = fmin - length;
                    if ( sign == '-' )
                            --leading;
            }
            if( sign == '-' && fill == '0' )
                    (*func)(farg,sign);
            if( leftjust == 0 )
                    for( i = 0; i < leading; i++ )
                            (*func)(farg,fill);
            if( sign == '-' && fill == ' ' )
                    (*func)(farg,sign);
            for( i = 0 ; i < length ; i++ )
                    (*func)(farg,str[i]);
            if ( leftjust != 0 )
```

```
                    for( i = 0; i < leading; i++ )
                            (*func)(farg,fill);
        }
}

LOCAL    _prt10(num,str)
         unsigned int num;
         char    *str;
{
         int     i;
         char    c, temp[6];

         temp[0] = '\0';
         for(i = 1; i <= 5; i++)  {
                 temp[i] = num % 10 + '0';
                 num =/ 10;
         }
         for(i = 5; temp[i] == '0'; i--);
         if( i == 0 )
                 i++;
         while( i >= 0 )
                 *str++ = temp[i--];
}

LOCAL    _prtl10(num,str)
         long    num;
         char    *str;
{
         int     i;
         char    c, temp[11];

         temp[0] = '\0';
         for(i = 1; i <= 10; i++)  {
                 temp[i] = num % 10 + '0';
                 num =/ 10;
         }
         for(i = 10; temp[i] == '0'; i--);
         if( i == 0 )
                 i++;
         while( i >= 0 )
                 *str++ = temp[i--];
}

LOCAL    _prt8(num,str)
         unsigned int num;
```

```
        char    *str;
{
        int     i;
        char    c;
        char    temp[7];

        temp[0] = '\0';
        for(i = 1; i <= 6; i++)  {
                temp[i] = (num & 07) + '0';
                num = (num >> 3) & 0037777;
        }
        temp[6] &= '1';
        for(i = 6; temp[i] == '0'; i--);
        if( i == 0 )
                i++;
        while( i >= 0 )
                *str++ = temp[i--];
}


LOCAL   _prt18(num,str)
        long    num;
        char    *str;
{
        int     i;
        char    c, temp[12];

        temp[0] = '\0';
        for(i = 1; i <= 11; i++)  {
                temp[i] = (num & 07) + '0';
                num = num >> 3;
        }
        temp[11] &= '3';
        for(i = 11; temp[i] == '0'; i--);
        if( i == 0 )
                i++;
        while( i >= 0 )
                *str++ = temp[i--];
}


LOCAL   _prt16(num,str)
        unsigned int num;
        char    *str;
{
        int     i;
        char    c, temp[5];
```

```
        temp[0] = '\0';
        for(i = 1; i <= 4; i++)  {
                temp[i] = "0123456789abcdef"[num & 0x0f];
                num = num >> 4;
        }
        for(i = 4; temp[i] == '0'; i--);
        if( i == 0 )
                i++;
        while( i >= 0 )
                *str++ = temp[i--];
}


LOCAL   _prtl16(num,str)
        long    num;
        char    *str;
{
        int     i;
        char    c, temp[9];

        temp[0] = '\0';
        for(i = 1; i <= 8; i++)  {
                temp[i] = "0123456789abcdef"[num & 0x0f];
                num = num >> 4;
        }
        for(i = 8; temp[i] == '0'; i--);
        if( i == 0 )
                i++;
        while( i >= 0 )
                *str++ = temp[i--];
}
```

Doprnt scans and writes the format string on its output, replacing occurrences
of "%..." with a character representation of an argument. For example, it replaces
occurrences of %o by the characters that give the octal representation of an argument, %d by characters for the decimal representation, and %x by characters for
the hexadecimal (base 16) representation. Whenever *doprnt* manufactures a character to be written, whether from copying the format string or from the converted
value of an argument, it calls a character-handling procedure to write the character. The flexibility of *doprnt* arises because the character-handling procedure is an
argument that can be different each time *doprnt* is called. The next section shows
some of the ways *doprnt* can be used.

19.4.1 Printf And Fprintf

The three procedures *printf*, *fprintf*, and *kprintf* all use *doprnt* to format values for output. The only difference, is the character-handling routine they pass to *doprnt*. *Printf* specifies *putc* as the character-handling routine, and the CONSOLE as the device to which characters should be written. When *doprnt* invokes *putc*, characters are placed in the tty output buffer using the standard Xinu tty device driver:

```
/* printf.c - printf */

#define OK        1
#define CONSOLE 0

/*------------------------------------------------------------------
 * printf  --  write formatted output on CONSOLE
 *------------------------------------------------------------------
 */
printf(fmt, args)
        char    *fmt;
{
        int     putc();

        _doprnt(fmt, &args, putc, CONSOLE);
        return(OK);
}
```

Fprintf also uses *putc* as the character-handling procedure, but passes it the device specified by its first argument instead of the CONSOLE device:

```
/* fprintf.c - fprintf */

#define OK      1

/*------------------------------------------------------------------------
 * fprintf  --  print a formatted message on specified device (file)
 *------------------------------------------------------------------------
 */
fprintf(dev, fmt, args)
        int   dev;
        char *fmt;
{
        int     putc();

        _doprnt(fmt, &args, putc, dev);
        return(OK);
}
```

19.4.2 Kprintf

Kprintf does much more than provide a convenient way to format a string: it operates independent of the rest of the system. To understand why such a tool should be built as early as possible, consider how difficult it is to debug an output driver if there is no way to print information. Even after the console I/O system is running, *printf* cannot be used to debug other interrupt handlers because it uses *putc* which may eventually *wait* for the buffer semaphore. Thus, a special-purpose output routine is needed that will never *wait*; *kprintf* serves that purpose.

To print formatted strings without enabling interrupts, *kprintf* uses polling. It still calls *doprnt*, but instead of passing the address of *putc*, it passes the address of *kputc*. When *kputc* needs to write a character, it polls until the device is idle, transmits the character, and polls until the device becomes idle again.

The code is found in file *kprintf.c*:

```
/* kprintf.c - kprintf, kputc, savestate, rststate */

#include <conf.h>
#include <kernel.h>
#include <io.h>
#include <slu.h>
#include <tty.h>


/*------------------------------------------------------------------------
 * kprintf  --  kernel printf: formatted, unbuffered output to CONSOLE
 *------------------------------------------------------------------------
```

```
 */
kprintf(fmt, args)                  /* Derived by Bob Brown, Purdue U.    */
        char *fmt;
{
        int     kputc();

        savestate();
        _doprnt(fmt, &args, kputc, CONSOLE);
        rststate();
        return(OK);
}


/*-------------------------------------------------------------------------
 *  kputc  --  write a character on the console using polled I/O
 *-------------------------------------------------------------------------
 */
LOCAL   kputc(device ,c)
        int     device;
        register char c;        /* character to print from _doprnt      */
{
        struct  csr     *csrptr;
/*T*/   int     slowdown;       /* added to delay output because VAX    */
/*T*/                           /* can't take it at 9600 baud           */
        if ( c == 0 )
                return;
        if ( c == NEWLINE )
                kputc( device, RETURN );
        csrptr = (struct csr *)devtab[device].dvcsr;   /* dev. address */
        while ( (csrptr->ctstat & SLUREADY) == 0 ) ;   /* poll for idle*/
        csrptr->ctbuf = c;
/*T*/   for(slowdown=0;slowdown<1000;slowdown++) ;
        while ( (csrptr->ctstat & SLUREADY) == 0 ) ;   /* poll for idle*/
}

LOCAL   int     savecrstat, savectstat;
LOCAL   char    saveps;
/*-------------------------------------------------------------------------
 *  savestate  --  save the console control and status register
 *-------------------------------------------------------------------------
 */
LOCAL   savestate()
{
        char ps;

        disable(ps);
```

```
        saveps = ps;
        savecrstat = (devtab[CONSOLE].dvcsr)->crstat & SLUENABLE;
        (devtab[CONSOLE].dvcsr)->crstat = SLUDISABLE;
        savectstat = (devtab[CONSOLE].dvcsr)->ctstat & SLUENABLE;
        (devtab[CONSOLE].dvcsr)->ctstat = SLUDISABLE;
}


/*-----------------------------------------------------------------
 * rststate  --  restore the console output control and status register
 *-----------------------------------------------------------------
 */
LOCAL   rststate()
{
        char ps;

        (devtab[CONSOLE].dvcsr)->crstat = savecrstat;
        (devtab[CONSOLE].dvcsr)->ctstat = savectstat;
        ps = saveps;
        restore(ps);
}
```

To prevent interrupts on the *CONSOLE* device (and interference from the lower half of the *tty* driver), *kprintf* calls procedure *savestate* to save the current device state before it begins, and procedure *rststate* to restore the state after it finishes.

Procedure *savestate* saves three values. It places the processor status in global variable *saveps*, the console receiver interrupt status in *savecrstat*, and the console transmitter interrupt status in *savectstat*. The saved values must be kept in global variables for two reasons: first, when procedure *savestate* returns, its local variables will disappear; second, the values will be restored by another procedure, so they must be accessible. *Savestate* and *rststate* must copy the saved processor status value from local to global memory because procedures *disable* and *restore* only work with local variables (the exercises suggest changes that eliminate copying).

19.5 Summary

Trapping and identifying unexpected interrupts, exceptions, and branches to location zero are important because they help isolate bugs that would otherwise be difficult to catch. Hence, building error detection routines early is essential, even if the routines are crude.

Another essential debugging tool consists of an output routine that masks interrupts and uses polling. In our case, the routine is called *kprintf*; it provides a way to print the values of variables and constants without relying on the conventional output device driver. *Kprintf* is especially useful for printing messages from within interrupt routines because the usual buffered output driver cannot be used there.

FOR FURTHER STUDY

Most books consider the issue of protection along with that of exception processing. Habermann [1976] and Calingaert [1982] are examples. Papers by Dennis and Van Horn [1966], Lampson [1969], and Fabry [1974] all consider protection mechanisms.

EXERCISES

19.1   Replace *panic* by a set of routines that merely halts the processor with an error code in register 0. How much space can you save?

19.2   How many locations does *panic* require on the user's stack to process an exception or illegal interrupt?

19.3   Experiment by calling *panic* from a C program. When the processor stops, compare the values printed for the registers and stack with those reported by ODT. Did *panic* correctly restore registers? Will it always restore registers correctly?

19.4   Design a mechanism that allows the executing process to catch exceptions.

19.5   Wire a switch so it will toggle DC power on the bus. Does it surprise you that the processor sometimes prints the power-fail message?

19.6   As implemented, *kprintf* violates the rule that says "no procedure should explicitly *disable* or *restore* interrupts unless it *disables* them on entry and *restores* them on exit." Rewrite *kprintf* and associated support routines so they follow the rule. Can you guess why they were designed in their current form?

19.7   Design another interface for *doprnt* that formats output and places it in a string.

20

System Configuration

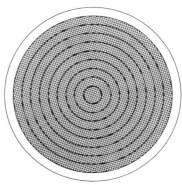

This chapter concludes our discussion of operating system design by answering two practical questions: how can the code built in earlier chapters be transformed to make it suitable for a system with different peripheral devices, and how can the code be collected into a so-called *kernel* that is isolated from user processes by the hardware's *system call* mechanism?

20.1 The Need For Multiple Configurations

When the system code is transformed to make it suitable for a particular set of peripheral devices, we say it has been *configured*; the result is often referred to as a *configuration*. The preceding chapters described the design process as if operating systems were built for one particular machine with a specific set of I/O devices. In reality, of course, a given operating system must run on a variety of hardware configurations, each with its own set of device and interrupt vector addresses. More importantly, devices are often combined on boards that limit the choice of addresses, so an operating system designer does not have complete freedom over them even if the hardware can be changed. For example, a system that contains 4 serial line units can have them on a single board, in which case the device addresses are contiguous, or they can be located on several boards, in which case it may not be possible to make the addresses contiguous.

Handcrafting a new system configuration for each machine would be costly, time-consuming, and error-prone. Xinu, like most systems, relies on a *configuration program* that helps reduce this cost by automating some of the chores. The program, called *config*, is not part of the system proper, and it will not be shown in detail. While the implementation is not important, understanding what *config* does is important: it takes as input a *specification* of the devices and parameters, and produces Xinu source files that generate the final object programs when compiled. Before discussing the input *config* expects and the general method it uses, the next section considers the entire configuration process.

20.2 Static vs. Dynamic Configuration

System configuration can be performed: when the system is generated (i.e. compiled and linked together), when the system is started (i.e., during bootstrap), or while the system is running. In general, postponing configuration makes the system more flexible but increases the overhead. The most advanced systems can reconfigure themselves dynamically as new devices are connected or old ones removed; the least advanced must be recompiled to accommodate even minor changes like switching the baud rate of a terminal.

The chief advantage of configuring at generation time (early) is that the memory image contains only those device drivers needed for devices that exist. Another advantage is that the system spends less time trying to identify hardware details during the bootstrap process because these details are bound into the code. The chief disadvantage of early configuration is that a system configured for one machine cannot run on any other (unless they are identical, including such small details as device and interrupt vector addresses).

Deferring configuration until system startup allows the designer to build more robust code because a single system can operate on several hardware configurations. During startup, the system locates devices, initializes interrupt vectors, establishes appropriate entries in the device table, and somehow correlates the devices with their drivers. It should be noted that the hardware on many machines limits the amount of configuration that can be deferred until startup. For example, devices on the 11/2 must be known by the system because it cannot determine their type or the location of their interrupt vectors at run-time.

Reconfiguring at run-time allows a system to adapt to changes in the hardware without stopping. Some systems keep all device drivers resident in main memory so they can associate new devices with an appropriate driver immediately. Others permit device drivers to be loaded on demand (and unloaded on request). In such systems, the hardware cooperates closely with the software to inform the system whenever a device or processor becomes ready, or a ready device becomes disabled.

20.3 The Details Of Configuration In Xinu

Like many systems, Xinu uses a mixture of configuration strategies. Because it is a small system designed to run on primitive hardware, much of the configuration occurs early. For example, devices and associated drivers must be specified when a system is generated. Even in a small system like Xinu, some of the configuration can be postponed until system startup. For example, the size of memory and the existence of a real-time clock are both tested after Xinu begins. Interrupt vector initialization also occurs dynamically, when the system calls the driver initialization routines.

Most of the differences between configurations of Xinu concern details of device addresses, interrupt vectors, and driver routines. Thus, the program *config*, responsible for producing a system given its specification, deals primarily with device configuration. It reads a specification file that describes the types of device drivers available as well as a list of specific devices, and produces as output files that contain the definition of a device switch table, and code to initialize it. We have already seen the output files, *conf.h* and *conf.c*, in Chapter 11. *Config* reads input specifications from the file named *Configuration*; its contents are shown below.

```
/* Configuration - (device configuration specifications) */

/* device "type" declarations plus disk file (df) */

tty:
        on SLU          -i ttyinit       -o ionull       -c ionull
                        -r ttyread       -w ttywrite     -s ioerr
                        -n ttycntl       -g ttygetc      -p ttyputc
                        -iint ttyiin     -oint ttyoin
dlc:
        on SLU          -i dlcinit       -o ioerr        -c ioerr
                        -r dlcread       -w dlcwrite     -s ioerr
                        -n dlccntl       -g ioerr        -p dlcputc
                        -iint dlciin     -oint dlcoin
dsk:
        on WIN          -i dsinit        -o dsopen       -c ioerr
                        -r dsread        -w dswrite      -s dsseek
                        -n dscntl        -g ioerr        -p ioerr
                        -iint dsinter    -oint dsinter
df:
        on DSK          -i lfinit        -o ioerr        -c lfclose
                        -r lfread        -w lfwrite      -s lfseek
                        -n ioerr         -g lfgetc       -p lfputc
                        -iint ioerr      -oint ioerr

    %

/* Device definitions starting with SLU devices */

CONSOLE         is tty  on SLU          csr=0177560 ivec=0060 ovec=0064
OTHER           is tty  on SLU          csr=0176500 ivec=0300 ovec=0304

/* Ring network block-mode input and block-mode output devices */

RING0IN         is dlc  on SLU          csr=0176510 ivec=0310 ovec=0314
RING0OUT        is dlc  on SLU          csr=0176520 ivec=0320 ovec=0324

/* Disk device */

DISK0           is dsk  on WIN          csr=0177460 ivec=0134 ovec=0134

/* Slots for files (not really devices) */

FILE1           is df   on DSK          csr=0       ivec=0     ovec=0
FILE2           is df   on DSK          csr=0       ivec=0     ovec=0
```

```
FILE3            is df    on DSK        csr=0       ivec=0      ovec=0
FILE4            is df    on DSK        csr=0       ivec=0      ovec=0

%


/* Configuration and Size Constants */


#define MEMMARK                        /* define if memory marking used*/
#define NNETS    1                     /* number of Xinu ring networks */
                                       /*  (remove if there are zero)  */
#define NPROC    10                    /* number of user processes     */
#define NSEM     50                    /* total number of semaphores   */
#define RTCLOCK                        /* system has a real-time clock */
#define VERSION  "6.1b (05/22/84)"     /* label printed at startup     */
```

20.3.1 Input To Config

The input to *config* is divided into three sections by occurrences of the separator character "%". Section 1 contains *type declarations* that identify major device types (e.g., *tty*). Section 2 contains *device declarations* that define device names (e.g., *CONSOLE*). Section 3 contains *constant declarations* that select system options (e.g., whether to use memory marking) or override default sizes and parameters (e.g., the number of processes). We will now consider the first two parts of the specification file in detail.

Device type declarations define a device type name, list the possible hardware mechanisms associated with that type, and give the default device drivers associated with each mechanism. For example, the type declaration:

```
tty
        on SLU          -i ttyinit    -o ionull     -c ionull
                        -r ttyread    -w ttywrite   -s ioerr
                        -p ttyputc    -g ttygetc    -n ttycntl
                        -iint ttyiin -oint ttyoin


        on HYP          -i hypinit    -o ionull     -c ionull
                        -r hypread    -w hypwrite   -s ioerr
                        -p ioerr      -g ioerr      -n hypcntl
                        -iint oddiin -oint oddoin
```

defines type *tty* to work on a serial line hardware unit, *SLU*, or a hypothetical hardware unit, *HYP*. If the device type is only used with a particular hardware unit, the phrase "*on* unit-name" can be omitted. Keywords *-i, -o, -c, -r, -w, -s, -g, -p, -n,* are abbreviations for the device driver functions *init, open, close, read,* *write*, *seek*, *getc*, *putc*, and *control*; they are used to associate a set of device driver routines with the type name. Similarly, keywords *-iint* and *-oint* specify the name of the input and output interrupt drive routines.

Declaring a device type serves two purposes. First, it provides an abbreviation so individual devices can be declared without writing down the set of driver routines again and again. Second it informs *config* that all the devices of a given type belong in a class, distinguished only by minor device numbers. Devices with the same type receive minor numbers in sequence starting at zero. Notice that the concept of "device type" has been separated from the concept of "hardware type" so an arbitrary set of devices can be thought of as a single type even if their hardware interface devices differ. Thus, there may be a general device type like *disk* and only one array of control blocks for *disk* devices, even though specific disks use slightly different lower-level driver routines.

The second part of the input specification file contains *device declarations*. Each device declaration declares one device by giving its name, its type, and information that is not supplied by the type (e.g., the interrupt vector address). If the device type has two or more sets of driver routines, the device declaration must also specify the hardware unit name with the phrase "*on* hardware-unit". For example, the declaration of type *tty* given above included two sets of drivers, one for "SLU", the other for "HYP". A device declaration for a console of type *tty* that runs on an SLU is written:

```
CONSOLE is tty on SLU  -csr 0177560 -ivec 060 -ovec -064
```

The declaration specifies an input interrupt vector address, 060, an output interrupt vector address, 064, and a CSR (Control and Status Register) address, 0177560. The information needed to fill in driver fields of the device switch entry for this device is taken from the device type, *tty*. For example, *config* will specify that, for device *CONSOLE*, the driver routine corresponding to *read* is *ttyread*.

Information like the names of driver routines and interrupt vector addresses can be specified in either the type declaration or the device declaration. Values in the device declaration override those given in the type declaration when both have been supplied for a particular device. For example, the declaration:

```
CONSOLE is tty on SLU  -csr 0177560 -ivec 060 -ovec 064 -g mygetc
```

specifies the CONSOLE device as before except that name *mygetc* is used for the *getc* driver instead of the default name *ttygetc*. Such a declaration might be made to test a new version of a driver before replacing the standard version.

20.3.2 Computation Of Minor Device Numbers

Consider the files that *config* produces. *Conf.h* contains the declaration of the device switch table, and *conf.c* contains the code that initializes it. For a given device, its *devtab* entry contains a set of pointers to the device driver routines that correspond to high-level I/O operations like *open*, *close*, *read*, and *write*. The entry also contains input and output interrupt vector addresses, and the device address. All this information comes from file *Configuration* in a straightforward way.

The device switch entry also contains a field that gives what we have referred to as the *minor device number*. Minor device numbers are nothing more than integers that distinguish among multiple real devices, all of which use the same device drivers. Our drivers use the minor device number as an index into the array of control blocks to associate a control block with each real device. We have assumed that the minor device numbers are assigned sequentially, starting at zero for each type of device. For example, Figure 20.1 shows how device ids and minor numbers are assigned on a system that has three *tty* devices and two *dlc* devices.

device name	device identifier	device type	minor number
CONSOLE	0	tty	0
RINGIN	1	dlc	0
RINGOUT	2	dlc	1
TERMINAL	3	tty	1
PRINTER	4	tty	2

Figure 20.1 An example of device configuration.

Notice that the three *tty* lines have minor numbers zero, one, and two, even though their device ids happen to be zero, three, and four. Program *config* assigns these minor device numbers based on the file declarations. To understand how it determines which minor number to assign to which device, we need to look closely at the input.

20.4 Configuring A Xinu System

To configure a Xinu system, the programmer edits file *Configuration*, adding or changing device information and symbolic constants as desired. Changing constants like *MEMMARK* that are used throughout the system will change the way system routines are compiled because each routine includes a copy of *conf.h* at compile time.

When run, *config* first reads and records the device type information. It then reads device declarations, assigns minor device numbers, and produces the source code in *conf.c* and *conf.h*. Finally, it appends definitions of symbolic constants from the third section of the specification file onto *conf.h*, making them available to other routines.

After *config* produces a new version of *conf.c* and *conf.h*, routines that include *conf.h* must be recompiled and grouped into library files. Most of the Xinu procedures reside in file, *libx.a*. The entire process is controlled by the UNIX utility program *make*, which automatically checks the modification dates and only recompiles procedures when necessary. *Make* also links together compiled versions of *lowcore.s*, *startup.s*, *initialize.c*, and *conf.c* and names them *xinu.o*. Thus, the lowcore area, the startup routine, the device switch, and all the routines they reference will be part of the memory image. When *libx.a* and *xinu.o* have been built, configuration is complete. To run a program, the user compiles it, binds it together with *xinu.o*, and resolves references to other system routines from the library.

20.4.1 Counting Devices

How does the system know how many devices exist? How does a driver know how many devices it controls? *Config* counts devices as it processes the specification. To pass the information on to other programs, it inserts defined constants in *conf.h* that specify the number of devices of each type, and the total number of devices. Constant *NDEVS* is an integer that tells the total number of devices. The device-independent I/O routines use *NDEVS* to test whether a device id corresponds to a valid device. Constants of the form N*xxx* tell the number of devices of type *xxx* (e.g., *Ntty* gives the total number of *tty* devices). The device driver routines can use these constants to declare the size of control block arrays.

20.5 System Calls And Procedures

Most hardware includes special instructions that programs use to call system routines. Even the LSI 11 includes them: *TRAP* and *EMT*. These instructions take an integer argument that specifies the desired system procedure. When executed, they trap to a dispatch routine just like an exception or device interrupt. The system call dispatch routine must examine the argument, *i*, and pass control to the system procedure that performs function *i*. The chief disadvantage of using the system call mechanism is that all system procedures must be present in memory, independent of whether they will be used at run-time. Loading procedures that are never used is a luxury that may not be viable on small systems. By defining such an interface, the designer places a distinct boundary between user code and system code, preventing users from adding more layers to the design easily.

The advantages of using special instructions to call system procedures are: the hardware mechanism may be more efficient than normal procedure calling mechanisms, and it allows a user program to be loaded into memory without knowing the exact addresses of system procedures. The latter may be important if the operating system needs to load new programs from disk dynamically. In systems that have hardware-assisted memory management, it may be necessary to use system call instructions to keep the user's address space separate from the system's address space.

How difficult is it to change Xinu to use hardware system call instructions? Not difficult at all, although it will force every system procedure to be present in every memory image. To make the change, the designer first chooses a set of system procedures that correspond to system calls. (Be warned that the hardware often limits the number of possible system calls, so it may not be possible to have more than sixty four). Each of these is assigned a number starting at zero. Calls to system procedures in the user's code must be mapped into a special system call instruction with the appropriate integer argument. This can be done by writing special assembler language routines that perform the mapping at run-time, or by having the compiler recognize the names of system calls and generate special code for them.

Building the system call dispatcher is also quite easy. The code consists largely of a branch table and a small routine that accesses the system call argument and uses it to select the appropriate branch from the table. Control passes to the individual system procedure, which executes and returns to the dispatcher. The dispatcher then returns control to the caller. Usually, the hardware's system call instruction disables interrupts when executed, and reenables them when the dispatcher returns.

20.6 Summary

This book has covered the fundamentals of operating systems design, including a look at the basic system components, the design process, and system configuration. We have seen components for: memory management, process management, process coordination, process synchronization, interprocess communication, intermachine communication, clock management, device management, device drivers, and a file system. This chapter discussed how a subset of the procedures can be selected to give a fixed set of system calls, and how the software can be reconfigured to accommodate changes in hardware devices.

Abstractions like processes and device-independent I/O are extremely powerful notions because they make it possible for programmers to deal with complicated computations. Knowing how to design and organize software that supports such abstractions is a skill that has many applications. Of course, some programmers will use this skill to build general-purpose operating systems for new machines, but others will apply the same skill to design such things as: run-time systems for concurrent programming languages, database systems that support concurrent transactions, and special-purpose systems for microprocessors. Independent of the application, the same general design procedure applies — by now the reader should have a firm grasp of that design procedure and the system it will ultimately produce.

FOR FURTHER STUDY

Few books or papers consider the topic of hardware or operating system configuration in detail. The memo by Kridle et. al. [1983] is a good example of the informal way configuration information is often disseminated; it also assumes that readers are more interested in configuring hardware for the operating system than configuring the operating system to fit their hardware.

Much has been written on the topic of portability. Miller [1978] discusses a portable UNIX system, while Cheriton et. al. [1979] considers a system designed to be portable.

EXERCISES

20.1   Replace part of the tty driver and reconfigure Xinu to use your routine.

20.2   Find out how other systems are configured. Read about IBM's SYSGEN procedure (See if you can find someone with first-hand experience).

20.3   Xinu reconfiguration takes much longer than necessary if every program is recompiled whenever *Configuration* changes. Write a *config* program that separates constants into several different include files to eliminate unnecessary recompilation.

20.4   Discuss whether a configuration program is worthwhile? Include some estimate of the extra effort required to make a system easily configurable. Remember that a programmer is likely to have little experience or knowledge about a system when it is first configured.

20.5   Xinu can be configured with or without a real-time clock easily. Identify other desirable configuration parameters.

Appendix 1

A Quick Introduction to C

C is a popular algol-like language with features that support systems programming. Although it cannot be explained or learned in ten minutes, a few pointers and some simple examples are usually sufficient to provide experienced programmers with a reading knowledge sufficient to understand the code in this book. A chart that explains the basics of C syntax and semantics in terms of Pascal follows a short list of the highlights of the language.†

1. Types are not as strict as in Pascal. Although later versions of the language are more strongly typed than early versions, compilers usually allow data types to be interchanged freely. One often sees arithmetic operations on characters, because declaring something to be a character is an easy (although nonportable) way of declaring a one-byte object.

2. There is no type *Boolean*. Nonzero is equivalent to *true*; zero is equivalent to *false*.

3. Like Pascal and PL/I, C has aggregate types *array* and *structure* (called *record* in Pascal). Unlike many languages, C has no notion of files.

4. C procedure declarations may not be nested, so it is not block-structured in the Algol, Pascal, or PL/I sense.

5. C does not distinguish *procedures* from *functions*. All procedures return a value; if the programmer does not specify one, the value returned will be nonsense. The calling program can ignore the returned value by invoking a procedure in a single statement, or use the returned value by invoking the procedure in an expression.

6. C supports recursive procedure calls.

7. The C syntax is concise. C uses left and right braces in place of PL/I's *do end* or Pascal's *begin end*.

8. Brackets [ ] denote subscripting, and parentheses ( ) denote procedure calls. If x is the name of an array, then x[i] refers to element i, but the

---

†For more details about C consult Kernighan and Ritchie [1978].

name x used without subscripts refers to the address of the first element (i.e., the address of x[0]). Similarly, a procedure name that appears without parentheses following refers to the address of the code for the procedure. Subscripts for an array of N elements range from 0 through $N-1$.

9. C has an extensive and powerful set of operators including such functions as bit-wise *shift, and, or, complement,* and *exclusive or.* Operators are often denoted by one or two special characters. Even operators that have side-effects return functional values. For example, the assignment operator assigns its right-hand operand to its left-hand operand, and returns the value assigned as in APL. Some surprises: = denotes assignment, == denotes test for equality, != denotes test for inequality, *x denotes *whatever x points to,* x++ has the same value as x, but has the side-effect of incrementing x after it has been accessed, ++x means *first increment x and then return its new value.*

10. C allows arithmetic on pointers, where the type of the pointer determines how the new address is computed. If x points to an object of size y bytes, then x+1 points to the "next" occurrence of the object (i.e., produces an address that is equivalent to adding y to the integer value of x).

11. Pointer arithmetic and array subscripting in C are curiously related. By definition, x[a] means "add" a to x, where addition is performed according to the rules of pointer arithmetic. The definition happens to make a[x] equivalent to x[a] if a is an integer and x is an array. It also means that if p points to x[5] then p+1 points to x[6] (provided p is declared to be a pointer to the type of object in x). Unfortunately, many C programs contain cryptic code that "walks" through an array by assigning a pointer the starting address and incrementing the pointer with ++.

12. Semicolons are statement terminators; they follow every statement except for compound statements. Like PL/I, but unlike Pascal, semicolons in C precede the keyword *else.* A semicolon by itself is a null statement.

13. The C macro preprocessor handles parameterized macros, allowing in-line expansion of code and substitution of symbolic constants in the program. The macro facility, which also provides for source file inclusion, is less powerful than that of PL/I, but more powerful than the *const* facility in Pascal. By convention, the names of symbolic constants are written in upper case; other names are written in lower case. Constants and data used by more than one source program are usually declared in a separate file and included in the source program at compile time. By convention, the names of included files end in ".h" (for *header*).

14. C supports separate compilation of procedures. In declarations, the keyword *static* limits the visibility of the declared name to the currently compiled file, providing a way to group procedures and data so that only

selected names are visible in the rest of the program. Whenever a procedure is loaded, the loader includes all procedures and data that were
compiled with it.

15. The keyword *extern* makes a declaration refer to an external object; all
references to a given external name refer to the same object independent
of the file in which the declaration occurred (like external variables in
PL/I or named common in FORTRAN). Declaring an object to be
external merely instructs the compiler to generate code to reference it as
such; the actual definition of storage for an external object is made by
writing a declaration outside of the scope of a procedure. External objects must be defined once no matter how many times they are declared.

16. In C, data can be initialized at compile time; by default, the initial
value of an external data object is zero.

17. Unlike the Pascal *case* statement that selects one out of n statements
(i.e., is an n-way conditional), the C *switch* statement is merely an n-
way branch. The switch expression is evaluated, and control transfers to
one of n branch points (called *cases*) as expected, but after the transfer,
execution continues falling though case after case until the program explicitly branches out of the switch statement. The usual way to branch
out is with a *break* statement, which causes flow of control to pass to
the statement following the switch. *Switch* statements can include a *default* label, equivalent to *otherwise* in some dialects of Pascal. Control
passes to the *default* if no other case is true.

18. Comments start with "/*" and end with the next "*/" as in PL/I.

19. Identifiers can contain letters, digits, or underscores; they must begin
with a letter or an underscore.

The following chart explains specific constructs in C by giving their equivalent
in Pascal. Notice, in particular, the powerful *for* statement, the array subscripting
(which extends from 0 through N-1, not 1 through N), and the unusual declaration
syntax.

C construct	explanation	Pascal equivalent
int a; char b; char *c; int (*x)();	declarations: integer character pointer to character pointer to procedure that returns integer	var a: integer; var b: char; var c: ↑char; -none-
char d[10]; char e[10][12]; char *f[5] char **g;	array of characters 2-dimensional array array of pointers pointer to pointer	var d: array[0..9] of char; var e: array[1..9,0..11] of char; var f: array[0..4] of ↑char; var g: ↑↑char;
´a´ ´\014´	character constant character constant with value 014 (octal)	´a´ -none-
"abc"	string constant Array of contiguous characters terminated by a null byte (i.e., 'a', 'b', 'c', '\0'). Newline and tab denoted by \n and \t. Value is the the address of the first character	-none- (some Pascal compilers use '...')
123 0123 0x123	decimal constant octal constant (has leading zero) hexidecimal constant	123 -none- (decimal value is 83) -none- (decimal value is 291)

struct x {
    int f1;
    char f2;
}
	structure (record)
	declaration with
	fields f1 and f2
		x = record
		    f1: integer;
		    f2: char
		end

struct x y[2];	y is array of struct x	var y: array[0..1] of x;
#define A v	symbolic constant	const A = v;
#define A(x) v(x)	parameterized macro	-none-
#ifdef A X #endif	conditional compilation code X is compiled only if symbol A defined	-none-
#ifndef A X #endif	negative conditional compilation; X compiled only if A not defined	-none-

C Construct	explanation	Pascal equivalent
#include *src*	source file inclusion (if *src* is "*path*" then path is relative to current directory; if *<path>* then relative to system directory)	-none-
=	assignment operator	:=
+ - * / %	arithmetic operators division (C does integer division on integers) modulus or remainder	+ - * / div -none-
var op= exp v += 9	operation and assignment example: add 9 to variable v	var := var op exp v := v + 9
== != > < <= >=	test equality test inequality test greater than test less than test less than or equal test greater than or equal	= <> > < <= >=
*x	pointer dereference (whatever x points to)	x↑
sizeof(x)	size of data object x in bytes	-none-
&x	address of object x (when used as a unary operator)	-none-
& | ~	bitwise and (when used as binary operator) bitwise or bitwise (1's) complement	-none- -none- -none-
&& || !	Boolean and Boolean or Boolean not (&& and || are evaluated left-to-right with early termination)	and or not (Pascal does not use early termination)
x[i]	array reference	x[i]

C construct	explanation	Pascal equivalent
s.f p−>f	reference to field f in structure s reference to field f in structure pointed to by p	s.f p↑.f
e ? a : b	conditional expression (if e is nonzero, value is a else value is b)	-none-
++x x++ −−x x−−	preincrement postincrement predecrement post decrement (when used in an expression ++x refers to the value of x after incrementing; x++ refers to the value before incrementing)	x := x + 1 x := x + 1 x := x − 1 x := x − 1
p(e1,e2,...,en)	procedure invocation	p(e1,e2,...,en)
while (exp) S;	indefinite iteration	while exp <> 0 do S
if (exp) S;	conditional	if exp <> 0 then S
if (exp) S1; else S2;	2-way conditional	if exp <> 0 then S1 else S2
{S1;S2;...;Sn;}	compound statement (note semicolons)	begin S1;S2;...;Sn end

for(S1;exp;S2)
   S3;
	indefinite iteration
	with initialization
	and reinitialization
	(S1, exp and S2 are
	optional − if exp is
	omitted, infinite loop
	results)
		S1;
		while exp <> 0 do
		  begin
		    S3;
		    S2
		  end

return	procedure return	finish executing procedure
return(exp)	return exp to caller as function value	*function name* := exp; finish executing function

name(formals)
declaration of formals
{
  declaration of
  local variables;
  statements;
}
	procedure declaration	procedure name(formals);
		declaration of locals;
		begin
		
		  statements
		
		end;

C construct	explanation	Pascal equivalent

type name(formals)
declaration of formals
{
   declaration of
   local variables;
   statements;
}
	function declaration	function name(formals) : *type*;
		declaration of locals;
		begin
		
		   statements
		
		end;

for(i=0 ; i<N ; i++) ...x[i]...	typical loop to search array x, assuming x has size N	for i := 1 to N do ...x[i]...
*x++	idiomatic expression for pointer x: its value is whatever x points to; x is incremented after the reference according to pointer arithmetic	-none-
(type)exp 1 + (int) &x	type casting the type of expression exp is changed. Example: make the address of x an integer before adding 1 to it (i.e., use integer, not pointer, arithmetic)	-none-
/*...*/	Comment	(*...*) or {...}

Appendix 2

Xinu Programmer's Manual

Version 6b

(XINU IS NOT UNIX)

The Xinu Programmer's Manual contains a description of the Xinu software. It has been divided into three sections, following the style of the *UNIX Programmer's Manual*. This introduction explains how to use the Xinu software to compile, download, execute, and debug a C program. It also contains a set of informal implementation notes that give the character of Xinu.

The body of the manual gives a terse description of Xinu procedures and the details of their arguments — it is intended as a quick reference for programmers, not as a way to learn Xinu. Section 1 describes cross-development commands that run on the host computer. These cross-compile, cross-assemble, cross-load, download, upload, and analyze programs. Section 2 describes Xinu system procedures that programs call to invoke operating system services. Section 3 describes procedures available from the standard libraries. (From the programmer's point of view, there is little distinction between library routines and system calls.)

As in the UNIX manual, each page describes one command, system call, or library routine; section numbers appear in the page footer as "(digit)" following the name of the program. Within a section all pages are arranged in alphabetical order. References have the same form as headers (e.g., "getc(2)" refers to the page for "getc" in section 2). Related commands are sometimes mentioned on one page (which may make it difficult for beginners to find them).

A Short Introduction To Xinu
and the Cross-Development Software

How to Use Xinu

Architecture. Xinu comes in two parts: a cross-development environment that runs on the host machine (usually a Digital Equipment Corp. VAX), and an independent system that runs on the microcomputer (usually a Digital Equipment Corporation LSI 11/2). The microcomputer is connected to the host over an asynchronous serial line like those used to connect terminals. From the point of view of the host, the microcomputer is simply another device that transmits and receives characters; from the point of view of the micro, the host is merely a console terminal that transmits and receives characters.

Overview. To run a program under Xinu, you create the source file on the host machine, and invoke cross-development software to compile and load the program along with the Xinu system. Once a complete memory image has been produced, it can be downloaded onto the microcomputer where it executes independent of the host. During execution, you invoke a program on the host that captures characters emitted by the micro and displays them on the terminal screen, and sends characters typed at the keyboard to the micro. Thus, your terminal on the host appears to be connected directly to the micro. If the micro crashes, it can be restarted without downloading (provided the crash did not destroy the program in memory). To help debug severe crashes, the contents of memory on the micro can be uploaded to a file on the host where a post-mortem program can analyze the state and report problems.

Cross-Development commands. The cross-development system contains a C compiler, linking loader, downloader, uploader, and post-mortem debugger as well as a few miscellaneous commands. The details can be found in section 1 of this manual. These commands probably reside in the Xinu "bin" directory on your system; the directory name must be part of your PATH for you to execute them. If they are not in directory /usr/Xinu/bin, consult whoever installed Xinu to find out the bin directory name and add it to your path.

Compiling programs. The command *cc11* works like the UNIX *cc* command. It invokes the C cross-compiler, cross-assembler, and cross-loader to translate C programs into a memory image. Like *cc*, the actions of *cc11* depend on the file names passed to it as arguments — names ending in ".c" are assumed to be C programs, those ending in ".s" are assumed to be assembler programs, and those ending in ".o" are assumed to be previously compiled object programs. Unless you specify otherwise, *cc11* compiles C programs, assembles assembler programs, and loads object programs to produce a memory image in file *a.out*. Normally, the memory image contains the Xinu operating system along with your program (you can ask *cc11* to leave out the operating system and just prepare a "stand-alone" program).

Downloading. Command *download* reads file *a.out*, and loads the memory image into the microcomputer (it will look for the memory image in a different file if you instruct it to do so). Usually, *download* is invoked with an argument "-a5" that causes the microcomputer to delay for five seconds before starting execution of the downloaded program.

Interacting with the Micro. The microcomputer on which Xinu runs is attached to the host like a peripheral device. The program *odt* "connects" your terminal to the microcomputer by relaying characters between the terminal and the device. Characters that arrive from the micro are sent to your terminal, while characters typed on your keyboard are sent to the micro. *Odt* can be invoked at any time, but it is most often used just after a *download* so you can see the output of the program as it runs. *Odt* will halt the microcomputer for you by "breaking" the console line if you type the 2-character sequence backslash (\) followed by null (CONTROL-@). To proceed again, type uppercase-P (see the LSI 11 manual for more information on the "odt" mode).

Debugging a crash. If the program running on the micro crashes, the cause of trouble may not be easy to spot. Help is available from a post-mortem debugger, *pm*. You must first execute command *upload* to copy the complete memory image from the micro into a file on the host. By default, the image file is named *core11*. After the *core11* file has been created, run command *pm* to cull through it and print out the system status. *Pm* uses both *core11* and *a.out* to diagnose the problem (as usual, the actual file names can be changed if you don't happen to like them).

An Example

Create a C program. For example, here is a C program that prints the string "Hello world." on the console terminal and exits. (*Printf* is a system (library) procedure that prints formatted strings on the console; other system commands are described in sections 2 and 3 of this manual):

```
/* example C program in file example.c */
main()
{
    printf("Hello world.\n");
}
```

Compile and Download. Cross-compile the program, download it onto the micro, and connect your terminal to the micro with the following commands:

```
cc11 example.c
download -a5
odt
```

The cross-compiler will compile the C program, and load it along with the Xinu system, leaving file *a.out* in your current directory. The downloader will copy the image from *a.out* into the micro and start it executing (after a delay of five seconds). During downloading, you will see a count of the bytes remaining as blocks are transferred. Finally, *odt* will connect your terminal to the micro (the 5-second delay leaves time for the VAX to start *odt*). When the micro begins execution you will see a few Xinu system startup messages followed by the program output. When all of your processes complete (in this case, when the single program terminates), you will see a system termination message. The output is:

```
Xinu Version 6.10b 7/6/83
57346 real mem
21268 avail mem
clock enabled


Hello world.


All user processes have completed.
```

Re-run the program. To re-run the program without downloading the micro again, type:

```
\ CNTL-@
1000G
```

The 2-character sequence backslash (\) null (CNTL-@) causes *odt* to halt the LSI 11 and place it in "ODT" mode. The LSI 11 responds with an at-sign prompt. The sequence "1000G" starts the machine executing at location 1000 (octal). To get out of *odt*, kill the process by typing the "DELETE" key (or Control-C if you use 4.2 bsd UNIX). Note that killing *odt* does not stop the micro — it merely disconnects your terminal.

Upload the memory. You may want to see what processes are (were) running. To retrieve the memory image and analyze it, run the commands:

```
upload
pm
```

Warning: *upload* destroys the contents of memory on the micro as it executes, so the micro cannot be restarted again after uploading. Also note that if you interrupt (i.e. kill) the uploader and then restart it, the image it retrieves will be incorrect.

Interpreting pm. *Pm* reports whether the program text has been changed and the status of each process. If the output from *pm* seems unreasonable, check for the following common errors. If significant portions of the program have been changed, it may mean a stack overflow occurred; totally meaningless process information often indicates that the overflow extended into the process table. Having only one or two bad process states in an otherwise meaningful set may indicate that the context switch ended up with no ready or current processes; this only happens if you modify the system code or add your own device driver. When experimenting with device drivers, look carefully at the status of the null process after a crash — if you find it sleeping, waiting, receiving, or suspended then you probably have a lower-half driver routine that removes the null process from the current/ready lists.

System Termination. Xinu may not always print the system termination message even if all your processes exit, because it interprets the term "user process" to mean "all processes except the null process." This can be confusing because the network software starts processes that never terminate (they continue forwarding frames even if the CPU is otherwise idle). Also remember that the tty driver will continue to echo characters even if there are no processes running to consume them.

Hints on restarting. The LSI 11 ODT command 1000G sets the program counter to 1000 and starts execution with interrupts *enabled*. Xinu disables interrupts immediately after it starts executing to avoid being interrupted before the system is ready. If an interrupt occurs before the LSI 11 can execute the first instruction, it may cause the system to crash (ungracefully). If your processor gives you trouble with the "G" command, then type the following three lines to restart Xinu:

```
RS/xxxxxx 340
R7/xxxxxx 1000
P
```

The LSI 11 will print octal values in place of xxxxxx. Note: no carriage return is used after the "P" command (consult the LSI 11 manual for more information).

Xinu Directory Organization

The Xinu software distribution tape, available from the publisher, contains all Xinu software from the book as well as the VAX cross-development and library software described in this manual. Source files and manual pages are included. To run the software on the distribution tape, you will need a Digital Equipment Corp. VAX computer running Berkeley 4.1bsd or 4.2bsd UNIX operating system, and at least one Digital Equipment Corporation LSI 11/2, LSI 11/03, or LSI 11/23 microcomputer.

Directories on the tape form a UNIX tree as described below. Usually, the Xinu software is rooted in the UNIX directory */usr/Xinu*, although this is not necessary. In the directory listing, a number in front of a name gives its level of nesting. The Xinu directory (denoted ".") resides at level 1. Directories immediately below it lie at level 2. Thus, manual pages for library commands are found at level 3 in directory *./man/man3*.

Within source directories, C programs are found in *file.c*, while complex subsystems have a directory of their own. For example, the C compiler resides in subdirectory *./src/cmd/cc11*, while the file *./src/cmd/size11.c* contains the entire source for thee "size11" command. Each source directory contains a *Makefile* that gives the UNIX utility *make* instructions for compiling and loading the programs in that directory.

Included files can be found in directory *./include*, which contains links to the Xinu system include files (which reside in directory *./src/sys/h*), as well as include files for the cross-development software.

As the directory chart shows, source files for Xinu itself are located in directory *./src/sys/sys* (a convention used by early UNIX systems). That directory also contains the *Configuration* file and the object version of *config*.

The tape comes with further instructions needed to install the software and connect an LSI 11 to the VAX.

```
1 .                     Xinu-directory (usually /usr/Xinu)

   2 /bin                All cross-development object programs

   2 /include            All include files

   2 /install            Installation shell script

   2 /man                All manual pages:
      3 /man1                for cross-development commands
      3 /man2                for Xinu system commands
      3 /man3                for library commands

   2 /src                All source files subdivided:
      3 /cmd                 cross-development software
      3 /lib                 libraries
      3 /sys                 Xinu and configuration:
         4 /con                  configuration program
         4 /h                    Xinu include files
         4 /sys                  Xinu and Makefile
```

Xinu Design Notes

(Updated 1/82, 3/82, 11/82, 3/83)

These are the notes kept during implementation; they are not designed as an accurate introduction to Xinu. In particular, deferred operations (e.g., deferred process termination) have disappeared from the book version along with the *pmark* process table entry even though they remain in version 5.

Some quick ideas:

- There are multiple processes.
- A process is known by its process id.
- The process id is an index into the process table.
- There are counting semaphores.
- A semaphore is known by its index in the semaphore table.
- There is a line time clock.
- The system schedules processes based on priority.
- The system supports I/O.
- For tty I/O characters are queued on input and output. The normal mode includes echoing, erasing backspace, etc.
- There is a frame-level data link communication package to make a ring of LSI 11's.
- There is a file system that supports concurrent growth of files without preallocation; it has only a single-level directory structure.
- There is a one-word message passing mechanism (on the 68000, a "word" is large enough to hold a pointer).
- There is support for self-initializing routines (memory marking) that makes the system serially reusable without requiring the kernel to explicitly call initialization routines.
- Processes can create processes, kill processes, suspend processes, restart processes, and change the priority of processes.
- There is no real memory management, but there are primitives for acquiring and returning memory from the global pool, and a way to suballocate smaller pools of fixed-size buffers.
- There is a configuration program, config, to generate a Xinu system according to specifications given.

Discussion of implementation:

0. Files. The system sources are organized as a set of procedures. For the most part, there is a file for each system call (e.g., chprio.c for the system call chprio). In addition to the system call procedures, a file may contain utility functions needed by that system call. Files which do not correspond to system

calls are listed below along with a brief description of each:

Configuration
> The file of device and constant information as edited by the user to describe the hardware; the config program takes this file and produces conf.c and conf.h files.

conf.h Generated constants including I/O and size constants; do not edit directly.

conf.c Generated file of initialized variables; do not edit directly.

kernel.h General symbolic constants; misc defined macros.

proc.h Process table entry structure declaration; state constants.

sem.h Semaphore table entry structure declaration; semaphore constants.

io.h General user-level I/O definitions.

slu.h Serial Line Unit CSR layout; I/O constants for slu's.

tty.h Tty line discipline control block, buffers, excluding sizes.

dlc.h Line discipline control block for asynchronous device used as network interface.

disk.h Disk driver control block.

dtc.h Data Technology Corp. SASI disk interface hardware register layouts.

xebec.h Xebec Corp. SASI disk controller register layouts.

frame.h Xinu ring network frame format definitions.

bufpool.h Buffer pool constants and format.

mark.h Memory marking table declarations.

mem.h Memory management free list format declarations.

ports.h Definitions for communication ports (queued interprocess rendevous points).

sleep.h Definitions for real-time delay software.

dir.h Layout of disk directory block.

iblock.h Layout of index block (i-block).

file.h Definitions of variables and constants used by the local file system routines.

q.h Q data structure declaration (see below); defined macros for q predicates.

queue.c Q manipulation routines.

resched.c Almost the inner-most routine (rescheduler). It selects the next process to run from the ready queue and fixes up the state. Calls ctxsw to switch contexts.

cxtsw.s The routine that actually changes the executing process into another one. A very small piece of assembler code with only one trick: when a process is saved, the execution address at which it restarts is actually the instruction following the call to ctxsw.

lowcore.s The loaded version of the low part of memory (interrupt vectors). All interrupt vectors are initialized by the loader to point to panic routines, and overwritten for valid devices at startup.

ioint.s   I/O interrupt dispatchers.

startup.s   Actual entry point (start) with code to set up C run-time environment and call high-level initialization.

initialize.c All external (global) variables, the null process (process 0, see below), and the high-level system initialization routine (e.g., to craft the process table entry for process 0).

userret.c   The routine to which user processes return (i.e. exit) if they ever do. Care should be taken so that userret never exits; it must kill the process that runs it because there is no legal return frame on the stack.

sizmem.s   Utility procedure to size main memory.

1. Process states. Each process has a state given by the pstate field in the process table entry. The state values are given by symbolic constants PRxxxx. PRFREE means that the process entry is unused. PRREADY means that the process is linked into the ready list and is eligible for the CPU. PRWAIT means that the process is waiting on a semaphore (given by psem). PRSUSP means that the process is in hibernation; it is not on any list. PRSLEEP means that the process is in the queue of sleeping processes waiting to be awakened. PRCURR means that the process is (the only one) currently running. The currently running process is NOT on the ready list. In addition to the actual state, there is a "mark" field (pmark) which indicates pending state changes. PMDEAD indicates that the process has been killed and should be removed as soon as it reaches the ready queue. PMSUSP indicates that the process has been suspended and should move to the suspended state as soon as it reaches the ready queue. PMNONE indicates no pending action.

2. Semaphores. Semaphores reside in the array semaph. Each entry in the array corresponds to a semaphore and has a count (scount), and state (sstate). The state is SFREE if the semaphore slot is unassigned, SUSED if the semaphore is in use. If the count is -p then the sqhead and sqtail fields point to a FIFO queue of p processes waiting for the semaphore. If the count is nonnegative p then no processes are waiting. More about the head and tail pointers below.

3. Suspension. Suspended processes are forbidden from using the CPU. They may remain on semaphore/sleep queues until they are to be moved to the ready queue. A call to ready(p), where p has been marked suspended, will NOT place it on the ready queue. It will merely result in p being placed in the suspended state. Suspending a process that is already on the ready queue will remove it. Suspending the current processes forces it to give up the CPU.

4. Sleeping. When a process calls sleep(n) it will be delayed n seconds. This is achieved by placing the process on a queue of jobs ordered by wakeup time and relinquishing the CPU. Every 60th of a second, an external line-time clock will interrupt the CPU and cause a clock interrupt routine to be called. To avoid extra overhead, 5 such interrupts are ignored before one is pro-

cessed. Thus, the granularity of clock counts is 1/10 of a second. The interrupt handler maintains a clock and moves processes back to the ready queue when their wakeup time has been reached. Notice that a process may put itself, but no one else, to sleep.

5.   Queues and ordered lists. There is one data structure for all heads, tails, and elements of queues or lists of processes: q[]. The first NPROC entries in q (0 to NPROC-1) correspond to the NPROC processes. If one wants to link process i onto a queue or list, then one uses q[i].qnext and q[i].qprev as the forward and backward pointers.

The remaining entries in q are used for the heads and tails of lists. The integer *nextqueue* always points to the next available entry in q to assign. When initialize builds the heads and tails of various lists, it assigns entries in q sequentially. Thus, the sqhead and sqtail fields of a semaphore are really the indices of the head and tail of the list in q. The advantage of keeping all heads and tails in the same data structure is that enqueuing, dequeuing, testing for empty/nonempty, and removing from the middle (eg., when a process is killed) are all handled by a small set of simple procedures (files queue.c and q.h). An empty queue has the head and tail pointing to each other. Since all real items have index less than NPROC, testing whether a list is empty becomes trivial. In addition to FIFO queues, q also contains ordered lists based on an integer kept in the qkey field. For example, processes are inserted in the ready list (head at position q[rdylist]) based on their priority. They are inserted in the sleep list based on wakeup time. Ordered lists are always in ascending order with the inserted item stuck in BEFORE those with an equal key. Thus, processes are removed from the ready list from the tail to get the highest priority process. Also, processes of equal priority are scheduled round robin. Since the sleep queues are serviced from the smallest to largest keys, items are removed from the head of the queue (equal keys do not matter for sleeps).

6.   Process 0. Process 0 is a null process that is always available to run or is running. Care must be taken so that process 0 never executes code that could cause its suspension (e.g. it cannot wait for a semaphore). Since Process 0 may be running during interrupts, this means that interrupt code may never wait for a semaphore. Process 0 initializes the system, creates the first user process, starts it executing the main program, and goes into an infinite loop waiting until an interrupt. Because its priority is lower than that of any other process, the null process loop executes only when no other process is ready. It uses a pause instruction while waiting to avoid taking bus cycles just in case dma devices are running.

Section 1: Cross-Development Commands

This section of the manual describes the program development commands that run on the host computer. They are used to prepare programs for execution under Xinu, transfer the memory image into the micro, and monitor execution. None of these programs (e.g., the C compiler) executes on the micro itself.

NAME

cc11 — cross compiler for the LSI-11

SYNOPSIS

cc11 [option] ... file ...

DESCRIPTION

Cc11 is a general-purpose script that invokes the C preprocessor, C cross-compiler, cross-assembler, and cross-loader to produce code for an LSI 11. *Cc11* is easier to use than invoking the processors individually because it passes the necessary arguments like library directories and keeps track of intermediate files automatically. By default, *cc11* leaves the result in a file named 'a.out' that is ready for downloading into the LSI 11 memory. **N.B.:** *cc11* produces object code in the PDP-11 UNIX format; as expected, it is incompatible with the VAX UNIX object code format.

By default, *cc11* preprocesses, cross-compiles, cross-assembles, and cross-loads a program; arguments can limit which steps it performs and change such things as the order in which libraries are searched.

Arguments whose names end with '.c' are taken to be C source programs; they are compiled, and each object program is left on the file whose name is that of the source with '.o' substituted for '.c'.

In the same way, arguments whose names end with '.s' are taken to be assembly source language and are assembled, producing a '.o' file.

Arguments whose names end with '.o' are combined with '.o' files produced from '.c' and '.s' arguments by the loader to produce an 'a.out' file.

Arguments whose names end with '.a' are taken to be libraries of '.o' programs, and are searched by the loader in the order specified.

Other arguments to *cc11* control the process as follows:

−c   Suppress the loading phase of the compilation, and force *cc11* to stop after producing '.o' files.

−o *output*
        Name the final output file *output*.

−v   Verbose output narrating each step of the compile. This is useful if you want to see what's going on.

−D*name*=*def*
−D*name*
        Define the *name* to the preprocessor, as if by '#define'. If no definition is given, the name is defined as "1".

−E   Run only the macro preprocessor on the named C programs, and send the result to the standard output.

−I*dir*   '#include' files whose names do not begin with '/' are always sought first in the directory of the *file* argument, then in directories named in −I options, then in directories on a standard list.

−L   If loading, include the standalone startup routine in preparation for downloading without Xinu. The default load sequence includes Xinu startup routines.

−O   Invoke an object-code improver as part of the C cross-compilaton.

−P   Run only the macro preprocessor on the named C programs, and send the result to corresponding files suffixed '.i'.

−S   Compile the named C programs into assembly language, and leave the assembler-language output on corresponding files suffixed '.s', without assembling or loading the result.

−U*name*

Remove any initial definition of *name*.

Other arguments are taken to be either loader option arguments, or C-compatible object programs, typically produced by an earlier *cc11* run, or perhaps libraries of C-compatible routines. These programs, together with the results of any compilations specified, are loaded (in the order given) to produce a file that may be downloaded to the LSI−11 for execution. Unless changed with the −o option, *cc11* leaves the result of the load in file 'a.out'.

Examples

To compile a C program and load it with the Xinu libraries, producing an image in 'a.out' that is ready for downloading:

        cc11 program.c

To compile C code in file f1.c and leave the object code in file f1.o:

        cc11 -c f1.c

To assemble code in file f2.s and leave the object code in file f2.o:

        cc11 -c f2.s

To compile C code in file f3.c and combine it with previously compiled code in file f1.o:

        cc11 f3.c f1.o

To load three previously compiled files f1.o, f2.o, and f3.o:

        cc11 f1.o f2.o f3.o

To compile and load the C code in file f4.c leaving the output in 'outfile' instead of 'a.out':

cc11 -o outfile f4.c

FILES

file.c	input C file
file.s	input or output assembler language file
file.o	input or output object file
a.out	loaded output
/tmp/ctm?	temporary compiler files
Xinu-directory/lib/cpp11	preprocessor
Xinu-directory/lib/c0.11	first pass
Xinu-directory/lib/c1.11	second pass
Xinu-directory/lib/c2.11	optional optimizer
Xinu-directory/include	'#include' files

DIAGNOSTICS

The diagnostics produced by C itself are intended to be self-explanatory. Occasional messages may be produced by the assembler or loader.

BUGS

Cc11 does not support arguments *-g*, *-w*, *-p*, *-R*, *-C*, *-B*, or *-t* that the VAX version handles.

SEE ALSO

as11(1), ld11(1), ranlib11(1), download(1), ar(1)

NAME

dd58 — copy a file to or from a TU58 connected to an asynchronous VAX line

SYNOPSIS

dd58 [option[=value]] ...

DESCRIPTION

The TU58 tape drive is a block-addressable, random access cartridge tape storage unit often used with LSI 11 microcomputers. The program *dd58* provides a way to write TU58 tapes from the VAX (e.g., to create a bootable system tape). It copies standard input to the TU58, or a given number of blocks from the TU58 to its standard output. Because the TU58 controller is a block-oriented interface that relies on the driver to supply data quickly, one should **never** use a terminal as standard input. Options are:

option	*values*
sam	set special addressing mode
-sam	disable special addressing mode (default)
verify	check data after reading or writing (default)
-verify	do not check data after reading or writing
maint	set maintenance mode
-maint	disable maintenance mode (default)
drive=*n*	use drive number *n* (default 0)
posit=*n*	reading or writing begins with tape block *n* (default 0)
count=*n*	read or write *n* bytes (default for *writing* is to end of file; this must be specified for reading)
read	read from the TU58 and write to the standard output
write	read from the standard input and write to the TU58
seek	position the TU58 drive at the given block number

For example, to put the file *x* on a tape cartridge at block 31, using special address mode, use

    dd58 sam posit=31 write < x

To read its first 512 bytes into the file *y*, use

    dd58 sam posit=31 count=512 read > y

DIAGNOSTICS

Error messages are printed on the terminal; they are self-explanatory.

NAME

download — load program into LSI—11

SYNOPSIS

download [file] ... [option] ...

DESCRIPTION

Download loads an absolute binary program image (PDP—11 a.out format) into the memory of an LSI-11/2 computer over an asynchronous line. After halting the LSI-11 with a break, *download* places a bootstrap in memory, and uses it to load the remainder of memory.

Loading the object program takes time proportional to the size of the program itself. It takes about two seconds to load 1000 bytes.

Download will normally leave the LSI 11 in ODT. The -a option requests *download* to auto-start the micro. The optional number N following -a, forces a delay of approximately N seconds before execution, allowing the user to reconnect the console port before output begins.

The bootstrap program is loaded 100 words beyond the end of the user's object program. If there is insufficient memory for the bootstrap and stack, this program will fail. When using the —n option, the user must assure that the bootstrap loadpoint has not changed since the last reload.

Download loads the user's program as specified in the command line. If no program name is given, *a.out* is used.

Options are:

—n   Do not preload the bootstrap program, assume it is already loaded.

—v   Verbose. Print details of the communications with the LSI-11/2.

—s   Silent. Print no information messages.

—a*[N]* Autostart. After loading, start the user's program running in the LSI-11. Optionally delay N seconds.

—lx   Use LSI number *x* as the LSI 11 for downloading. If this option is not specified, download selects the LSI-11 that the user has on reserve, or a free one if none is reserved. E.g. —*l9*.

—b *f* Use file *f* as the bootstrap program.

FILES

/dev/LSI.i LSI 11 device connections
/tmp/LSI-* Lock files for auto-select
Xinu-directory/lib/dl default bootstrap loader

NAME
    ld11 — LSI 11 cross-loader for the VAX

SYNOPSIS
    ld11 [option] file ...

DESCRIPTION

Ld11 combines several object programs into one, resolves external references, and searches libraries. In the simplest case several object *files* are given, and *ld11* combines them, producing an object module which can be either executed or become the input for a further *ld11* run. (In the latter case, the −**r** option must be given to preserve the relocation bits.) By default, *ld11* leaves its output on file **a.out**.

The argument routines are concatenated in the order specified. The entry point of the output is the beginning of the first routine unless altered by the −**e** option.

If any argument is a library, it is searched exactly once at the point it is encountered in the argument list. Only those routines defining an unresolved external reference are loaded. If a routine from a library references another routine in the library, and the library has not been processed by *ranlib11* (1), the referenced routine must appear after the referencing routine in the library. Thus the order of programs within libraries may be important. If the first member of a library is named '__.SYMDEF', then it is understood to be a dictionary for the library such as produced by *ranlib11*; the dictionary is searched iteratively to satisfy as many references as possible.

The symbols '_etext', '_edata' and '_end' ('etext', 'edata' and 'end' in C) are reserved, and if referred to, are set to the first location above the program, the first location above initialized data, and the first location above all data respectively. It is erroneous to define these symbols.

Ld11 understands several options. Except for −**l**, they should appear before the file names.

  −**s**   'Strip' the output, that is, remove the symbol table and relocation bits to save space (but impair the usefulness of the debugger). This information can also be removed by *strip11(1)*.

  −**u**   Take the following argument as a symbol and enter it as undefined in the symbol table. This is useful for loading wholly from a library, since initially the symbol table is empty and an unresolved reference is needed to force the loading of the first routine.

  −**l***x*   This option is an abbreviation for the library name 'Xinu-directory/lib/lib*x*.a', where *x* is a string. If that does not exist, *ld11* tries '/usr/lib/lib*x*.a'. A library is searched when its name is encountered, so the placement of a −**l** option is significant.

−x   Do not preserve local symbols (i.e., symbols not declared .globl) in the output symbol table; only enter external symbols. This option saves some space in the output file.

−X   Save local symbols except for those whose names begin with 'L'. This option is used by *cc11(1)* to discard internally generated labels while retaining symbols local to routines.

−r   Generate relocation bits in the output file so that it can be the subject of another *ld11* run. This flag also prevents final definitions from being given to common symbols, and suppresses the 'undefined symbol' diagnostics. The idea is that several object files may be combined into one large one using −r without losing information.

−d   Force definition of common storage even if the −r flag is present.

−n   Move the data areas up to the first possible 4K word boundary following the end of the text. Designed for systems that share text, this option only wastes space when used with Xinu -- it should not be specified except for debugging.

−i   Important that it not be used on an LSI 11/2. It causes the text and data areas to be allocated from separate address spaces (i.e. the data area relocation begins at location 0).

−o   The *name* argument after −o is used as the name of the output file, instead of **a.out**.

−e   The following argument is taken to be the name of the entry point of the loaded program; location 0 is the default.

−O   Not to be used on an LSI 11/2. It makes the file an overlay.

−D   The next argument is a decimal number that sets the size of the data segment.

FILES
   Xinu-directory/lib/lib*.a libraries
   a.out   output file

SEE ALSO
   as11(1), ar(1), cc11(1), ranlib11(1)

NAME

lorder11 — find ordering relation for an LSI 11 object library

SYNOPSIS

lorder11 file ...

DESCRIPTION

Argument *file* is the input consisting of one or more object files or library archives (see *ar*(1)). The standard output is a list of pairs of object file names, meaning that the first file of the pair refers to external identifiers defined in the second. The output may be processed by *tsort*(1) to find an ordering of a library suitable for one-pass access by *ld*(1).

This brash one-liner intends to build a new library from existing '.o' files.

    ar cr library `lorder11 *.o | tsort`

The need for lorder11 may be vitiated by use of *ranlib*(1), which converts an ordered archive into a randomly accessed library.

FILES

*symref, *symdef
nm11(1), sed(1), sort(1), join(1)

SEE ALSO

tsort(1), ld11(1), ar(1), ranlib11(1)

BUGS

The names of object files, in and out of libraries, must end with '.o'; nonsense results otherwise.

NAME
  LSIunlock — release lock on an LSI 11

SYNOPSIS
  LSIunlock [-lx]

DESCRIPTION
  LSIunlock releases the caller's currently reserved LSI 11, making it available
  for others to use. Reservations expire after 10 minutes of idle time even if
  LSIunlock is not used. Argument *x* forces *LSIunlock* to cancel the reservation
  on LSI 11 number *x* no matter who holds the reservation. Users are assumed
  to cooperate and not release reservations capriciously.

SEE ALSO
  lusers(1)

NAME

lusers — list users holding reservations on LSI 11s

SYNOPSIS

lusers

DESCRIPTION

Lusers lists the users who hold reservations on LSI 11s. Each line of output contains the LSI 11 number, the user who holds it, and the idle time, rounded to the nearest minute. Reservations are made by *download*(1), *upload*(1), and *odt*(1).

FILES

/tmp/LSI-* Lock files.

SEE ALSO

LSIunlock(1)

BUGS

Lusers lists reservations and idle time based on lock file times which may not be quite accurate. LSIs with more than 10 minutes of idle time are listed even though the reservation software considers the reservation to have expired.

NAME

nm11 — print name list for object file produced by cc11

SYNOPSIS

nm11 [—agnopru] [file ... **]**

DESCRIPTION

Nm11 prints the name list (symbol table) of each object *file* in the argument list. If no *file* is given, the symbols in 'a.out' are listed.

Each symbol name is preceded by its value (blanks if undefined) and one of the letters U (undefined), A (absolute), T (text segment symbol), D (data segment symbol), B (bss segment symbol), C (common symbol), or f file name. If the symbol is local (non-external) the type letter is in lower case. The output is sorted alphabetically.

Options are:

—a   Include all symbols in candidates for printing; normally symbols destined for UNIX's *sdb* (1) are excluded.

—g   Print only global (external) symbols.

—n   Sort numerically rather than alphabetically.

—o   Prepend file or archive element name to each output line rather than only once.

—p   Don't sort; print in symbol-table order.

—r   Sort in reverse order.

—u   Print only undefined symbols.

NAME

odt — connect VAX tty to LSI—11 console (odt) line

SYNOPSIS

odt [-lx]

DESCRIPTION

Odt connects a terminal on the VAX to an LSI 11 tty line so the output of the LSI 11 is sent to the terminal and characters typed at the terminal are sent to the LSI 11. *Odt* sets the LSI 11 tty to raw mode, and the VAX terminal to cbreak mode. The connection can be broken by killing the odt process (e.g., by typing CONTROL-C or DEL depending on your tty setting).

When *odt* receives a backslash from the terminal, it switches to raw mode to read one character, after which it switches back to cbreak mode. The backslash escape allows the user to send characters like DEL to the LSI 11 even though they are normally interpreted as signals. As a special case, an escaped null character (octal 0) causes *odt* to force the LSI line into a break condition for 1 second. This is useful for trapping the LSI 11 into ODT mode.

FILES

/dev/LSI.i default LSI 11 connection
/tmp/LSI-* Lock files

NAME

pm — Xinu post mortem debugger

SYNOPSIS

pm [**-p**] [**-s**] [**-t**] [*txtfil* [*corfil*]]

DESCRIPTION

Pm performs a post mortem given a core image from an LSI 11 running Xinu. It takes as input the memory image (in LSI 11 a.out format) that was *down-load*ed, and the core image (in LSI 11 core format) that was *upload*ed, and prints the following information:

Differences between the text portions (program instruction areas) of the file before downloading and after uploading. Except for interrupt vectors which are initialized at run-time, differences indicate that instructions were accidentally overwritten. Interrupt vectors lie below location 1000 (octal).

C traceback of the executing process, based on Xinu's *currpid*.

C traceback of all other processes.

The status of all semaphoresa; if a semaphore is in use and the count indicates that there are processes waiting, the list of waiting processes is printed along with an actual count. Backward links are checked for consistency.

The status of tty devices, including the buffer head and tail pointers along with buffer contents.

By default, *pm* takes the downloaded image from file *a.out,* the uploaded image from file *core11,* and produces all of the above output. *Pm* always prints information about the current process. If the following flags are present, *pm* prints only the information requested.

-p   dump the process table.

-s   dump the semaphore table.

-t   dump the tty tables.

Optional arguments *txtfil* and *corfil* can be specified to change the files used as the downloaded and uploaded image.

SEE ALSO

download(1), upload(1)

BUGS

Pm may fault when given garbage files (e.g., a badly damaged core file) because it references symbols in the core image based on values obtained from the a.out file without checking their validity.

NAME

ranlib11 — convert LSI 11 cross-archives to random cross-libraries

SYNOPSIS

ranlib11 archive ...

DESCRIPTION

Ranlib11 converts each *archive* to a form which can be loaded more rapidly by the LSI 11 cross-loader, by adding a table of contents named **__.SYMDEF** to the beginning of the archive. It uses *ar*(1) to reconstruct the archive, so that sufficient temporary file space must be available in the file system containing the current directory.

SEE ALSO

ld11(1), ar(1)

BUGS

Because generation of a library by *ar* and randomization by *ranlib11* are separate, phase errors are possible. The cross-loader *ld11* warns when the modification date of a library is more recent than the creation of its dictionary; but this means you get the warning even if you only copy the library.

NAME

size11 — size of an 11 object file

SYNOPSIS

size11 [objectfile ...]

DESCRIPTION

Size11 prints the (decimal) number of bytes required by the text, data, and bss portions, and their sum in hex and decimal, of each object-file argument. If no file is specified, **a.out** is used.

SEE ALSO

ld11(1)

NAME

strip11 — remove symbols and relocation bits from 11 object file

SYNOPSIS

strip11 name ...

DESCRIPTION

Strip11 removes the symbol table and relocation bits ordinarily attached to the output of the assembler and loader. This is useful to save space after a program has been debugged.

The effect of *strip11* is the same as use of the −s option of *ld11*.

FILES

/tmp/stm?   temporary file

SEE ALSO

ld11(1)

NAME

subEIS — substitute code for LSI 11 extended instructions

SYNOPSIS

subASH
subASHC
subMUL
subDIV

DESCRIPTION

These programs read an LSI 11/2 assembly language listing from the standard input, replace opcodes from the Extended Instruction Set (EIS) with a call to a library subroutine that simulates them, and write the new listing on the standard output. They are used mainly as filters for compiling LSI 11/2 programs for machines without the EIS chip.

Each program checks for a different instruction; *subMUL* checks for (and replaces) *mul* instructions, *subDIV* checks for (and replaces) *div* instructions, *subASH* checks for (and replaces) *ash* instructions, and *subASHC* checks for (and replaces) *ashc* instructions. The resulting assembly language program must be loaded with the library *libeis.a* , which contains the routines called.

SEE ALSO

cc11(1), EIS(2)

DIAGNOSTICS

The condition codes are correctly set by the above calling sequence.

BUGS

Setting the condition codes accounts for most of the work these routines perform. Unfortunately, they are so slow that most programs, including Xinu are almost unusable on an 11/2 without the EIS hardware.

NAME

tu58 — routines to access TU58 tape drives attached to the VAX

SYNOPSIS

topen(drive, mode, name)
char *drive;
int mode;
char *name;

tclose(dn)
int dn;

tseek(dn, offset, whence)
int dn;
int offset;
int whence;

tread(dn, buf, nbytes)
int dn;
char *buf;
int nbytes;

twrite(dn, buf, nbytes)
int dn;
char *buf;
int nbytes;

#include <tu58io.h>
tioctl(dn, request, arg)
int dn;
int request;
union tio *arg

#include <tu58errno.h> extern int terrno; tperror(str) char *str;

DESCRIPTION

These routines manipulate a TU58 tape drive unit that is attached directly to the VAX. They are obtained by loading the library *lib58.a*. These routines do all the tape controlling including mutual exclusion of users (but *not* that of a user's processes).

The TU58 has two drives on one controller. These routines treat each drive as a separate file; that is, each must be opened individually, operations may be intermixed, and they can be closed in any order.

Topen opens drive *drive* for reading (if *mode* is 0), writing (if *mode* is 1) or for both reading and writing (if *mode* is 2). *Drive* is the address of a string of ASCII characters representing the drive number; only the first character is used. Legal drive names are "0" and "1". *File* is the name of the port to which the TU58 is attached; if given as NULL, the port *ldev/LSIfast* is used.

The opened drive is positioned at the beginning (block 0), and is opened with the verification bit set and the special addressing and maintenance modes cleared. (To change these, see *tioctl*, below.) The returned drive descriptor must be used for subsequent calls for other input-output functions on the drive. On error, -1 is returned.

Given a drive descriptor *dn* returned from a *topen* call, *tclose* closes the associated drive. If all drives on the TU58 are closed, it also releases the unit. Note that this routine is *not* invoked automatically; it must be called explicitly.

Given a drive descriptor *dn* returned from a *topen* call, and the address *buf* which is the location of *nbytes* contiguous bytes into which the input will be placed, *tread* will read *nbytes* bytes into the buffer. The number of characters read, or -1 (on error), is returned. Note that reading begins at a block boundary, and that there is no concept of "end of file".

Given a drive descriptor *dn* returned from a *topen* call, and the address *buf* which is the location of *nbytes* contiguous bytes which are to be written to the drive, *twrite* will write *nbytes* bytes from the buffer to the drive. The number of characters written, or -1 (on error), is returned. Note that writing begins at a block boundary,

Given a drive descriptor *dn* returned from a *topen* call and a request *request*, *tioctl* will either alter a characteristic of the drive, or return information about the drive. Legal requests are:

request	effect
TU58SSAM	set special addressing mode
TU58CSAM	clear special addressing mode
TU58SVFY	set verification mode
TU58CVFY	clear verification mode
TU58SMTM	set maintenance mode
TU58CMTM	clear maintenance mode
TU58SPOS	set new position; unlike *tseek*, this does not move the tape, but the next operation will take place at the current position. *Arg* is a pointer to an integer, which is the new block number.
TU58GDCB	return the drive control block. This copies the drive control block into the locations pointed to by *arg*; the structure is defined in *Xinu-directory/include/tu58io.h*.

On error, *tioctl* returns -1; on success, 0. The requests are defined in the include file *Xinu-directory/include/tu58io.h*.

ERROR HANDLING

Errors are handled uniformly; if the operation failed, the attempted command is aborted and an error flag is returned. This flag is always -1. To obtain more detailed error messages, there is a routine *tperror* which prints its argument string, followed by a brief message describing the last error that occurred. There is an external variable, *terrno*, that contains a code number indicating the last error. Its values are in *Xinu-directory/include/tu58errno.h*.

There is one error that will not return an error code, even though *terrno* is set (and so *tperror* will report it); namely, if the operation succeeded but retries were necessary. This is a TU58 error code; the only routine that ever sends something more than once is the routine that initializes communications between the VAX and the TU58.

AUTHOR

Matt Bishop (*mab*)

BUGS

Sometimes the TU58 does not respond to an initialization command. When this happens, check the connections and try again.

NAME

upload — copy LSI 11 memory to VAX

SYNOPSIS

upload [options] ... [[min addr] max addr]

DESCRIPTION

Upload copies the contents of an LSI 11 memory onto a file on the VAX. By default the image is placed in file core11.

Arguments *min addr* and *max addr* limit the image to specific addresses.

Options include the following:

  −o   Output file. Take the next argument as an output file name in place of *core11*.

  −v   Verbose. Print the details of communications between the LSI 11 and the host.

  −s   Silent. Print no information messages.

  −n   Noload. Assume the uploader code already resident in the LSI 11.

  −lx   LSI number. Use LSI number *x* for uploading. If this option is not specified, *upload* selects the LSI 11 that the use has reserved.

  −a   a.out file. Take the next argument as the name of the object file in place of a.out.

FILES

/dev/LSI.i LSI 11 device connections

/tmp/LSI-* Lock files for auto-select

{Xinu-directory}/lib/ul default bootstrap loader

BUGS

Upload reads the contents of some memory locations with ODT and then overwrites them with a bootstrap program; if aborted, it cannot be restarted because data has been lost.

Section 2: System Calls

The Xinu operating system kernel consists of a set of run-time procedures to implement operating system services on an LSI 11/2 microcomputer. The system supports multiple processes, I/O, synchronization based on counting semaphores, preemptive scheduling, and communication with other machines. Each page in this section describes a system routine that can be called by a user process.

Each page describes one system call, giving the number and types of arguments that must be passed to the procedure under the heading "SYNPOSIS" (by giving their declaration in C syntax). The heading "SEE ALSO" suggests the names of other system calls that may be related to the described function. For example, the "SEE ALSO" entry for system call *wait* suggests that the programmer may want to look at the page for *signal* because both routines operate on semaphores.

In general, Xinu blocks processes when requested services are not available. Unless that manual page suggests otherwise, the programmer should assume that the process requesting system services may be delayed until the request can be satisfied. For example, calling *read* may cause an arbitrary delay until data can be obtained from the device.

NAME

chprio − change the priority of a process

SYNOPSIS

int chprio(pid,newprio)
int pid;
int newprio;

DESCRIPTION

Chprio changes the scheduling priority of process *pid* to *newprio*. Priorities are positive integers. At any instant, the highest priority process that is ready will be running. A set of processes with equal priority is scheduled round-robin.

If the new priority is invalid, or the process id is invalid *chprio* returns SYSERR. Otherwise, it returns the old process priority. It is forbidden to change the priority of the null process, which always remains zero.

SEE ALSO

create(2), getprio(2), resume(2)

BUGS

Because *chprio* changes priorities without rearranging processes on the ready list, it should only be used on waiting, sleeping, suspended, or current processes.

NAME

close — device independent close routine

SYNOPSIS

int close(dev)
int dev;

DESCRIPTION

Close will disconnect I/O from the device given by *dev*. It returns SYSERR if *dev* is incorrect, or is not opened for I/O. Otherwise, *close* returns OK.

Normally tty devices like the console do not have to be opened and closed.

SEE ALSO

control(2), getc(2), open(2), putc(2), read(2), seek(2), write(2)

NAME

control — device independent control routine

SYNOPSIS

int control(dev, function, arg1, arg2)
int dev;
int function;
int arg1, arg2;

DESCRIPTION

Control is the mechanism used to send control information to devices and device drivers, or to interrogate their status. (Data normally flows through getc(2), putc(2), read(2), and write(2).)

Control returns SYSERR if *dev* is incorrect or if the function cannot be performed. The values returned otherwise are device dependent. For example, there is a control function for "tty" devices that returns the number of characters waiting in the input queue.

SEE ALSO

close(2), getc(2), open(2), putc(2), read(2), seek(2), write(2)

NAME

create — create a new process

SYNOPSIS

int create(caddr,ssize,prio,name,nargs[,argument]*)
char *caddr;
int ssize;
int prio;
char *name;
int nargs;
int argument;   /* actually, type machine word */

DESCRIPTION

Create creates a new process that will begin execution at location *caddr,* with a stack of *ssize* words, initial priority *prio,* and identifying name *name. Caddr* should be the address of a procedure or main program, If the creation is successful, the (nonnegative) process id of the new process is returned to the caller. The created process is left in the suspended state; it will not begin execution until started by a resume command. If the arguments are incorrect, or if there are no free process slots, the value SYSERR is returned. The new process has its own stack, but shares global data with other processes according to the scope rules of C. If the procedure attempts to return, its process will be terminated (see KILL(2)).

The caller can pass a variable number of arguments to the created process which are accessed through formal parameters. The integer *nargs* specifies how many argument values follow. *Nargs* values from the *arguments* list will be passed to the created process. The type and number of such arguments is not checked; each is treated as a single machine word. The user is cautioned against passing the address of any dynamically allocated datum to a process because such objects may be deallocated from the creator's run-time stack even though the created process retains a pointer.

SEE ALSO

kill(2)

NAME

getc — device independent character input routine

SYNOPSIS

int getc(dev)
int dev;

DESCRIPTION

Getc will read the next character from the I/O device given by *dev*. It returns SYSERR if *dev* is incorrect. It returns the character read (widened to an integer) if successful.

SEE ALSO

close(2), control(2), open(2), putc(2), read(2), seek(2), write(2)

NAME

getmem,getstk — get a block of main memory

SYNOPSIS

char *getmem(nbytes)
int nbytes;

char *getstk(nbytes)
int nbytes;

DESCRIPTION

In either form, *getmem* rounds the number of bytes, *nbytes,* to an even-word multiple, and allocates a block of *nbytes* bytes of memory for the caller. *Getmem* returns the lowest word address in the allocated block; *getstk* returns the highest word address in the allocated block. If less than *nbytes* bytes remain, the call returns SYSERR.

Getmem allocates memory starting with the end of the loaded program. *getstk* allocates memory from the stack area downward. The routines cooperate so they never allocate overlapping regions.

SEE ALSO

freemem(2), buffer(3)

BUGS

There is no way to protect memory, so the active stack may write into regions returned by either call; allocations returned by *getstk* are more prone to disaster because they lie closest to the dynamic stack areas of other processes.

NAME

getpid — return the process id of the currently running process

SYNOPSIS

int getpid()

DESCRIPTION

Getpid returns the process id of the currently executing process. It is necessary to be able to identify one's self in order to perform some operations (e.g., change one's scheduling priority).

NAME

getprio — return the scheduling priority of a given process

SYNOPSIS

int getprio(pid)
int pid;

DESCRIPTION

Getprio returns the scheduling priority of process *pid*. If pid is invalid, *getprio* returns SYSERR.

NAME
>   kill — terminate a process

SYNOPSIS
>   **int kill(pid)**
>   **int pid;**

DESCRIPTION
>   *Kill* will stop process *pid* and remove it from the system, returning SYSERR if
>   the process id is invalid, OK otherwise. *Kill* terminates a process immediately.
>   If the process has been queued on a semaphore, it is removed from the queue
>   and the semaphore count is incremented as the process had never been there.
>   Processes waiting to send a message to a full port disappear without affecting
>   the port. If the process is waiting for I/O, the I/O is stopped (if possible).
>
>   One can kill a process in any state, including a suspended one. Once killed, a
>   process cannot recover.

BUGS
>   At present there is no way to recover space allocated dynamically when a pro-
>   cess terminates. However, *kill* does recover the stack space allocated to a pro-
>   cess when it is created.

NAME

mark, unmarked — set and check initialization marks efficiently

SYNOPSIS

#include <mark.h>

int mark(mk)
MARKER mk;

int unmarked(mk)
MARKER mk;

DESCRIPTION

Mark sets *mk* to "initialized", and records its location in the system. It returns 0 if the location is already marked, OK if the marking was successful, and SYSERR if there are too many marked locations.

Unmarked checks the contents and location of *mk* to see if it has been previously marked with the *mark* procedure. It returns OK if and only if *mk* has not been marked, 0 otherwise. The key is that they work correctly after a reboot, no matter what was left in the marked locations when the system stopped.

Both *mark* and *unmarked* operate efficiently (in a few instructions) to correctly determine whether a location has been marked. They are most useful for creating self-initializing procedures when the system will be restarted. Both the value in *mk* as well as its location are used to tell if it has been marked.

Memory marking can be eliminated from Xinu by removing the definition of the symbol MEMMARK from the Configuration file. Self-initializing library routines may require manual initialization if MEMMARK is disabled (e.g., see BUFFER(3)).

BUGS

Mark does not verify that the location given lies in the static data area before marking it; to avoid having the system retain marks for locations on the stack after procedure exit, do not mark automatic variables.

NAME

open — device independent open routine

SYNOPSIS

int open(dev);
int dev;

DESCRIPTION

Open will establish connection with the device given by *dev*. It returns
SYSERR if *dev* is incorrect or cannot be opened. Normally it is not necessary
to open a "tty" device.

SEE ALSO

close(2), control(2), getc(2), putc(2), read(2), seek(2), write(2)

NAME

panic — abort processing due to severe error

SYNOPSIS

int panic(message)
char *message;

DESCRIPTION

Panic will print the character string *message* on the console, dump the machine registers and top few stack locations, and halt the processor. It uses *kprintf* rather than *printf,* so it may be called anywhere in the kernel (e.g., from an interrupt routine that may be executed by the null process). Typing **P** after the processor halts will cause panic to restore the machine state and continue, so it is possible to examine locations with ODT after the processor halts, and still restart processing.

There are alternate entry points to *panic* that are invoked by branch to location zero, illegal interrupts, or processor exceptions (traps).

SEE ALSO

kprintf(3), printf(3)

NAME

   pcount — return the number of messages currently waiting at a port

SYNOPSIS

   int pcount(portid)
   int portid;

DESCRIPTION

   Pcount returns the message count associated with port *portid*.

   A positive count p means that there are p messages available for processing. This count includes the count of messages explicitly in the port and the count of the number of processes which attempted to send messages to the queue but are blocked (because the queue is full). A negative count p means that there are p processes awaiting messages from the port. A zero count means that there are neither messages waiting nor processes waiting to consume messages.

SEE ALSO

   pcreate(2), pdelete(2), preceive(2), preset(2), psend(2)

BUGS

   In this version of Xinu, SYSERR has the value -1 which corresponds to a legal port count. *Pcount* should be modified to report negative counts as large positive integers or to return a nonstandard value for SYSERR. Ugh.

NAME

pcreate — create a new port

SYNOPSIS

int pcreate(count)
int count;

DESCRIPTION

Pcreate creates a port with *count* locations for storing message pointers.

Pcreate returns an integer identifying the port if successful. If no more ports can be allocated, or if *count* is nonpositive, *pcreate* returns SYSERR.

Ports are manipulated with PSEND(2) and PRECEIVE(2). Receiving from a port returns a pointer to a message that was previously sent to the port.

SEE ALSO

pcount(2), pdelete(2), preceive(2), preset(2), psend(2)

NAME

pdelete — delete a port

SYNOPSIS

int pdelete(portid, dispose) int portid; int (*dispose)();

DESCRIPTION

Pdelete deallocates port *portid*. The call returns SYSERR if *portid* is illegal or is not currently allocated.

The command has several effects, depending on the state of the port at the time the call is issued. If processes are waiting for messages from portid, they are made ready and return SYSERR to their caller. If messages exist in the port, they are disposed of by procedure *dispose*. If processes are waiting to place messages in the port, they are made ready and given SYSERR indications (just as if the port never existed). *Pdelete* performs the same function of clearing messages and processes from a port as preset(2) except that *pdelete* also deallocates the port.

SEE ALSO

pcount(2), pcreate(2), preceive(2), preset(2), psend(2)

NAME

preceive — get a message from a port

SYNOPSIS

char *preceive(portid)
int portid;

DESCRIPTION

Preceive retrieves the next message from the port *portid*, returning a pointer to the message if successful, or SYSERR if *portid* is invalid. (The sender and receiver must agree on a convention for passing the message length.)

The calling process is blocked if there are no messages available (and reawakened as soon as a message arrives). The only ways to be released from a port queue are for some other process to send a message to the port with psend(2) or for some other process to delete or reset the port with pdelete(2) or preset(2).

SEE ALSO

pcount(2), pcreate(2), pdelete(2), preset(2), psend(2)

NAME

preset — reset a port

SYNOPSIS

int preset(portid, dispose)
int portid;
int (∗dispose)();

DESCRIPTION

Preset flushes all messages from a port and releases all processes waiting to send or receive messages. *Preset* returns SYSERR if *portid* is not a valid port id.

Preset has several effects, depending on the state of the port at the time the call is issued. If processes are blocked waiting to receive messages from port *portid*, they are all made ready; each returns SYSERR to caller. If messages are in the port they are disposed of by passing them to function *dispose*. If process are blocked waiting to send messages they are made ready; each returns SYSERR to its caller (as though the port never existed).

The effects of *preset* are the same as *pdelete*, followed by *pcreate*, except that the port is not deallocated. The maximum message count remains the same as it was.

BUGS

There is no way to change the maximum message count when the port is reset.

SEE ALSO

pcount(2), pcreate(2), pdelete(2), preceive(2), psend(2)

NAME

psend — send a message to a port

SYNOPSIS

int psend(portid, message)
int portid;
char *message;

DESCRIPTION

Psend adds the pointer *message* to the port *portid*. If successful, *psend* returns OK; it returns SYSERR if *portid* is invalid. Note that only a pointer, not the entire message, is enqueued, and that psend may return to the caller before the receiver has consumed the message.

If the port is full at the time of the call, the sending process will be blocked until space is available in the port for the message.

SEE ALSO

pcount(2), pcreate(2), pdelete(2), preceive(2), preset(2)

NAME

putc — device independent character output routine

SYNOPSIS

int putc(dev, ch)
int dev;
char   ch;

DESCRIPTION

Putc will write the character *ch* on the I/O device given by *dev*. It returns SYSERR if *dev* is incorrect, OK otherwise.

By convention, *printf* calls *putc* on device CONSOLE to write formatted output. Usually CONSOLE is zero.

SEE ALSO

close(2), control(2), getc(2), open(2), read(2), seek(2), write(2)

NAME

read — device independent input routine

SYNOPSIS

int read(dev, buffer, numchars)
int dev;
char *buffer;
int numchars;

DESCRIPTION

Read will read up to *numchars* bytes from the I/O device given by *dev*. It returns SYSERR if *dev* is incorrect. It returns the number of characters read if successful. The number of bytes actually returned depends on the device. For example, when reading from a device of type "tty", each read normally returns one line. For the tu58, however, each read returns one block.

SEE ALSO

close(2), control(2), getc(2), open(2), putc(2), seek(2), write(2)

NAME

receive — receive a (one-word) message

SYNOPSIS

int receive()

DESCRIPTION

Receive returns the one-word message sent to a process using SEND(2). If no messages are waiting, *receive* blocks until one appears.

SEE ALSO

preceive(2), psend(2), receive(2)

NAME

resume — resume a suspended process

SYNOPSIS

int resume(pid)
int pid;

DESCRIPTION

Resume takes process *pid* out of hibernation and allows it to resume execution. If *pid* is invalid or process *pid* is not suspended, *resume* returns SYSERR; otherwise it returns the priority at which the process resumed execution. Only suspended processes may be resumed.

SEE ALSO

sleep(2), suspend(2), send(2), receive(2)

NAME
scount — return the count associated with a semaphore

SYNOPSIS
int scount(sem)
int sem;

DESCRIPTION
Scount returns the current count associated with semaphore *sem*. A count of negative p means that there are p processes waiting on the semaphore; a count of positive p means that at most p more calls to wait() can occur before a process will be blocked (assuming no intervening sends occur).

SEE ALSO
screate(2), sdelete(2), signal(2), sreset(2), wait(2)

BUGS
In this version, SYSERR has the value -1 which corresponds to a legal semaphore count, so *scount* should be modified to report negative counts as large positive integers.

NAME

screate — create a new semaphore

SYNOPSIS

int screate(count)

int count;

DESCRIPTION

Screate creates a counting semaphore and initializes it to *count*. *Screate* returns the integer identifier of the semaphore if successful, SYSERR if no more semaphores can be allocated.

Semaphores are manipulated with WAIT(2) and SIGNAL(2) to synchronize processes. Waiting causes the semaphore count to be decremented; decrementing a semaphore count past zero causes a process to be blocked. Signaling a semaphore increases its count, freeing a blocked process if one is waiting.

SEE ALSO

scount(2), sdelete(2), signal(2), sreset(2), wait(2)

NAME

sdelete — delete a semaphore

SYNOPSIS

int sdelete(sem)

int sem;

DESCRIPTION

Sdelete removes semaphore *sem* from the system and returns processes that were waiting for it to the ready state. The call returns SYSERR if *sem* is not a legal semaphore; it returns OK if the deletion was successful.

SEE ALSO

scount(2), screate(2), signal(2), sreset(2), wait(2)

NAME

seek — device independent position seeking routine

SYNOPSIS

int seek(dev, buffer, position)
int dev;
char *buffer;
long position;

DESCRIPTION

Seek will position the device given by *dev* after the *position* character. It returns SYSERR if *dev* is incorrect, or if it is not possible to position *dev* as specified.

Seek cannot be used with devices connected to terminals.

Note that the position argument is declared *long* rather than *int*.

SEE ALSO

close(2), control(2), getc(2), open(2), putc(2), read(2), write(2)

NAME

send,sendf − send a (one-word) message to a process

SYNOPSIS

int send(pid, msg)
int pid;
int msg;

int sendf(pid, msg)
int pid;
int msg;

DESCRIPTION

In either form, *send* sends the one-word message *msg* to the process with id *pid*. A process may have at most one outstanding message that has not been received.

The form *send* returns SYSERR if *pid* is invalid or if the process already has a message waiting that has not been received. Otherwise, it sends the message and returns OK.

The form *sendf* differs from *send* only in that it forces the message *msg* to be sent to the process even if it means destroying an existing message that has not been received.

SEE ALSO

preceive(2), psend(2), receive(2)

NAME

signal,signaln — signal a semaphore

SYNOPSIS

int signal(sem)
int signaln(sem,count)
int sem;
int count;

DESCRIPTION

In either form, *signal* signals semaphore *sem* and returns SYSERR if the semaphore does not exist, OK otherwise. The form *signal* increments the count of *sem* by 1 and frees the next process if any are waiting. The form *signaln* increments the semaphore by *count* and frees up to *count* processes if that many are waiting. Note that signaln(sem,x) is equivalent to executing signal(sem) x times.

SEE ALSO

scount(2), screate(2), sdelete(2), sreset(2), wait(2)

NAME

sleep,sleep10 — go to sleep for a specified time

SYNOPSIS

int sleep(secs)
int sleep10(tenths)
int secs;
int tenths;

DESCRIPTION

In either form, *sleep* causes the current process to delay for a specified time and then resume. The form *sleep* expects the delay to be given in an integral number of seconds; it is most useful for longer delays. The form *sleep10* expects the delay to be given in an integral number of 1/10 seconds; it is most useful for short delays.

Both forms return SYSERR if the argument is negative or if the line time clock is not enabled on the processor. Otherwise they delay for the specified time and return OK.

Sleeping is not the same as hibernation (see SUSPEND(2)). In particular, sleeping processes cannot be awakened until they time out.

SEE ALSO

suspend(2)

BUGS

The maximum sleep is 32767 seconds (about 546 minutes, or 9.1 hours). Sleep guarantees a lower bound on delay, but since the system may delay processing of interrupts at times, sleep cannot guarantee an upper bound.

NAME

sreset − reset semaphore count

SYNOPSIS

int sreset(sem,count)
int sem;
int count;

DESCRIPTION

Sreset frees processes in the queue for semaphore *sem,* and resets its count to *count.* This corresponds to the operations of sdelete(sem) and sem=screate(count), except that it guarantees that the semaphore id *sem* does not change. *Sreset* returns SYSERR if *sem* is not a valid semaphore id. The current count in a semaphore does not affect resetting it.

SEE ALSO

scount(2), screate(2), sdelete(2), signal(2), wait(2)

NAME

   suspend — suspend a process to keep it from executing

SYNOPSIS

   int suspend(pid)
   int pid;

DESCRIPTION

   Suspend places process *pid* in a state of hibernation. If *pid* is illegal, or the
   process is not currently running or on the ready list, *suspend* returns SYSERR.
   Otherwise it returns the priority of the suspended process. A process may
   suspend itself, in which case the call returns the priority at which the process is
   resumed.

   Note that hibernation differs from sleeping because a hibernating process can
   remain on I/O or semaphore queues. A process can put another into hibernation; a process can only put itself to sleep.

SEE ALSO

   resume(2), sleep(2), send(2), receive(2)

NAME

wait — block and wait until semaphore signalled

SYNOPSIS

int wait(sem)
int sem;

DESCRIPTION

Wait decrements the count of semaphore *sem,* blocking the calling process if
the count goes negative by enqueuing it in the queue for *sem.* The only ways to
get free from a semaphore queue are for some other process to signal the semaphore, or for some other process to delete or reset the semaphore. *Wait* and
signal are the two basic sychronization primitives in the system.

Wait returns SYSERR if *sem* is invalid. Otherwise, it returns OK once freed
from the queue.

SEE ALSO

scount(2), screate(2), sdelete(2), signal(2), sreset(2)

NAME

    write — write a sequence of characters from a buffer

SYNOPSIS

    int write(dev, buff, count)
    int dev;
    char *buff;
    int count;

DESCRIPTION

    Write writes *count* characters to the I/O device given by *dev,* from sequential locations of the buffer, *buff. Write* returns SYSERR if *dev* or *count* is invalid, OK for a successful write. Write normally returns when it is safe for the user to change the contents of the buffer. For some devices this means write will wait for I/O to complete before returning. On other devices, the data is copied into a kernel buffer and the write returns while it is being transferred.

SEE ALSO

    close(2), control(2), getc(2), open(2), putc(2), read(2), seek(2)

BUGS

    Write may not have exclusive use of the I/O device, so output from other processes may be mixed in.

Section 3: Library Procedures

This section of the manual describes the procedure (functions) available to programs from the standard libraries. C programmers will recognize some of the
C-library functions (esp., those that manipulate strings). Be careful: not all
procedure arguments are like those in UNIX.

NAME

freebuf, getbuf, mkpool, poolinit — buffer pool routines

SYNOPSIS

int freebuf(buf);
char *buf;

char *getbuf(poolid);
int poolid;

int mkpool(bufsiz, numbufs)
int bufsiz, numbufs;

int poolinit()

DESCRIPTION

The routine *poolinit* initializes the entire buffer pool manager. It may be ignored as long as the MEMMARK option has been included in the Xinu Configuration file. Without MEMMARK, *poolinit* must be called once, before any other buffer manipulatiion routines.

Mkpool creates a pool of *numbufs* buffers, each of size *bufsiz,* and returns an integer identifying the pool. If no more pools can be created, or if the arguments are incorrect, *mkpool* returns SYSERR.

Once a pool has been created, *getbuf* obtains a free buffer from the pool given by *poolid,* and returns a pointer to the first word of the buffer. If all buffers in the specified pool are in use, the calling process will be blocked until a buffer becomes available. If the argument *poolid* does not specify a valid pool, getbuf returns SYSERR.

Freebuf returns a buffer to the pool from which it was allocated. *Freebuf* returns OK for normal completion, SYSERR if *buf* does not point to a valid buffer from a buffer pool.

BUGS

At present there is no way to reclaim space from buffer pools once they are no longer needed.

NAME

EIS — extended instruction set for the LSI-11/02

SYNOPSIS

jsr pc,times2

jsr pc,over2

jsr pc,shift2

jsr pc,cshft2

libeis.a

DESCRIPTION

This library contains assembly language routines to simulate LSI-11 multiply, divide, arithmetic shift, and arithmetic shift combined instructions. Normally, an assembly language listing should be filtered through the programs *subMUL*, *subDIV*, *subASH*, and *subASHC* to replace any of the extended instructions with the proper calling sequence. (The command *cc11* does this.) The resulting assembly language program must be loaded with this library, which contains the routines called.

These routines do *not* use the C calling conventions. The multiply routine is called by:

```
mfps      -(sp)                / push psw
mov       A,-(sp)             / push multiplier
mov       R,-(sp)             / push multiplicand
jsr       pc,times2           / call mul simulation routine
mov       (sp)+,R             / save low word of product
mov       (sp)+,R+1           / save high word of product
mtps      (sp)+               / put in new psw
```

where the instruction being mimicked is "mul A,R" and R is an even-numbered register (if R is odd, change the "mov (sp)+,R" to "tst (sp)+" and the "mov (sp)+,R+1" to "mov (sp)+,R"). The division routine is called by:

```
mfps      -(sp)                / push psw
mov       A,-(sp)             / push divisor
mov       R,-(sp)             / push high word of dividend
mov       R+1,-(sp)           / push low word of dividend
jsr       pc,over2            / call div simulation routine
mov       (sp)+,R+1           / save remainder
mov       (sp)+,R             / save quotient
tst       (sp)+               / reset stack pointer
mtps      (sp)+               / put in new psw
```

where the instruction being mimicked is "div A,R". The arithmetic shift routine is called by:

```
mfps      -(sp)                / get psw
mov       A,-(sp)             / push shift count onto the stack
mov       r0,-(sp)            / push number to be shifted onto the stack
jsr       pc,shift2           / call the simulation routine
```

```
    mov         (sp)+,r0              / save the result
    tst         (sp)+                 / reset stack pointer
    mtps        (sp)+                 / put in new psw
```

where the instruction being mimicked is "ash A,R". The arithmetic shift combined routine is called by:

```
    mfps        -(sp)                 / get psw
    mov         A,-(sp)               / push shift count onto the stack
    mov         r0,-(sp)              / push high word onto the stack
    mov         r1,-(sp)              / push low word onto the stack
    jsr         pc,shift2             / call the simulation routine
    mov         (sp)+,r1              / save the low word
    mov         (sp)+,r0              / save the high word
    tst         (sp)+                 / reset stack pointer
    mtps        (sp)+                 / put in the new psw
```

where the instruction being mimicked is "ashc A,R".

FILES
{Xinu-directory}/lib/libeis.a
{Xinu-directory}/bin/subMUL
{Xinu-directory}/bin/subDIV
{Xinu-directory}/bin/subASH
{Xinu-directory}/bin/subASHC

SEE ALSO
cc11(1), subEIS(1)

DIAGNOSTICS
The condition codes are correctly set by the above calling sequence.

NAME

fgetc, getchar, — get character from a device

SYNOPSIS

#include <io.h>

int fgetc(dev)
int dev;

int getchar()

DESCRIPTION

Fgetc returns the next character from the named input *device*.

Getchar() is identical to *getc(CONSOLE)*.

Note that *fgetc* is exactly equivalent to *getc*.

SEE ALSO

getc(2), putc(2), gets(3), scanf(3),

DIAGNOSTICS

These functions return the integer constant **SYSERR** upon read error.

NAME

fputc, putchar— put character to a device

SYNOPSIS

#include <io.h>

int fputc(dev, c)
int dev;
char c;
putchar(c)

DESCRIPTION

Fputc appends the character *c* to the named output *device*, and returns SYSERR if device is invalid; it is defined to be *putc*(2).

Putchar(c) is defined as *putc(CONSOLE, c)*.

SEE ALSO

getc(3), puts(3), printf(3)

NAME

gets, fgets — get a string from a device

SYNOPSIS

#include <io.h>

char *gets(s)
char *s;

char *fgets(dev, s, n)
int   dev;
char *s;
int   n;

DESCRIPTION

Gets reads a string into *s* from the standard input device, CONSOLE. The string is terminated by a newline character, which is replaced in *s* by a null character. *Gets* returns its argument.

Fgets reads *n*−1 characters, or up to a newline character, whichever comes first, from device *dev* into the string *s*. The last character read into *s* is followed by a null character. *Fgets* returns its second argument.

SEE ALSO

getc(2), puts(2), scanf(3), fread(3),

DIAGNOSTICS

Gets and *fgets* return the constant pointer **SYSERR** if an error results.

BUGS

Gets deletes a newline, *fgets* keeps it, all in the name of backward compatibility.

NAME

 printf, fprintf, sprintf — formatted output conversion

SYNOPSIS

 printf(format [, arg] ...)
 char ∗format;

 fprintf(dev, format [, arg] ...)
 int dev;
 char ∗format;

 sprintf(s, format [, arg] ...)
 char ∗s, format;

DESCRIPTION

 Printf writes formatted output on device *CONSOLE*. *Fprintf* writes formatted output on the named output *device*. *Sprintf* places formatted 'output' in the string *s*, followed by the character '\0'.

Each of these functions converts, formats, and prints its arguments after the format under control of the format argument. The format argument is a character string which contains two types of objects: plain characters, which are simply copied to the output stream, and conversion specifications, each of which causes conversion and printing of the next successive *arg printf*.

Each conversion specification is introduced by the character %. Following the %, there may be, in the following order,

— an optional minus sign '—' which specifies *left adjustment* of the converted value in the indicated field;

— an optional digit string specifying a *field width;* if the converted value has fewer characters than the field width it will be blank-padded on the left (or right, if the left-adjustment indicator has been given) to make up the field width; if the field width begins with a zero, zero-padding will be done instead of blank-padding;

— an optional period '.' which serves to separate the field width from the next digit string;

— an optional digit string specifying a *precision* which specifies the maximum number of characters to be printed from a string;

— the character l specifying that a following **d**, **o**, **x**, or **u** corresponds to a long integer *arg*. (A capitalized conversion code accomplishes the same thing.)

— a character which indicates the type of conversion to be applied.

A field width or precision may be '∗' instead of a digit string. In this case an integer *arg* supplies the field width or precision.

The conversion characters and their meanings are

dox   The integer *arg* is converted to decimal, octal, or hexadecimal notation respectively.

c   The character *arg* is printed. Null characters are ignored.

s   *Arg* is taken to be a string (character pointer) and characters from the string are printed until a null character or until the number of characters indicated by the precision specification is reached; however if the precision is 0 or missing all characters up to a null are printed.

u   The unsigned integer *arg* is converted to decimal and printed (the result will be in the range 0 through 65535 on the LSI-11 for normal integers and 0 through 4294967295 for long integers).

%   Print a '%'; no argument is converted.

In no case does a non-existent or small field width cause truncation of a field; padding takes place only if the specified field width exceeds the actual width. Characters generated by *printf* are printed by *putc*(2).

Examples

To print a date and time in the form 'Sunday, July 3, 10:02', where *weekday* and *month* are pointers to null-terminated strings:

        printf("%s, %s %d, %02d:%02d", weekday, month, day, hour, min);

SEE ALSO

    putc(2), scanf(3)

BUGS

    Very wide fields (>128 characters) fail.

NAME
>   puts, fputs — put a string on a stream

SYNOPSIS
>   **puts(s)**
>   **char *s;**
>
>   **fputs(dev, s)**
>   **int dev; char *s;**

DESCRIPTION
>   *Puts* writes the null-terminated string *s* on the output device *CONSOLE* and appends a newline character.
>
>   *Fputs* writes the null-terminated string *s* on the named device *dev*.
>
>   Neither routine writes the terminal null character. They return *SYSERR* if *dev* is invalid.

SEE ALSO
>   gets(3), putc(3), printf(3), read(2), write(2)

BUGS
>   *Puts* appends a newline, *fputs* does not; there is no good reason for this.

NAME

qsort — quicker sort

SYNOPSIS

qsort(base, nel, width, compar)
char *base;
int (*compar) ();

DESCRIPTION

Qsort is an implementation of the quicker-sort algorithm. The first argument
is a pointer to the base of the data; the second is the number of elements; the
third is the width of an element in bytes; the last is the name of the comparison
routine to be called with two arguments which are pointers to the elements being compared. The routine must return an integer less than, equal to, or
greater than 0 according as the first argument is to be considered less than,
equal to, or greater than the second.

NAME

   rand, srand — random number generator

SYNOPSIS

   srand(seed)
   int seed;

   rand()

DESCRIPTION

   Rand uses a multiplicative congruential random number generator with period 2^{32} to return successive pseudo-random numbers in the range from 0 to $2^{31}-1$.

   The generator is reinitialized by calling *srand* with 1 as argument. It can be set to a random starting point by calling *srand* with whatever you like as argument.

NAME

scanf, fscanf, sscanf — formatted input conversion

SYNOPSIS

scanf(format [, pointer] . . .)
char *format;

fscanf(dev, format [, pointer] . . .)
int dev;
char *format;

sscanf(s, format [, pointer] . . .)
char *s, *format;

DESCRIPTION

Scanf reads from the standard input device *CONSOLE*. *Fscanf* reads from the named input *device*. *Sscanf* reads from the character string *s*. Each function reads characters, interprets them according to a format, and stores the results in its arguments. Each expects as arguments a control string *format*, described below, and a set of *pointer* arguments indicating where the converted input should be stored.

The control string usually contains conversion specifications, which are used to direct interpretation of input sequences. The control string may contain:

1.   Blanks, tabs or newlines, which match optional white space in the input.

2.   An ordinary character (not %) which must match the next character of the input stream.

3.   Conversion specifications, consisting of the character %, an optional assignment suppressing character *, an optional numerical maximum field width, and a conversion character.

A conversion specification directs the conversion of the next input field; the result is placed in the variable pointed to by the corresponding argument, unless assignment suppression was indicated by *. An input field is defined as a string of non-space characters; it extends to the next inappropriate character or until the field width, if specified, is exhausted.

The conversion character indicates the interpretation of the input field; the corresponding pointer argument must usually be of a restricted type. The following conversion characters are legal:

%   a single '%' is expected in the input at this point; no assignment is done.

d   a decimal integer is expected; the corresponding argument should be an integer pointer.

o   an octal integer is expected; the corresponding argument should be an integer pointer.

x   a hexadecimal integer is expected; the corresponding argument should be an integer pointer.

s   a character string is expected; the corresponding argument should be a character pointer pointing to an array of characters large enough to accept the string and a terminating '\0', which will be added. The input field is terminated by a space character or a newline.

c   a character is expected; the corresponding argument should be a character pointer. The normal skip over space characters is suppressed in this case; to read the next non-space character, try '%1s'. If a field width is given, the corresponding argument should refer to a character array, and the indicated number of characters is read.

e f   a floating point number is expected; the next field is converted accordingly and stored through the corresponding argument, which should be a pointer to *float*. The input format for floating point numbers is an optionally signed string of digits possibly containing a decimal point, followed by an optional exponent field consisting of an E or e followed by an optionally signed integer.

[indicates a string not to be delimited by space characters. The left bracket is followed by a set of characters and a right bracket; the characters between the brackets define a set of characters making up the string. If the first character is not circumflex (^), the input field is all characters until the first character not in the set between the brackets; if the first character after the left bracket is circumflex (^), the input field is all characters until the first character which is in the remaining set of characters between the brackets. The corresponding argument must point to a character array.

The conversion characters **d**, **o** and **x** may be capitalized or preceded by **l** to indicate that a pointer to **long** rather than to **int** is in the argument list. Similarly, the conversion characters **e** or **f** may be capitalized or preceded by **l** to indicate a pointer to **double** rather than to **float**. The conversion characters **d**, **o** and **x** may be preceeded by **h** to indicate a pointer to **short** rather than to **int**.

The *scanf* functions return the number of successfully matched and assigned input items. This can be used to decide how many input items were found. The constant **EOF** is returned upon end of input; note that this is different from 0, which means that no conversion was done; if conversion was intended, it was frustrated by an inappropriate character in the input.

For example, the call

       int i; float x; char name[50];
       scanf("%d%f%s", &i, &x, name);

with the input line

       25   54.32E−1   thompson

will assign to *i* the value 25, *x* the value 5.432, and *name* will contain *'thomp-son\0'*. Or,

>   int i; float x; char name[50];
>   scanf("%2d%f%*d%[1234567890]", &i, &x, name);

with input

>   56789 0123 56a72

will assign 56 to *i*, 789.0 to *x*, skip '0123', and place the string '56\0' in *name*. The next call to *getchar* will return 'a'.

SEE ALSO
getc(2), printf(3)

DIAGNOSTICS
The *scanf* functions return **SYSERR** on end of input, and a short count for missing or illegal data items.

BUGS
The success of literal matches and suppressed assignments is not directly deter-minable.

NAME

strcat, strncat, strcmp, strncmp, strcpy, strncpy, strlen, index, rindex — string operations

SYNOPSIS

char *strcat(s1, s2)
char *s1, *s2;

char *strncat(s1, s2, n)
char *s1, *s2;

strcmp(s1, s2)
char *s1, *s2;

strncmp(s1, s2, n)
char *s1, *s2;

char *strcpy(s1, s2)
char *s1, *s2;

char *strncpy(s1, s2, n)
char *s1, *s2;

strlen(s)
char *s;

char *index(s, c)
char *s, c;

char *rindex(s, c)
char *s, c;

DESCRIPTION

These functions operate on null-terminated strings. They do not check for overflow of any receiving string.

Strcat appends a copy of string *s2* to the end of string *s1*. *Strncat* copies at most *n* characters. Both return a pointer to the null-terminated result.

Strcmp compares its arguments and returns an integer greater than, equal to, or less than 0, according as *s1* is lexicographically greater than, equal to, or less than *s2*. *Strncmp* makes the same comparison but looks at at most *n* characters.

Strcpy copies string *s2* to *s1*, stopping after the null character has been moved. *Strncpy* copies exactly *n* characters, truncating or null-padding *s2;* the target may not be null-terminated if the length of *s2* is *n* or more. Both return *s1*.

Strlen returns the number of non-null characters in *s*.

Index (*rindex*) returns a pointer to the first (last) occurrence of character *c* in string *s,* or zero if *c* does not occur in the string.

NAME

swab — swap bytes

SYNOPSIS

swab(from, to, nbytes)
char *from, *to;

DESCRIPTION

Swab copies *nbytes* bytes pointed to by *from* to the position pointed to by *to,* exchanging adjacent even and odd bytes. It is useful for carrying binary data between LSI 11's and other machines. *Nbytes* should be even.

Bibliography

AHO, A. V., P. J. DENNING, and J. D. ULLMAN [Jan. 1971], Principles of Optimal Page Replacement, *Journal of the ACM,* 18(1), 80-93.

AHO, A. V., J. HOPCROFT, and J. D. ULLMAN [1974], *The Design and Analysis of Computer Algorithms,* Addison-Wesley, Reading, Massachusetts.

AHUJA, V. [1982], *Design and Analysis of Computer Communications Networks,* McGraw-Hill, New York.

ANDREWS, G. R. [Oct. 1981], Synchronizing Resources, *ACM Transactions on Programming Languages and Systems,* 3(4), 405-430.

BANINO, J. S., C. KAISER, and H. ZIMMERMANN [Oct. 1979], Synchronization for Distributed Systems using a Single Broadcast Channel, *Proceedings of the First International Conference on Distributed Computing Systems,* 330-338.

BASKETT, F. [Oct. 1971], The Dependence of Computer System Queues Upon Processing Time Distribution and Central Processor Scheduling, *Proceedings of the Third ACM Symposium on Operating System Principles,* 109-113.

BAYER, R., R. M. GRAHAM, and G. SEEGMULLER (EDS.) [1978], *Operating Systems — An Advanced Course,* Springer-Verlag, Berlin.

BAYS, C. [Mar. 1977], A Comparison of Next-Fit, First-Fit, and Best-Fit, *Communications of the ACM,* 20(3), 191-192.

BELADY, L. A. [1966], A Study of Replacement Algorithms for a Virtual-Storage Computer, *IBM Systems Journal,* 5(2), 78-101.

BELADY, L. A., R. A. NELSON, and G. S. SHEDLER [June 1969], An Anomaly in Space-Time Characteristics of Certain Programs Running in a Paging Machine, *Communications of the ACM,* 12(6), 349-353.

BELADY, L. A., and C. J. KUEHNER [May 1969], Dynamic Space Sharing in Computer Systems, *Communications of the ACM,* 12(5), 282-288.

BELL, C. G., and A. NEWELL [1971], *Computer Structures: Readings and Examples,* McGraw-Hill, New York.

BOURNE, S. R. [July-August 1978], The UNIX Shell, *Bell System Technical Journal,* 57(6), 1971-1990.

BRINCH HANSEN, P. [April 1970], The Nucleus of a Multiprogramming System, *Communications of the ACM,* 13(4), 238-241 and 250.

BRINCH HANSEN, P. [1972], A Comparison of Two Synchronizing Concepts, *Acta Informatica,* 1(3), 190-199.

BRINCH HANSEN, P. [July 1972], Structured Multiprogramming, *Communications of the ACM,* 15(7), 574-578.

BRINCH HANSEN, P. [1973], *Operating System Principles,* Prentice-Hall, Englewood Cliffs, New Jersey.

BRINCH HANSEN, P. [Dec. 1973], Concurrent Programming Concepts, *Computing Surveys,* 5(4), 223-245.

BRINCH HANSEN, P. [June 1975], The Programming Language Concurrent Pascal, *IEEE Transactions on Software Engineering,* SE-1(2), 199-207.

BRINCH HANSEN, P. [1977], *The Architecture of Concurrent Programs,* Prentice-Hall, Englewood Cliffs, New Jersey.

BRINCH HANSEN, P. [1983], *Programming a Personal Computer,* Prentice-Hall, Englewood Cliffs, New Jersey.

BULL, G. M., and S. F. G. PACKHAM [1971], *Time Sharing Systems,* McGraw-Hill, London.

BUNT, R. B. [Oct. 1976], Scheduling Techniques for Operating Systems, *Computer,* 9(10), 10-17.

BUXTON, J. N., and B. RANDELL (EDS.) [1970], *Software Engineering Techniques,* NATO Science Committee, Brussels.

CALINGAERT, P. [1982], *Operating System Elements: A User Perspective,* Prentice-Hall, Englewood Cliffs, New Jersey.

CCITT [1978] — Recommendation X.25, Geneva.

CERF, V., and R. KAHN [May 1974], A Protocol for Packet Network Interconnection, *IEEE Transactions of Communications,* Com-22(5).

CHERITON, D. R., M. A. MALCOLM, L. S. MELEN, and G. R. SAGER [1979], Thoth a Portable Real-Time Operating System, *Communications of the ACM,* 22(2), 105-115.

CLARK, D. D., K. T. POGRAN, and D. P. REED [Nov. 1978], An Introduction to Local Area Networks, *Proceedings of the IEEE,* 66(11), 1497-1517.

COFFMAN JR., E. G., and L. KLEINROCK [April 1968], Computer Scheduling Methods and Their Countermeasures, *Proceedings of the AFIPS Spring Joint Computer Conference,* 11-21.

COFFMAN JR., E. G., and L. KLEINROCK [Oct. 1968], Feedback Queuing Models for Time-Shared Systems, *Journal of the ACM,* 15(4), 549-576.

COFFMAN JR., E. G., and P. J. DENNING [1973], *Operating Systems Theory,* Prentice-Hall, Englewood Cliffs, New Jersey.

CORBATO, F. J. [May 1969], PL/1 as a Tool for System Programming, *Datamation,* 15(5), 68-76.

CORBATO, F. J., J. H. SALTZER, and C. T. CLINGEN [1972], Multics — The First Seven Years, *Proceedings of the AFIPS Spring Joint Computer Conference,* 571-583.

CRISMAN, P. A. (ED.) [1965], *The Compatible Time-Sharing System: A Programmer's Guide, Second Edition,* MIT Press, Cambridge, Massachusetts.

CUTTLE, G., and P. ROBINSON (EDS.) [1970], *Executive Programs and Operating Systems,* Macdonald, London.

DENNING, P. J. [1967], Effects of Scheduling on File Memory Operations, *Proceedings of the AFIPS Spring Joint Computer Conference,* 9-21.

DENNING, P. J. [May 1968], The Working Set Model for Program Behavior, *Communications of the ACM,* 11(5), 323-333.

DENNING, P. J. [Sept. 1970], Virtual Memory, *Computing Surveys,* 2(3), 153-189.

DENNING, P. J. [Jan. 1980], Working Sets Past and Present, *IEEE Transactions on Software Engineering,* SE-6(1), 64-84.

DENNING, P. J. [Oct. 1980], Another Look at Operating Systems, *Operating Systems Review,* 14(4), 78-82.

DENNING, P. J., T. D. DENNIS, and J. A BRUMFIELD [Oct. 1981], Low Contention Semaphores and Ready Lists, *Communications of the ACM,* 24(10), 687-698.

DENNING, P. J. [April 1982], Are Operating Systems Obsolete?, *Communications of the ACM,* 25(4), 225-227.

DENNIS, J. B., and E. C. VAN HORN [March 1966], Programming Semantics for Multiprogrammed Computations, *Communications of the ACM,* 9(3), 143-155.

DIJKSTRA, E. W. [1965], Cooperating Sequential Processes, *Technical Report EWD-123,* Technological University, Eindhoven, the Netherlands; reprinted in (Genuys [1968]), 43-112.

DIJKSTRA, E. W. [Sept. 1965], Solution of a Problem in Concurrent Programming Control, *Communications of the ACM,* 8(9), 569.

DIJKSTRA, E. W. [May 1968], The Structure of the THE Multiprogramming System, *Communications of the ACM,* 11(5), 341-346.

DIJKSTRA, E. W. [1971], Hierarchical Ordering of Sequential Processes, *Acta Informatica,* 1(2), 115-138; reprinted in (Hoare and Perrott [1972]), 72-93.

DION, J. [Oct. 1980], The Cambridge File Server, *Operating Systems Review,* 14(4), 26-35.

FABRY, R. S. [July 1974], Capability-Based Addressing, *Communications of the ACM,* 17(7), 403-412.

FLETCHER, J. G., and R. W. Watson [Nov. 1982], Report UCID-19294, Lawrence Livermore Laboratory, Livermore, California.

FREEMAN, P. [1975], *Software Systems Principles,* Science Research Associates, Palo Alto, California.

FRIDRICH, M., and W. OLDER [Dec. 1981], The Felix File Server, *Proceedings of the Eighth Symposium on Operating Systems Principles,* 37-46.

GENUYS, F. (ED.) [1968], *Programming Languages,* Academic Press, London.

GRAY, J. [Jan. 1977], Network Services in System Network Architecture, *IEEE Transactions on Communications,* COM-25(1), 104-116.

HABERMANN, A. N. [July 1969], Prevention of System Deadlocks, *Communications of the ACM,* 12(7), 373-377 and 385.

HABERMANN, A. N. [Mar. 1972], Synchronization of Communicating Processes, *Communications of the ACM,* 15(3), 171-176.

HABERMANN, A. N. [1976], *Introduction to Operating System Design,* Science Research Associates, Palo Alto, California.

HABERMANN, A. N., L. FLON, and L. COOPRIDER [May 1976], Modularization and Hierarchy in a Family of Operating Systems, *Communications of the ACM,* 19(5), 266-272.

HOARE, C. A. R. [1972], Operating Systems: Their Purpose, Objectives, Functions and Scope, in (Hoare and Perrott [1972]), 11-19.

HOARE, C. A. R. [Oct. 1974], Monitors: An Operating System Structuring Concept, *Communications of the ACM,* 17(10), 549-557; Erratum in *Communications of the ACM,* 18(2) [Feb. 1975], 95.

HOARE, C. A. R. [Aug. 1978], Communicating Sequential Processes, *Communications of the ACM,* 21(8), 666-677.

HOARE, C. A. R., and R. H. PERROTT (EDS.) [1972], *Operating Systems Techniques,* Academic Press, London.

HOFRI, M. [Nov. 1980], Disk Scheduling: FCFS vs. SSTF Revisited, *Communications of the ACM,* 23(11), 645-653.

HOLT, R. C., G. S. GRAHAM, E. D. LAZOWSKA, and M. A. SCOTT [1978], *Structured Concurrent Programming with Operating System Applications,* Addison-Wesley, Reading, Massachusetts.

JOHNSON, S., and D. M. RITCHIE [1981], The C Language Calling Sequence, *Computer Science Technical Report* No. 102, Bell Laboratories, Murray Hill, New Jersey.

KAHN, R. [Nov. 1972], Resource-Sharing Computer Communications Networks, *Proceedings of the IEEE,* 60(11), 1397-1407.

KATZAN, H. [1973], *Operating Systems: A Pragmatic Approach,* Van Nostrand-Reinhold, New York.

KERNIGHAN, B. W., and D. M. RITCHIE [1978], *The C Programming Language,* Prentice-Hall, Englewood Cliffs, New Jersey.

KNUTH, D. E. [1968], *The Art of Computer Programming, Volume 1: Fundamental Algorithms,* Addison-Wesley, Reading, Massachusetts.

KNUTH, D. E. [1973], *The Art of Computer Programming, Volume 3: Sorting and Searching,* Addison-Wesley, Reading, Massachusetts.

KOSARAJU, S. [Oct. 1973], Limitations of Dijkstra's Semaphore Primitives and Petri Nets, *Operating Systems Review,* 7(4), 122-126.

KRIDLE, R., W. JOY, and S. LEFFLER [Jan. 1983], Hints on Configuring VAX Systems for UNIX, Revised for 4.2BSD, *Technical Memo,* EECS Department, University of California at Berkeley, California.

LAGALLY, W. [1978], Synchronization in Layered Systems, in (Bayer *et. al.* [1978]).

LAMPSON, B. W. [May 1968], A Scheduling Philosophy for Multiprocessing Systems, *Communications of the ACM,* 11(5), 347-360.

LAMPSON, B. W. [1969], Dynamic Protection Structures, *Proceedings of the AFIPS Fall Joint Computer Conference,* 27-38.

LAMPSON, B. W., and H. E. STURGIS [May 1976], Reflections on an Operating System Design, *Communications of the ACM,* 19(5), 251-265.

LANG, C. A. [1969], SAL — Systems Assembly Languages, *Proceedings of the AFIPS Spring Joint Computer Conference,* 543-555.

LANG, C. A. [1970], Languages for Writing Systems Programs, In (Buxton and Randell [1970]), 101-106.

LAUESEN, S. [July 1975], A Large Semaphore Based Operating System, *Communications of the ACM,* 18(7), 377-389.

LISTER, A. M. [1979], *Fundamentals of Operating Systems,* Macmillan, London.

MADNICK. S. E., and J. J. DONOVAN [1974], *Operating Systems,* McGraw-Hill, New York.

MCNAMARA, J. [1977], *Technical Aspects of Data Communications,* Digital Press, Digital Equipment Corporation, Bedford, Massachusetts.

METCALFE, R. M., and D. R. BOGGS [July 1976], Ethernet: Distributed Packet Switching for Local Computer Networks, *Communications of the ACM,* 19(7), 395-404.

MILLER, R. [Feb. 1978], UNIX — A Portable Operating System, *Proceedings of the Australian Universities Computer Science Seminar,* 23-35.

MYERS, G. J. [1978], *Advances in Computer Architecture,* John Wiley & Sons Inc., New York.

NEEDHAM, R. M. [1979], System Aspects of the Cambridge Ring, *Proceedings of the Seventh Symposium on Operating System Principles,* 82-85.

NEUMANN, P. G., L. ROBINSON, K. N. LEVITT, R. S. BOYER, and A. R. SAXENA [June 1975], A Provably Secure Operating System, *Technical Report,* Stanford Research Institute.

ORGANICK, E. I. [1972], *The Multics System: An Examination of its Structure,* MIT Press, Cambridge, Massachusetts.

PATIL, S. [Feb. 1971], Limitations and Capabilities of Dijkstra's Semaphore Primitives for Coordination Among Processes, *Technical Report,* Massachusetts Institute of Technology.

PETERSON, J., and A. SILBERSCHATZ [1983], *Operating System Concepts,* Addison-Wesley, Reading, Massachusetts.

PIERCE, J. R. [1972], Networks for Block Switching of Data, *Bell System Technical Journal*, 51.

POSTEL, J. [1981], DARPA Internet Program Protocol Specification, *RFC 790-796*, USC Information Science Institute, Marina del Ray, CA.

PRESSER, L. [Mar. 1975], Multiprogramming Coordination, *Computing Surveys*, 7(1), 21-44.

RICHARDS, M. [1969], BCPL: A Tool for Compiler Writing and System Programming, *Proceedings of the AFIPS Spring Joint Computer Conference*, 557-566.

RITCHIE, D. M., and K. THOMPSON [July 1974], The UNIX Time-Sharing System, *Communications of the ACM*, 17(7), 365-375; revised and reprinted in *Bell System Technical Journal*, 57(6), [July-August 1978], 1905-1929.

SAMMET, J. E. [Sept. 1971], Brief Survey of Languages Used in Systems Implementation, *ACM SIGPLAN Notices*, 6(9), 2-19.

SAXENA, A. R., and T. H. BREDT [June 1975], A Structured Specification of a Hierarchical Operating System, *Proceedings of the ACM International Conference on Reliable Software*, 310-318.

SHAW, A. C. [1974], *The Logical Design of Operating Systems*, Prentice-Hall, Englewood Cliffs, New Jersey.

SHORE, J. E. [Aug. 1975], On the External Storage Fragmentation Produced by First-Fit and Best-Fit Allocation Strategies, *Communications of the ACM*, 18(8), 433-440.

SNA [1975], *IBM System Network Architecture — General Information*, IBM System Development Division, Publications Center, Department E01, P.O. Box 12195, Research Triangle Park, North Carolina, 27709.

STONE, H. S. [1972], *Introduction to Computer Organization and Data Structures*, McGraw-Hill, New York.

STONE, H. S. (ED.) [1975], *Introduction to Computer Architecture*, Science Research Associates, Palo Alto, California.

STONE, H. S., and S. H. Fuller [June 1973], On the Near Optimality of the Shortest-Latency-Time-First Drum Scheduling Discipline, *Communications of the ACM*, 16(6), 352-353.

STONE, H. S. [1980], The Coming Revolution in Operating Systems Courses, *Operating Systems Review*, 14(4), 72-77.

SWINEHART, D., G. MCDANIEL, and D. R. BOGGS [Dec. 1979], WFS: A Simple Shared File System for a Distributed Environment, *Proceedings of the Seventh Symposium on Operating System Principles*, 9-17.

TANENBAUM, A. S. [1976], *Structured Computer Organization*, Prentice-Hall, Englewood Cliffs, New Jersey.

TANENBAUM, A. [1981], *Computer Networks: Toward Distributed Processing Systems*, Prentice-Hall, Englewood Cliffs, New Jersey.

TEOREY, T. J. [1972], Properties of Disk Scheduling Policies in Multiprogrammed Computer Systems, *Proceedings of the AFIPS Fall Joint Computer Conference*, 1-11.

TSICHRITZIS D. and P. BERNSTEIN [1974], *Operating Systems,* Academic Press, New York.

WARD, A. A. [1980], TRIX: A Network-Oriented Operating System, *Proceedings of COMPCON,* 344-349.

WARWICK, M. [1970], Introduction to Operating System Concepts, in Cuttle and Robinson [1970, Chapter 1].

WATSON, R. W. [1970], *Timesharing System Design Concepts,* McGraw-Hill, New York.

WEIZER, N. [Jan. 1981], A History of Operating Systems, *Datamation,* 119-126.

WILHELM, N. C. [Jan. 1976], An Anomaly in Disk Scheduling: A Comparison of FCFS and SSTF Seek Scheduling Using an Empirical Model for Disk Accesses, *Communications of the ACM,* 19(1), 13-17.

WILKES, M. V. [1975], *Time-Sharing Computer Systems,* Third Edition, Macdonald, London.

WILKES, M. V., and D. J. WHEELER [May 1979], The Cambridge Digital Communication Ring, *Proceedings Local Area Computer Network Symposium.*

WIRTH, N. [Jan. 1968], PL360 — A Programming Language for the 360 Computers, *Journal of the ACM,* 15(1), 37-74.

WIRTH, N. [1976], *Algorithms + Data Structures = Programs,* Prentice-Hall, Englewood Cliffs, New Jersey.

WIRTH, N. [Jan.-Feb. 1977], Modula: A Programming Language for Modular Multiprogramming, *Software-Practice and Experience,* 7(1), 3-35.

WULF, W. A., D. B. RUSSELL, and A. N. HABERMANN [Dec. 1971], BLISS: A Language for Systems Programming, *Communications of the ACM,* 14(12), 780-790.

XEROX [1981], Internet Transport Protocols, *Report XSIS 028112,* Xerox Corporation, Office Products Division, Network Systems Administration Office, 3333 Coyote Hill Road, Palo Alto, California.

Index